An Academic Life

An Academic Life

A Memoir

HANNA HOLBORN GRAY

Princeton University Press

Princeton and Oxford

Published by Princeton University Press,
41 William Street, Princeton, New Jersey 08540

In the United Kingdom: Princeton University Press,
6 Oxford Street, Woodstock, Oxfordshire OX20 1TR

press.princeton.edu

Jacket design by Faceout Studio, Charles Brock

Jacket image courtesy of the Special Collections Research Center,
University of Chicago Library

Library of Congress Cataloging-in-Publication Data

Names: Gray, Hanna Holborn, author.
Title: An academic life : a memoir / Gray, Hanna Holborn.
Description: Princeton, New Jersey : Princeton University Press, 2018. | Series: The William G.
Bowen memorial series in higher education | Includes bibliographical references and index.
Identifiers: LCCN 2017036151 | ISBN 9780691179186 (hardback)
Subjects: LCSH: Gray, Hanna Holborn. | University of Chicago—Presidents—Biography. | Women
historians—United States—Biography. | Women college teachers—United States—Biography.
| Women in higher education—United States. | BISAC: BIOGRAPHY & AUTOBIOGRAPHY / Educa-
tors. | BIOGRAPHY & AUTOBIOGRAPHY / Women. | BIOGRAPHY & AUTOBIOGRAPHY / Personal
Memoirs. | EDUCATION / History. | EDUCATION / Higher. | EDUCATION / Leadership.
Classification: LCC LD925.G73 A3 2018 | DDC 378.0092 [B]—dc23 LC record available at
https://lccn.loc.gov/2017036151

British Library Cataloging-in-Publication Data is available

This book has been composed in Gentium Plus

Printed on acid-free paper. ∞

Printed in the United States of America

1 3 5 7 9 10 8 6 4 2

Contents

List of Illustrations   vii

Preface   ix

Acknowledgments   xv

1   From Berlin and Heidelberg to Exile in London   1

2   The Search for Academic Work in Exile:
    London and New York   23

3   The Academic Émigrés in America   46

4   Growing up in New Haven and in Washington, DC   64

5   An Education at Bryn Mawr College   91

6   A Year at the University of Oxford   115

7   Graduate Study and Teaching at Harvard   133

8   The First Round in Chicago and Evanston   169

9   The Yale Years   203

10   President of the University of Chicago   236

11   Finale   274

      Notes   299

      Select Bibliography   305

      Index   315

List of Illustrations

Section 1 (following p. 124)

1. Ludwig Holborn

2. Hajo Holborn with sister, Louise, and mother

3. Hajo Holborn at Heidelberg

4. Bettmann home

5. Siegfried Bettmann

6. Annemarie Bettmann Holborn

7. Hans Bettmann

8. Letter from Hajo to Annemarie Holborn

9. US immigration visa

10. Hajo, Annemarie, and Hanna Holborn

11. Holborn family and home

12. Hanna and Frederick Holborn

13. Hajo and Frederick Holborn with Friedrich Meinecke

14. Holborn family and Friedrich Meinecke

15. Certificate of US citizenship

16. Hajo Holborn, June 20, 1969

Section 2 (following page 204)

17. Hanna Holborn Gray and Kingman Brewster

18. Yale Class Day 1978

19. Hanna Holborn Gray and President Gerald Ford

20. Kingman Brewster, Bart Giamatti, and Hanna Holborn Gray

21. Robert Maynard Hutchins

22. Amos Alonzo Stagg, T. Nelson Metcalf, and Robert Maynard
    Hutchins

23. Hans Rothfels

24. Edward Levi, Hanna Holborn Gray, John Wilson, and George Beadle

25. University of Chicago presidential inauguration

26. Hanna Holborn Gray and Chicago mayor Michael Bilandic

27. Hanna Holborn Gray, Neil Rudenstine, and Nelson Mandela

28. Raisa Gorbachev, Hanna Holborn Gray, and others

29. Charles Gray, President George H. W. Bush, Barbara Bush, and
    Hanna Holborn Gray

30. Sir George Solti with Charles and Hanna Gray

31. David Rockefeller and Hanna Holborn Gray

32. Hanna and Charles Gray

Preface

As daughter and granddaughter, sister and niece, and finally spouse of an academic, I have lived in the university world all my life. My parents were among the émigrés who left Central Europe after Hitler's accession to power and ultimately settled in the United States, a group that came to have a substantial influence on American higher education as it had in turn on them. While the intellectual migration of the 1930s has been extensively studied, more attention has been devoted to the remarkable men (and, occasionally, women) associated with the creative and performing arts who were often well known to the general public than to the scholars who joined the faculties of colleges and universities without, in most instances, becoming visible outside their institutions or disciplines of learning.[1]

Yet another topic has come recently to scholarly attention, that of the "second generation" represented by the refugees' children who were born in Europe and educated mainly in the United States.[2] I belong to that cohort, growing up in two cultures and schooled to some degree in two academic traditions.

Over my lifetime and a career of some sixty-five years, I have seen, as did the generation of my parents through an even sharper lens, that even in wholly new contexts of time and place and intensity, the basic questions that affect universities have remained endlessly to be rediscovered, redefined, reargued, and debated anew in altered circumstances and in changing eras for higher education. Those have to do, most significantly, with questions of the universities' mission, of their requisite autonomies and their relation to government, to political and social movements, and to societal expectations and demands, as well as with questions of academic freedom and freedom of thought and expression within the academy. They include also issues of governance, of the balances between teaching and research, and between undergraduate and professional education, and matters concerning the desirable purposes and outcomes, and hence the content, of higher education.

In the memoir that follows, I have tried to describe something of the European background and its academic traditions that shaped my family and had a lasting effect on my own development and outlook on the world as to some degree a citizen of two cultures. I have tried to situate my parents' experience within the broader history of the intellectual migration and its consequences for the first, as for the second, generation. I have attempted also to characterize the ways in which the essential questions that surround higher education have recurred and taken form in my own observation and, indeed, in my own life as a student, teacher, and university administrator even in the midst of the significant changes that have occurred during my lifetime.

One of those changes has to do with the role of women in higher education. My professional career began at a time when relatively few women had the opportunities I was given. I graduated from college in 1950 and received my PhD in 1957. The number of women in my generation who had been able to complete their PhDs without interruption was relatively small. As we came into our late thirties and forties, now ready for senior positions within the academic world and elsewhere, a number of women of my generation became "firsts." I was a "first" as a teaching fellow and tutor and instructor and assistant professor of history at Harvard, and again, in 1961, as an assistant professor of history at the University of Chicago. When I became dean of the arts and sciences at Northwestern in 1971, then provost at Yale in 1974, and finally president at the University of Chicago in 1978, these appointments of a woman to executive positions at major research universities were regarded as exceptional and drew a degree of media attention that astonished me. The stories, of course, all took the theme of the "first woman" to do this or that; reporters never seemed to take any interest in my views on education or other relevant topics.

I had set out with the ambition to become a professor of history and never imagined that I would want to take on administrative positions or other assignments outside the classroom. Doing so was not part of some grand design. Instead, and over the course of time, with great good luck in being in the right place at the right time, as well as with the support of family, teachers, and colleagues, one thing simply led quite surprisingly—and interestingly—to another.

We are all, no doubt, aware that choices made will constrain or close off others, but it is, I think, more important to remember that every choice made will open up totally unanticipated options and opportunities. I have concluded that this truth will remain permanently hidden to youth, however hard one tries to convey it. One needs to experience its reality in order to learn that every decision or step one takes when starting out is not necessarily, indeed is not likely, a final destination. My own life did, however, come full circle when I returned to the faculty after leaving the president's office at the University of Chicago.

In appointing me its president, the University of Chicago, often regarded as a conservative institution, had taken a step about which its trustees and faculty seemed not to fuss at all. I was never treated as a different species or made to feel that my gender caused alarm. At my inauguration, which because of its novelty drew much media attention, the chairman of the board introduced me by saying that I was the first—and here he paused as the audience awaited the inevitable end of his sentence—foreign-born president of the university.

My account of the status of women provides an incomplete commentary on what remains an incomplete story that will appear to some a narrative of progress and to others one of a still-unending process. From my perspective, I have felt remarkably fortunate to have witnessed and participated in a powerful transformation that, however incomplete, has forever changed the possibilities and assumptions that shape women's lives.

That transformation, in turn, is part of a wider shift still very much in progress, one that originated to some extent with the GI Bill after World War II: namely, the changing demography of higher education and its widening availability to a broader spectrum of the population. The composition of student bodies came to mirror the middle class more generally.

Institutions were opening doors to individuals once excluded or limited by quotas, for example, to Jewish students. By the sixties, coeducation was coming to be adopted where it had not existed, and women were being admitted in greater numbers where it had already been the rule. At the same time, colleges and universities were giving new attention to expanding the diversity of their communities through the recruitment of minority group members to their student populations and, importantly, also to their faculties. That process, always slow and now concerned with addressing the recruitment of lower-income students as well, is of course anything but complete. Nevertheless, altogether, there has been a significant shift in the social backgrounds of students and faculties alike. Not only has this changed the character of academic institutions; it has created both new benefits and new tensions in their relationship to federal and state government as well, given the intersection of public policy priorities, public funding, and their accompanying regulations.

Another significant development, in this case a tide that has turned over the last fifty years or so while still leaving its distinct imprints on the sand, has been the ebbing of America's romance with higher education since the days when the GI Bill symbolized an enthusiastic faith in the power of education as a central engine of social mobility, key to the capacity for creating an increasingly meritocratic society of strengthened democratic virtue. The infatuation has faded, even though a considerable attachment remains, faith succeeded by increasing doubt about the costs and outcomes and behaviors of contemporary higher education.

I began my training for the academic profession at a time now wistfully (and somewhat mistakenly) called a golden age, and retired in what may eventually be deemed an age of bronze. As a historian, I know that such judgments are usually flawed, and that it is all too tempting to whitewash and idealize the past in order to bemoan and reject the present. Nonetheless, there do exist cycles of better and worse times, and there is much to arouse concern, despite so many remarkable achievements, in some of the pressures and passions, both internal and external, that universities are encountering today.

The universities with which I have been associated have been private research universities that scarcely represent the whole of American higher education with its many different kinds and levels of institutions, public and private. My account of university life, my reflections on the roles of university presidents, and the concerns I discuss inevitably focus on what I know best. I have attempted, in relating something of my life as a university president, to give a sense of the intensity and complexity of academic life and administration. Those have grown over my time as academic institutions have taken on more tasks and obligations and have seen the demands of learning accelerate their growth.

My final chapters remain autobiographical in their source while giving greater emphasis to the institutional histories in which I played some part. I hope that through these histories one can discern larger conditions and developments of an academic universe always in flux and always, however different the historical contexts of the moment, confronting anew the enduring questions and challenges of institutional purpose and intellectual integrity, creativity, and freedom for which universities exist.

Acknowledgments

My first debt is to the late William G. Bowen, admired friend, outstanding university and foundation president, who encouraged me to pursue the project of a memoir and who read drafts of early chapters with immense generosity and insight. My colleague Harry Davis also provided such encouragement and gave his time and judgment unstintingly in reading and discussing further drafts, always ready to do more and with a light editorial touch always on point. I owe much to David Nirenberg for his close reading and helpful suggestions, and to other friends and colleagues, including Nancy Maull, James Shulman, Judith Shapiro, Joan Leonard, and David Epstein. Liv Leader has been indispensable in dealing with every need from securing library books and documents to technology support and proofreading. I am indebted also to the three anonymous readers whose very courteous comments were of great use. At Princeton University Press, Peter Dougherty has been the most constructive, supportive, and permissive editor one could hope for, and Jessica Yao at every moment a cheerfully responsive source of assistance, guidance, and information. My warmest thanks to all.

An Academic Life

1

From Berlin and Heidelberg
to Exile in London

My parents, both born in 1902, came from families of what is usually called the *Bildungsbürgertum* (loosely translated as "educated upper bourgeoisie"), whose members constituted a recognizable group in early twentieth-century Germany. Theirs was a universe of generally prosperous civil servants and professional people, as well as some in the world of business. They were university educated, well traveled, cultivated lovers and supporters of the arts and of the German humanistic tradition, with a high respect for learning, and not always immune to a belief in the superiority of German culture. Jewish families of this cohort, to which my mother belonged, were in large numbers assimilated, having usually converted at some point to Christianity in the later years of the nineteenth century, secular in outlook, and regarding themselves as patriotic German citizens.

My father's father, Christian Friedrich Ludwig Holborn (usually known as Ludwig), was a well-known research physicist, specializing in thermodynamics, who became a director and also board member (together with such luminaries as Albert Einstein and Max Planck) of the Imperial Institute of Physics and Technology (Physikalisch-Technische Reichsanstalt, now the Physikalisch-Technische Bundesanstalt Berlin). He died in 1926, shortly before my parents' marriage. Son of a gymnasium (secondary school) instructor (and married to the daughter of another), he had earned his doctorate at Göttingen. Ludwig Holborn's career seems to have progressed smoothly and steadily. The impressive certificates, now in my possession, conferring annual appointments, regular promotions, and various honorific awards, signed by both the emperor and a succession of chancellors, testify amply to his solid and secure position. After World War I and the abolition of the monarchy, the institute retained its "Imperial" title while coming under republican auspices and struggling to maintain its stature of renown under the economic circumstances of postwar Germany.

My grandfather was a liberal in politics and a stout defender of the Weimar Republic; my father was much engaged in political discussions at home throughout his youth. My grandmother Holborn, of Frisian stock (Friesland, on the North Sea coast, is both Dutch and German; hence my father's name of Hajo), was a quite conventional academic wife and woman of her class with a finishing school education and few intellectual interests. The family lived a comfortable existence in the Charlottenburg area of Berlin in a substantial house set in the institute's spacious garden. In a memorial tribute to my father, his close friend and fellow student Dietrich Gerhard remembered his visits to the Holborn home as occasions for entering an "oasis in the midst of the turbulence of Berlin."[1]

My mother's family was Jewish by origin on both sides. Her father was a professor of medicine at the University of Heidelberg, like my other grandfather a prolific author of scientific papers, a man of broad cultivation with a passion for music, literature, art, and travel. Born in Bayreuth, Siegfried Bettmann held a strong dislike for Wagner. I am not sure when he or my grandmother's family converted to Lutheranism. She, like my other grandmother, had been given only a typical young ladies' education. Married at a very young age, she then received an advanced introduction to the arts and humanities from her husband, whose cultural interests and tastes became hers as well. My grandfather was a patriarchal figure who ruled with a distinct force of personality. He seemed very stern to me, but I did recognize that he was witty as well. His medical pronouncements fortified his moral judgments; good health was aligned with virtuous behavior (thus, for example, mountain climbing was good for your character as well as your body, not to mention its spiritual and aesthetic benefits).

Household chores at the large Bettmann house on the Kronprinzstrasse (now the Dantestrasse) were performed by an array of helpers. My grandmother had never cooked when she came to the United States, but she had managed an extensive household, and she had read widely, was thoroughly versed in classical music, had visited the major museums of Europe, and knew the principal cities, landscapes, landmarks, and vacation resorts of the Continent. Already sixty when she came to America, she accepted her new life in a new country uncomplainingly, with an exemplary grace and fortitude and an extraordinary self-discipline. There remained always about her an aura of stateliness and privilege, yet she was in essence a quite unassuming lady of the Old World who inspired immediate courtesy. Something about her made people straighten up and mind their manners in her presence.

The Bettmanns' environment differed considerably from that of the Holborns' Berlin. Heidelberg was a tight-knit university community celebrated for its picturesque setting on the Neckar River, its iconic castle, its romantic myths, and a long academic tradition that outstripped Berlin by centuries. My grandparents were part of a circle of friendships among professors and professionals who saw themselves as cultural leaders in a relatively homogeneous world where the people who counted knew one another. Such eminent figures as Max Weber belonged to this circle. My grandfather sent a death mask of Weber to my father, who stored it in his study cabinet together with a photograph of Weber lying on his bier. I peeked at these occasionally in my youth, finding the whole idea of death masks ghoulish but this one oddly fascinating. Despite his admiration for the great sociologist, my grandfather was said to have commented, when after her husband's death Marianne Weber published a memoir, that he now understood the rationale behind the Indian custom of suttee.

The world in which my parents were raised was hardly idyllic, certainly not after 1914. They experienced the Great War and the deprivations of its later period, Germany's defeat and the continuing resentment and backlash over the terms of the Versailles Treaty, the country's economic disasters, from hyperinflation to the Depression (with a brief period of recovery and greater normalcy between 1925 and 1929), the revolution of 1918–19 that culminated in a republican government unable to provide any lasting stability or peace and that lacked for any widespread support. They witnessed political assassinations and social unrest, widespread unemployment, the conflict of right-wing and left-wing extremes, a political impasse that spawned conditions verging on civil war, with open violence on the streets and paramilitary armies serving the major parties that conducted lawless mayhem. My parents' contemporaries were too young to have fought in the war, but old enough to feel and to be disillusioned by its impact on what had seemed a fairly stable, predictable, and satisfying existence.

Both my parents attended excellent humanistic gymnasiums, steeped in the study of Greek and Latin, and both received their PhD degrees from the Friedrich Wilhelm University (now the Humboldt University) of Berlin. I have the registration booklets in which they inscribed the titles of the lectures and seminars taken semester by semester, accompanied by the signatures of the professors who taught them. Among those are the signatures of such giants of scholarship as Friedrich Meinecke, Ernst Troeltsch, Adolf Harnack, and Karl Holl (for my father); Ulrich von Wilamowitz-Moellendorff, Eduard Meyer, and Eduard Norden (for my mother).

My grandfather Bettmann was determined that his daughters should get a good education and be prepared, if they wished, for careers. Both excelled in and finished their gymnasium programs, among the very few girls still in their gymnasium class at the final scholastic level, and both went on to university. Their father required them to attend housekeeping school beforehand; he wanted to make sure that, even with advanced degrees, they would continue to be marriageable. While her sister, Gertrude, sowed some wild oats in Weimar Berlin, my mother, Annemarie, immersed herself in a sobersided pursuit of graduate study in classical philology and in courtship with the young historian whom she was to marry after receiving her PhD in 1926.

My mother was an ardent supporter of the Weimar Republic and a left-of-center Social Democrat, a partisan consistently loyal to her cause but not an activist. She was and remained a deeply idealistic person, with an ascetic streak and a perfectionist's conscience, by no means humorless—on the contrary, no one enjoyed humor more—but opposed to superficiality and materialism where she thought seriousness and profundity of thought should prevail, as, for example, in choosing literature to read or a play to attend. Her standards and expectations of conduct and accomplishment, for herself and for those around her, were very high indeed. She was extremely economical, always anxious about money even after the clouds had lifted. She never quite recovered from the shocks of the Weimar inflation (while at university she received her allowance in suitcases of cash delivered weekly by a maid sent to Berlin by her father; the mark changed value very rapidly), the fears born of the Depression, the loss of the resources that had to be left behind in Germany, and the need to start all over again from scratch amid the insecurities of the early years in America. At the same time, she quietly and generously assisted other refugees and to my knowledge helped at least two who had lost their refugee parents to complete their college educations.

My mother's own ambition was to become an instructor in a classical gymnasium. Her dissertation, which had to be composed and published in Latin, took on the controversial subject of the "pseudo-Sallust." Her thesis argued that two letters to Julius Caesar and an invective against Cicero attributed by tradition to the historian Sallust were in fact genuinely his. Today's consensus, alas, holds that the weight of evidence shows this conclusion to be mistaken, although some very significant scholars had thought those writings authentic. But my mother's Latin was superb. Early in their marriage, she and my father coedited a volume of selected works by Erasmus that is still widely cited for the excellence of the texts she established. It was a source of some sadness that, although she taught and tutored in Latin and Greek whenever she could and also worked at translation, she could not find a lasting position that would allow her fully to realize her evident learning and talent.

That was one of the prices my mother paid for the emigration to America. It made her still more fiercely anxious that her daughter have the opportunities she missed. My mother was always busy, from the outset of their marriage, in assisting my father's work—typing, editing, preparing indexes—and she held a number of middle-level jobs in a variety of research centers around Yale; she also worked at the OSS (Office of Strategic Services, a forerunner of the contemporary CIA) in Washington during the war. But her true pleasures came in studying and analyzing and learning everything she could about languages and in rereading the classics, both ancient and modern. She was a romantic humanist with a deep veneration for the achievements of high scholarship and a strong desire to serve its goals; she could imagine no higher vocation than that of scholarship. When, shortly before her death and failing in memory, she asked me what I was doing, and I replied that I was president of the University of Chicago, she sighed and said, in German, "Oh dear, and I thought you had a talent for *Wissenschaft!*"

My father's report cards from the Kaiserin-Augusta-Gymnasium zu Charlottenburg show that his work was generally deemed satisfactory in all subjects except, most unfortunately, English. At university he became something of a prodigy, studying medieval and modern European history, church history, and religious thought while moving with unusual speed toward his degree. As his principal field he chose modern history and made rapid progress in the seminar of Friedrich Meinecke, who saw him as an especially promising student and gave him his fullest support.

Friedrich Meinecke was regarded as one of the truly outstanding historians of his time. A man of immense learning and range, his major works dealt with the history of ideas, relating this to the developments of political history. His book on the idea of "reason of state" and its history (*Die Idee der Staatsräson*, translated into English as *Machiavellism: The Doctrine of Raison d'État and Its Place in Modern History*) is probably now the best-known of his works. Editor for almost forty years of the principal German historical journal, the *Historische Zeitschrift*, and chairman of the Imperial Historical Commission (Historische Reichskommission), a prominent figure in public life, Meinecke retired in 1932 and was forced in 1934 and 1935 to resign from his other posts under pressure from the Nazi regime. He lived in "inner exile" from 1935 to 1945 when he returned to his home in a devastated Berlin and helped found the Free University of Berlin, becoming its first rector. One of the few academic elders of my father's youth to survive into the postwar age, he died in 1954. He left behind a still-debated legacy, having argued that the catastrophe of the Third Reich was the tragic consequence of the "special path" (*Sonderweg*) taken by Germany over its longer history, in contrast to that of Western Europe, citing also Germany's difficult geopolitical situation and a series of unforeseen and determining contingent events. My father was, with some sorrow, sharply to criticize the implication he saw in this interpretation that Germany and the Germans might be to some degree excused, if what had transpired was partially the result of inexorable historical forces beyond their control, from some share of a collective guilt.[2]

Meinecke attracted a great many gifted students to his seminar. In a university world that was dominantly conservative in the political and social outlook of its professoriate, rigidly hierarchical in its structures and policies, resistant to change in its institutions, and continuingly inhospitable to Jews or people of liberal republican views, Meinecke took on an unusual number of such persons and treated them with tolerance and respect. Gerhard Masur, one of his students, actually heard the seminar referred to as "the Jews School."[3] In addition, Meinecke did not insist that his students share his opinions and was supportive of those who went in new directions of historical method and interpretation that differed from his own. Nor, unlike most professors, did he insist on handing them their dissertation topics.

Meinecke had concluded that the republic, however unsatisfactory and however tempting it might be to yearn for the good old imperial days, had realistically, if without enthusiasm, to be accepted. Adherents to this position were called "rational" or "prudent" republicans (*Vernunftrepublikaner*). In his view, one had to commit to the new state while hoping for reforms that might strengthen its effectiveness by diminishing the role of a weak multiparty parliamentary system and increasing the power of an elected president. His moderate stance and toleration attracted many who were further to the left than he in a university environment that was highly politicized, and in which, despite the role in university appointments taken by the federal government and those of the states that were of a more liberal tenor, leftish candidates were suspect and could easily be passed over and even denied an academic future.

My father's fellow students were of differing political persuasions, mainly, but not exclusively, on the republican left. My parents and many of their contemporaries were critics of a university system they considered unresponsive to the possibilities and needs of a democratic society and weighed down by outmoded and obstructive traditions and practices. They wanted to diminish the privileges and forms of power assumed by the small elite of an old academic guard whose authority they found excessive and whose scholarship might be seen as serving flagrantly partisan ends. While these Young Turks were relatively tempered in their public rhetoric, and indeed in wanting to introduce reforms from within, they looked forward with some impatience to helping bring about change in the academic universe.

It is not surprising to find that a disproportionate number of the German historians who emigrated in the 1930s were Meinecke students, given his openness to both Jewish students and political dissidents. The best known among them, in addition to my father, were Dietrich Gerhard, Felix Gilbert, Hans Rothfels, Hans Rosenberg, Gerhard Masur, and Hans Baron (and there were more).[4] Each of these men struck out in his own scholarly directions, but all showed Meinecke's influence and retained their veneration for their *Doktorvater* and pride in the training they had received. Meinecke did not produce a "school" of history, but he provided a model of scholarship and taught a profound respect for scholarly integrity and for a breadth of inquiry that marked them all.

For my father, Meinecke's instruction and example were important in many ways. He shared with his mentor a great love of teaching and a belief in giving his students the greatest possible freedom. He was drawn to serious engagement with intellectual history, while coming to believe that Meinecke's approach to the history of ideas isolated ideas too much from their social context, and that the field required an integration of political, social, and other dimensions   that ideas should not be treated as entities with lives of their own but understood in their historical contexts. He developed quite a different style of intellectual history while building to some extent on Meinecke's pathbreaking foundation. He thought, as did Meinecke, that the historian should be at once an objective scholar and a scholar engaged in and having some influence on the course of public affairs. My father, deeply preoccupied with the troubling developments around him and anxious to act on his convictions, found himself conflicted. He was set on achieving success in the academic profession, but he could not entirely quell an ambition to enter public life. At twenty-two he wrote to Dietrich Gerhard: "Despite occasional doubts . . . I believe in my calling as a historian and will never abandon it. But at the same time I am tempted to participate directly in public life, a desire so powerful that my peace of mind is sometimes shaken. You are no doubt right that the two tendencies are basically quite compatible and can perhaps even be integrated as a single whole. For now I will press on with my studies; that is at present my only option in any case."[5]

I would characterize my father as at once a realist and an optimist, a supremely intelligent man with an unerring sense for the central issues posed in any question and with a capacity for finely balanced analytic judgment. His considerations rested on an unyielding sense of the complexity of things, and an insight into the differences and conflicts of positions and interests that informed them, while never giving way to simple relativism or to the acceptance of the unacceptable. He was under no illusion that complicated problems would solve themselves or just disappear; he believed, at the same time, that most problems were susceptible to hard thought and effort, and that one could have some confidence in finding reasonable, if not necessarily perfect, solutions for most situations, and in finding ways to ameliorate incrementally what could not be changed quickly or at all. Always thoughtful, judicious, and intellectually far-ranging, he delighted in searching discussion and vigorous debate. He disdained all forms of oversimplification. His optimism in the face of the personal difficulties and of the harsh events and evils encountered in his experience and observation of the world enabled him not to falter before the challenges of emigration, to possess a robust pleasure in the gifts of civilized living, and to take special delight in his network of friendships, many dating from his time in Berlin and Heidelberg. Felix Gilbert, in a memorial tribute, spoke of his friend's leading virtue as that of an unwavering loyalty and reliability toward friends and colleagues over the course of a lifetime.[6]

My father's memory was quite remarkable. It was as though he could recall every performance of every opera or symphony or chamber group he had ever attended. He had a profound love for and knowledge of classical music. His interest in every aspect of the academic world was inexhaustible. He possessed a taste for travel, good food and drink, and conservative neckties. He liked going places on just about everything that moved—cars, trains, ocean liners, planes—and, in the days when it mattered, knew the railway schedules in detail and the schedules (published in the daily *New York Times*) of the comings and goings of the ocean liners sailing to and from New York. Sending off correspondence destined for Europe would be timed precisely to a ship's departure date.

My father's general good cheer and easy sociability belied to some degree an inner tension and a strong drive toward achievement and recognition. He was successful, and acknowledged as unusually precocious in his profession, at an early age. He began his career on the first rung of the academic ladder as a *Privatdozent* (equivalent to an assistant professor in our terms) at the University of Heidelberg—at twenty-four, the youngest in Germany. He had already published not only his dissertation, on a topic in diplomatic history dealing with German-Turkish relations in the era of Bismarck, but a number of articles and two editions of diplomatic documents as well. He went on to gain his *Habilitation*; this process requires a substantive work of scholarship and examination by the relevant faculty to provide a postdoctoral certification for eligibility to teach at a university. It is the postdoctoral *Habilitationsschrift*, rather than the PhD dissertation, that is essential to qualifying for an academic career in Germany. For this work my father turned to writing a historical biography of Ulrich von Hutten (published in English as *Ulrich von Hutten and the German Reformation*), the sixteenth-century German knight, humanist, cultural nationalist, and early defender of Luther, offering a new interpretation of that figure and of the relation between humanism and Reformation thought in a blend of intellectual, social, and political history.

My parents established their household in Heidelberg. My brother, Frederick, was born in 1928 and I in 1930; my grandparents were delighted to have grandchildren close by. My parents entered into Heidelberg's absorbing academic culture, finding pleasure in friendships with interesting colleagues, among them two in particular who were to share the experience of emigration, the Sanskrit scholar Heinz Zimmer and the philosopher Erich Frank. They had close relations with some of the senior faculty also, as with the philosopher Karl Jaspers and the sociologist Alfred Weber, and my father particularly with Hans von Schubert, whom he admired greatly, and whose book on the sixteenth-century figure Lazarus Spengler and the Reformation in Nuremberg he was to bring to publication in 1934. But my father did not much admire and had somewhat thorny relations with Willy Andreas, senior professor of Reformation and modern European history who oversaw his *Habilitation* and made clear that the young *Privatdozent* was, and should never forget to conduct himself as, subordinate to the Herr Professor. My father found him temperamental, demanding, and intolerant. Andreas was a conservative nationalist who held office as rector of the university when the Nazis came to power in 1933. He welcomed the new regime as Germany's "destiny," cooperated in purging the university of Jewish and politically dissident professors in 1933–34, wrote to Goebbels (who had earned his degree with supervision from a Jewish professor at Heidelberg) that he would be happy to help him in countering "foreign anti-German propaganda," and, while not a party member, remained in place throughout the Third Reich.[7]

In the years that followed, my father's scholarship continued to embrace both nineteenth-century and Reformation history while widening even more to include international relations, political thought, twentieth-century European (especially German) history, and the philosophy of history. In 1929 Meinecke, on behalf of the Imperial Historical Commission,

selected him to undertake a history of the formation of the Weimar constitution, with full access to the archives. This invitation presented a great
opportunity to explore extensive but still little-known materials, to collect
new sources, and to interview figures who been actors in the course of the
Weimar Republic's foundation. It also offered a subject that spoke directly
to political questions of particular interest and concern to the historian
himself, and he accepted with enthusiasm. Not surprisingly, taking on this
project made my father yet more suspect in the eyes of right-wing scholars and opponents of the republic. He embarked with energy on a series
of interviews and on finding pamphlets and other literature that bore on
his subject. But the book was never completed. He had to leave Germany
before finishing his research, although it was well along and he did make
use of his findings in a number of articles. The rare collection of pamphlets
on Weimar that he brought with him to America now resides in the Yale
University Library.

In 1931 my father left Heidelberg to become Carnegie Professor of International Relations and History at the Hochschule für Politik in Berlin,
also holding a lecturer's appointment at the Friedrich-Wilhelm University
of Berlin. His chair had been established by the Carnegie Endowment for
International Peace, and that connection, together with the Hochschule
itself, brought him into networks that were to be of great importance to his
future. It also opened the opportunity to combine his political and historical interests in a progressive institution of higher education.

The Hochschule was a kind of experiment. It represented a new kind of
academy of higher education in Germany, one that reflected the new times
in which it was created.

The school was founded in 1920 with the assistance and backing of such
academic luminaries as Troeltsch, Meinecke, and Weber, and such liberal
politicians as Theodor Heuss (its first director of studies and later, from
1949 to 1959, the first president of the Federal Republic of Germany). It
was planned as a private and independent institution separate from the
state-run universities (although there were many joint appointments with
the University of Berlin in particular) and with a major program of adult

education. The Hochschule was to have three principal goals: (1) education for citizenship, an education for the public that was open to adults while also accepting younger learners, including those who had never received the *Abitur* conferred after graduation from a gymnasium (classes were held in the evening); (2) training for public service, in the hope of helping develop a knowledgeable senior civil and diplomatic service; and (3) scholarly and policy-related research in political science and international affairs broadly construed as disciplines in their own right.

The school's mission included reaching out to the general public with conferences, newspaper articles and columns, radio talks, and publications, providing a political education for an informed citizenry. The training of public servants came to involve a number of specialized programs, whether for social workers, journalists, trade unionists, or Foreign Office candidates. The principle guiding research was that it be conducted in an objective and scientific manner and, above all, in the nonpartisan spirit and method of *Überparteilichkeit* (being above parties). The school claimed its political neutrality to be a unique characteristic. It admitted students and appointed faculty of diverse political views and party affiliations. Many were Jewish. The school tended toward the liberal center and left, but it was home to some conservative faculty as well. The Hochschule was nonetheless generally regarded as left-wing and was from the outset attacked by rightist parties, journals, and groups as politically biased, even communist in orientation, staffed by Jewish advocates of dangerous views.[8]

The Hochschule aimed to serve the society of the "new" Germany, to reinforce civic commitment and understanding, to propagate the values of a healthy political community, and so to enrich and strengthen the future of the republic. The formative outlook of the school emphasized the value of political engagement for both teacher and scholar. Its faculty consisted of a full-time core together with a large number of visiting and part-time lecturers, including some very prominent politicians and government officials, and leaders drawn from the professions.

Among the scores of public lecturers sponsored by the school were many who came from other countries as well. The founders of the school were intent on helping Germany escape from intellectual and international isolation. They were anxious to participate in the wider world community of those concerned with international affairs, and above all with such issues as disarmament and the League of Nations. The school welcomed many foreign students who attended for a time or came to lectures (among them George Kennan, who attended lectures on the Soviet Union). In its research program, the school was anxious to create something of a center for a new discipline of political science and of international relations as academic subjects in their own right.[9]

Although the school was private and insisted on its independence, it did receive support from the Prussian government and, in the lingering Depression, became increasingly dependent on its public funding. It had also to deal with the government bureaucracy and the opposition of traditional universities in order to receive accreditation, so full certification came late. Even so, the school played a distinctive and significant role, and it attracted the interest of philanthropic organizations abroad, in particular of the Carnegie Endowment for International Peace and the Rockefeller Foundation. Both became major investors in the school; both offered a new set of connections and assistance to the leaders and scholars who were, beginning in the spring of 1933, to become refugees abroad.

The Carnegie Endowment was most interested in the international affairs side of the Hochschule and in helping create a collaboration of effort in that area both between individuals and institutions and across borders. Carnegie hoped to influence public opinion toward a peaceful world. It established a European Center and a chair in Paris, and supported the Royal Institute for International Affairs (Chatham House) in London and the Geneva School for International Affairs, helping the Hochschule come into regular association with both.

The Rockefeller Foundation directed its grants especially to the school's social scientific research. That was in accordance with the foundation's concern with working to ease the intellectual isolation that affected postwar Germany, and with strengthening cooperation and communication among scholars and scientists internationally. These aims were achieved partly through grants to universities in the United States and institutions abroad (for example, the London School of Economics), and partly through a highly influential program of fellowships that brought American scientists and scholars to German universities (as well as other European countries) and Germans to America and England. In addition, its Division of the Social Sciences pursued the priority of developing and strengthening the social sciences as fields of inquiry, with social scientists leading departments and research centers dedicated to their own fields. The importance of these contacts, the existence of such relationships already in place before the Central European migration, the connections to a number of institutions and acquaintance with a number of colleagues abroad, and not least the presence of foundation officials in Europe who observed developments there—all of this made a considerable difference, one that helped improve the fate of a significant group of academic refugees.

The ethos and program of the Hochschule must have been very appealing to my father. He was back in Berlin and at the university, with easier access to the main archives he needed for his work on Weimar and now active at the center of current events, while enjoying a position at a progressive institution of higher learning. He was one of a group of younger men joining the elders who had founded the school. These colleagues included Sigmund Neumann and Franz Neumann, two major scholars who were to have considerable influence in the field of political science in the United States, and whose key works dealt with the development, impact, and characteristics of National Socialism and with Weimar's multiparty and parliamentary systems and their weaknesses. The younger men were, on average, of greater scholarly distinction and more geared to pursuing fundamental research than were their seniors, but they participated in the school's other programs as well.

Some 50 percent of the entire Hochschule faculty were to emigrate after April 1933. Seven went to the University in Exile; they became the core of the Graduate Faculty of the New School for Social Research.[10] One might recognize a few parallels between the Hochschule and the New School. Among other prominent members, Sigmund Neumann went to Wesleyan,

Franz Neumann to Columbia, and Arnold Wolfers (director of studies at the Hochschule in my father's time) to Yale.

At the Hochschule my father gave and then published public lectures on such politically sensitive subjects as "The Origins of the Weimar Constitution as a Problem of Foreign Policy" (*Die Entstehungsgeschichte der Weimarer Verfassung als aussenpolitisches Problem*) and on Article 231 of the Versailles Treaty in his "War Guilt and Reparations at the Paris Peace Conference of 1919" (*Kriegsschuld und Reparationen auf der Pariser Friedenskonferenz von 1919*).[11] He participated in a number of international conferences and in the project of defining the field of international relations as it might be understood in disciplinary terms. He became acquainted with a number of people outside Germany, in part through his Carnegie connections as well as through visitors and students from abroad.

My father had come to the Hochschule at a time rapidly darkening for the supporters of democracy and the rule of law. The Hochschule faculty increasingly felt the impact of political battles that came to be internalized within the school itself as student politics mirrored and mimicked those of the world outside its walls. Hitler's party had surged with dramatically larger numbers of Reichstag deputies in the September 1930 elections; they were now second only to the Social Democrats. As the crisis of the Depression escalated still further, vast unemployment had overtaken the country and intensified its social unrest and disorder. The issue of reparations was increasingly at the forefront of the German and international political and economic agenda; the burden of reparations was seen by many Germans as the root cause of all that had gone wrong, and they laid the blame for their problems on intransigent foreign powers (and, in some cases, on their conspiratorial allies, identified as Jews). Those who saw little hope for their own future were ready to enact within the universities their resentful sense of being helpless victims of alien forces determined to destroy a Germany governed by the weakest of leaders and the least effective of political institutions.

By 1931, the Weimar Republic's Chancellor Brüning had invoked the emergency decree powers written into the Weimar constitution; his coalition was governing with broad executive authority and very little popular support. Brüning's successor as chancellor, Franz von Papen, in his rule by emergency decree and by his extraconstitutional abolition of the Prussian government, merging Prussia into the central state, caused still greater alarm among those fearful that the republic was being replaced by an authoritarian state. A short-lived ban on the paramilitary organizations attached to political parties had been lifted, and open violence, all too rarely curbed by the police and the courts, became the norm.

Berlin's public spaces were filled with mass meetings, the city's streets with constant marches and demonstrations and, very often, with hard-fought battles, especially between brown-shirted Nazis and Communists. Jews were being subjected to increasing and frequently physical harassment and intimidation. In the universities, the disruption of classes, boycotts and shouting down of teachers, and vilification hurled against liberal and Jewish faculty became common occurrences. It has been rightly said that "it was the students who formed the vanguard of the Nazi campaign against the universities," and that "while most professors condemned the rowdyism of the Nazi students, . . . they sympathized with their motives and were anxious not to be thought to be out of touch with the current mood or to appear 'political.'"[12] Students were to play, and were asked by the party to play, a central role in the "purification" of universities and in the public displays of book burning in 1933.

The Hochschule prided itself on remaining a calmer and more orderly place as compared to the universities, but it had to pay close attention to the various student organizations associated with political parties in order to maintain the peace, and it saw disturbing outbursts of student rhetoric directed against members of the faculty and the academic posture of the school itself. Communist and Nazi students alike called for "parity" in the teaching of certain subjects. In 1932 Communist students objected to the presentation of the Soviet Union by a specific lecturer; Nazi students produced a leaflet excoriating the school as "un-German" and "saturated with foreigners and Jews" and "Marxist" professors. Faculty members tried to moderate these conditions and to create educational opportunities from such events by organizing lectures, forums, and discussions around the issues being raised.

Public accusations of political bias were at the same time mounting in volume. Hochschule students tended to the left, with Social Democrats in the majority, but after the accession of the von Papen government in 1932, the rightist organizations took heart and were heard more loudly. A National Socialist *Bund* had been established at the school in 1931, and it began to participate in student elections in 1932. These Nazi organizations were making substantial gains generally at the universities. It took somewhat longer at the Hochschule, but in the end, the Nazi organization, calling in the Berlin SA (the *Sturmabteilung*, known as Storm Troopers or Brown Shirts) to help with hostile demonstrations, took over student government just as had its parent party in capturing the government of Germany.[13]

In October 1932 my father spoke in Leipzig. The occasion was a meeting of university professors who had come together as the Weimar Circle of German University Teachers (Weimar Kreis der Deutschen Hochschullehren), a group created in support of the Weimar Republic in an environment of higher education ruled more generally by conservative opposition to or, at best, by a passive or lukewarm acceptance of the struggling republic. My father's topic was "Weimarer Reichsverfassung und Freiheit der Wissenschaft" (The Weimar Constitution and the Freedom of Learning).[14]

He focused his discussion on Article 142 of the republic's constitution. That article reads: "Die Kunst, die Wissenschaft und ihre Lehre sind frei. Der Staat gewährt ihnen Schutz und nimmt an ihrer Pflege teil" (The arts, knowledge and its teaching are free. The state guarantees their protection and takes responsibility for their cultivation).

The lecture described how this clause had evolved, and analyzed its import for the current situation in Germany. My father argued that only within a genuinely democratic society and legitimate free state could the academic and artistic freedoms guaranteed by this constitutional right be sustained, that the two were linked closely together ("freie Wissenschaft und freier Rechtsstaat sind auf besondere Weise verknupft").[15] He pointed to recent political developments as threatening to end in the emergence of a one-party authoritarian state, maintaining that the greatest and indeed imminent danger did not lurk in the extreme Left, however much the Communists were to be feared, but was arising actively from the extreme Right represented by the National Socialists and their allies. After a sharp critique of the Nazi Party's ideology and conduct, he ended his lecture with a warning that their victory would inevitably mean the death of academic and artistic freedom in Germany.

The Leipzig lecture was published as a pamphlet in January 1933. On the 30th of that month Hitler became chancellor, and the swift, systematic demolition of the Weimar constitution was underway. By July that document had become a dead letter as the regime proceeded step-by-step to consolidate its dictatorial power, sweeping away civil rights and political dissent, the freedoms of the academy, artistic expression, and the press, while also mounting and encouraging harsh anti-Jewish actions. February and March saw successive waves of terror under the SA's aegis.

On April 7, 1933, the regime issued the "Law for the Restoration of the Professional Civil Service" (Gesetz zur Wiederherstellung des Berufbeamtemtums). Its provisions covered everyone who held civil service status. That, of course, included all university faculty members, given the German system of state universities. The law specified that Jews (with exceptions for men with a record of honorable military service in World War I or who had lost sons or fathers in the war) and persons who were "politically unreliable" be dismissed.

My father belonged quite clearly to the category of the politically unreliable, and his position at the University of Berlin was at once untenable. In addition, my mother was Jewish by race. The edict of 1933 did not originally outlaw "Aryan" persons with Jewish spouses; that was to come a bit later, and with the passage of the Nuremberg Laws in 1935 non-Aryans were also stripped of citizenship and the exemption for Jewish veterans removed. But my parents found the handwriting on the wall perfectly legible. They read it correctly. Equally important, the Hochschule für Politik, condemned by the regime as a nest of leftists and Jews, was also under attack.

Already on April 3, 1933, a form letter of termination had gone out to the Hochschule faculty informing them that the school would be formally dissolved on April 27. The Hochschule was taken over almost at once and placed under Goebbels's jurisdiction, becoming a training school in Nazi ideology for future party leaders.[16]

On April 1 there had taken place a planned boycott, national in scope, of Jewish businesses and Jewish practitioners of law and medicine and other professions. On that morning my mother's brother, Hans Bettmann, a young and outspoken lawyer, was roughed up by brown-shirted SA men and dismissed from the court in Heidelberg where he was already serving as a junior magistrate. He went to his parents' house and was outraged to see at the entrance a group of SA men and anti-Jewish placards denouncing his physician father. A concentration camp (it was the first) had just opened at Dachau to receive—the term used was "in protective custody"—the growing swarms of political prisoners. Hans Bettmann anticipated that he would shortly be placed under arrest, likely to be imprisoned there. That afternoon, he shot himself.[17]

His death, and his written statement, as one who had considered himself a patriotic German, of defiance, anger, and despair received wide publicity and became a symbol both of opposition to the regime and of its utter futility.

By the end of summer, my father had departed for England, not to return—and then as an American citizen—until after World War II. His life as an émigré had begun. He was one of some eleven or even twelve hundred scholars and scientists, representing perhaps 16 percent of all academics throughout Germany, who had left or been dismissed from their institutions since April. Another thousand (at least) were to follow. Academics were to constitute about 2,200 out of the 11,000–12,000 members of the intelligentsia—scholars, teachers, researchers, physicians, lawyers, journalists, writers, publishers, artists, architects, musicians, actors, filmmakers, and the like—who went into exile.

Not all who were let go from their positions left Germany, or did so immediately, and some who did imagined that they might be returning home again in the foreseeable future. Not all believed at first that the Nazi regime would last for long or that, if they chose to depart, they would face permanent exile. Some even hoped that they could somehow be exempted from the worst harassments at home. Those who left Germany (and, later, fled from Austria and other Central European countries) were often to find themselves moving from one country to another and then still another, coming to rest only after a period of years and after enduring unstable conditions of life and frequently daunting prospects. About half the German academic refugees came ultimately to America, many after detours to other places, especially France, England, and Palestine, but also to such destinations as Turkey, Shanghai, and Cuba, among others.

In general, the erstwhile university colleagues of the dismissed professors sat by in silence. There were singularly few attempts to offer support or to protect and retain even the most distinguished fellow faculty. Yet an official party publication announced that

the victory of the revolution in higher education has, with few exceptions, been achieved with no credit due to the university teachers and on occasion in direct opposition to them. The official upholders of German scholarship felt themselves committed to a concept of scholarship whose ideas of absolute objectivity derive from a rationalism which has long been superseded. . . . The academic representatives of classical liberalism were bound to respond with instinctive hostility to a movement which had adopted as its programme . . . the synthesis of scholarship and politics.[18]

Academic freedom had indeed died with the republic. In his inaugural lecture as rector of the University of Freiburg in May 1933, the philosopher Martin Heidegger had declared: "The much praised 'academic' freedom shall be driven out of Germany's universities, for this freedom, being merely negative, was not genuine. What it meant primarily was unconcern, was a capricious exercise of intentions and inclinations, was non-commitment."[19]

On the eve of departure, my father wrote to Dietrich Gerhard (who was later also to emigrate):

We do not want to be forced to violate in any way what we regard as our life's work and as an obligation to our heritage and our intellectual goals. . . . Naturally, things may (and probably will) develop in such a way that we might have to begin again from scratch. . . . For now, the situation simply calls for one to remain true to one's profession and to oneself and, in this spirit, to make the best of one's fate. So I am trying to think of our journey as a kind of education and study trip, one that will eventually bring us back home again.[20]

2

The Search for Academic Work in Exile

London and New York

In London my parents found a boardinghouse run by Quakers sympathetic to the plight of German refugees and welcoming to other foreigners as well, an international home at Russell Square. My mother had taken the children to Heidelberg to live with her parents and a nanny and then spent most of the autumn in London, acquiring a sense of life in the city, its landmarks and thriving culture, together with its fog and damp and soot and chill. She returned for another month in the winter of 1934 before my father sailed for America in late February. My parents hoped that England would be their next home, in a country close to the Continent, within reach of family, and at least recognizably European. Other acquaintances had also fled to London; they would not be without friends from their German world and were already sharing their lives in London with a group of them. My father had also arranged for his sister, Louise, to study at the London School of Economics; she traveled back and forth between London and Berlin, providing an ongoing link to both families, as did my mother's brother-in-law, a Berlin banker who frequently had business in London. My parents worked hard at learning English at a language school, my father more slowly than my mother. But he persevered and gradually came to feel that he was making progress.

My knowledge, such as it is, of my father's life in London and New York and of my mother's existence in Germany during the greater part of that time, comes largely from the letters he wrote her at least several times a week when they were apart, as well as from letters he wrote to his sister, Louise, and his mother and, finally, from letters written by my mother to Louise and to her mother-in-law and her parents. The omissions from their contents are almost as informative as what is included. They contain no passages on the Nazi regime and almost none on politics or current international events. Very rarely are colleagues or friends still in Germany mentioned by name. There are, however, many references to sending further news by a friend or relative who will soon be visiting Germany. In other words, some of the most critical matters that were constantly on my parents' minds could not be noted in correspondence; letters could be (and were) opened by censors, imperiling the recipients or others mentioned.

The letters suggest also that my father tried valiantly to keep up his family's morale, and perhaps his own as well, to persuade them and himself that all would be well, that he would, finally, gain command of the English language and secure a future in which they would be reunited. But moments of frustration do sometimes emerge as various opportunities seem to slip away, despite all the contacts, kindnesses, and diligent attempts to make something happen. Such moments are always followed by words of hopefulness and understanding of the need for patience and the sense that things will, truly, turn out for the best.

There is a considerable contrast between my father's letters from London and those he wrote from America. In the first instance, my mother had spent a good deal of time in London, could visualize his surroundings, and had met many of the people about whom he wrote. It was familiar territory. But America was a different story, and my father kept telling her how hard it was to give a really thorough and vivid account of what he was seeing and whom he was meeting, and of what life in America was actually like. He felt the inadequacy of his words in trying to convey across the Atlantic the intense and constantly evolving experiences and impressions that he was finding so preoccupying. At the same time he was hoping to persuade her that the move to the United States was not only necessary, but something to which to look forward. Once reunited, he said, they would have to spend days just talking and talking. He wished he could be talking over with her now the various options and problems and ideas with which he was dealing.

My father's London letters recount interesting and sometimes comical meetings with scholars such as R. H. Tawney, the esteemed economic historian and Christian Socialist, whom he described as living in complete disorder, surrounded by precarious piles of books and papers, slippers, teacups, and tobacco tins, intent only on learned conversation, and Arnold Toynbee, director of Chatham House, whom he described as another kindly English gentleman, then totally caught up in issues of international cooperation and peace. My father thought it characteristic, however, of the British academic scene that the three principal figures in the study of international relations were all classicists by training—Toynbee himself, Zimmern at Oxford, and Barker at Cambridge. My father talked of long walks and talks in Hyde Park with Felix Gilbert and with Franz Neumann, of the unfamiliar customs surrounding Christmas as it was celebrated in his boardinghouse, of receptions and lectures he attended where he met new acquaintances, and of having gone to the theater in the quiet Christmas week to see *Mass für Mass* (*Measure for Measure*). While understanding almost none of the English, he found it a wonderful performance.

Both my parents at first found London overwhelming—the size, the traffic, the noise and confusion, the pervasive coal dust and freezing dampness and enveloping fog—and then, once they had mastered the map of the Underground and acquired tickets to read at the British Museum Library, began to feel more at ease in the city. My mother's letters describe the routines of daily life, the rooms and furnishings so different from the Biedermeier style to which she was accustomed, the not-very-competent maids, the fellow boarders, and the amiable Quaker landlords. She speaks of their going to many lectures related to history and to classics, in part in order to extend their knowledge of English. She reported having gone to a movie that featured a "new, very unusual actress" named Katharine Hepburn. She wrote repeatedly of how much she loved London's parks and museums. Both she and my father wrote about the news they had of their children, who seemed to be doing well. It appears, said my father in collo-quial German, that his daughter was turning out to be the kind of person who "will certainly not let anyone take the butter from her bread."

My father could afford his life while searching for a position because the Carnegie Endowment had suspended its chair at Berlin and continued to pay his professorial salary in London for the academic year. He was able to pursue his own work at a desk at Chatham House and to make contact with people there, as well as others who had had some association with the Hochschule or Carnegie or their affiliates, and through them also to broaden his access to other academic figures in England. He hoped espe-cially for guidance from the Carnegie officer in Paris and was somewhat disappointed by the response that he should not be too hopeful, given the large number of candidates and the small number of positions available in either England or the United States. The president of the Carnegie Endow-ment was Nicholas Murray Butler of Columbia University. Professor James Shotwell of Columbia had been the first Carnegie-sponsored lecturer in Berlin, and my father thought these connections might prove of special weight. In addition, he was in regular touch with the Academic Assistance Council in London.

The council, renamed the Society for the Protection of Science and Learning in 1936, had been established in 1933 by William Beveridge, then director of the London School of Economics, with prominent academic leaders as patrons. Its goal was to help German scholars and scientists who had been forced out of their universities and research institutes by intro-ducing them to individuals who could perhaps be of assistance, and to in-stitutions that might have something to offer. The organization acted as a source of information and of small grants that could tide someone over or allow someone to travel to a place that might have a position available. The council did not directly connect people to jobs, nor did it pay salaries or fund positions. It was rather a networking organization that gave out valuable information and advice. Despite its attempts, the council was not able to help place any historian at a university during this time. In 1933 the council's director was Walter Adams, who later became director of the London School of Economics.[1]

British immigration policies were highly selective; most émigré visas were issued for restricted temporary stays of no more than a year. Already in April of 1933, the minute of a cabinet meeting reported its decision

[to] try and secure for this country prominent Jews who were being expelled from Germany and who had achieved distinction whether in pure science, applied science, such as medicine or technical industry, music or art. This would not only obtain for this country the advantage of their knowledge and experience, but would also create a very favorable impression in the world, particularly if our hospitality were offered with some warmth.[2]

"Prominent" was the operative word. British immigration policy required would-be refugees to demonstrate that they had a job in hand or at least "visible means of support"; entry permits were ordinarily for limited stays only. Adherence to this policy was fortified by the continuing Depression and the fear, intensified by the country's unemployment rate, of losing jobs to foreigners, as well as by a widespread public dislike and suspicion of foreigners. Germans, for obvious reasons, were especially unpopular, and anti-Semitism was endemic. The assumption was that most refugee scholars would and should ultimately leave—that England was, so to speak, a way station toward final immigration elsewhere.

The Academic Assistance Council wanted to help find places for and to retain only the most renowned of the newcomers. Those already in that category were likely to be of a senior generation, and the significant contingent of distinguished émigrés who remained in England did indeed achieve great success and acclaim. In addition, the British academic world was relatively small, vacancies few, the Depression effect financially difficult for universities to cope with, and opportunities limited. The greatest number of successful immigrants at the outset, though not of course all, came from the natural sciences (members of this distinguished group were later to be awarded a large number of Nobel Prizes and other honors). It was the children who accompanied their families and finished their education in England who, not surprisingly, were to find a generally higher degree of success and acceptance. Nonetheless, in the years 1933–35 the AAC did help a significant number of academic émigrés find places of some sort (many in secondary schools).[3]

After visiting Cambridge University, my father wrote of its beauty and of how incredible he found the "mixture of wealth and asceticism, tradition and open-mindedness (*Aufgeschlossenheit*), together with much dust of the centuries and many hoary relics. It is at once extremely attractive and quite strange."

The émigré scholars of the Hochschule's younger generation and their contemporaries were gratefully admiring of England and at the same time surprised by the insularity they found in its academic culture. They thought the British university system narrowly elitist and marked by an unbending conservatism. They were often dismayed by the Conservatives in government who failed to see the evils of the Nazi regime, and by the isolationist pacifism of a Labor Party that seemed to have no will to fight against those evils. Looking back on his three years in London, Franz Neumann described these reactions:

> A clean break—psychological, social, and economic—had to be made. But England was not the place to do it. Much as I (and all the others) loved England, her society was too homogeneous and too solid, her opportunities (particularly under conditions of unemployment) too narrow, her politics not agreeable. One could, as I felt, never quite become an Englishman.[4]

A major assistance organization for émigré scholars had also been founded in the United States in 1933. Known as the Emergency Committee in Aid of Displaced German (later, Foreign) Scholars, it soon developed a fruitful relationship with Adams and his Academic Assistance Council. The Emergency Committee was headed by Stephen Duggan, president of the Institute for International Education in New York, with a board consisting

of presidents of colleges and universities and other leading academic figures. Its procedures differed significantly from those of the Academic Assistance Council, for the Emergency Committee was engaged directly in
the process of placing refugee scholars at academic institutions and contributing financially to their compensation.[5]

The Emergency Committee would first decide which scholars to assist;
its criteria had to do with judgments about the intellectual quality, work,
and promise of the individual émigré and his or her capacity ultimately to
qualify for a tenure-track position. The committee had generous funding
from the Rockefeller Foundation and received gifts from other foundations
and individuals as well. It would circulate a list of scholars to a number of
institutions for their evaluation and, if the college or university showed
interest (or if it presented the committee with a candidate on its own initiative), would offer, as a kind of challenge grant, to pay half the person's
salary if the institution paid the rest and if the institution could promise
that in one or two years it would consider the candidate for a permanent
position. These conditions were often flexibly adapted to particular circumstances, and quite a few renewals were approved.

The records of the Emergency Committee, now housed at the New York
Public Library, show a very long list of applicants of whom only a relatively small percentage could be chosen for the committee's support. But
the committee made a huge difference, as did the New School for Social
Research, which was simultaneously recruiting refugee scholars to the
University in Exile with its own funding. The Institute for Advanced Study
in Princeton was also bringing émigrés to its new campus, and the New
York Institute for Fine Arts began to welcome a number of refugee art
historians. And a number of universities, especially when looking to the
natural sciences, required no intermediary when initiating appointments
directly through their normal procedures, although they might request
grants from the committee if other means of support were not immediately within reach. The Emergency Committee's work extended to scientists, social scientists, and humanists, but many scientists in particular did
not go through the committee at all. A considerable number of the scholars

who had fled to England were referred to the committee by the Academic Assistance Council and with both endorsements were able to reach the United States with positions already in hand.

At the same time, there were many obstacles in the way of academic appointments in the United States. American universities, too, were suffering badly from the effects of the Depression; they were letting younger faculty go and sometimes reducing faculty salaries. There was concern about giving positions to foreigners when young American scholars went without them. A pervasive anti-Semitism marked the American academic world. The supporters of bringing émigré scholars into that world worried that their presence would provoke an aggravated hostility to Jews as well as to foreigners perceived as unfairly replacing Americans. The Emergency Committee and its supporters spoke of the need for caution and for not drawing too much attention to their work. When challenged, they justified their mission as helping not only the refugees, but the universities themselves and American culture more generally.

Beyond these concerns, there was the problem of American immigration laws that set quotas by country of origin. Astonishingly, quotas for Germany went unfilled in all but one year of the 1930s. Visas were hard to secure, with long delays encouraged by the resistance of many State Department leaders and officials to admitting Jewish refugees. In addition, not all leaders of universities were advocates of the refugee cause or felt a special sense of urgency or priority about it, at least before the Kristallnacht of November 1938 captured their attention in a new and much more urgent way. Those who did want to help often lacked the resources to do so. There existed a considerable range of sentiment among the leaders of academic institutions on the question. But after the brutal horrors of Kristallnacht, the reservations of those who had been reluctant to take an institutional stance, like Harvard's President Conant, began swiftly to vanish.

As it began its work in the spring of 1933, the Emergency Committee sent a letter to fifteen universities inviting each to recommend the name of a displaced scholar it would like to appoint, and stating that the committee would obtain necessary funding from the Rockefeller Foundation to make this possible. Only Harvard did not take up the offer. President Conant's reservations had to do with his belief that young American scholars and scientists would be supplanted, possibly by mediocre or at any rate not stronger foreigners; he feared that the appointment process itself would be attenuated in order to make way for a political cause, and that his institution might be seen as taking a political stance. He did not object, he said, to candidates who happened to be émigrés being proposed through the regular procedures initiated by departments or faculties to make the best possible appointments. But, in a revelatory moment, when asked by a research executive at DuPont about the quality of a Jewish chemist under consideration at the company, he replied that he was "rather against bringing him over. . . . My own personal feeling is that we shall not help the cause of American science any by filling up the good positions in this country by imported foreigners . . . I think a deluge of medium and good men of the Jewish race in scientific positions . . . would do a lot of harm." While in 1938 Conant became a committed advocate for a movement to help rescue Central European scholars (and while Harvard had in fact made some remarkable appointments of émigrés), the views he expressed in 1933 and 1934 say something about the situation in those early years of the migration.[6]

American immigration law did, however, contain an exemption from the national quotas for teachers, so long as they met certain requirements before being admitted: exemptions were granted to immigrants who had taught for two years in a row directly before emigrating, could claim an already-guaranteed job in hand in the United States, and could offer a sponsor's affidavit from a US citizen affirming that this person would be financially responsible for the immigrant should that become necessary. This exemption turned out to be a godsend for a number of the émigré scholars who managed to procure positions in advance and so were eligible to become nonquota immigrants. My own visa, issued by the American consulate in Stuttgart, identifies me as such.

In January of the new year 1934 Walter Adams informed my father that he had come to the conclusion that my father would better suited to and

more likely to acquire a research than a teaching position in England, and
that the outlook for historians was in any case dim at best. Adams also told
him that Stephen Duggan was visiting London, and encouraged him to ask
for a meeting. My father did so and learned that Duggan was extremely
skeptical that he, or indeed any young scholar, would find any job in the
United States. It would be foolish to make the trip, said Duggan. But my
father was not ready to give up his goal of university teaching. He was determined to try his luck in America and insisted on doing so almost at once.
Duggan relented sufficiently to let the Emergency Committee office know
that my father was on his way, even while warning him again how remote
his prospects seemed to be.

Somehow, my father was confident he could succeed. He booked passage
on the White Star SS *Olympic*, thinking that he could at least attempt to
use the contacts he had in America with the Carnegie Endowment and the
Rockefeller Foundation. He wrote to individuals of his acquaintance like
Harvard's Carl Joachim Friedrich, whom he had known in Germany, and
former Hochschule colleagues like Arnold Wolfers, now already at Yale,
and the military historian Alfred Vagts, son-in-law of the renowned American historian Charles Beard and resident in Connecticut. He was ready to
reap whatever benefit he could from such networks and to expand them as
much as possible. Adams, always ready to be of assistance, had given him
a number of names and letters of introduction. He also carried with him
letters of recommendation from Meinecke and other historians familiar
to American scholars. He wrote ahead to everyone he could think of, and
made plans to stay with his brother and family in New Jersey, close enough
to commute to New York.

My father's brother, Friedrich—my Uncle Fritz—had emigrated not long
after World War I. As an army officer he had been seriously wounded; permanently lame, he had then attended the University of Göttingen to study
physics. Finding no future in postwar Germany, he had joined the RCA research laboratories in New York. My father had not, I think, seen him for at
least ten years and had never met his three children.

My father loved his ocean voyage, even in February. He wrote with great delight about the ship, the excellent service, the pleasures of his deck chair and being brought afternoon tea, the vistas of the Atlantic and its changing moods. As America came closer, a huge storm broke out at sea and a big snowstorm on land so that the ship's landing had to be delayed. It stopped well short of the harbor with a view of the coast from its decks.

My father's description has remained with me: he saw in the distance the illuminated figure of the Statue of Liberty and, still further away, the lights of New York, and he realized, as the dream life of the ship was about to end and reality to intrude, that he knew so little of the enormous country he was about to enter, and that so much would now depend on the workings of sheer chance in a new and mysterious world. He would now have in earnest to embark on the task he had set for himself. The pleasant trip over, he was at once nervous and excited. He wrote also of the beauty of that night—cloudless, starry, freezing, an almost full moon. I recalled his words when attending the Statue of Liberty's rededication fifty-two years later during the celebration of its centennial, sitting in the stands on Governor's Island and watching as across the water the flame of the torch, relit, shot suddenly high into the air on a similar night, clear, starlit, moonlit, and cold even though it was July.

The *Olympic* finally docked on March 1, and my father went immediately to work on his agenda. He visited the Carnegie Endowment and Rockefeller Foundation offices on March 2, and the Emergency Committee's office the next day. There he met Duggan's staff of one, a young assistant who was actually left pretty much in charge. His name was Edward R. Murrow; two years later he moved to CBS and began a famous career in news broadcasting. Accepting the Albert Einstein Commemorative Award in 1957, Murrow spoke of his time with the committee:

> When Hitler and his henchmen chopped off the highest branches of the German academic tree, those scholars sought exile in many countries. There was established in this country a small committee to aid in the

placement of these scholars in American universities. . . . It was my privilege to prepare lists of the displaced German scholars, to circulate them to American universities, and then to go before the committee with applications for considerable sums of money to finance the first few years of their residence in this country. Several scores of scholars came and became part of our academic communities from Seattle to Boston. . . . In presenting applications to the committee I was never once asked: "Is this man a Jew?" The only question was: Is he a competent scholar of standing or promise? Are his services sought by an American college or university? . . . In those days . . . we used to talk of the cross-fertilization of cultures that might result from this migration and hope that American students would be stimulated. These men and women represented every academic discipline, and I have been fortunate enough to see the human dividends that have been produced by their labors. . . . I can only add that my own small part in that operation has given me more satisfaction than anything I have ever done.[7]

The two young men hit it off at once, and Murrow (whose name my father at first kept misspelling as Murro, thus somehow giving him a quite different persona) said he was sure he could help find what my father needed. He was indefatigable in his support, and my father's morale and increasing sense of possibility were fortified by the friendship and working relationship that they established so quickly. Within a week Murrow had already arranged for him to visit Washington (American and George Washington Universities), Princeton, and Harvard, while my father had set plans through his other contacts for visits to Columbia, the New School, and Yale. He was a little alarmed when Murrow mentioned the University of Chicago as a possibility, hoping it would not be necessary even to visit.

My father began writing his observations about America, the people he met, the universities he visited, the customs he noted, and the cities and landscapes he encountered from day one. New York astonished him. He admired the skyscrapers, was struck by the city's division into ethnic groups, and could scarcely believe the ceaseless hyperactivity all around. He disliked it at first, describing the city as ugly but wonderfully situated between its two rivers and endowed with some beautiful things. The climate, he said, was dreadful. He did, however, come over the course of his visit and ever after to love the city and its cultural riches, although London long took first place in his affections. At the beginning, he wrote that it was hard to distinguish between "what was New York and what was America." His nostalgia for London persisted: "There are things in London that one searches for here in vain. . . . That *duft* of the centuries cannot be found here. Nonetheless my impressions of America are excellent. One can do a great deal here, and the *Landschaft* as a whole is magnificent." He was beginning to urge his sister, too, to think about leaving London for America.

In the United States for only several days, my father wrote to my mother that he was quite sure they would be able to come to America, and that it was a place where it would be possible to "live in the surroundings of nature." He thought, with a bit of bravado, that it might take five or six weeks to achieve some certainty, and that (a theme to be reiterated in almost every message) my mother would really like it in America. They might be able to find a small house to live in not too far from a town and should definitely bring their own furniture from Germany (another topic often discussed, one that gave plausible and concrete form to the idea of moving to America even when it was still entirely speculative).

"I have to say," my father wrote, "that I like America. There are indeed things that we would never have here; one sees that to be so as I did the other day in New York talking with Tillich."

Within ten days of his arrival in New York my father was staying with Arnold and Doris Wolfers in New Haven and writing his impressions of Yale. "Yale," he reported, "is a remarkable university! The opulence of its campus must be unique and so, too, the manner in which the students and many of the faculty live. While the imitation of Oxford is somewhat hard to take, the campus is nonetheless extremely handsome, almost out of this world. The New England character of the place is in stark contrast to New

York's mix of nationalities, and although the towns are not very pretty, the landscape is really attractive, certainly a lot more beautiful than the surroundings of Berlin."

Walter Adams had given my father a letter of introduction to Yale's Professor Wallace Notestein, an eminent historian of seventeenth-century England and of the British Parliament. He exercised considerable influence in the university and especially with the provost (later to be president), Charles Seymour, a diplomatic historian who had been at the Paris Peace Conference and was anxious to develop a strong program of modern European history as well as a degree in international relations at Yale. Notestein was equally anxious to find a sixteenth-century and Reformation scholar for his department. He took an immediate liking to my father and began, while realizing that there was of course no money for appointments, to plot a strategy. Wolfers, who knew my father and his work well (he had, after all, recruited him to the Carnegie Chair at the Hochschule) and who was in the early phases of founding his program in international relations at the university, was ready to join the plan. My father seemed to be a triple threat, fulfilling all three priorities. He had already published extensively in each of the fields. As it happened, the then-current issue of the *American Historical Review* contained a favorable review of my parents' edition of Erasmus. It was too early to know whether anything might come of all this, my father cautioned, but his hopes began to grow, and his ambition to land at a leading university rose with them. So, too, he wrote, did his belief that he had found a country in which they could start over and have a decent life and meaningful work, where their children would thrive, and where they would all enjoy a garden, good air, and a beautiful natural environment. These would compensate for what they would not have. "Americans are very good-natured and friendly, but somewhat superficial and limited. Their intellectual (*geistiger*) life is less intense and focused than, for example, that of the English. . . . And it is pitiful to see how few stores, even first-class ones, have a good inventory of books. Nor can the newspapers here be compared to the English ones." My father's dissatisfaction with the quality of the press in America began on day one.

Having formed these judgments only ten days after disembarking in New York, my father told his wife a week later that he couldn't wait to see her reactions to all the things he already liked about America. Maybe she would even learn to drive and become independent like Mrs. Roosevelt. He announced his intention to start driving lessons as soon as possible; this skill would be important for life in America. His spirits high, he wrote that Columbia was definitely out since it lacked resources for an appointment, and the Emergency Committee (i.e., Murrow) was not about to give them any, probably a good thing since, nice as the people he'd met had been, they weren't great scholars and Columbia was something of a mess. On the other hand, Yale continued to look promising: the deans made a good impression, as did the historians, the proximity of ocean and mountains was great, and one would just have to accept the campus architecture despite its distressingly fake neo-Gothic. He reported that his English was much improved, and that he was even receiving some compliments on it. As to further impressions: he thought the situation in the United States, not only its economy but its political tendencies, were at a critical stage, and that there was some softening of confidence in FDR. In addition, he was surprised to find so little interest in or news about European affairs in the United States, no matter how preoccupying domestic problems might be. These last passages represent one of the few instances in which my father mentioned politics in his letters to Germany. It is clear that he was following the American scene with great fascination. Clear, too, that his judgments of intellectual quality contained no element of grade inflation.

Traveling to Washington, my father found strong interest expressed by the two universities. He now felt that he had secure fallback positions but would prefer, if possible, to end up in New England. Harvard was next on his itinerary. A letter from Notestein informed him that in the meantime, only two weeks since his visit, both the Yale history department and the dean of the graduate school had recommended his appointment; now they awaited the provost's approval. It seemed, said my father, almost too good to be true, but he began to feel a mild euphoria while sternly reminding himself not to expect too much too soon.

From Cambridge my father wrote of how impressive he found Harvard and how helpful his old acquaintance Carl Joachim Friedrich was being on his behalf. The students seemed excellent, the faculty in general very good, and he felt quite at home. But Harvard's large history department (which he somewhat surprisingly assessed as very solid but lacking anyone of truly first rank) already had professors in the fields of sixteenth-century, modern European, and diplomatic history, so he found it less likely that they would be interested in his coming or that there would be a longer future there. Harvard, my father wrote, was indescribable:

> Until now, I had not imagined it possible for so richly endowed a university actually to exist. College after college, library, institute after institute: I have never seen anything like this. Everything is handsomely built and for its purposes, quite beautiful, at any rate more so than Yale's neo-Gothic. Yale is ridiculously wasteful; Harvard keeps within more appropriate bounds. There's no doubt, too, that the student body is better than Yale's.

Even so, he went on, it would be hard, if it came to that, to choose between Harvard and Yale. If push came to shove and he had to choose, he would actually probably take Yale. And so he did, I think above all because he saw there an opportunity to build the fields of his interest where they either had not existed or had not had substance before. For this (and for the house, garden, landscape, and good air he kept promising my mother) he was willing to swallow his curious aversion to the American collegiate neo-Gothic. He told my mother, who had long hoped that England would be their final destination, that Yale was in fact "much more English" than Harvard, and the German influence more pervasive. And he began to give her instructions for preparing to move overseas: what to do with the books and their other possessions, as well as what furniture to bring.

He also sent her a long description of Yale's organization—the residential colleges, Yale College and its dean (who, he pointed out, was a classicist who had studied in Munich, Freiburg, and Leipzig), the graduate school with its seminars (on a German model, he said) and its dean, the faculties that in America were called departments or schools, the lecture and course system, the provost and president and the boards of trustees that were called corporations at Yale and at Harvard. Very different, my father observed, from the German university structure, more like the English, although the state universities were more similar to the German model and were at present suffering greater financial problems than were the privately endowed ones. This was an introductory lecture on the American university scene centered on Yale and his barely suppressed expectation of an appointment there. To learn more, my father suggested that my mother read the relevant chapter in volume 2 of Bryce's *American Commonwealth*. I have no idea whether Bryce was on their shelves in Heidelberg, but it was clear that my father had become quickly well informed on the new and, to him, more progressive kind of academic institution he was likely to join.

Before the final outcome of his search, my father had paid a visit to Princeton. He started this journey from Boston on a boat that he described as a miniature steamship (and indeed the picture on the letterhead is very impressive). A kind of mini-*Bremen*, with cabins for its passengers, it sailed overnight to New York. This was to become, while it lasted, his favorite way of going to and from Boston (one could embark at the New Haven harbor), where he was also to teach regularly and gain an additional source of income at the Tufts University's Fletcher School of Law and Diplomacy, founded in 1933 as a graduate school of international affairs.

Princeton appeared interested in having my father join the departments of history and political science, and he found everyone extremely pleasant and friendly. But the university did not feel right to him. Here is his account:

Princeton is actually the most beautiful of all the places I've seen—from the point of view of landscape and setting, unimaginably lovely. It has a wonderfully pastoral and peaceful environment. The actual scholarly strength of Princeton lies in the natural sciences. The history department is not very broad in range and its faculty rather weak, and the department of politics one can forget about. As a result there are hardly any graduate students in these programs and the undergraduates, even more than is the case at Yale, are the pampered children of the top one thousand. . . . Despite its attractions, I would prefer not to go there; Princeton has difficult problems of atmosphere that would be very hard to tolerate.

My father was told by Murrow that the Emergency Committee would support whatever choice he made once offers were actually in hand; the two had many talks about Yale versus Harvard. My father's friendship and many discussions with Murrow also enabled him to bring to Murrow's attention the situation of several other German scholars who were hoping to move from England to America; he was especially concerned about Sigmund Neumann, for whom a position was happily found that spring at Wesleyan. My father became a regular consultant in the committee's work. He could write about all this to his sister, Louise, who was in London and in touch with his émigré friends there, as he could not to my mother, given the sensitivity of referring in letters to Germany to the regime or its university policies, or of naming the names of scholars who had fled or were soon to flee.

He could also share with his sister the interesting news that on April 3 the front page of the *New York Times*, which despite his disdain for American newspapers he read religiously, featured a long article on the return of Nicholas Murray Butler from Europe. In those days passengers considered important were interviewed on the piers immediately after their ships had docked. The story revealed, to my father's delight, that the Carnegie Chair had been removed from Berlin. "Hitler Bars Work of Carnegie Fund," read the headline, with the subheading "Dr. Butler Reveals Chair at Berlin School Is Suspended—Fostered Liberal Forum." Butler was asked to speak about the conditions of academic life in Germany. In his response, he was clear that they were certainly not good, but he was very cautious about saying too much, apparently still believing that change for the better might yet come, and that the Carnegie Endowment might return to its work in Germany. About Butler my father was less delighted, referring somewhat sarcastically to his posture as an oracle of world politics ("welt-politische Orakel").

On the 19th of April my father learned that Yale had presented his name to the Emergency Committee for funding; the committee in turn requested a grant from the Rockefeller Foundation. By the end of the month my father had decided on Yale as the right choice, and all had been accomplished. My father's six and a half weeks in America had come to a surprisingly productive conclusion.

The outcome seemed a kind of miracle. My father was very conscious of his good fortune and aware also of the possible resentments that could be provoked by the insertion of foreign scholars into a tight academic market. But he thought that if the foreigners represented, as he felt he did to some degree, fields that were otherwise not cultivated or well developed in American universities, then they were not taking anyone else's places. He believed he owed his good fortune to the special support of the Emergency Committee and such sponsors as Wolfers and Friedrich, and to the fact that his work was already known, at least by those in the major universities who wanted to expand their programs in European history.

My father's situation was in some ways atypical when compared to that of the majority of émigrés in the areas of history and political science. Given the depth of anti-Semitism that prevailed in its institutions, it is quite certain that, had he been Jewish, his search would have been unlikely to end in a department of history in the Ivy League. On a more positive note, he was and probably showed himself at once far more adaptable and open to an unfamiliar American academic culture than were some others, for whom letting go of the high professorial status characteristic of their German world and taking up new tasks, such as the teaching of American undergraduates, could prove more difficult. In addition to good luck and to their relative youth, combined with excellent scholarly records, those who came early and were fairly quickly successful in finding positions benefited greatly, as my father's example demonstrates, from their association with already-existing networks and personal contacts. They benefited also from the prospects they held out of introducing fields that the universities to which they went and the disciplines themselves were ready to embrace and build into academic strengths. These émigrés' willingness to adjust to a new academic universe might have been born of necessity, but it was reinforced by the terrible disillusionments they had suffered with the state of their own universities, however alien or exotic the American academic world might sometimes seem.

My Aunt Louise became another academic émigré, and an unusual one. She had had a good gymnasium education and then, at the age of twenty, married a much older East Prussian mine proprietor in what turned out to be a very unhappy union. Divorce was unthinkable, indeed scandalous, in her mother's worldview, and Louise turned to her brother for help; they remained close throughout their lives. She had always wanted a university education, something thought unnecessary for women in her circle, and he assisted her in obtaining a divorce and returning to Berlin to attend a school of social work founded by a progressive group of women whose politics were those of the Weimar left wing. She became active in social work and teaching, and in women's causes. Later she also attended lectures at the Hochschule für Politik. After its Nazification she went to England and was able to attend the London School of Economics, traveling back and forth between England and Germany to look after her widowed mother.

After my family's emigration, my father persuaded his sister to come to America to study. Despite her lack of a university degree, at an older age, and with a very uncertain grasp of English, she arrived from London and was admitted to the PhD program at Radcliffe. She was awarded the degree in political science at the age of forty in 1938 and went on to teach at several women's colleges before settling at what was then the Connecticut College for Women as a much-prized professor and as a noted scholar of international immigration studies. After retirement, she became a senior scholar at the Radcliffe Institute for Independent Study (now the Radcliffe Institute for Advanced Study). She wrote histories of both the International Refugee Organization and the UN High Commission for Refugees, and received the Golden Fridtjof Nansen Ring, awarded by Norway for exceptional service on behalf of refugees. Her English, to the delight of all who encountered her, remained sui generis: she would speak of reading Shakespeare "in the English translation" and exhort us to "stop running around the shrub and do the business."[8]

My mother's sister, Gertrude, arrived with her daughter in 1936 and took up residence in New York, sometimes with and sometimes apart from a husband who found exile difficult and degrading, having been used to prosperity and executive status. Later in life he found a new career in cybernetics at George Washington University, and they came together again.

My grandmother Bettmann arrived from Switzerland by way of Genoa in 1941. She and my grandfather had stayed on in Heidelberg after my grandfather's forced retirement, subjected to the various restrictions, rules, and indignities that were increasingly imposed on non-Aryans. They had hoped to go to America but were unable to get visas. My retired grandfather could not meet the qualification of having taught for two years in a row in the immediate past; my parents were not yet American citizens and therefore were not eligible, under the immigration laws, to provide an affidavit for them. After Kristallnacht, it became clear to my grandparents that they had to leave Germany at once. Helped by a number of friends who took real risks on their behalf, they prepared to emigrate, going first to Zurich.

They quickly sold their large Heidelberg house; the proceeds of the sale were sequestered by the government, as was their bank account. But at least, my grandmother wrote from Switzerland, she had been able to bribe an official into letting her take her silver, which could then be sold abroad. Ordinarily, she said, Jews were allowed to take with them only one spoon, one knife, and one fork each, and even that was about to change.

From the safety of Zurich, my grandmother wrote that the situation from which they had escaped was incredible; one now had actually to believe the unbelievable. "Bestiality," she said, now ruled in a world suffused with insecurity, dread, and fear of being consigned to a concentration camp. Many of their acquaintances in Germany had been arrested; others had left or were waiting, in trepidation, to find a refuge.

In Zurich the Bettmanns rented a room, which they described as airy and spacious, in a private house. They met a number of times with the US consul, and attempts were made to help them from America, but visas were still not to be had. Nonetheless, they remained hopeful and convinced that they would have a future life in America. They attended lectures, socialized with a widening circle of friends and visitors, read every newspaper they could buy, went to the museums and the numerous well-stocked book-stores, while always on tenterhooks for news from Heidelberg (the reports became steadily worse) and America. They tried to read as much English as they could and one evening decided to attend an American film. This was not a success. Although they took pride in understanding almost all the spoken English, my grandfather wrote that the plot was so stupid that he feared they would never understand American "fun."

He died in Switzerland the following year. My grandmother, having pretty much lost everything, managed to retain hope. In mid-1941, now sixty years old, with a visa finally in hand, and with sponsorship from my now-naturalized parents, she arrived in New York. She was to live here for the next thirty-three years, becoming an American citizen like the rest of us, without ever becoming quite as American. But she definitely came to love her adopted country and, after a life of upper-middle-class prosperity and comfort, to adapt without complaint or, so far as I could tell, regret, to her vastly changed circumstances.

To me, it is a constant source of amazement and admiration to be re-minded of what my parents and so many other refugees accomplished. They had to start all over again in a new world and culture, to become accustomed to a new social position, to write and lecture and speak in a new language, to experience the uncertainties of advancing or succeed-ing in new, quite unfamiliar academic settings, to master the conditions and details of a kind of daily life very different from that which they had in their earlier years taken comfortably for granted. My parents' sense of mission and their unshakable belief in the worth of intellectual and po-litical freedom, of learning and intellectual accomplishment, created a strong foundation for their lives as émigrés. Their comparative youth and their readiness to see the positive elements in a university system much less tradition bound than that of Germany, and less susceptible to direct interference from the state, made them more open than many to embracing an American academic ethos. And their good fortune in starting out in a supportive academic environment, even without solid guarantees of a permanent future, gave them an advantage in coming to terms with the problems that exile inevitably brought with it.

3

The Academic Émigrés in America

In 1946, at the age of eighty-four, Friedrich Meinecke had returned to Berlin. He was engaged in the project of establishing the Free University of Berlin and, in a letter to my father, asked whether he would be willing to return to Germany in order to help restore the country's shattered historical profession. My father, looking back on what had now become twelve years of exile, responded:

> In general, I would like nothing better than to help German historians to rebuild historical studies in Germany, and you may call on me any time you think I could be of help. . . . However, I would not consider accepting an appointment at a German university. Our children are American children. They have spent all their formative years in this country, and if we went back to Germany, they would be exiles. Knowing what that means, we certainly would not want them to go through that experience unnecessarily. Moreover, we have not become American citizens in name only. We are deeply devoted to the country of our adoption. We have been happy here after going through the first years of difficult adjustment. I have been particularly lucky in attracting a large number of unusually good students. Some of them are already teaching in various places; others, delayed by the War, will soon start their academic careers. I believe it to be my function in life to finish the task of helping to educate and train a new generation of college teachers of European history in this country, and I feel that by doing this I shall contribute at least indirectly to maintaining or rebuilding German historical research.[1]

My father was not alone in his views. By and large the academic refugees had come to see their exile as permanent and America as their home. While the end of the war opened the opportunity to reverse their emigration, it also opened greatly enriched opportunities in the expanding academic world of America itself.

Most of the academic refugees were anything but enthusiastic about remigration in the immediate postwar period. Efforts in Germany to bring back scholars who had been forced to flee were met by the German university authorities and faculties with resistance, with indifference at best, dislike and hostility at worst. The refugees saw that an old guard continued to dominate university professorships, and they could easily observe that the program of "de-Nazification," intended to remove the worst offenders from their university positions, was achieving meager results. Nor were the conditions of a country whose cities lay in ruins, whose economy was broken, and whose people resented their fate, attractive to contemplate, especially for refugees who had by now achieved some sense of security and comfort in their American milieu. In addition, the sentiments about America that my father expressed were widely shared, and the refugees' children had indeed become American. Over time, some of the émigrés did return and did make a considerable difference, most notably for their students, in the homeland. They often retained their ties in the United States, arranging to hold appointments simultaneously in both countries. Still, there were some, like Adorno and Horkheimer of the Frankfurt School, who had never felt truly at home in the United States and were glad to leave exile behind as soon as they could do so.

Finally, there were those who, like my father, would not think of returning but began to visit and to become involved as advisers and active participants in the German academic scene, hoping to help plan the institutions of a democratic state and to reform German academic life, to foster and guide the development and careers of a new generation of younger German scholars, and to create constructive ties and understanding between their two countries. My father was a regular visitor to Germany; the American representative in the international committee overseeing the publication of German Foreign Office documents; a consultant to the US high commissioner for Germany and the State Department; author of a report (negative and pessimistic in its findings) on the state and prospects of German higher education and what needed, if at all possible, to be done; a mediator who brought together people from government, the diplomatic services, and the universities with American counterparts. He had a very wide network in Germany, starting with his Hochschule colleague Theodor Heuss, who became the first president of the Federal Republic.[2]

The extensive literature on the intellectual migration of the 1930s has devoted predominant attention to the outstanding artists, architects, writers, composers, playwrights, musicians, and filmmakers who ended up primarily on both coasts of the United States. It is estimated that some twelve thousand émigrés might belong to the category of "intellectuals," defined to include artists, writers, lawyers, doctors, journalists, and freelancers as well as scholars. Approximately two thousand of this group were (or became) academics by profession.[3]

A great deal has been said about the impact of the émigré scholars on American higher education, somewhat less about the influence of American academic culture on the refugees in turn. Of course the academic worlds of these professors, and hence the influences to which they were exposed, underwent massive changes over the longer period of their residence and assimilation. The contrast between European and American university life was clearly very great. They experienced a changing American society in the '30s and, later, the transformative consequences of the New Deal, the era of World War II and its effects, the Cold War, and the conflicts of the '60s here and abroad. They witnessed also the revolution in American higher education that followed the war: the expansion of higher education and the influence of federal funding, the impacts of McCarthyism and later of student radicalism on American campuses. They saw the rise of American scholarship and science to a position of leadership in many areas and the transition of American higher education from an earlier quasi-provincialism to a broadly international outlook and role. Their contributions were important in that process. In the meantime they had in turn come to be strongly influenced by their adopted environment.

It is scarcely possible to generalize about the academic émigrés, given the immense diversity of personalities, disciplines of learning, individual careers, and fortunes (or misfortunes) in exile that marked their histories. Yet their members shared significant experiences in their backgrounds and in the courses of their exile that, at the very least, created an abiding sense of community founded in a recognition of what they shared.

There would always exist a space hard to bridge between the émigrés and those born in the country of their adoption. The émigrés of the first generation had in common with one another the histories they had been forced so abruptly to leave behind in another world of family, education, institutions, ways of life, and cultural assumptions, not to mention the more recent events of persecution and unforeseen exile. Many had been part of the same networks or had known one another as fellow students or colleagues. In their new world they could learn something about, but they had not lived, the formative backgrounds of their American associates; they could not take the same legacies and intuitive understandings for granted. That distance could never be narrowed completely.[4]

Their children, members of my so-called second generation, possessed neither the parents' histories to make their own nor that of their new compatriots, except indirectly and incompletely. On the other hand, the members of the second generation were beneficiaries of a gift, sometimes problematic but ultimately a very rich one: that of living, at least for some time, in or with two cultures as they became full Americans, always to be marked by a sometimes-subtle difference from their American peers. They, too, could recognize one another, though one cannot call them a community. The most comprehensive survey of this generation attributes to its members a distinctly unusual degree of educational accomplishment and professional success in their lives and careers. One of the study's findings is that second-generation persons who arrived between 1933 and 1945 are some fifteen times more likely to be listed in *Who's Who in America* than are native-born Americans of the same age group. For women the odds were found to be more than double those of their American-born contemporaries.[5]

By and large, the academic refugees had come to embrace the American academic world. They preferred its institutions to the rigid, hierarchical, and authoritarian universities they had left behind and had hoped to reform. While marking the downside and the imperfections of the American system—the taint of its continuing anti-Semitism even well after the war, the exposure to intrusiveness from political and funding quarters, the unevenness of quality, the excesses of campus life—they had never lost their profound sense of the evil that had driven them to emigration, and of the evils that arise from the politicization of universities and the destruction of institutional autonomy and of academic freedom it provokes.

It was not by accident that a number of those who opposed the imposition of a loyalty oath on faculty of the University of California should have come from the ranks of refugee scholars, or that some of them left the university. Nor is it surprising that, with some well-known exceptions like Herbert Marcuse, refugee scholars were so often among those especially alarmed by the rhetoric and actions of the radical Left of the 1960s that yearned to transform universities into instruments of social revolution. Whatever their own individual political persuasions, the refugees had seen the consequences of that kind of aspiration all too clearly. They cared above all about sustaining the integrity of the universities' central mission: to provide the space and the support for freedom of thought and expression, scholarship, and learning, and they believed these values were under threat. They had escaped from a society in which those freedoms had been crushed to a world in which the universities, however imperfect, held out their essential autonomy as a guiding principle of their existence. The émigrés were committed to this American academic ethos. They were deeply aware of its potential fragility, and they wanted to see it preserved and strengthened. In that, too, they played a role as they shared the lessons they had so painfully learned before their migration.

It is not surprising that many of the émigrés wrote autobiographies and memoirs. They felt it important to preserve and to pass on their personal histories and to make sense of the larger history they had witnessed. The émigrés' memoirs convey vivid pictures of their initial environments, their families and earlier lives, their awakening to politics and to the overwhelming disturbances of World War I and its disillusionments; of Germany's defeat and its aftermath, patriotic loyalties betrayed, ideals of liberal democratic reform crushed, and even modest expectations of a decent life violently reversed. The memoirs speak to many common themes rooted in the experience of exile and adjustment to new circumstances and cultures. The broad outlines of that process, its difficulties and triumphs, are quite similar for all, familiar to those who had passed through the first shocks and uncertainties of their arrival in an alien environment to achieve some sort of security and ease with their new surroundings and the demands of their new beginnings. My own family's experience reflects those patterns, but it is certainly not the case that our family, or any other, can be taken as "typical" of the émigrés generally.

The majority of the first generation were highly educated and assimilated Jews who came from prosperous backgrounds in which the values of intellectual activity and of immersion in music, art, and literature had a special worth. Their families tended to be well traveled and to see themselves as cosmopolitan in outlook, while regarding German culture as preeminent and often disdaining much of American culture as superficial, commercialized, and insulated from the larger and higher traditions of European civilization. They had a deep need to cling to and advocate the cultural values that accompanied and in multiple ways defined them. And they shared a deep longing to pass those values on to their children, to see them sustained in the next generation even as they watched their children become Americanized.

Many factors differentiated the processes of adaptation to the United States and their outcomes. Some people found it hard to adapt at all. Some remained captives of nostalgia and longing for an idealized lost world. Some lost their basic confidence and hope for the future and never quite recovered. Some found it almost too difficult to accept the lowering of their social status, so elevated in Europe, together with the financial hardships they had to endure. For some their chosen careers could not be continued. Some experienced the humiliation of having at least for a time to accept menial work in order to survive. Some tended to seek out and to live or work in enclaves of their own kind, most notably in New York, where, for example, the Graduate Faculty of the New School for Social Research exhibited some attributes of a Central European colony.

There were professors whose spouses continued to serve them as Herr Professors around whom all had to revolve, but there were wives who worked at low-level jobs to support their families, and wives who embraced what they thought a greater freedom of self-expression and independence as working women. The ages at which people immigrated generally made a considerable difference to their capacity for gaining the flexibility needed to accommodate a new life. Those who came early might find a comfort with that life somewhat easier to attain than did those who followed. Those who could not bear watching their children become, to a greater or lesser degree, separated in language and outlook from themselves might have an especially difficult time. The strength, or lack of strength, of any given family mattered greatly, as did an openness to trying to understand the larger society that was now theirs, a willingness to participate in its customs and arrangements, and the impulse to explore new cultures.

Pure luck and the contingencies of timing were always very much at work. Refugees found places at a surprising number of historically black colleges.[6] Some found places at a number of small and less prestigious liberal arts colleges, where they could not teach graduate students, but where they made a very large and usually appreciated difference (there were always a few whose personalities, sense of entitlement, or belief in the superiority of everything European did not endear them to their colleagues). Some changed their professional disciplines. This was especially true of men trained as lawyers who could not practice or be licensed in the entirely different American legal system, and who became political scientists (for example, Franz Neumann and Karl Loewenstein) or teachers of the Central European history they knew well. A few were able to find positions as scholars of jurisprudence, comparative law, Roman or canon law, or history of law. Medical doctors could not practice unless they were relicensed, not an easy task (and one that required new study and then service as poorly compensated interns, etc.) but successful for some; others found positions as teachers of biological subjects. There were many immigrant scholars who had to take menial jobs, at least at the outset, or who had to abandon their academic aspirations altogether.

The émigré scholars exercised no single influence. Their impact on the disciplines of learning varied greatly. It can be more directly assessed in such fields as those of the natural sciences, mathematics, and some of the social sciences, for science generally already constituted an international community with many existing interconnections and professional relationships. Visits, conferences, exchanges, fellowships and postdoctoral periods abroad, and the leading scientific publications had long brought scientists into a shared universe. The academic refugees' influence can be discerned more clearly also in such fields as economics, political science, sociology, and the history of art and of music than in such areas as literature, philosophy, or classics. There were indeed, however, distinguished émigré scholars of these last three fields who played important roles in strengthening and deepening their disciplines in this country, and who created schools of thought and method within them. The study of literature, of course, then existed primarily as that of national bodies of writing; the refugees whose impact is most visible were those who brought comparative literature to a new status and helped found new degree programs in this area.

It has often been observed that émigré scholars were most warmly welcomed and most influential in those areas that were most ready to embrace, and had already perhaps started to embrace, the disciplinary approaches in which the newcomers specialized, thus bringing new strengths to universities, departments, and fields of learning that were ready to accept and benefit from their contributions. In general, one can say that American higher learning in the humanities and social sciences was rendered less parochial and far more cosmopolitan by the presence and influence of the refugees who brought with them a tradition of culture that emphasized breadth of learning, the humanistic values of what the Germans call *Bildung*, a classical education, and a universe of experience and perspective that made themselves felt by their students and associates. This translated into an enriched and searching intellectual outlook, referred to by Carl Schorske as an enormous influence on the "cultural formation" of his scholarly generation.[7]

It is important to observe that the émigrés, too, gained new horizons and new perspectives in their intellectual outlooks and scholarship. Thus my father, in introducing his *History of Germany*, a three-volume work that summarized his interpretation of every significant question of German history that he had pondered and assessed over the course of his scholarly life, wrote that his transformation into an American had given him a broader perspective on all things German and on his view of European history in general. He spoke also of moving increasingly to a comparative history approach in his thinking and analysis, and he came to emphasize that in his teaching as well.

It is as mentors, I think, that the historians had their greatest legacy. Their breadth of learning and of interests was remarkable and made itself felt. My father, for example, taught and wrote widely in the areas of intellectual history and the history of the Renaissance and Reformation as well as of the modern era, German history from medieval times onward, modern international relations, and philosophy of history. The historians conveyed a somewhat new focus in their conception and practice of intellectual history, regarded by many as a European import. They also made Central European history a critical subject alongside English and French history, and emphasized both the study of Europe as a whole and the sweep of its history.

At the same time, the historians varied in the periods they chose and in the approaches they represented, from the economic history championed by Hans Rosenberg to the history of ideas espoused by historians like my father, so they cannot be identified with a single school of thought or with founding one form of historical scholarship. While émigré scholars such as Hans Baron, Felix Gilbert, and Paul Oskar Kristeller were major figures in the field of Renaissance history and its growth in America, each of these men brought a different approach and substance of interpretation to his studies of that era. Altogether, the historians played a significant role as intellectual models in ways to which their students have testified. In the end, and as in the case of most scholars, however distinguished their work, their most enduring influence flowed through their role as educators and cultural role models, not only for their students, but also for others with whom they were in contact.

One can see that the refugee scholars of German history, however differing their individual narratives and analyses, were preoccupied with a common underlying question: How had the history they had experienced and observed in their own lives come to happen? Was Nazism the inevitable outcome of a distinctively German tradition, and if so, how far back did it extend: to Luther? to Bismarck? What were its ultimate sources? Was German history that of a *Sonderweg*, a distinctive evolution peculiar to German history that distinguished Germany's character and development from those of the Western European states? Did geography play a special part in its destiny? Did Germans have an innate impulse toward authoritarian forms of government? What had gone wrong with the Weimar Republic? Why could it not establish deeper roots? Why could democracy not have commanded genuine allegiance among more of the republic's citizens? Was Hitler an aberration, one who had seized power for contingent reasons, or did he and his regime represent something that went deeper into the core of German history? The German historians were, in short, absorbed in the study of the foundations of fascism in their homeland. They wanted to move away from the strongly politicized accounts and interpretations of an existing historiography, and to assess the course of German history in the context of Europe—and now of the New World—as a whole. All this represented a significant style of modern European history that the exiles helped imbed in the American historical profession.

Of course the situation of émigrés was never static. People continued to develop over time and to experience new influences. Their opinions and attitudes, their personal satisfactions or preoccupations quite naturally underwent changes large and small; their knowledge of and interest in all things American, and American higher education especially, grew decisively. The developments that took place in the decade of the thirties and the postwar years had powerful effects on their lives. Many refugees had been active during the war in various Washington agencies or in the armed forces. One center of their activity had been the Office of Strategic Services, and especially its Research and Analysis (R&A) Branch, where German refugee scholars, working side by side with American scholars drawn from many institutions, brought their expertise to the gathering and interpretation of intelligence related to Germany as well as contributing to the larger planning for postwar policies concerned with governing and (so it was hoped) transforming a defeated state into a healthy democracy. My father was the OSS liaison with the State and War Departments in this effort and later wrote a book on the subject, *American Military Government: Its Organization and Policies*, published in 1947.

The mix of scholars at the OSS created what they christened the "OSS University" and established an influential network that was to have an impact on their professions for a considerable time to come. Young men, many of whom who had started their graduate studies or who were on their way to doing so when the war began, found themselves in close contact with European émigrés from whom, as they testified, they learned immensely. The friendships and professional ties among members of the different generations of the R&A, both native and new Americans, endured over the subsequent decades. The OSS experience wielded a discernible influence on the careers and mind-set of the graduate students returning to finish their degrees after the war, their intellectual directions and destinations shaped in part by their association with the European members of the Research and Analysis Branch.[8] H. Stuart Hughes recalled the OSS as his "second graduate education" and described the subculture of the R&A Branch as "an ongoing if ever-interrupted seminar."

The rapid growth of higher education after 1945 created extensive opportunities for academic and research appointments that had not existed earlier, and the situation for some who had lacked good positions, or any secure professional positions at all, improved greatly in the postwar era as their learning came into demand. Some gradual erosion of the anti-Semitism that had barred Jews in any proper number from the academy was to a degree fostered by the presence and assimilation of scholars who had fled the Nazis. The new internationalism, the events of the war, and the widespread experience of serving in the military abroad had helped create a greatly increased interest in European studies, all of which re-dounded to the benefit of the European scholars. And in the meantime, the academic exiles had become, in the main, genuine (if not always uncritical) Americans as well as respected colleagues within the academic world.

The Yale to which my father came in 1934 was in many ways provincial and turned in on itself, an institution alarmingly anti-Semitic in its atti-tudes and policies, a male, college-dominated university that showed a considerable gap between its collegiate and scholarly cultures, and a com-munity that was only partially aware of developments in Central Europe. The president, James Rowland Angell, was the first (and since then only) of its presidents to have had no Yale degree. The Yale over which he presided, with a faculty composed to a large extent of Yale degree holders, regarded him as an outsider. The much-revered William Lyon Phelps had remarked before Angell's appointment that were he to imagine a non-Yale man as president he would "feel exactly as a Catholic would feel if a Mohammedan were elected Pope."[9]

President Angell brought a new emphasis to the Graduate School of Arts and Sciences and to the role of scholarship and research at Yale. The Yale of the thirties was turning increasingly into a university, however much some of its loyal and tradition-minded college faculty may have clung to their fa-miliar culture and Yale's collegiate identity, even as the residential colleges gave a new and in some ways deepened focus to undergraduate life.

Angell and his provost, the historian Charles Seymour, sought to strengthen the faculty by making first-rate appointments through the graduate school and to lessen the independence of the college from central oversight—and to attenuate the college's dominance—by consolidating to a new degree the university's central administration. Angell gained considerable success on both fronts.

In 1934 Yale's history department (Seymour's original home and one to which he gave much attention) had been known primarily as a bastion of American and English history. The department benefited in the thirties from growth in both numbers and quality, and it was in this atmosphere that my father became a member of the graduate school faculty and was given encouragement to deepen and expand the area of modern and Central European history. A few other émigré scholars received appointments at the same time—Arnold Wolfers, specialist in international relations (a program in which my father also taught) who had been my father's senior colleague at the Hochschule für Politik, had arrived the year before; the Assyriologist Albrecht Goetze and lawyer/political scientist Karl Loewenstein (later and for many years at Amherst) were given visiting appointments in 1934.

My parents were welcomed by a number of people who were conscious of and very much concerned about developments in Germany and the plight of academic refugees, and who were anxious to be helpful. Some of them, in the midst of an academic community that was quite conservative in political as in university matters, were very liberal and deeply involved in social causes (some of them in fact found the New Deal insufficiently progressive and voted for Norman Thomas). They were generous in their support of the émigré newcomers. A number of more conservative colleagues were very helpful also, including even some with strongly isolationist or at least noninterventionist views. One of those was the English historian Wallace Notestein, a close friend until he discovered in 1940 that my father intended to cast his first vote as a citizen for FDR and a third term. On this ground Mr. Notestein stopped speaking to my father, asserting that he had assisted him to escape from fascism only to see him now try to impose a dictatorship on this still barely free country. It was only many years later when they met accidentally in the men's room of the Hall of Graduate Studies that their conversations resumed. Another helpful (and strongly anti-interventionist) colleague was the American diplomatic historian Samuel Flagg Bemis, who kindly called us up one Christmas in Cold War days to let us know that he had received secret knowledge of a Russian plan to attack the United States on the holiday. He urged us to seek immediate shelter, apparently rating us as worth saving.

While his primary appointment was in the graduate school, my father's undergraduate lecture courses turned out to be surprisingly popular. I still encounter former students who remember him fondly. They were charmed by my father's accent and by learning their modern European history from a modern European. They presumably also liked the fact that he was not the hardest of taskmasters. Like many of the other émigré scholars I knew, my father was delighted to find so many young men who seemed interested in his subject, and he tended not to overwork them. The most extreme case of this syndrome I can recall is that of a refugee professor of Roman law at Harvard who was astonished, but ecstatic, to see so many fine, rather large boys flood into his classroom to take up the study of Roman law—the entire football team was onto Roman law for some reason, causing an early instance of grade inflation.

When it came to graduate students, however, my father was absolutely rigorous and demanding, setting standards that helped elevate the professional aspirations and accomplishments of his students, and that helped define the field of modern German and Central European history in the American academic world more generally. By the end of his life, my father had supervised some fifty-five PhD recipients who held, or had held, positions in history departments across the country. He was also the first foreign-born historian to become president of the American Historical Association, and Yale's history department was now known as a leading academic center for the study of modern European history.

My father's first years at Yale were, as he wrote to Meinecke, difficult, given the tasks of learning the ways of an American university and the teaching of undergraduates, having to write lectures in a still imperfectly mastered language, and trying to carry forward his scholarly work while dealing with financial needs that meant additional teaching as a regular visitor at the Fletcher School of Law and Diplomacy of Tufts University, and also trying to make all the other adjustments necessary for managing American life itself. His letters to his sister, Louise, describe both the stresses of his situation and his characteristically optimistic determination to succeed.

From the time of his arrival in the United States, my father had become active in working to aid other refugees to establish themselves in America. The refugees began to form a community based both on shared pasts and on their current experience of coming to terms with America and its culture. In the same letter, my father wrote to Meinecke:

> Relations among the German colleagues are . . . very pleasant; they are all quite different from one another, but all are very willing to help one another. With the rarest of exceptions, incidentally, the Americans are entirely approving about their growing numbers. That's very gratifying to all of us.[10]

An earlier émigré, Alfred Vagts, a military historian who had not emigrated for political reasons but had come to the United States, married the daughter of Charles Beard, and settled comfortably in Connecticut, left this description:

> In various ways we émigré scholars remained "Verschworene" [sic], sworn band helping one another as far as our reach went, telling one another of academic openings where such occurred, giving applicants a good character; keeping silent where there might be something discredible [sic], in American eyes, as to their past.[11]

Vagts wrote these words in an unpublished memoir; the last comment was followed by his recital of a juicy piece of gossip about an affair conducted by one of the refugee scholars. He was not the kindest of commentators, but he did feel a deep sense of belonging to a larger family of exiles, and he was generous in his assistance to many in what was a kind of mutual aid society. Those already settled helped and helped advise the new arrivals. In my family's case, our guest room was often their first home as they searched for positions. The children inherited the outgrown clothes of other young refugees. The émigrés frequently raised money to tide people over or to enable an individual's travel to interviews or reconnaissance at colleges and research institutions around the country. They visited one another often. Our home became a gathering place for some of this larger family, especially those who came to be resident in New Haven and New York, our living room a kind of salon for many lively meetings and discussions among the clan.

As with so many families, the community of refugee scholars, for all its powerful sense of a unified identity and an enduring commitment to mutual support and collaboration, was not without its tensions, conflicts, strong disagreements, and personal feuds. Some were jealous of those whom they saw as gaining greater success in their professional opportunities and careers than they themselves had been able to find, attributing the good fortune of others to luck and political savvy and their own disappointments to the unfairness of life. But the larger sense of community consistently outweighed such internal dissension when it came to the major concerns that mattered for their common purposes.

Emigration affected my father's scholarship not only in its broadening perspectives but also in the fundamental consequence that he no longer had access to the German archives on which much of his work had depended. He was never again able to pursue archival research. In addition, he now had to learn to write in English. He was naturally less prolific during the first period of his American career, and, although he published steadily, it was only after the war and the interruption caused by his service in the OSS that he could again write in greater volume. Some of what he published was designed to reach a larger reading public. For example, his *The Political Collapse of Europe* (1951), expanding on ideas first laid out in an article in *Foreign Affairs*, landed him on the cover of the *Saturday Review of Literature* and became a staple of courses on modern Europe. Its argument— that after the two world wars Europe's political system had disintegrated, that the European states had ceased to be Great Powers and had given way to the new constellation of two superpowers, the United States and the USSR—seems evident now, but it had not been historically analyzed with the same clarity and immediacy then. While embarking on his ambitious *History of Modern Germany*, he continued to publish work displaying the wide range of his interests, from the ancient Greeks and their ideas of history to the diplomacy of the Weimar Republic and the character of Nazi ideology. At the same time, an article, "Der deutsche Idealismus in sozialgeschichtlicher Beleuchtung" (translated as "German Idealism in the Light of Social History"), which appeared in the *Historische Zeitschrift* in 1952, considered the question of whether and how a distinctive German historical evolution had differentiated German from Western European culture in the basic social and intellectual developments of the nineteenth century. Among his many essays, this article came to be read and cited with particular frequency among German historians. The blend of social and intellectual history that he advocated and that this essay demonstrated was as significant to historians as was its argument that Germany's development had in fact taken a separate path in which social class and a dominant view of state power had combined to create a characteristic orientation toward power and human rights that differed from the directions emerging from Western Europe. In his presidential address at the American Historical Association's annual meeting of 1967, he laid out at length his conception of intellectual history and the importance of analyzing the development of political and other ideas as situated within the social and political fabric of their time, responsive to its historical realities, rather than as abstract sequences of thought.[12]

My father's strong interest in politics and in finding a role in public affairs lasted throughout his life. After the war he was able to realize a portion of this commitment in a new way, by becoming an adviser to General Clay during Clay's service as high commissioner for the US military government of occupied Germany. He served as an adviser to the State Department on German affairs until his death, and as a well-known figure who could offer informal but useful assistance in conferring with German leaders in government and elsewhere to the end of helping pave a path to constructive relationships between American and German individuals and institutions. While disappointed that the university reforms he had advocated and hoped might transform higher education in a new Germany failed sufficiently to materialize, he became active also in helping forge linkages between academic groups in the two countries. He found much satisfaction as well in becoming something of a mentor to a number of the young German historians who were emerging in the 1950s and 1960s and used his government and other contacts to help expand exchange programs and fellowships and to encourage young German academics' entry into the international scholarly community.

Recognized increasingly for his work in Germany as well as his academic stature, my father died in Bonn in June 1969 on the night after he received the first Inter Nationes Prize, an award bestowed on the occasion of the twentieth anniversary of the Federal Republic of West Germany to recognize his contribution to international understanding, specifically in his influence on people and policies having to do with American-German relations. His last public talk was a brief speech of acceptance that ended thus: "One of the finest experiences in my career was that I was always able to act in the fullest identity with both my American responsibilities and my German past. . . . At this moment, then, let me thank not only all my German friends but also all my American friends for what as a whole I consider a happy life."[13]

4

Growing up in New Haven and in Washington, DC

When our family arrived in America on the SS *Olympic* in August 1934, the ship docked at midnight after sailing past a brightly lit Statue of Liberty. It was intensely exciting, the latest I had ever been up, and I remember my hat flying away into the harbor as we stood on deck watching the ship's deliberate progress as it was towed toward the pier. This vivid memory may be regarded as suspect, since I was not quite four years old at the time, but its details were so often repeated as part of family lore that it was reinforced in my personal sense of a significant past moment, always to be preserved.

As our very large quantity of luggage was processed through customs, my brother burst into tears when the inspector opened a trunk revealing on top a pair of his lederhosen with a hole in their seat. Frederick thought the uniformed official was a policeman who would at once bar him from entry to America. Once outside the customs shed we were welcomed by Uncle Fritz. He drove us to New Jersey, where I awoke the next morning to the stares of several older cousins who spoke no German and teased me for my ignorance of English.

From there we went to New Haven, where my parents had rented a house in the Spring Glen section of Hamden, a suburb just north of the city. (Some six years later they had a larger home designed by a Yale architecture professor built nearby.) There my brother and I began to live a childhood that was in some ways an American suburban life in an American academic setting, and in others a life shaped by the ethos, expectations, and practices of our European household.

My parents' strong desire to adapt to their new world, to see it in a positive light, but without sacrificing the values of their European culture, had a huge impact on both my brother and me. We were encouraged to learn the language quickly, to embrace school and find American friends. My parents did not, as did some of their friends, confine themselves essentially to the company of other European émigrés. They adapted better than many others to the reduced social status that came with moving from the German academic system of the Herr Professor to the more democratic American one, and they very much liked the greater informality of this new world.

At the same time, we continued at home to speak German, to celebrate holidays (especially Christmas) and other occasions in the German way, to listen, under my father's instruction, to classical music in the German manner, and to read German books. Before the war we went twice to Europe, stopping in London and Paris, where we were taken (sometimes dragged) to the museums and landmarks, and then going on to the Engadin in Switzerland. There, in Sils Maria, we stayed with our Heidelberg grandparents and were governed by my grandfather's rather severe discipline. He had very firm and precise views on how and where to hike, what to read, what to eat, and when and how to speak. He assigned reading and tested us with oral exams on books and subjects that he wanted to be sure we would learn something about. I particularly recall his insistence that we read and discuss *Nathan der Weise*. We had to work diligently; our summer studies under his tutelage felt more demanding than those of our quite rigorous school in New Haven. In contrast, a week's visit to my father's mother at a resort hotel in Grünwald required only good manners and polite conversation, as my grandmother spent the day sitting comfortably on the veranda. We did eat well.

Another strong influence came from the network of academic refugees that developed and grew in the years after our arrival. As our family had come early and had a settled home, colleagues and friends who came later

often passed through our house on their way to their next stop (unfortunately often only a temporary destination). Our living room became, both
then and later, a meeting place for exiled friends. The many gatherings
of Central European academics there remain vivid memories. My brother
and I were directed to sit in the corner and listen. We were told that many
of these people were absolutely remarkable, and that we should always
remember them. Some members of this network taught at Yale, prominent
among them the literary critics and comparative literature scholars René
Wellek and Erich Auerbach and, for shorter periods, the composer Paul
Hindemith, the economist Jakob Marschak, and the philosopher Ernst Cassirer. Hindemith invited me to examine his collection of instruments and
hear him play. Later I learned to drive from an instructor who seemed to
have been turned permanently ashen by his terrifying (and unsuccessful)
attempt to teach his art to the Hindemiths.

Mrs. Cassirer was an accomplished seamstress, and one summer, scandalized by my mother's complaint about my stubborn resistance to sewing,
she determined that she would teach me. I would go to the Cassirers' apartment, where she would talk and talk while cutting out patterns. She would
then finally open the door to the philosopher's study, where, looking with
his great mane of white hair like a movie producer's vision of a philosopher, and writing steadily in a flowing script without ever crossing out a
word, Cassirer was at work. "Ernstli," his wife would say, "Himbeer Saft,
bitte." And he would go obediently to the kitchen, pour raspberry syrup
into three glasses, add water, and join us for savoring this treat and for
kindly conversation. I never did really learn to sew, however; Mrs. C., while
chattering away, did all the work.

Visitors included nonacademics as well as scholars—for example, the
writer Hermann Broch—but most were academics. Among other regular
visitors I remember most clearly Heinrich Zimmer, the Sanskrit scholar
who died young, and his wife, the daughter of Hugo von Hofmannsthal;
the art historians Erwin Panofsky (the great scholar of iconography, professor at the Institute for Advanced Study) and his wife (they were known
as Pan and Pandora) and Richard Krautheimer (professor at Vassar); the

theologian Paul Tillich (then at the Union Theological Seminary in New York); the philosophers Hannah Arendt (then at the New School), Herbert Marcuse (then with the International Institute for Social Research in New York; he could not stand Arendt and always referred to her as "die Blaustrumpf," the bluestocking), and Erich Frank; the political scientists Franz Neumann (author of *Behemoth*, the influential Marxist analysis of National Socialism and professor at Columbia), Sigmund Neumann (at Wesleyan), and Karl Loewenstein (at Amherst); the sociologist Albert Salomon (professor at the New School); and the Renaissance scholar Paul Oskar Kristeller (leading scholar of humanism and professor of Italian and philosophy at Columbia). The historians included Felix Gilbert (a wanderer through various institutions but without a regular academic position before the war), Theodor Mommsen (the medievalist, also without a regular position at the time), Dietrich Gerhard (a scholar of European and comparative history who became professor of European history at Washington University in St. Louis), Fritz Epstein (without a faculty position before the war, he worked as a bibliographer at Harvard's Widener Library), Hans Rosenberg (influential historian of early modern and modern Germany with a specialty in economic history, then at Brooklyn College and later at Berkeley), Ernst Kantorowicz (medievalist and author of a well known and controversial biography of Frederick II and of *The King's Two Bodies* on the ideology of medieval kingship, finally at the Institute for Advanced Study), and Ludwig Edelstein (professor of the history of ancient philosophy and medicine at Johns Hopkins). Both Kantorowicz and Edelstein held appointments at Berkeley from which they resigned at the time of the loyalty oath controversy, having refused to sign the oath. Gilbert and Mommsen, with my father's support, held temporary research positions at Yale; otherwise they depended on temporary jobs, Mommsen (descendant of the great historian of Rome) at a prep school (I think Groton). A majority of these historians had been students of Friedrich Meinecke.

I remember with special clarity our excitement in 1936 when Professor Meinecke came to the United States to receive an honorary degree at Harvard's tercentenary celebration. My parents were proud to have my father's renowned *Doktorvater* stay at our house; they introduced him not only to Yale but to some of the surroundings they found so beautiful along the Connecticut shore and in the northwestern part of the state. I recall a festive picnic in the Kent Falls State Park, and I have photos of my father and Meinecke and his namesake, my brother Frederick, standing by the secondhand Ford, recently purchased, that was my father's pride and joy, a kind of symbol for having really taken to life in America—and one he could demonstrate to his foreign visitor as he drove him about.

The conversations in my parents' living room covered all kinds of intellectual and political topics, some of which I could scarcely understand in my early years. There was of course a tremendous amount of talk devoted to the international situation, to developments in Germany and on the Continent more generally, and to the New Deal. I was much encouraged, at a very early age, to learn all I could about both domestic and international politics and, when the war began, to follow its course. I became an ardent interventionist. I believed that Franklin Delano Roosevelt was a truly great man, and assumed that he was the permanent leader of the United States; I could imagine no other. My earliest political education was conducted carefully by my brother, a precocious expert in both domestic and international affairs. I could scarcely claim much in the way of any actual knowledge and sometimes became badly mixed up—I remember, for example, that my brother had to explain to me at the age of six that Mussolini's victories in Ethiopia were not to be applauded and that Il Duce was as bad as Hitler.

The large personalities I observed and the debates to which I listened were a significant part of my education. In addition, the academic refugees conveyed their strong sense of community, and my brother and I saw ourselves as children of this familiar and collaborative tribe. In moving to Washington in 1943 to serve full-time in the OSS until 1945, my father joined a number of other refugees assigned to the Research and Analysis Branch. I encountered again such familiar people as Franz Neumann and Herbert Marcuse, and was introduced to some new faces, Otto Kirchheimer (another political scientist originally associated with the Institute for

Social Research and later with the New School) prominent among them. There were others in different sections of the OSS. Once again, in Washington, our living room was the site of many gatherings of the clan, and by then I was old enough to take most of it in.

Learning to live with two cultures was an always-evolving process for the first as for the second generation, although the second generation came of course to be far more firmly rooted in the new culture as their real home. The experience of the members naturally varied, and yet there was something recognizable about us, something we had in common. Among my very good friends of the second generation were the historians John Clive and Klaus Epstein, the economist Henry Rosovsky, the psychologist Lotte Bailyn, and the political scientists Susanne Rudolph and Judith Shklar. We shared a recognizable identity.

On our arrival in Spring Glen, my six-year-old brother was sent to the local public school. It was hard to enter that totally unfamiliar environment, and without knowing its language, but he learned English by some process of osmosis and taught it to me. Then, having learned to read and write the language, he passed these accomplishments on to me also, with the consequence that I was later found overqualified for first grade.

Fred had already, like all little German boys, been addicted to the Wild West stories of the German author Karl May. He was at first disappointed to find no heroic Indians or cowboys in our neighborhood. But soon we visited the historian Charles Beard and his family in Washington, Connecticut, and they took us to a Mohawk reservation close by. Mr. Beard explained to us something of the history of the Mohawks and their association with this region of Connecticut, and my brother was appeased.

We lived in a German home, surrounded by Biedermeier furniture, German books and records and pictures and knickknacks. It amazes me to think of how much we brought to America, including even gooseberries that had been put up in jars in Heidelberg, and that were served as dessert in Hamden for many years. After my father's death, I discovered that he had brought along and preserved several bottles of 1920s Rothschild. The wine was still outstanding in 1969, and we drank it reverently.

My parents were used to having help at home, and a wonderful Mrs. Nallinger, born in Bavaria, did most of the housekeeping and cooking (of course with German recipes); she also helped look after the children. My mother thought I should learn housekeeping early. As a young child, I was given a book called *Mutter's kleine Hilfsreiche* (Mother's Little Helper), the didactic tale of a young girl that reached its first suspenseful climax when she was taught to iron, beginning with a handkerchief. I learned the same way, and all the housekeeping rules that I was (and remain) disciplined to observe were detailed and demanding. For dish drying, we had a row of towels, one for glass, another for silverware, yet another for china, still another for cooking implements, and so on. All had their purposes in letters beautifully hand stitched on them, part of my mother's trousseau that included everything monogrammed by hand, sheets with buttonholes designed to be affixed to buttons sewn on blankets, exquisite napkins and tablecloths. For cleaning, we used specialized tools that had to be wielded in a certain order. We had straw mattresses that came in three pieces and had to be aired every day with the window open, as did all the bedding; goose-down covers had to be pounded with a special paddle (also imported from the old country).

My parents had done a very clever thing: they told us we would learn proper English before they did, and we should correct their English; in turn, they would correct our German. This gave us, we felt, an important role, and it also made us proud of being bilingual so that we kept up our German. For many of the émigré children, that was the last thing they wanted, and they became "American" by speaking only English and losing command of German altogether. The difference between those who wanted to adapt fully to their new surroundings and those who were reluctant to do so (or whose parents were reluctant to let go) was sometimes mirrored in the presence or absence of an accent.

Our parents insisted that we read the German classics and that we speak only German on Sundays. But finally my mother heard me kicking the stairs as I came down them one Sunday, muttering loudly, "Goddamn it, another goddamned Sunday," and began to fear that she was raising a monster. By then, however, my German was quite firmly implanted. As time passed, we moved between the two languages, even in the same paragraph, with scarcely a thought.

We were occasionally embarrassed by our parents' accents. The German émigrés, while always hoping to improve their English, dealt with the problem by telling inside jokes, which we loved. For example, one story, often repeated, that always made everyone roar with laughter, was about a refugee in London who went to the grocer's and asked for "bloody oranges." "We have no oranges for juice," was the answer. Whereupon the lady turned to her companion and said "Ach, siehmal, jetzt werden sie auch hier anti-semitisch" (Oh, look, now they're becoming anti-Semitic here, too). Another cited the translation from the Lutheran Bible of the passage "The spirit is willing, but the flesh is weak," as "The ghost is eager, but the meat is tender."

My parents loved much about America—its political system, its freedom, its relative informality, its diversity. But they were leery of American popular culture and anxious that we share the high European culture in which they were steeped. The comics were strictly forbidden. We did not go to movies, except for such carefully selected ones as *Fantasia*, with its dramatization of Beethoven's Pastoral Symphony, and (for me) *Journey for Margaret*, with its wholesome attitude toward virtue's triumph over the sorrows of wartime. We were not allowed to listen to radio, except for the New York Philharmonic, the NBC Symphony, and the *University of Chicago Roundtable of the Air*. Fortunately, my father at some point discovered, and fell for, the Sunday evening comedians: Jack Benny, Fred Allen, Edgar Bergen (with Charlie McCarthy and Mortimer Snerd), and I was permitted to join him for these wonderful programs. I loved these so much that I had a brief period (in eighth grade) of wanting to become a radio comedienne.

In our German cuisine, we were forbidden white bread (Wonder Bread was considered the epitome of barbarism) and a number of other such unhealthy products. We were also—this was not, perhaps, typically German but advocated by my grandfather who, as a doctor, was deemed to have unarguable authority—not allowed hot baths (decadent) or pillows or to sleep in a curled-up position (ruinous to posture; we were woken up and straightened out if found to sleep in this mode). For a time, our clothes were German too, quite literally. My brother suffered the humiliation of lederhosen and I of dirndl dresses, sent from my grandmother's seamstress in Heidelberg. The ladies of New Haven clucked over how adorable these were, while we squirmed self-consciously. But after my grandparents left Germany for good, we began to look more like (but still not exactly like) the other children at school.

At friends' houses, I luxuriated in eating sandwiches made with white bread, in having no requirement to finish what was on my plate, and in listening to afternoon radio serials like *Stella Dallas*. Sometimes I read comic books and, with great caution, chewed gum. But I did not confess these sins on returning to the more austere environment of my own home.

Despite restrictions designed to keep us from the corruptions and superficialities of popular culture, we were given freedoms unknown to other children. We could read whatever we wished in the well-stocked library at home, and were encouraged to keep up with the newspapers. We could roam about and explore and visit, so long as we turned up at a stated time and did what we needed to do on time, and we could go to school on our own. School was the most important thing. Education was everything, and my parents sacrificed for the best education they could give us at the excellent private elementary school, the Foote School, in New Haven, followed by prep school for my brother and private high school for me. It was clear to us that doing well at school mattered tremendously, and that our futures, and some guarantees for those futures, were at stake. Academic and intellectual achievement was prized above all else. That was very much a common experience for the second generation.

Spring Glen was a pleasant residential suburb, leafy and solid. It had extensive open spaces that began gradually to fill up with comfortable houses placed on good-sized lots over the years of our residence there. Climbing around the construction sites was one of the forbidden pleasures of childhood, and watching the moving vans disgorge their contents as new neighbors arrived a regular entertainment. The hills and fields and ponds around us made it possible to sled, ski, and skate in the winter, to ride our bicycles pell-mell downhill and circle lazily around the neighborhood in other seasons. Autumns were marked by the scent of burning leaves that had been raked and piled at the curb. That aroma lingers in my memory together with the sound of distant shouts from the Yale Bowl as my friend Harriet and I spent Saturday afternoons playing Robin Hood in New Haven's Edgewood Park. Summers were marked by the scent of freshly cut grass. They were filled with time spent at the nearby beaches along Long Island Sound, swimming and learning to sail, weeks at day camps in the area and later at sleepaway summer camps. After the start of the war, when we could no longer travel to Europe, we enjoyed several family stays in Greensboro, Vermont, that set an unforgettable standard for the perfect summer retreat, given the natural beauties of the landscape and the pleasures of the lake, of hiking, and of horseback riding, as also of long days immersed in reading whatever could be found in the village's little public library, and of Sunday concerts at the waterfront.

The house in which my family lived for almost thirty years was situated about a half mile from the principal artery, Whitney Avenue, that runs directly into the center of downtown New Haven. My brother and I attended private school in the city. We always took the same Whitney Avenue number 10 bus and saw the same people who got on from the same corners and sat in the same seats (one of them was Thornton Wilder) and nodded to one another. The route passed by Lake Whitney and the location of the Armory, a factory for the production of muskets constructed by Eli Whitney, inventor of the cotton gin. Downtown, the bus passed through the principal intersection of Church and Chapel Streets and ended at the railway station, an architectural landmark that housed New Haven's best restaurant. It was a point of pride that all trains had to stop in New Haven because this was the location where steam had to be exchanged for electricity, and vice versa. The New York, New Haven and Hartford Railroad built its headquarters across the way; it was New Haven's first tall building—seven stories, with a fine view, from the top floor, of the city and its surroundings. We went there on a school tour and were greatly impressed by New Haven's first high-rise. We also visited the Winchester Repeating Arms factory. In my school days, New Haven still had a significant industrial base, and the arms factory was its leading manufacturing site.

New Haven is called the Elm City. It was indeed full of elm trees when we first lived there. The legendary hurricane of 1938 (huge and destructive, especially at the shore, but even in our own backyard) destroyed many of those; elm disease was to kill the rest later on. I well remember the downed trees that were blocking many of the streets on the day after the storm. We had trouble getting to the Foote School for our first day on the peaceful and brilliant morning that dawned after the dark and noisy violence of our first (but not our last) hurricane.

The New Haven of the thirties was a small and, in the parts we knew, attractive city with some handsome residential areas of large houses and gardens on the hilly side and the East Rock area, and with neighborhoods to the south of more modest homes and of many two-family houses in the area east of Whitney Avenue. We were almost unaware of sections that were not so nice; they were walled off by dead-end streets that blocked access to the poorer sections and the segregated black neighborhood. The New Haven Green created a classic city center with three churches on one side, civic buildings (public library, courthouse, and city hall) around the corner on another, and stores on the remaining spaces. The Edward Malley department store, a sort of local Marshall Field's, anchored the commercial district. The House of Hasselbach, a block or two away, served as a favorite destination for tea and baked treats; it was considered an appropriate location for children suitably accompanied or, when they had reached a certain age, on their own. A wonderful library, musty and old-fashioned, called the Young Men's Christian Institute, became my favorite hangout. For a small subscription, one could take out any book or read all day undisturbed in the reading room. The public library allowed the young to read only children's books, but the YMCI let one read anything it had on the shelves. Next door, at David Dean Smith's record store, one could spend infinite amounts of time in the listening booths discovering and playing records; purchase was not mandatory. A few blocks north was the old New

Haven Arena where, enrolled as a member of the Skating Club, I learned figure skating, with the incessant practice of figure eights preceding the increasingly more difficult exercises. At the end of each session our group would rush to the arena's bar where a tough-talking bartender served us cocoa topped with melting marshmallows. One memorable year, wearing clown costumes, we served as chorus for the Ice Capades, whose performance (and ours) at the arena was a big event in New Haven.

The city's politics seemed stable and predictable. The mayor's office was traded back and forth in regular rotation between an Italian Republican (New Haven had a very large Italian population and claimed to have the best, and perhaps the first, pizza in America) and an Irish Democrat. The city's social leadership, on the other hand, was decidedly WASP. It included bankers, lawyers, doctors, and businessmen—many of them, of course, Yale graduates—as well as gentlemen from the university, often prosperous, confident in their distinguished genealogies. For the families, the New Haven Lawn Club functioned as a prized institution where children were taught dancing, manners, and tennis, where young women held their debuts, and where annual events, from balls to dinners to championship tournaments, framed a calendar of the seasons. My family was scarcely eligible for membership had they even wished it. Instead, I took my dancing and swimming lessons at the local YWCA, an unpretentious setting where I met lots of real New Haveners and participated in much simpler celebrations.

A large number of our schoolmates took music lessons. For piano, Mrs. Nahum was the most sought-after teacher. She lived in a beautiful house close to the Foote School, with a studio attached to a room filled with books, where on weekends she held a special music school for her pupils. We learned something about the history of music, individual composers and their work, the various instruments and how they were used and played, and the different forms and styles of musical composition. Mrs. Nahum was an ardent lover of opera. Each year she had us concentrate on a single opera—the first time it was *Carmen*, the second, *The Magic Flute*—and had us learn both the score and the libretto and listen to various recordings before leading us to the Metropolitan Opera in New York for a matinee performance. We were entranced by the rich interior of the opera house, then still on Broadway at Thirty-Ninth Street, by the artists on-stage, and by our sense of hearing and seeing and finding in full realization an opera about which we had come to feel almost possessive. Decades later, when I came to Yale as provost, Mrs. Nahum insisted that my husband and I accompany her to a performance at the Met and that we first study the extensive materials she sent as homework. The three of us drove to New York and consumed an elegant dinner she had prepared, complete with silver and glassware, while tailgating, as though we were at the Yale-Harvard game, in a parking lot near the opera house.

New York, for all of us, was The City. I thought that what was meant to happen when you grew up was that you moved to New York, finally liberated from a backwater like New Haven. My family went there for the museums, concerts, and theater, and to shop and visit friends (often fellow refugees). My school took us there for the Museum of Natural History (and its awe-inspiring display of the astronomical universe) and the Metropolitan Museum (when we were studying the Egyptians, the Egyptian galleries, when we turned to classical civilization, the Greek collections, and so on). In the later thirties my mother's sister, my Aunt Gertrude, emigrated to New York, and I was able frequently to stay with her and sample what seemed to me the sophisticated delights of a city that made New Haven look not just dull but quite unsuitable for someone anxious to arrive at adulthood and do something with her life. The lifeline of the New York, New Haven and Hartford Railroad offered an easy escape route to the real city. It was an even speedier trip then than now, since the rail bed was in much better shape. In those days you had just the right amount of time before reaching your destination, as Connecticut flew by outside, to enjoy the dining car with its spotless white tablecloths, heavy cutlery and china, good cuisine, and attentive waiters.

New Haven did have an absorbing history that stimulated our interest in the colonial past. Especially fascinating was the story of the regicidal judges (Whalley, Goffe, and Dixwell, all with streets named after them) who had voted for the execution of Charles I. The three who fled to New Haven at the Restoration were hidden for some time in the Judges' Cave on West Rock, and Dixwell later lived in a house on the Green.

And of course we had museums and concerts and theater in New Haven too, the bulk of these provided by Yale. We spent hours in the Yale Art Gallery and at the Peabody Museum of Natural History, whose dinosaurs never lost their drawing power. Beyond North Haven, around Mt. Carmel, there was preserved an actual dinosaur footprint that we examined on occasional expeditions; once you saw it there wasn't much more to see, but it made a good picnic spot. As for theater, we took pride in the Shubert, where plays destined for Broadway had their first tryouts (and where they might also die for good). From time to time famous actors and actresses could be glimpsed on College Street; they stayed at the Taft Hotel next door to the theater, both immortalized in the film *All About Eve*.

In New Haven, the university seemed at once dominant and almost entirely separate. The external walls formed by the buildings of the Old Campus west of the Green surrounded an alien world, as did the closed courtyards of the recently constructed residential colleges. To ordinary citizens, Yale students seemed to be stereotypically rich boys who led lives of unimaginable privilege and who caused trouble and damage carousing on the streets.

The Yale College of the thirties was, of course, an all-male institution. The majority of its students were prep school graduates from prosperous families, many embedded in tight networks already formed by school and family. They bonded further through major extracurricular activities like the *Yale Daily News* and the Political Union, and through the secret societies like Skull and Bones. It was a world in which, although some of the elite compiled outstanding academic records, gentleman's Cs abounded. They had no difficulty in going on to the Harvard or Yale Law Schools as they had not, indeed, had any difficulty in reaching Yale College. That was still true, I found, in the later '40s when I had a summer job in the Yale College Dean's Office (and it was still true, too, of Harvard undergraduates I taught in the '50s).

The dean, whose Yale year was inscribed on his license plate, was a graduate of Phillips Academy Andover, and he assigned me a project to examine

the performance of Andover alumni at Yale. I discovered, not to his pleasure, that they performed on average somewhat below the norm for their
Yale classmates. I believe he suppressed my report. Almost seventy students from Andover, as I recall, were admitted to Yale annually (about the
same number of Exeter boys to Harvard, I think). I learned also from the
freshman records that I was given to review and summarize for the dean
how difficult it was for a boy from the Bronx High School of Science and
similar schools—boys with excellent records, high scores, and strong recommendations—to be admitted to Yale. The admissions records were part
of each file, and there I read the reports of interviewers (some of them
members of the Yale faculty), who would make such comments as "A good
specimen of his type," or who would mention the facial characteristics of
Jewish candidates. The prep school boys could generally get in just on the
recommendation of a headmaster.[1]

Shortly after our arrival in Hamden, I was made one Sunday afternoon
to dress in my party best and instructed to behave myself especially well,
or else. A large black car drove up, and from it emerged President James
Rowland Angell and Mrs. Angell. They stayed for tea and German cake. In
those days, the president and his wife paid a call on every newly appointed
senior member of the faculty. That was not too onerous a duty in the fall
of 1934, during the Depression, and in a year when only one full professor
and two associate professors were appointed to Yale College, and one full
professor, two visiting professors, and one associate professor to the graduate school.[2]

A few weeks later, we received another visit, this time from the provost, Charles Seymour (he became president in 1937) and his wife. Thus, at
the age of four, I met both the president and the provost of Yale, without
of course understanding anything about them. I am amused to think of
my later time as provost and interim president at Yale. And I was simi-
larly amused to learn that Mr. Angell had spent a considerable time at the
University of Chicago, where he served as dean of the faculties, as vice
president, and, for one year, as acting president. Had Chicago's then president, Harry Pratt Judson, taken the hint, Mr. Angell would very likely have

succeeded him. It was he who made Robert Maynard Hutchins, at the age of twenty-six, dean of the Yale Law School, and while he recommended him, then aged twenty-nine, to the University of Chicago trustees as their next president, he also cautioned them that Hutchins was not perhaps quite mature enough for the role.

Kay Angell became a good friend after my return to New Haven (she was Mr. Angell's younger second wife). She was a vibrant, generous, strong-willed, larger-than-life character who loved entertaining, knew everyone, had an opinion about everything, and kept up a lively interest in the affairs of both Yale and the city. Kay was instrumental in establishing the Culinary Institute of America in New Haven (it later decamped to Hyde Park, New York) and she enjoyed the discomfiture caused by its students wearing "CIA" sweatshirts around the campus neighborhood during the times of radical protest at Yale in the 1960s.

As a child, I believed that Yale was clearly one of the most important and esteemed institutions in the world. Most of my friends were also academic offspring, and we followed the fortunes of the Yale teams (although the girls did not attend football games, they learned from their brothers and adopted their heroes, like Albie Booth, as their own) with an intense and loyal attention. My parents were totally puzzled by American sports and by the role of athletics at the university. Nor would it have occurred to them ever to watch a school game in which their offspring were playing. Children were to do children's things on their own. Skiing and tennis and skating my parents could understand; football, basketball, and baseball they could not. The one baseball game they ever attended, the Harvard-Yale game in the week of my brother's graduation from Harvard, they went to out of a sense of duty because it was on the program of events, but it was a disaster; they had no idea what was going on, and vanished after the third inning.

Yale professors were fellows of colleges, my father of Jonathan Edwards, and every Christmas season before the war JE held a party for the fellows and their families. Young men in black tie sang "God Rest Ye Merry Gentlemen" and similar carols from the holly-decked dining hall balcony. Santa

Claus appeared and presented a gift to each child. One year McGeorge Bundy was assigned as my student escort (both he and his brother Bill took courses with my father) and my present turned out to be a water pistol that I aimed at him for the rest of the evening. He was very polite about this, but he remembered, as I discovered when I was a very junior faculty member and he the dean of the Faculty of Arts and Sciences at Harvard.

The Foote School became my much-beloved school from the fourth grade on, and I continue to think it the best educational experience ever. Founded by Mrs. Foote, a redoubtable Bryn Mawr graduate with Bryn Mawr standards as her beacon, it was both rigorous and mildly progressive in allowing students to go at their own rate in a variety of subjects, such as math. It was coeducational not only in classes but, until the sixth grade, in sports and always in the round-robin baseball and soccer played during recess. The arts were emphasized: music (primarily choral), visual art (drawing, painting, art appreciation), and drama. I loved being on the stage and can remember my first role: I wore a yellow costume, lay down on the floor, and was tripped over by a small boy, after which I rose and said, "My name is Banana Peel. I am a menace to public safety." My brother, who was two grades ahead of me, brilliant, quiet, and very shy, shone as an actor and shed his normal demeanor when on the public stage. He was Prospero in *The Tempest* (I, on the other hand, always the clownish one, played Caliban). He was an acclaimed St. George slaying the Dragon in the medieval English mystery plays that we repeated at every Christmastime; I acted the Dragon in my year. Every year we feverishly wondered which girl and boy would be selected as Mary and Joseph to star in the medieval mystery drama that depicted the story of Christ's birth. The winners represented the nearest equivalent to prom queen and king we had at our school.

Another major tradition was May Day, a combination of performance (including both sword and Maypole dancing, rehearsed for weeks beforehand) and garden party. It took place on the extensive lawns of the Yale secretary's house down the street from Foote's. The secretary was known as "Caesar" Lohmann and much feared by us for his name and lofty position in the university. I once found in the provost's office files a letter he had written to Yale's secretarial staff, graciously granting them the afternoon—but not the morning—off on the Saturday before Easter as a special favor.

We had first-rate teachers at Foote's. Some were Yale faculty wives. The most memorable teacher, I think for all Foote graduates, was Mrs. Margaret Hitchcock, wife of a self-effacing Yale professor, who spent her entire career as the fearsome and creative English teacher for the upper grades. A Bryn Mawr graduate who encouraged me to attend her alma mater, she was uncompromising and frighteningly direct in her critical judgments and in her love—and her ability to communicate this quality—for literature. She was a demon for correct pronunciation and grammar, and a severe editor of our weekly essays. She wasted no words in cataloging our deficiencies. Decades later on my return to New Haven, I spoke to a ladies' reading club that Mrs. Hitchcock presided over. Terrified of speaking in her presence, I had never been more nervous. She approached me afterward and, to my relief, said, in her familiar booming voice, "That was quite good, Hanna. You didn't split a single infinitive."

I think it often happens that the single most influential teacher people have encountered in school is an outstanding English teacher who awakened students to the beauties and complexities of literature and to the world of ideas. That happened to me again at the Sidwell Friends School in Washington with a remarkable woman, Mrs. White, who seemed to live her subject and invite us to share in her total engagement with it. Alas, she disappeared from the school not long after I left, the victim of an abusive marriage and a chaotic life.

The Foote School required French from the early grades on. We began Latin in seventh grade. We read our first Shakespeare, I think it was *Julius Caesar*, in sixth grade, as we were studying Roman history. Before that, of course, came the Egyptians and the Greeks. Medieval history and literature dominated seventh grade; American history and literature (beginning with Puritan texts) the eighth. Every eighth-grade class was given the project of reading and creating a large illustrated map of *The Pilgrim's Progress*.

By the time of graduation from Foote's, we had completed advanced algebra; we had read widely, including the essential novels of Dickens and a great deal of English poetry, and were reading French classics as well; and in general we had had a good education in writing and grammar. When my family moved to Washington in 1943 and I was sent to the Sidwell Friends School, an excellent school then as it is now, I was once again considered overqualified, this time for the first year of high school, and put in the sophomore class. I was the youngest in my class and became accustomed to being younger than my classmates wherever I was, with the curious result that I have always thought of myself since as younger than I am.

The Foote School had an English headmistress, Mrs. Winifred Sturley, whom we revered, and who helped make us into little Anglophiles. Her educational standards and tastes came from her English background, and these were reinforced when, in 1940, a largish contingent of English schoolchildren, mostly from Oxford, were sent to live with families, primarily but not exclusively connected with Yale, for the duration of the war.

The Foote School was transformed by the presence of so many English children, and Mrs. Sturley was determined that they should not have fallen behind their peers when they returned home at war's end; this had an effect on the level of our curriculum as well. Deep and lasting friendships and memories arose out of the English invasion of New Haven. When I arrived to study at Oxford, I found many hospitable friends there. A few of the evacuated children stayed or returned to live in the United States. In the main, the temporary migration was a success that added to our education in every way. It also brought the war still more vividly home to us. In addition, Mrs. Sturley invited girls in the upper grades to learn knitting and come to her home twice a week after school. There we knit Bundles for Britain (ours were wool liners to be worn under helmets). For a time, when Finland was under attack, we knit for the Finnish ski troops as well. I have no idea whether these minor items were ever received by even a single fighting man, but we certainly felt as though we were somehow contributing to the war effort.

At my graduation from the Foote School, I gave a talk on behalf of my class that was meant to be amusing. The next day my father summoned me to his study and offered a comprehensive critique of my performance.

If you want to be a radio comedienne, he said (and that was, indeed, my ambition at the time), these are the things you need on work on.

My parents took any announcement of future career interests very seriously and expected us to pursue such goals with purpose and discipline. I had already acquired a Gilbert chemistry set during a brief period of thinking I'd become a scientist; I used it to perform the most rudimentary experiments and create quite safe small explosions in our basement. And I had a library of books about science, including more than one biography of Mme Curie. Indeed, I had books galore on many subjects and an excellent collection of English literature. European books, together with great swaths of ancient texts and works on history, religion, philosophy, art, and music as well as literature, were stocked on my parents' overflowing shelves. For some reason, the scholar Julian Obermann, who obviously knew little about children, had given me a Loeb volume of Plato for my tenth birthday, and I set it in a place of honor, just because the Greek looked so impressive. I read voraciously, sometimes finishing a book and then flipping it over to read again from the beginning. From science, I moved on to the aim of becoming a novelist or an international journalist, perhaps both.

My parents continued to advise me to prepare myself with hard work and commitment for whatever seemed my career choice of the moment. It never occurred to me, or I think to them, that I might not come to have a profession. The one thing I knew was that I absolutely would not, like everyone else in my family, become a teacher; I was determined to steer clear of such a fate.

On Monday, December 8, 1941, I was scheduled to give the seventh-grade geography class report on Japan but was shouted down and barred from proceeding. Instead the class discussed that day's declaration of war and FDR's words before Congress. From then on, we became increasingly aware of older brothers and other relatives enlisting or being drafted, of Yale changing dramatically as students left for the armed forces and as a variety of military programs came to be located on campus, and of faculty fathers disappearing to Washington and other places, some secret. Everyone had to have blackout curtains and ration books for food and gas. The railway station and the trains were crowded with soldiers and sailors. Patriotic posters starring Uncle Sam were everywhere.

On my very first date, asked out by my classmate Bobby Nangle, and chaperoned by his mother, we went to a war bond rally. It was held at Yale's Woolsey Hall, where we sat through a long program presented by a large group of star entertainers, singers, comedians, and others who were traveling the country to market war bonds. They sold like hotcakes that night. I still have one.

At home there was installed in my father's study an ultrapowerful shortwave radio with an unusual antenna that is still visible after all these years. He was to monitor and then report on what he found significant points and trends in official German broadcasts, forwarding his findings to the intelligence service of the State Department. My parents had acquired US citizenship in January 1940 (they were pleased to have it conferred on the anniversary of Hitler's becoming chancellor), so my father could now receive security clearance.

But there was a problem: we were harboring an enemy alien. My grandmother Bettmann had managed to leave Europe on an Italian liner in the spring of 1941 and had come to live with us. Enemy aliens were regarded as potential recruits to the dreaded fifth column about which we were incessantly warned by Uncle Sam posters. They were not allowed to have binoculars in their possession—binoculars were considered obvious tools of the spy trade. So my grandmother handed over to my father, to be locked up for the duration, three pairs of pearl-inlaid opera glasses. Nor could enemy aliens travel more than forty miles from their place of residence without permission from the Department of Justice. My grandmother liked to shop at G. Fox in Hartford, forty-three miles from door to door, and as a law-abiding lady she obeyed this rule whenever she needed a pair of gloves or shoes, no doubt causing a huge waste of time and manpower at the department.

Finally, enemy aliens were forbidden to own or listen to shortwave radio—the ultimate instrument of enemy espionage. My father dealt with this problem by having my grandmother stay in her room with her door closed while he, too, closed his study door; this was meant to solve the problem of having a potential intelligence agent and a probable enemy spy under the same roof. I was often permitted to listen with him and so heard, despite often erratic and always scratchy reception, speeches made by Hitler and Goebbels and others. There would be long periods of silence and then the playing, over and over again, of the German shortwave's theme music from *The Magic Flute*: "Üb immer Treu und Redlichkeit." At some point my father would switch to the BBC, and we would get newscasts, in those first years very depressing, about the Blitz and the most recent events of the war. Occasionally we could hear, and be awed by, Winston Churchill's voice.

In 1941 and 1942 my father went regularly to Washington as a consultant. Finally, after the Office of Strategic Services was organized to serve as the central intelligence agency for wartime, he went on leave from Yale to become a full-time member of the OSS in the Research and Analysis Branch, among other tasks serving as liaison between the OSS and the State Department for the planning of postwar military government in Germany.[3] The division of R&A was heavily manned by academics, including a number of Central European émigrés (as indicated earlier, Franz Neumann, Marcuse, and Kirchheimer among them) and American historians of Europe (the leading Harvard historian of modern Europe William Langer was in charge of the division). Other members included political scientists and a number of young men in uniform who had been graduate students before the war (such as Leonard Krieger, Carl Schorske, and H. Stuart Hughes). The section came to be seen as having created an important academic network and served as a kind of informal graduate school of European history and culture that wielded a considerable influence on the careers and the outlook of the graduate students returning to complete their degrees after the war, their intellectual directions and destinations very much influenced by their interaction with the European refugees.

My mother, when we moved to Washington, also had a job at the OSS; I never learned what she did. And my Aunt Louise was in some way connected. I later found all my relatives named as CIA spies on a Soviet list that purported to out all such people. Their address was noted as "233 Santa Fe Ave., The United States of America."

Wartime Washington seemed filled to capacity. We were fortunate to find a row house adjoining Rock Creek Park not far from the National Zoo. With open windows, one could hear the distant roar of lions and the shrieks of caged animals. The Sidwell Friends School was so crowded, expanded to bursting point by the temporary population explosion of wartime, that high schoolers had to eat their lunches on a third shift, and an awful lunch it was.

In some respects, Washington suffered a dearth of cultural events as compared to New Haven. Theater was almost nonexistent; the most visible ones were a burlesque house and several movie theaters downtown. But I loved the city and had the freedom to roam about. The National Gallery was a wonderful destination, and on Sundays I went to the splendid chamber concerts performed by the Budapest String Quartet in the gallery's interior courtyard. There were of course other museums and plenty of historical monuments to visit, not to mention the zoo and the park and the general excitement of an urban environment full of activity. A good public library was right down our street, and I was permitted to register at and to use the Library of Congress for school "research" papers.

The Sidwell Friends School was highly international in outlook and composition, with students from everywhere: children of diplomats, of men posted to Washington from a myriad of countries for military and war-related assignments, and of people recruited to serve in the wartime agencies. Children of Supreme Court justices and of members of Congress and the cabinet added to the mix of transient and long-term Washingtonians. The Quaker tradition of the school was scarcely reflected in the religious affiliations of its students, but the Quaker ethos had a significant influence. It stressed tolerance and thoughtfulness and a certain kind of simplicity and calm, and it held out a high standard of intellectual achievement as something commendable and good in itself as well as for the social good.

Our headmaster, for whom the students had little use or respect and who, I believe, was later let go under a cloud, was of course a Friend, and we used to mock what we deemed the pinched and pretentious and self-righteous way in which he presided over the mandatory meetings held in the gymnasium. I found these hopelessly boring and spent my time looking at the numerous insignia of colleges and universities reproduced on the walls, wondering which one was for me and wishing that time would pass by more quickly.

I was once called before the headmaster to be disciplined for publicly announcing to our French teacher, Mademoiselle O'Sullivan, that her accent was simply terrible. It was not a pleasant experience. I was suspended from French class and made to perform a Canossa-like penance at its doors. And once, on a Memorial Day, I made the mistake of rising in meeting to point out that every other school in Washington was marking the holiday, but that Sidwell was apparently not up to honoring those who had died for their country. This did not go over well, especially with the Friends, who were, after all, pacifists, and a teacher immediately rose to have an "inspiration" on an entirely different subject. Later at Bryn Mawr, another Quaker foundation but one that had been essentially secularized from an early time, I came to realize how important the ethos of the school had been to the development of my own sense of values.

Adolescence hit me pretty hard in those years, with its powerful dreams of independence and achieving something of note and its strong fear of social failure, with its certainty about the hopeless weaknesses of familiar adult authority and its belief in the prospect of discovering new ways of thought that would challenge the old-fashioned views of one's elders. I tried out being less of a liberal than my parents and recall being sent away from the dinner table after arguing too heatedly in defense of Chiang Kai-shek (the pretty but empty-headed daughters and an intelligent niece of T. V. Soong, then ambassador to the United States, were acquaintances at school, and I had bought into their party line). I spent time sneaking away to forbidden movies and going regularly against school rules to a Hot Shoppe across Wisconsin Avenue with fellow hedonists. There we indulged in hamburgers, milk shakes, and endless teenager chatter.

Etched in my memory is the afternoon of April 12, 1945, when we heard the news of President Roosevelt's death. It seemed unbelievable. That weekend it was learned that the president's casket was to be taken by motorcade from the White House to Union Station for its final journey to Hyde Park. No time was given. I went to the Mall, where for several hours on the most beautiful of spring afternoons an ever-enlarging crowd gathered, waiting expectantly, strangers talking quietly with one another. It was the first time, I think, that I had seen black and white people mingling naturally and engaged emotionally with one another in this totally segregated city, an intensely moving occasion. The motorcade finally came past, first the hearse and then we could just glimpse Mrs. Roosevelt in one car and other family members in those that followed. Struck by the historic moment I had witnessed, I decided to keep a journal. A description of that afternoon was its first, and last, entry. And not too long after, on May 8, I was again at the Mall, this time for a noisy celebration of V-E Day.

College was in the air. My brother graduated that June from prep school and was on his way to Harvard. I was envious and yearned for independence. It was not clear that I would be allowed to apply anywhere the following year because of my age and, truth to tell, my SATs were not at all impressive. But two of the Seven Sisters (it was simply assumed that one would attend one of those) were willing to interview me, Bryn Mawr and Smith, at both of which my parents had some connections through academic friends, and I through teachers.

From Washington I was sent to visit Bryn Mawr and was startled to come upon young women wearing gauzy long white dresses with garlands around their heads; some were guiding oxen, real oxen, around the campus. It was Bryn Mawr's traditional May Day celebration, as I later learned, and it left a weird first impression. Mrs. Hitchcock had arranged that I be interviewed by her classmate, Katherine McBride, the college's president. After I was ushered into her rather intimidating presence, she looked at me for what seemed an eternity of silence with an X-ray vision that I thought could see right through me, and finally spoke. "Why don't you go to Wellesley?" she asked. I was ready to run. It turned out that she was trying to put me at ease, in her fashion, since she knew that my Aunt Louise was then teaching at Wellesley. But it was not an auspicious beginning, although I came to admire her greatly and to strive for her approval.

Among the Seven Sisters, Bryn Mawr was known (and often derided) as a college for "bluestockings." It was not chic for young women to be too obviously intellectual or to place too much value on doing well in school or to be seen studying too seriously, and since Bryn Mawr girls had a reputation for being guilty on all counts, many seniors were reluctant to apply.

I guessed that Smith would probably be more to my taste and found that confirmed when visiting its campus the following fall. It seemed so very sophisticated. The girls all appeared to be wearing cashmere sweater sets and pearls and plaid skirts and kneesocks and saddle shoes. They could have stepped right out of the pages of *Mademoiselle*, and they exuded a far greater worldliness than had the garlanded ox drovers. Worldly was definitely what I wanted.

Returning to the suburbs of New Haven after enjoying urban life in Washington seemed a letdown. The Prospect Hill School, where I enrolled for the final year of high school, was a sad departure, I thought, from the cosmopolitanism of the Sidwell Friends School. Prospect Hill was a very small all-girls' private high school (later merged, as was our competitor Miss Day's School, into the formerly all-boys' Hopkins School). There were just eleven in my class. The school was located in what had been the monkey house (you can imagine the interminable and tired jokes on this subject) for Yale laboratories situated nearby. It was directly across the street from the university's science quadrangle.

The principal form of entertainment at recess was to watch and, if you dared, greet Yale undergraduates passing by on their way to class or lab, until our headmistress announced one morning that the gates were to be shut at all times while school was in session, so that, as she elegantly put it, "the girls of the Prospect Hill School not be considered meat for the young men of Yale to feast their eyes upon." It was, however, considered proper for us to attend the tea dances given for Yale freshmen to which we were invited by Mrs. Seymour, the president's wife. At one of these we were all blown away by the looks and flair of a dashing young man named Ricky Cochrane. To my astonishment, some fifteen years later, I found that my principal colleague in Renaissance and Reformation history at the University of Chicago was the now very scholarly and very ascetic Professor Eric Cochrane.

Prospect Hill was less challenging than had been my previous schools, but my class in American history was taught by a law student who was outstanding, an enormously gifted and demanding teacher who whetted my interest in history. I hope he became a law professor. I took to playing hooky from time to time, escaping to the public library on the Green for long periods of reading; at the time I was into contemporary literature.

The entire senior class was impatient to leave school and to leave home. Finally came the day on which we received our college results. I was admitted to both Bryn Mawr and Smith and with great excitement told my father that I would be attending Smith.

No, he said, you are going to Bryn Mawr.

And so I did.

5

An Education at Bryn Mawr College

Every college and university regards itself as "special"; each owes to its history the presence of distinctive characteristics that remain embedded in a culture that, however modified and refined, retains the imprint of its origins and early development, a kind of institutional DNA. In the case of the particular persona of Bryn Mawr, it had a graduate school from the outset, and the college focused always on high scholarship and the training of women for scholarly pursuits, intellectual fulfillment, and personal independence. These characteristics offer a key to the ethos of the college and to the criteria and expectations associated with its faculty. Bryn Mawr differentiated itself from the other six Sisters by making advanced degrees a critical feature of its program. The legacy of the Society of Friends and its spirit in the thinking and composition of the original board and leadership of the institution marked another influence unique to this women's college.

In its first dean and second president, M. Carey Thomas, who worked together with the first president, James Rhoads, to design the educational standards and programs of the college, Bryn Mawr had a strong-willed feminist and formidable advocate for the higher education of women. Her views had been formed in part by her having been denied the possibility of pursuing a PhD in an American university and her contempt for the quality of most men's colleges, which she found little better than midlevel prep schools. She was determined that a Bryn Mawr education be better than that afforded by these pitiful colleges. She was determined also that young women of intelligence be freed to concentrate on intellectual goals. To this end she decreed that they be provided with a wide range of services; students should not, in her opinion, be wasting their time on such female duties as making their own beds or serving their own meals.

Legends of the awesome Miss Thomas were still current in my day. We were a little disappointed to hear that her famous remark, "Only our failures marry," was probably never uttered (she *might* have said, "Our failures only marry"), and we were unsure whether she had really forbidden the Bryn Mawr name to be mentioned in any public engagement or wedding announcement. It was alleged that when one of her favorite students (and in my time professor of history), Helen Taft Manning, daughter of President Taft, was marrying a fellow Yale graduate student, Miss Thomas had sent a wire the night before the wedding containing just one word, "Reconsider!" A very handsome Sargent portrait of Miss Thomas dominated the reading room in the library that bore her name; her spirit seemed to hover over this center of college life.

Bryn Mawr did not abandon its own demanding entrance examinations until very late, one of the last colleges to recognize the SATs. Elementary Latin was not offered during my time since at least three years of Latin were required for entrance. Examinations in two languages were required for graduation; taken as the misnamed "orals" they had originally been, they demanded translation in both directions. (A friend who had had excellent French throughout her school days and had traveled extensively in France was somehow unable to pass the French oral until the last gasp in her senior year, having memorably rendered "train of thought" as *chemin de fer de pensée* in an unsuccessful earlier attempt. The authorities were less charmed by this phrase than they should have been.) Also required were English composition, a yearlong course in introductory science (I foundered in the shoals of Biology 101), a yearlong course in English or Latin or Greek or biblical literature, and a yearlong course in the history of philosophy. A course in the social sciences was added only in the '50s. Grades were numerical and averages calculated to three decimal points. There was no Phi Beta Kappa at Bryn Mawr. It was argued that all BMC graduates were really worthy, and I blush to recall that when an alumnae group called on the college to accept PBK, I wrote an editorial in the *College News* opposing such a move, saying it would "gild the lily."

Student life, too, had its distinctive features. Bryn Mawr was proud of having created the first student self-government among its peers. Rules, policies, and discipline governing all aspects of student life—parietal hours, for example—were set by students themselves, and a sturdy civic spirit prevailed. I was not a very good citizen; the virtuous clichés of these community activities were not for me, and I was never a candidate for the offices that, after strenuous competitions, conferred glory on the leaders of each class. Nor was I a meticulous observer of rules. But, in Bryn Mawr's good tradition, I was on the whole left alone to follow my own bent rather than made to conform. I was not inclined to dance around the Maypole, either, or to roll a hoop down Senior Row as proper Bryn Mawr girls were meant to, but even these transgressions were more or less forgiven. I did not, however, make myself more popular with the administration by flying a Soviet flag one May Day from the tower of Taylor Hall, the principal administration and classroom building. Pictures of this outrage were featured on the front pages of the Philadelphia newspapers. The college's reputation as "pinko" was held in some quarters to be confirmed, and President McBride's belief in freedom of speech (although no statement of any kind was implied by my prank) was severely tested.

My extracurricular activities were mostly confined to the *College News* and to the part-time jobs, reserved for scholarship students, in which I earned my spending money. Those jobs were not overtaxing and were in fact quite interesting. One was in the college's news office, another in the bookstore, and yet another involved showing the slides for Professor Rhys Carpenter's introduction to the archaeology of ancient Greece (a wonderful course; my task made me automatically also an auditor). An especially attractive job was as a lunchtime waitress at the Deanery (once the extraordinary home of M. Carey Thomas, filled to the gills with expensive and exotic objects, and at that time the college's guesthouse) where many of the faculty lunched. The opportunity to observe the faculty at play and, if one was lucky, to overhear some of their conversation gave much fodder for thought and gossip. We talked constantly about the faculty, and especially about certain members (men, in the main) and speculated about their lives, so this was no small matter. Faculty-student marriages were not unheard-of, and while not encouraged, such relationships were not forbidden. In general, encounters on campus between men and women were meant to be decorous. If one were to entertain a young man in one's room, the door had to be left open, and the hours of such visitations ended early. The occasional contravention of this rule raised eyebrows. But the most exciting event of my college years was the wedding of our dean. It had not occurred to us that an actual dean might yet be eligible for romance and marriage.

Sports were required in the first two years, and participation in athletics was much recommended. Although I had enjoyed sports in school, my enthusiasm waned after I experienced what was meant to be a singular privilege, that of playing field hockey under the iron discipline of the famous (in admittedly restricted circles) Constance Applebee. She was, so to speak, the Amos Alonzo Stagg (an icon of the football world and of the University of Chicago) of women's field hockey and lacrosse. Miss Applebee, an Englishwoman who died just short of her 108th birthday, had introduced women's field hockey to the United States in 1901 and had been appointed Bryn Mawr's director of outdoor sports by Miss Thomas in 1904. After a renowned career she had retired, but in my years in college she had returned as a visiting coach, something she gave up at the age of ninety-six. Then in her midseventies, she could outrun most of us. Despite the many testimonies to this icon's being a kind, if rather crusty, person, that was a side I never saw. Instead, she would poke at me with her stick and shout, "Get down the field, you dirty Greek!" The source of this slur remains a mystery to me. I understand that the less offensive "Put both claws on your stick, you one-legged turnip," was one of her favorite exhortations. In any case, I withdrew from hockey as soon as that was legally permitted. There were actually others who prospered under Miss Applebee's tutelage and remembered her fondly. The majority of students, however, tended to abandon physical education as early as they could. Athletics was regarded as both time-consuming and unfashionable, and most young women would not want to be caught dead exercising.

For all its reputation as a haven for bluestockings, Bryn Mawr was also described as a "Society College." The college's most famous alumna was Katharine Hepburn, and her unique accent, often called a "Bryn Mawr accent" (but I think hers alone), was thought representative of its snobbish and upper-class population.

The majority of students came from private schools, whether such feeder boarding schools as the Milton Academy or private schools like New York's Brearley or Baltimore's Bryn Mawr School. Their backgrounds ranged from very comfortable to wealthy. Many of the first-year girls from New York were entering their debutante season, and during the fall they could be glimpsed in their fur coats leaving campus for the city and the weekend parties that preceded their own debutante balls. We could go away for as many weekends as we chose. Haverford, so ran the usual (and inaccurate) story, was for weekdays only. The weekend traffic was high at all times, directed most heavily toward Princeton and Yale, followed by Harvard and Dartmouth.

Freshmen who came from certain families, including most of those with alumnae mothers, were already on their arrival at college asked to special teas and receptions given by some of the grandes dames of the Main Line. Those of us not part of this inner circle knew at the outset that we were, and were likely to remain, in some respects outsiders to a slightly mysterious "society."

A *Saturday Evening Post* article of 1949 spoke of Bryn Mawr's "academic hauteur" but added, "Bryn Mawr girls note with relief that the old picture of the Bryn Mawr Type—wholesome girls from Our Better Families, with more I.Q. than maddening allure—is fading."[1]

Surrounding Bryn Mawr, and all along the Main Line, expansive estates and large houses with perfectly kept gardens projected great collective affluence in a landscape of memorable beauty, especially during the flowering of spring. The commercial section of Bryn Mawr village was quite small. At the center of its town square sat a statue of Columbus bearing a plaque that read, "Dedicated to the memory of Christopher Columbus by his grateful fellow citizens of the Main Line." In my time the village had only two places where we could hang out, a movie theater that we attended for just about every film that came along, many of them enjoyably and hilariously bad, and a hamburger joint that provided a gourmet alternative to dormitory food (weekly Philadelphia scrapple might have been the worst). Liquor was of course forbidden (and so were cars). Being caught drinking in the village bar, as happened to some, was about as scandalous as you could get.

We went to Philadelphia especially for the excellent symphony orchestra concerts and for dates with young men who took us to dinner and dancing. The Paoli Local, then serving the Main Line with two Philadelphia stations (Broad Street and 30th Street) evoked for me an air of mystery and romance. The train announcer called out each stop by name, culminating in a final "Paoli and the West." The West out there seemed an invitation to something unknown and adventurous, although in Philadelphia it probably just meant Harrisburg. At the Bryn Mawr station, each arriving train was met by a man with a lantern whom we called Diogenes, and who walked behind us to the campus. We had great freedom; we also existed in a thoroughly protective environment.

Helicopter parents were unheard of. Communications arrangements with my mother specified that I was to call home, collect, every other Sunday at the lowest rate. My mother kept a three-minute egg timer by the telephone; she hung up when the sand had reached bottom, no matter where we might be in conversation. Letters took up the slack. But she was still responsible for laundry, since coin-operated machines did not then exist in the dorms, and laundry was sent home and returned in specially designed boxes by Railway Express.

At the college we were served by the black maids and porters who annually presented the musical (and, I felt, embarrassing) "Maids and Porters Show." The maids ran a sewing and alterations bureau in addition to serving all three meals on fresh white tablecloths in the dining rooms attached to each dormitory, cleaning our rooms, and changing our beds. One of the staff was "on bells" at the entrance to each hall to fetch us to the phone when called—we had no phones in our rooms—and to take care of whatever was needed, whether to announce visitors or inform someone that a taxi was waiting. Given the level of services we enjoyed, it is perhaps not surprising that board fees were substantially higher than the tuition price (tuition was $550 my first two years, $650 the second two; the corresponding board fees ranged from $650 to $850 and then $800 to $1,000, depending on the type of room you had).

In my entire time at college, we had only two black students, both daughters of prominent fathers. The college had a kind of Southern feel. It still astonishes me that, with a generally liberal faculty and a Quaker tradition, Bryn Mawr could have been so seemingly remote from the critical issues of race and class.

There were, however, a number of other large issues that shaped much of Bryn Mawr's world in the later forties and early fifties. I went to college at a time when the end of the war had left a conflicted legacy for women students. Women had held increasing numbers of responsible positions during the war and had in larger numbers than ever before experienced what a career might be like, and what larger opportunities might exist for women in pursuit of careers. At the same time, the tug toward resuming a more "normal" existence, the powerful drive toward reestablishing family life and supporting the men who had returned from war, was pressing also.

The postwar era brought with it, too, a strong emphasis on and an intense belief in the importance of higher education, a powerful conviction that an improved democracy and healthier social order rested on extending higher education to all who might benefit, that the better educated the world, the better the world could be made. The GI Bill began an educational revolution for men who might not otherwise have attended college, and with it a demographic expansion in the universe of higher education that was to have consequences for women as well as men. Bryn Mawr and its sister colleges wanted to do their bit and invited men on the GI Bill to enroll; there were initially five men in my class. (Bryn Mawr had already opened its graduate school to men in 1931.)

Enrollments in colleges and universities, including the women's colleges, grew immensely in the war's immediate aftermath, and Bryn Mawr's leadership became acutely concerned about the increased size of the college (602 undergraduates and some 175 graduate students in the academic year 1949–50, the largest numbers ever) and what this would mean for its resource needs and the sustenance of its community tradition.

In addition, war's end was accompanied by a new internationalism that, it was hoped and believed, could also be a stimulus to world peace and reconciliation. Support for the United Nations ran high. A branch of the World Federalists was active on campus among its more left-wing students (a relative term, considering what that came to mean later). Its chair wrote to a great many prominent figures (the pope, Winston Churchill, etc.) to ask them their thoughts on how to attain international understanding. There were few replies, but she did hear from George Bernard Shaw and was cast into despair. "The best way to promote international understanding," he wrote, "is for everyone to stay home."

The rise of interest in international relations drove new curricular initiatives and student organizations. During my senior year, West Point—I think in part to show itself to be a serious institution of learning and not just a military school—sponsored a conference on international affairs to which two students from each of fifty colleges were invited. Typical of Bryn Mawr, the college sent me, a Renaissance history major, and a Greek concentrator, my friend and classmate Emily Townsend (later in life, as Emily Vermeule, a distinguished professor at Harvard). Everyone else at the conference was majoring in political science or international relations. We listened to prominent speakers and participated in intense, sometimes combative, debates on questions related to current developments, ultimately winding up in late-night sessions devoted to writing majority and minority reports on just about every theme that sparked controversy in the geopolitical universe of our day, writing as though the solution would depend critically on our conclusions and recommendations. It was exhilarating. Out of this experience there emerged a network (though we did not know the word or realize that we had networked, exactly) of people who encountered one another many times and in many settings later on. It was at West Point, for example, that I first met the political scientist Susanne Hoeber Rudolph. We met again as graduate students at Harvard and afterward were close colleagues, together with our husbands, at the University of Chicago. There were many others of the West Point conferees spread around the country and pursuing careers in academia and public service who remained members of a group that could communicate instantly and on familiar terms.

Internationalism was not something new at Bryn Mawr. The college enjoyed a long tradition of Europeans on the faculty and as visitors, as well as a significant presence of foreign students, augmented by the Graduate School of Arts and Sciences. During the '30s, President Park had been more vigorous than most university and college presidents in her condemnation of the Nazi regime and its war against Jews and political dissidents.[2] She served on the board of the Emergency Committee for the Relief of Displaced German Scholars, and she did what was possible in a small college with a small faculty to bring exiled scholars to Bryn Mawr, as well as supporting a program, launched partly at the initiative of Bryn Mawr students, to establish scholarships for refugee students. It was in the '30s that two exceptionally eminent women academics, both of whom died far too soon after their arrival, came to Bryn Mawr: Emmy Noether, recognized as the greatest woman mathematician, indeed quite simply one of the greatest mathematicians, of the past century, and Eva Fiesel, an Etruscan philologist, linguist, and classicist (and close friend of my mother's). Hertha Kraus, a leader in the field of social work, who had converted to Quakerism as a university student in Germany and had served Konrad Adenauer's administration when he was mayor of Cologne, arrived at Bryn Mawr in 1936; her presence elevated the reputation of the Graduate School of Social Work. In addition, a number of other refugee scholars visited or spent shorter periods of time at Bryn Mawr in the '30s and early '40s. Another distinguished scholar, Richard Bernheimer, arrived in the early '40s and remained a very influential teacher of art history when I was at college.

The postwar period saw the appointment of two outstanding scholars who had come as refugees to the United States in the '30s: Felix Gilbert

in history and Erich Frank in philosophy. Both were long-standing friends
of my parents from their past in Germany and part of the community of
displaced scholars who remained in continuing contact. Gilbert, together
with my father a student in Meinecke's seminar at Berlin, was a man of an
extraordinary breadth of learning and cultivation whose influence was felt
throughout the college. His considerable range included both teaching and
publication in the fields of Renaissance, modern European, Russian, and
American diplomatic history. He belonged to the extended Mendelssohn
family, and after the war the joke went that in Germany the occupiers had
found three categories of natives: Nazis, non-Nazis, and cousins of Felix
Gilbert. I had the privilege of taking just about every course he gave and
of benefiting from his generous supervision of my honors work. When invited in 1948 to become a professor at the Institute for Advanced Study, he
declined, writing to Robert Oppenheimer, then the institute's director, that
he found teaching "a novel and inspiring experience" and felt that it was
too "important for the clarification of my ideas on history" to give it up.
After accepting the institute's invitation in 1962, he paid tribute to Bryn
Mawr, writing to President McBride about "the remarkable interest which
the College takes in the personal well-being of members of the faculty," and
adding that "Bryn Mawr . . . is a unique place where it is good to live and
to work." Later he spoke of his positive sense of "the continued existence
of an attitude which had been strong and dominant in Bryn Mawr from
the beginnings of the college: the combination of a progressive political
outlook with the view that scholarship is an enterprise reaching far beyond national borders and based on cooperation of all nations. One might
perhaps say that the refugee problem which the Nazi policy had brought
about was a test of these convictions and Bryn Mawr's record was good."[3]

Erich Frank had been Martin Heidegger's successor at Marburg University when Heidegger moved to Freiburg. Frank was dismissed in 1935. He
was an amazing lecturer who had given the college's distinguished Flexner
Lectures, published as *Philosophical Understanding and Religious Truth*, after
which Bryn Mawr was eager to recruit him. Frank was an unusually kind
and lovable person; these qualities seemed to animate his every interaction

with others. He was very popular with students, who carefully transcribed his words while having some difficulty with his German accent. I had to explain that his description of St. Augustine as having an "agonized face" according to my classmates' notes actually referred not to the saint's physical appearance but to his *faith*. Frank's teaching of the required course in the history of philosophy opened a whole new subject and way of thinking to many of us who had had no idea of what philosophy might really be about before this introduction.

The college was active in recruiting students from abroad. We came to know, and to learn from, one or two girls coming from displaced persons' camps, and a few students from Germany and Japan—in the latter two cases, it was still early days for students from former enemy countries to be on an American campus. A group of ten quite impressive German women, already graduates, spent a year on campus as part of a cultural exchange project, and we had many opportunities to talk and become acquainted with them and with the stories of their experiences of war and a despised regime.

I had felt rather guilty when arriving at Bryn Mawr for having been awarded a scholarship designated for foreign students, worrying that I might be seen as admitted under false pretenses. From time to time in the very first days I tried speaking to staff members in a German accent, hoping to be accepted as a legitimate non-American.

In domestic politics, Bryn Mawr students tended to be Republican, an inheritance from their families. Some, in a mild form of rebellion, became Democrats, but not very many, although many more, judging from class notes in the *Alumnae Bulletin*, seem since to have moved in that direction. Most of us, of course, were not old enough to vote; you had to be twenty-one. A small number of my classmates swerved leftward and supported Henry Wallace in the election of 1948. On the day after that election, there were few smiles to be seen among my fellow students. They had been fully prepared to welcome Thomas Dewey as their president and were stunned by Truman's unexpected victory. Only the faculty, and a few students like me, seemed cheerful—indeed, extremely cheerful—on that day.

The postwar era saw the development of the Cold War, of the Red Scare, and of a growing preoccupation with the consequences and destructive threats posed by nuclear weapons. It saw the continuing outgrowth of an alliance that had been forged in wartime between government funding and academic research and training, as well as new forms of government funding undertaken in the name of national defense and directed to language and area studies as well as the support of higher education. Related to this alliance, and as domestic anticommunism and its politics came to be carried to new extremes, there also emerged deeply significant problems that posed great dangers to academic freedom and its sustenance. Some resonance of these developments touched the college directly. We were there when loyalty oath requirements were first imposed in California, and were sympathetic to those who protested and resisted the oath in the conflicts that ensued at Berkeley. Bryn Mawr, acting on principle, ultimately refused to accept federal fellowships that required such oaths, and was willing to forfeit the funds to which they were attached. The Alger Hiss story began to unfold, and the FBI visited campus in search of correspondence that might have been written on the famous typewriter on which Whittaker Chambers claimed classified secrets had been copied to be passed to the Russians. (Priscilla Hiss was an alumna.) The HUAC and Senator McCarthy began their aggressive hunt to root out Communists and "fellow travelers." Among those alleged to have been guilty of treasonous conduct was Owen Lattimore, a scholar of China and brother of Bryn Mawr's Professor Richmond Lattimore, best known for his translations of Greek drama and of Homer.

It is often thought that mine was, in the fifties, the "silent" generation, characterized by a passivity and conservatism and acceptance of the status quo that stood in stark contrast to the activism that followed in the sixties. It is true that we were not usually marchers and public protesters in the style of the sixties and that many young women of my generation were not particularly engaged with politics and/or with the reformist movements of the time at all. But a significant number were highly critical of the trends, dilemmas, and developments they discerned in their contemporary world. Nor were all simply quiet observers, as witness those who stayed committed to movements like nuclear disarmament or world federalism in an environment where those came under heavy suspicion and attack as potentially "subversive." Our student forums and publications, and much of our discussion with faculty and with visiting speakers, returned again and again to these debates, to the need for supporting academic freedom, and to the threats now posed to the essential imperatives of higher education in both teaching and research. The students preoccupied with such issues tended to congregate around a liberal center, as did the faculty. One huge change marking the sixties lay precisely in the fierce attack mounted by radical protesters against that center and the broad consensus it had represented, to the bewilderment of liberal academics who had regarded themselves as sympathetic to the protesters' concerns.

It is often thought, too, that feminism was born only in the sixties and with the civil rights movement. But that is true only if you neglect the feminism of earlier generations that had in fact built a lasting foundation for the multiple feminisms of the sixties and afterward, and that had created the distinctive forms and aspirations of the women's colleges. Those institutions now require new or renewed defenses of their existence in a world almost entirely devoted to coeducation. Such reflections have in turn again helped revive interest in thinking about the purposes of liberal education itself.

My first assignment in English Composition was to read *General Education in a Free Society*, the report known as the "Red Book" written by a Harvard faculty committee that outlined the goals, and a curriculum to fulfill them, for Harvard College in the postwar age. I was so clueless that I failed to discern why we should be studying this official report, decked out in fulsome prose, rather than reading some great literary work as we embarked on serious collegiate study. Only gradually did I come to understand it as a historical document that expressed much of the hope, optimism, openness to wider intellectual horizons that characterized thinking about education at the time of its composition. The report embraced the acquisition of a common, largely Western and democratic, culture. Its recommendations for general education looked to shaping the citizens and leaders of an improved society.

Those recommendations were not, in the end, fully accepted at Harvard despite its introduction of general education requirements, but they had a considerable influence on the wide-ranging discussions of liberal education that were taking place elsewhere as well. And the Red Book has continued to serve as a classic text in the endless battles over the curriculum that have recurrently roiled discussion of higher education in the decades that followed. Those debates have come to include subjects and opinions that were scarcely at issue in 1946—for example, the place of global and non-Western studies, of ethnic and gender studies, of internships and community service, of online learning. Nonetheless, they remain at heart debates, conducted in changing contexts, about the aims of education, about the outcomes to be hoped for, about the balance of general and specialized learning, about the relative weight of free choice and required learning in the process of becoming educated, and, finally, about the things that are most worth knowing or pursuing intellectually over the course of a lifetime. In the end, they look to defining the kind of culture and society we want, and the kind of human models we construct as ideal persons to be shaped through education.

The faculty clearly thought we should start getting educated by learning to think about education and its goals, an excellent purpose that initially went right over my head. The faculty did not think we should necessarily accept what the Red Book said, and indeed its prescriptions were quite different from those represented by our own curriculum and by the general spirit of the college that assumed the liberal arts to be first and foremost a good in themselves, even if they had a social benefit as well.

There is some irony in the fact that the women's colleges could be (and, I think, can continue to be) in some sense the best or most single-minded advocates for the liberal arts in their purest form. In the case of women's education, after all, the colleges did not then believe it their first priority to talk, as did the Ivy institutions, about the preparation of "leaders" or, in the first instance, about the professional benefits of such an education. We were not expected to be busy building résumés. Women were not, it was assumed, necessarily being prepared for vocational or worldly success, or for going out into the world to run it. Not that such outcomes were unthought-of or entirely neglected, but the two priorities were reversed, and the claims of liberal learning as an educational value in itself were seen as paramount, a much-debated tradition that has lasted under what are now very different circumstances.

In my college days we talked a great deal about the purposes of the education we had chosen, both in terms of learning itself and in trying to define the ultimate value of education for women. Most of us were looking toward marriage but also toward careers. Some of my contemporaries knew exactly what they wanted, whether medicine or law or graduate school or school teaching or journalism or publishing. Many of us had less specific ideas about the future but hoped to be finding satisfying jobs, and many of us thought that the world of publishing would be the right place to start, whether at a magazine like *Time* or at a publisher like Alfred Knopf (in either case as intelligent assistants serving the coffee and carrying around the glue pots that were understood to be essential to the higher journalism and to literary production, and then rising in the organization). Such jobs were thought especially appropriate for female college graduates, in part because they would be dealing with, or at least close to, writing and books and ideas, in part because these were seen as genteel occupations, something to do before marriage intervened. A surprising number found such jobs.

We were a little vague about how we were going to combine careers and families. We imagined that we would need to drop out of the workplace for a time, but we were by no means unaware that there were difficult choices to be made, and that not all young men of our acquaintance would be sympathetic to our aspirations. We knew, of course, that the world in general was certainly not prepared to deal with us as we would like to be dealt with, that at least some pioneering might be necessary. We saw ourselves as empowered by our education and encouraged by our teachers to gain effective independence and resilience, and as able to act on the incontestable knowledge that we were intellectually equal to men. Looking now at the lives of my classmates, I see that a very large percentage went on to substantial careers as well as continuing to perform important volunteer service, a good number at later stages of life. We tended to get married fairly soon after graduation, much earlier than is customary nowadays, and often to get some specialized or advanced training later. At the same time, we believed that freedom of choice as to what kind of life we might lead, let alone the unforeseeable directions or pressures of individual circumstance, meant that the domestic path and the work of volunteer service were equally valuable outcomes. That view has frequently put people on the defensive as the next generation's view of women's liberation came all too often to suggest that only one choice could be considered correct or laudable.

The newer freedom for women, which has so greatly enlarged their realm of choice and opportunity, has not, of course, simplified women's lives. But this modern condition has surely enriched their lives, so long as it is not used to rationalize new conformities, or to encourage unproductive resentment or passivity in the face of the perceived difficulty of its consequences, or to suggest that the individual is defined by a single choice, like that of conventional career success, rather than by the deeper measures contained in those qualities of mind, perspective, sympathy, and imagination through which women may realize their independent natures. And those, I hope, may be at least in part an outcome of a liberal arts education for men and women alike.

Bryn Mawr did not allow students to marry while in college. Mine was a class of 158 at entrance, 133 at graduation. Some had transferred elsewhere (usually to New York and Barnard); a few had been expelled or had dropped out of college altogether. The rest had disappeared by marriage. And it is perhaps symbolic that a large portion of the student population spent endless hours knitting—even during class—and playing bridge, as though sending signals of a more conventional attachment or submission to contemporary expectations of women's futures.

The president of Wellesley College spoke one evening on the subject of higher education for women. Mildred McAfee Horton had commanded the WAVES during the war, and we anticipated a brisk exposition from a woman warrior. To our indignation, she talked of how the graduates of women's colleges would make better mothers, helping educate their children at a higher level, imbuing them with respect for civilized values. They would also become fine leaders of PTAs as well as bringing their knowledge and taste to service on museum boards. That provoked me to write an editorial claiming that such weak and outmoded views would never be uttered by our president, and that the individualism cultivated at Bryn Mawr would fortify us against surrender to Mrs. Horton's stereotypical description of educated women's roles in the prevailing culture. Hers was in fact a more representative version of a point of view quite common in the public attitudes and pronouncements of the day.

Bryn Mawr offered us a wealth of visitors and speakers. In my first year, Arnold Toynbee, who was then all the rage, delivered the Flexner Lectures (a series of special prominence at Bryn Mawr), and while I was not, as I had hoped to be, impressed by his ideas, my reaction made me start thinking about the philosophy of history and the different ways in which the shape, direction, and meaning of history have been conceived. In the same year, a conference on Leibniz somewhat surprisingly put my father together in a session with Leo Strauss. I could not understand a thing they said, but watched bemused while my father, very tall, and Mr. Strauss, very short, sat on a kind of swing (one of Miss Thomas's delights) in the Deanery that might at any moment have tipped them out. We had politicians and educators, theologians and poets, novelists and practitioners of the arts. Of special prominence I recall Eleanor Roosevelt coming to receive the college's M. Carey Thomas Award and Dean Acheson speaking at the commencement of 1949.

The high point for me was hearing T. S. Eliot read from his work in a hauntingly thin and world-weary voice. Asked the "meaning" of a poem, he answered, in the same voice, that he had not the faintest idea. The next morning, thanks to being assigned as interviewer for the *College News*, I had breakfast with Mr. Eliot, and this led to an invitation to visit him in London, which I did occasionally during my time in England; he was very kind to the young. Dylan Thomas stayed up all night drinking at the home of Professor Mary Woodworth, a deceivingly schoolmarmish lady when first encountered who turned out to be full of surprises (as an undergraduate, she had fled secretly to a nearby cemetery to smoke and was, we heard, responsible for Bryn Mawr becoming the first of the women's colleges to allow smoking for their students). Marianne Moore was a Bryn Mawr graduate much favored. But above all, our visitors were scholars, and our student paper set out to cover and to try to give a faithful summary of every lecture. That was an education in itself, offering an introduction to the work and thought of some remarkable minds.

Bryn Mawr's faculty seemed pretty well balanced between men and women. One striking picture I took away from the college was that of men and women working together as colleagues in a common cause. Renowned women academicians in those days, with a few exceptions here and there, were likely to pursue their vocation at the women's colleges, not at the major universities. I assumed that, were I to become a professional academic, I would do the same. Today the outstanding women scholars with whom I studied—certainly the classicist Lily Ross Taylor or the biologist Jane Oppenheimer, for example—would be holders of chairs at leading research universities. Other faculty members of that quality, like Rhys Carpenter or Felix Gilbert, were men who prized the academic environment of the college, and who, together with their colleagues, were active scholars who taught at every level from the introductory course to the graduate seminar.

Bryn Mawr was especially strong in the fields of Greek, Latin, archaeology, and history of art. It was excellent in the sciences, mathematics, and psychology as well as in history, philosophy, English, and French; it had less depth in the social sciences, although political science, especially given the increased interest in international politics, was on the rise, as was anthropology. Non-Western cultures were scarcely represented in the curriculum. Russian language and history came to be added, for obvious reasons, in the immediate postwar era. For similar reasons, physics became a quite popular major among the sciences, with chemistry a close second. A bit of new curricular breadth resulted from some early, if very limited, collaboration among Bryn Mawr, Haverford, and (more rarely) Swarthmore in appointments, as in Russian with Haverford and medieval history with Swarthmore, but this was far removed from the extensive tri-college cooperation that is so essential to the strength, and to the ongoing health and flourishing, of the three liberal arts colleges today.

I found myself on unexpectedly shaky ground in my freshman year. Everyone seemed well ahead of me in Latin; I was backward and clumsy in biology; my imagined skills in writing were not appreciated. My confidence received a little boost only from History 101, Introduction to the History of Europe. I was surrounded by people smarter than I was and socially far more advanced. At the same time it was exciting to be part of an intellectually lively group of students and to participate in the discussions about life, politics, and the world in general that preoccupied us and stretched our horizons and our sense of growing adulthood. In my second year, despite some tremors of sophomore slump, I had caught up to some extent and was engaged by some wonderful courses.

The apex of my undergraduate education was to study Tacitus, Livy, and Lucretius with Lily Ross Taylor. Every one of my teachers was highly competent, every one of them a scholar, each one knew his or her students and wanted to help them succeed. What set Lily Ross Taylor apart was a singular and vital connection to her subject, her distinctive breadth of intellectual curiosity, and her passionate, rigorous, and effective way of communicating the essence of Roman history and literature, and of demonstrating the relationships among seemingly disparate texts, subjects, and events. Our advanced Latin classes were small (I think six was the largest) and held in her apartment. At some point tea would be served. By the end, whenever that happened (time was not kept), the floor by Miss Taylor's armchair would be strewn with books she had pulled off her shelves in order to read out some favorite passage or answer some question or make some new observation that had just occurred to her. She taught us to read, which is to hear, Latin poetry as it should be read and heard, and had us memorize and recite quite a bit of Lucretius; those lines are still etched in my memory.

Miss Taylor's standards were formidable. Proud of a paper I had written, I looked eagerly for her comments and found only this: "I have checked all your footnotes and found them accurate." Crushed, I consulted another professor about what this indicated and was told it was actually a compliment. Some years later my husband and I had the great experience of visiting Miss Taylor when she served as director of the American Academy in Rome, and spending an entire day with her at the Forum—the most extraordinary passage into the ancient past one could imagine.

Entering the library on a winter evening of my second year at Bryn Mawr, I underwent a kind of epiphany. The heavy doors closed behind me with their usual solid thump, the familiar worn wooden steps gave off their usual creak, the distinctive odor of books was in the air, and before me lay the reading room with its green-shaded lamps and individual reading carrels. I suddenly realized that I could be happy to do this every night for the rest of my life, and that I was, and would now hope to become, an academic despite myself.

History became my major field, Latin my second area of concentration. It had become clear to me that I understood and thought about the world best by trying to understand how its institutions and cultures had come to be what they were. Renaissance intellectual history offered the link to a question that very much engaged me. What might be understood by the "revival" of antiquity, the ways in which the ancient past was interpreted and reinterpreted in other, quite different eras, the uses and adaptations to which its texts and figures were put, and the reasons behind looking to the classical world as a source of lessons for the present? To what degree do different uses and interpretations of the past in different eras illuminate the questions confronted and solutions offered by intellectuals seeking to understand and prescribe reforms for their own times?

For the Renaissance, Machiavelli was an obvious figure to study, as I did for my senior project. As a senior writing a thesis, one was admitted to the holiest of places in the library, the history seminar room, otherwise re-stricted to graduate student use. Every department had such a room, lined with the essential reference materials for its subject, and having, of course, a fine oval table at its center. Working there gave me an unrealistic sense of what graduate school might be like, as though advanced study would always allow a peaceful and reflective pursuit of the higher scholarship in sites designed for one's support and comfort and for intellectual exchange with fellow students.

Oddly, given Bryn Mawr's unique Graduate School of Arts and Sciences, we had little contact with its students other than those who were resident heads in the dormitories. They bore the slightly sinister title of wardens. Bryn Mawr had yet another group of graduate students in its Graduate School of Social Work and Social Research. Undergraduates tended to view all graduate students as a rather strange and unusually pale tribe from a distant planet. But it was clear that the PhD program was important, and that its existence had something to do with bringing together and retain-ing the scholarly faculty whom we admired.

I was and remain always moved by the solemn formula pronounced with the conferral of the PhD—at Bryn Mawr, as at the University of Chi-cago, a welcome to the "ancient and honorable company of scholars." Bryn Mawr's commencement ceremony featured the hooding of each candidate while the title of his or her dissertation was being read out. In my year, the most memorable event of the ceremony occurred when the unfortunate degree recipient was introduced with the title "A Study of Retired Civil Servants in Montgomery County Broken Down by Age and Sex."

More recently the college has reviewed its graduate programs, reduc-ing their numbers and reconfiguring their organization. A graduate school that initially welcomed and encouraged women to take up advanced study had in some ways fulfilled that purpose. Happily, women were no longer excluded from graduate schools in the universities that had been so slow to acknowledge their existence, and those universities could mount pro-grams of much greater range and depth than could the college through its relatively small departments. As in the case of the undergraduate colleges, now competing with universities and colleges that had become coeducational and having to reexamine and perhaps restate their case for women's colleges, so in that of a Graduate School of Arts and Sciences whose initial mission had been realized, it was time to consider the rationale for its survival. The answer has been to be at once selective and interdisciplinary in range by laying out a distinctive set of graduate programs that cross departmental boundaries and aim to build on Bryn Mawr's best academic strengths. The long-term future remains a puzzle.

After graduation, my association with the college continued over a long stretch of time, first as a substitute lecturer in the history department in 1953–54 when Felix Gilbert was on leave, and later, from 1977, as a member of the board of trustees (and for ten of those years, as its chair).

The year of teaching was grueling and instructive, with three courses to be designed from scratch. It was an excellent introduction to teaching full-time, and it certainly confirmed my choice of vocation before I then went on to write my dissertation. The students were both challenging and responsive, the schedule unremitting, and my learning curve very steep. I remember that for one course I had prepared three lectures in advance; during the first class, I found myself turning the page and, in horror, going on to lecture number two, with a terrible sense of having already fallen behind.

The college was not very different in essence from what it had been during my time as a student, and the political issues, as the McCarthy hearings took place (the first television I ever watched, in a common room of the college to which the faculty rushed the moment their classes ended), were very much the same. But it was quite new to see the college, and after having had a little experience elsewhere, from a different standpoint and to be a temporary junior colleague of those who had recently been my teachers.

By the time that I became a member of its board some twenty-four years later, both the college and, of course, the world of higher education itself, had changed in countless ways. In the meantime, I had married, completed my PhD, and taken up the academic profession. I had also served in administrative positions and on higher education boards, commissions, and committees. I had had a broad range of opportunities to observe that changing world, primarily at the universities where I studied and worked. In reconnecting to Bryn Mawr, I could now gain some insight into how those changes had affected this liberal arts college and others as well.

For the women's liberal arts colleges, there was increasingly a concern not just for their appeal to young women, but for their survival in the face of the coeducational competition, as well as for finding an ongoing justification for their existence. In a number of instances, women's colleges had turned or were talking of turning to coeducation, as had Vassar among the Seven Sisters.

My period of board service at Bryn Mawr coincided with one of transition for the board as for the college. The majority of members at the outset were alumnae for whom membership was an extension of their commitment to volunteer work on behalf of nonprofit organizations; other members were alumnae who had professional careers and men who cared, as did their fellow trustees, about higher education for women and the health of the college going forward. By the end of my time, the majority of new members were women with careers of their own. Those who came from the voluntary sector were less anxious to have meetings move quickly and efficiently, and somewhat more inclined to see almost all the business of the college as theirs as well. Their devotion to the cause was total; their experience of the delicate line between management and board responsibilities sometimes less than perfect. For the trustees in general, two things that stand out are (1) the different role played by college and university boards: the former often need the constructive participation in college affairs of people who have an expertise that a small college cannot support on its own (hence the larger role played by such boards in planning and overseeing capital projects, for example); and (2) the impact of Bryn Mawr's communitarian culture that brought faculty, student, and staff representatives to sit in on the full meetings of the board as well as its appropriate committees. These practices could occasionally inhibit sensitive discussions in densely filled rooms, but by and large they succeeded in establishing lines of communication and understanding between trustees and the college as a whole that, however incomplete (especially in times of financial hardship and the need to make tough choices), helped create an important sense of trust and common purpose that enhanced Bryn Mawr's distinctive strengths.

6

A Year at the University of Oxford

A confirmed Anglophile from childhood on, I had always wanted to study in England. Oxford was, to my mind, the pinnacle of universities, celebrated in fiction as in scholarship, the home of dreaming spires, glorious eccentrics, the highest academic standards, centuries of tradition, and every intellectual resource. I was awarded a Fulbright Scholarship to England and was assigned to St. Anne's College, one of Oxford's five women's colleges. My plan was to do my graduate work there and—so I daydreamed—become a fellow of an Oxford college like Somerville (which I imagined would resemble the college pictured in Dorothy Sayers's *Gaudy Night*). My actual knowledge of what really to expect was in fact quite slight, and as the year unfolded, I learned that rather than stay on, as I could easily have done with Fulbright generosity, I would do better returning home to graduate school and taking up the fellowship I was already guaranteed at Radcliffe.

I had failed to do my homework. Oxford was not the place to pursue Renaissance intellectual history, nor was it a place, at my stage of learning, to pursue the broader advanced studies that would equip me for my profession. It was a place to take another undergraduate degree, and I didn't want to do that. I had not paid sufficient attention, either, to what Virginia Woolf had to say about women and Oxford. It was there (and afterward at Harvard) that I first really experienced what discrimination toward women in academic life could mean. I had evidently lived a very sheltered life.

But I would not have missed that Oxford year for anything. Once I had things figured out, it became an exceptionally good time, and a wonderfully instructive one. Among other things, I learned, with the full force of discovery, that I was American and should stop acting as though I were not or as though I somehow belonged on the European side of the ocean, however comfortable I might be there. I learned much about Oxbridge and British education, both higher and lower. I found myself among interesting and talented people of all sorts who became, in many cases, friends for life. I traveled extensively and came to love the many landscapes of the British Isles, as well as to become acquainted with London, to feel at home there and love it above all cities. I enjoyed the theater, opera, and musical life and museums of London and Oxford, the riches of Blackwell's and other bookstores, the round reading room and the manuscript room of the British Museum, and the unique library of the Warburg Institute with its air of having been transported from Germany, people and contents alike, to remain in a kind of cocoon of its own. I traveled to the Continent, explored and came to love Paris too, visited Germany and a little of my family's past, and spent most of a summer in Italy with Florence as my base for studying Italian and Renaissance literature, with Tuscany and Rome the sites of further exploration and discovery.

In September 1950 the Fulbright Scholars who were bound for England and France were sent off on the SS *America* for Southampton and Le Havre. Thus we got to know most of our cohort before landing. I've always wondered what happened to the innocent Southerner who said that he was anxious about his French but fortunately was going to the south of France; I do hope that his accent worked out. My cabinmate, Isabel Gamble, became one of my closest friends. She was then a Radcliffe graduate student on her way to Cambridge to begin a dissertation on Milton. Later she taught at Bryn Mawr and Harvard, a fine writer and teacher who married another good friend, Wallace MacCaffrey, a historian of Tudor England. They became the first tenured couple at Harvard.

The many students of English literature on the ship gossiped, not very kindly, about their travel companion, Norman Podhoretz, as a kind of wunderkind, and about his reputation as a special protégé of Lionel Trilling; he was a conversation piece even then. Some were also eagerly looking forward to sitting at the feet of F. R. Leavis at Cambridge. Leavis's virtues were hotly debated; he was a subject of almost cult-like fascination as both person and critic. I saw him once, attending a lecture he gave at Oxford in a hall overflowing with disciples and disputants. He looked a bit grubby in open shirt and sandals and with uncombed hair. Leavis seemed to expect not just agreement, but adulation, from his audience. He gave a dogmatic sermon on Leavisite critical standards and judgments, a kind of summary of what he had written and preached elsewhere.

We arrived in Southampton and were ushered onto the boat train that took us to London, where we were to stay for a three-day orientation. The dinner served on the train was a sobering introduction to the contemporary English cuisine and to the menus I was to find at my college (the men's colleges did a little bit better). The tiny serving of meat was unidentifiable, as were the "greens"; the fruit tart consisted of an impenetrable dough and a few berries still containing their pits. We were brought by the Fulbright staff to what I remember, probably in error, as Nutbrown House, and our orientation began, conducted by rather officious young bureaucrats hoping to rise in the State Department.

We were immediately issued our ration cards. Austerity still prevailed in the England of 1950–51. Rationing was strict, including very little meat and butter. Strangely, one received a pound of sugar and of chocolate per month; I gave most of mine away to housemates who had grown up without meat and other solid food and had acquired a huge hunger for sweets, often living on an extremely unhealthy diet where sweets were the only items with real taste. That also made tea, where cakes and breads with jam could be consumed in large quantities, an exceptionally important meal.

London was gray as could be. The sights and signs of destruction were everywhere; pyramids of rubble still stood on many streets. There was little fuel; good clothing was hard to come by; a feeling of constriction was in the air. On the streets, people looked tired, pale, and anxious; in the thinly stocked shops, service was often slow and crabby. London fogs, the "pea soupers," added to the sense of gloom. The Attlee government seemed uninspired and uninspiring. It had done its work of introducing social legislation and institutional change in a hard time, had fallen into internal squabbling, and was soon to give way to the Conservatives in the general election of 1951.

At the same time, one could see the work of reconstruction going forward. Preparations were underway for the Festival of Britain that took place in the summer of 1951. It was intended to celebrate a forthcoming era of peace and achievement, and the Royal Festival Hall, one of its major projects, was now rising on the south bank of the Thames. This was an important initiative in bringing modern architecture to the city. One of its architects was Peter Moro, son of my grandparents' friends and neighbors in Heidelberg. When my grandmother returned for a postwar visit, she and Frau Moro, who had known one another for over fifty years, agreed delicately to address one another as *Du* rather than with the formal *Sie*. I often visited Peter and his aristocratic English wife, and saw the hall at various stages of construction, spending many hours sitting and listening in different locations during its acoustical testing.

Rich musical offerings pierced the London darkness. From recitals in Wigmore Hall to operatic productions at Covent Garden, with plenty of chamber and symphonic music in between, there was always a program one was eager to attend. I remember as a highlight a wonderful performance of *Meistersinger* conducted by Sir Thomas Beecham. It was a fine period, too, for the theater. We went to the Old Vic (and to Stratford) for great servings of Shakespeare; Chekhov was another much-performed playwright. We saw great acting: Laurence Olivier and Vivien Leigh, Ralph Richardson and John Gielgud, Michael Redgrave and Alec Guinness, Sybil Thorndike and Margaret Rutherford, among others. At Oxford, too, we found theater in a thriving condition.

Our band of Fulbright Scholars had arrived in England and at our universities at a time when anti-American sentiment ran strong and deep, especially so, it seemed, in the academic world but by no means confined there. Resentment and hostility took many forms. There was enormous concern about America's entry into the Korean War that began in the summer of 1950, and about "the bomb," a fear that a belligerent and arrogant

America might blow up the world, a larger uncertainty about the nuclear future and its controllers. Many saw the Cold War as a conflict provoked by America or at least thought the blame equally divided between the two superpowers. The growing awareness that Britain was no longer the Great Power it had been, and that its fortunes depended in so many ways on the policies and actions of its ally, played a considerable role. The gap between American prosperity and British austerity loomed large. Americans were often stereotyped as loud, boorish, boastful, provincial, uneducated, and naive, as likely to try to throw their weight around, as insensitive to the more advanced and complex cultures of England and the Continent. Simultaneously there existed an endless fascination with all things American and a desire to come to know America itself directly, mingled with a concern over a spreading "Americanization" of British culture.

I found that my contemporaries at Oxford frequently thought I couldn't be an American. I didn't quite fit their image of one, having had a good classical education and having interests in literature and the arts. So (and this was meant, I think, as politesse) it was sometimes concluded that I must be Canadian. Being a citizen of the Commonwealth would explain one's being somewhat civilized. Oxford had quite a few students from Canada, Australia, and New Zealand, often anxious to show themselves to be genuinely British and cosmopolitan and not always eager to return home. Many were postgraduates sent by their universities to obtain an Oxford DPhil and résumé before coming back to take up their academic careers. Among the Americans, Rhodes Scholars of course had a special place. Rhodes House invited the Fulbright Scholars to many events. I attended a dance there at which Princess Margaret was the honored guest. She behaved with an indifferent hauteur and made a rather unpleasant impression. I think I offered her my very last curtsy.

St. Anne's had been founded in 1879 as the Oxford Society of Home Students and was only now receiving its charter as a college, despite having for some time been a residential entity with both senior and junior common rooms and with academic and administrative buildings. St. Anne's had bought up a number of large houses between the Woodstock and Banbury

Roads as student residences, and I was assigned to one on the Woodstock Road. Since then St. Anne's, like the other women's colleges, has gone co-educational. It has become one of Oxford's largest, with a handsome campus and many new buildings on the familiar space. At 55 Woodstock, we were overseen by one Miss Amelia Naseby Saxby who was like a caricature of the impoverished gentlewomen and nannies of British fiction, always ready to tut-tut and to cast a severe eye on her charges, and deeply needing her proper status and hence her worth to be acknowledged. We had to rise when she entered the room and observe a respectful silence when she spoke.

The principal of St. Anne's, the Honorable Eleanor Plumer, was the daughter of a field marshal, and it showed. New students were invited to an evening at her home and were seated in a semicircle around her armchair. To each one of us she addressed a question or comment. To me, she said that she understood that in America people put ice in their tea; was this really true? Yes, I replied, iced tea was a popular summer drink. How extraordinary, she said, drawing out the second syllable. And that was as close as she and I ever came to conversation. Even so, I had many brief communications from her in writing. The rules of the college required one to be in by 10:00 p.m.; three times a term, on application to the principal, one might stay out until 11:00. Once a year, for a Commemoration Ball, one could stay out all night (which I did, greeting the dawn with aching feet at Magdalen Bridge).

My housemates were mostly in my age group, at nineteen and twenty, but they seemed almost more like schoolgirls in experience and conduct. Even our seemingly more sophisticated Belgian demonstrated an unusual naïveté. Hoping to earn some spending money, she put up a sign in central Oxford offering "French Lessons" and was stunned by the phone calls that followed. The girls appeared, while working conscientiously, to stick cautiously to the instructions given by their tutors. The tutorial system, for all its considerable strengths, did not necessarily encourage imagination and independence of thought, and much of it was pointed toward performance, based on a strict syllabus, on the final examinations ("Schools") that determined the class of degree, from first to fourth, of each graduate. Every college competed to have high performers on those.

There were of course many superb tutors and outstanding students all around, but one found also those of more average talents. Some tutors might be burned out after years of ten or more sessions a week. And while British students had had a more advanced education at school than their American counterparts, many would have benefited from a broader curriculum as they matured intellectually in their undergraduate years. I did not, in short, find my education inferior. But I did find a lot of brilliant contemporaries who were off the charts.

Also off the charts was the drinking among male undergraduates, including some who got firsts. I had never seen anything like it, even at the Princeton clubs on collegiate weekends. The idea was to get destructively drunk and break things; that was thought the greatest kind of fun. Now, reading about the undergraduate careers of dons like Hugh Trevor-Roper and his friends, it is incomprehensible to me how these men drank so much and accomplished as much as they did. Some held luncheon parties where they consumed a good deal of wine, rode to hounds afterward, and started all over again in the evening.

The St. Anne's fellows were a smaller group than now and included a few women who had a kind of schoolteacher's attitude toward students. I was assigned a "moral tutor," a historian who in her two major works had discovered that both the banana and the Christmas tree had entered England and its culture earlier than commonly believed. She was a kind and unworldly person of great goodwill who was happy if there was nothing much about which to advise.

Marjorie Reeves, a historian whose work on mysticism, heresy, and millenarianism in the later Middle Ages remains significant today, was perhaps St. Anne's leading scholar. The most striking member of the St. Anne's senior common room was Iris Murdoch, tutor in philosophy, emerging novelist, and subject of ceaseless gossip and speculation. All sorts of rumors followed her about. Her spectacular looks, striking hair, and bohemian costumes made her an exotic figure in the brisk but bland environment of St. Anne's.

St. Anne's sent many of its students out of college to tutors elsewhere. The history curriculum allowed a choice of one or two special fields for examination. One was the Italian Renaissance, with a syllabus centered on Machiavelli's *Prince* and on the *Chronicles* of a mediocre writer named Del Porto. I began a round of visits and discussions with a host of dons in an attempt to find someone who might supervise me for a graduate degree. I began with Cecilia Ady at St. Hugh's College. She had been instrumental in creating the special field, and she had written widely on Italian Renaissance history, primarily in the form of biographies of such figures as Lorenzo de' Medici and the Bentivoglio dynasty of Bologna, together with a history of Milan under the Sforza. But she did not believe there was such a thing as intellectual history. Next I had conversations with Alexandre Passerin d'Entrèves, who held a chair of Italian literature, but his principal work was in political philosophy and he was not interested in my kind of historical project. Then there was Hugh Trevor-Roper, who actually did write about Erasmus and one or two other humanists and who took me for a term, but he did not much like teaching girls, especially American ones (although he became more attentive after realizing that he knew my father and his work), and thought only an undergraduate degree made sense for them.

I was finally given up to the good offices, such as they were, of C.A.J. Armstrong, then dean of Hertford College. He was a large, self-indulgent, and seemingly indolent man (but with a respectable list of publications) who was said to be so prosperous that he poured sherry rather than water down upon undergraduates making noise under his windows late at night. I had in the meantime found a subject for what might become a DPhil thesis, and while it had nothing to do with Armstrong's field, which was Burgundian history and the Wars of the Roses, he was perfectly willing to hear me talk about it and ask me a few questions from time to time.

My topic came out of an interest in examining the reception and uses of Machiavelli in sixteenth-century England. I found an early instance in the case of William Thomas (d. 1554), who had scarcely been studied. Thomas had spent time in Italy, learned Italian, and come across Machiavelli's writings. He wrote an Italian grammar (the first English one) and a history of Italy, the latter containing much material cannibalized, plagiarized, and summarized from Machiavelli's *History of Florence*. On his return to England, Thomas became a clerk of the Privy Council and, hoping to become a political adviser to His Majesty, sought favor with the young King Edward VI by drawing up a series of precepts dealing with correct political behavior, stolen mostly from *The Prince*. An execrable poet, Thomas wrote that "women's rule the wealth turn shall / of the realm, quite upside down." Having lost all preferments on the accession of Queen Mary, he took part in Wyatt's Rebellion and was subsequently executed for treason.

Thomas's manuscripts and other relevant materials are held in the British Museum Library. When I went to get a reader's card there, I was told I was too young (you had to be twenty-one, and I had just turned twenty). To my intense embarrassment, I burst into tears and was then astonished at the effect, which was to have the official hastily offer me a card after all.

There was no such thing as a graduate program at Oxford other than the project of a dissertation, one to be written pretty much in isolation. The doctorate was not required for an academic career. One's time in residence could involve attending whatever lectures were being given, and that was entirely up to individual choice and inclination. I attended an excellent class in paleography and a number of lectures on medieval and early modern England. The bone-chilling cold of the lecture halls made it almost impossible to take notes; one had to wear gloves. (The same was true of the college rooms, heated, if that's the right word, by small gas fires into which one had to deposit shillings for an hour or two of warmth.)

During one term I participated in what was called a seminar (really a kind of upper-level discussion group with no special research to be done) on Marx given at All Souls College jointly by Isaiah Berlin and G.D.H. Cole, two men with very different views on Marx. Each session was a chapter in an ongoing debate between them, with the austere socialist Cole soberly attempting to fend off the irreverent and witty comments of Berlin, a man who talked faster than anyone I've ever known. Cole was always there early to chat with students. Berlin would bustle in at the last minute, his pajama pants peeking out from under the bottom of his exquisitely tailored pin-striped trousers. It was great comedy. Few of the students, of whom I think there were about a dozen, ventured to speak at all, with the exception of Jim Billington (later librarian of Congress, then a Rhodes Scholar).

I came to know a number of the German refugee scholars who held positions at Oxford, and also became acquainted with émigrés in London, where there existed small and distinct colonies of refugees, one of them centered at the Warburg Institute. The refugees in England constituted a group as diverse as were those elsewhere. The history of the Central European immigration in England and its impact is of great consequence in many fields. Out of that group came 18 Nobel Prize winners, 16 knighthoods, 71 members of the Royal Society, and 50 fellows of the British Academy.[1]

My own impressions at that time of my youth were that the émigrés living in England had in general undergone an experience somewhat different from that of the new Americans. It was noticeable, for example, that many more of the British second generation had Anglicized their names and had sometimes repressed their Jewish heritage when trying for entrance to the "good" schools and to Oxbridge. A gifted young man of my generation, the son of refugee parents, with whom I frequently went out at Oxford, had Anglicized his name; he was in fear of being somehow found out by those whom he considered anti-Semitic and even xenophobic fellow students.

Young men of the second generation who would have been eligible for military service, and who had every incentive to join the war against Nazism, had found themselves interned on the Isle of Man and then in Canada or Australia as enemy aliens. During the period in 1940–41 when England was swept by acute fear of an imminent German invasion, older refugees were often interned also. Max Perutz, who later in life was made a Commander of the Order of the British Empire and who won a Nobel Prize in Chemistry in 1962, wrote about his experience as an internee. "To have been arrested, interned, and deported as an enemy alien by the English, whom I had regarded as my friends," he said, "made me more bitter than

1. My grandfather Ludwig Holborn in his Berlin study.

2. My father with his sister, Louise, and mother before leaving for London, 1933.

3. Hajo Holborn at Heidelberg in his late twenties.

4. My grandparents Bettmann's villa in Heidelberg.

5. My grandfather Siegfried Bettmann as I knew him in the late 1930s during summers in Switzerland.

6. My mother, Annemarie Bettmann Holborn, in 1926.

7. My mother's brother, Hans Bettmann, 1933.

8. My father's letter to my mother on his last day aboard the SS *Olympic*, anchored outside New York's harbor in February 1934.

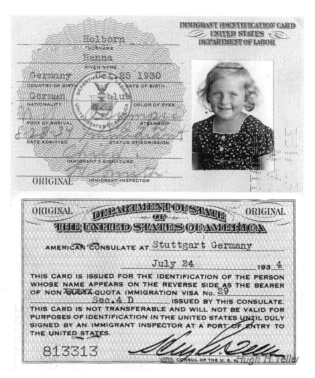

9. My visa issued at the American consulate in Stuttgart for immigration to America, 1934.

10. With my parents after our arrival in Hamden in September 1934.

11. Our first house in Hamden, Connecticut, and our first car, a secondhand Ford, with my father in the driver's seat.

12. With my brother, both of us still in German outfits, at home in Hamden, Connecticut, around 1937.

13. My father, brother Frederick, and his godfather, Friedrich Meinecke, on the Yale campus in 1936.

14. Friedrich Meinecke on his visit in 1936 at Kent Falls State Park, Connecticut, with my parents and their children.

15. My naturalization paper, issued in 1949, when I was a student at Bryn Mawr.

16. My father on the last day of his life after receiving the Inter Nationes award in Bonn, June 1969.

to have lost freedom itself. Having first been rejected as a Jew by my native Austria, which I loved, I now found myself rejected as a German by my adopted country."[2]

Together with others who were to become prominent either in England or in the United States (since most refugees were admitted only temporarily to England and went on, encouraged to do so by English immigration policy, to other countries, especially the United States), Perutz helped organize a university in his Canadian internment camp. Here internees could participate in remarkable courses given by such figures as the mathematician Hermann Bondi (later knighted after serving as chief scientist of the Ministry of Defense) and the physicist Klaus Fuchs (later unmasked as a spy who had passed on to the Russians information of an extremely sensitive nature, including the design of the plutonium bomb, from Los Alamos). Once released, Perutz became a citizen, contributed strongly to the Allies' wartime scientific effort, and then pursued an extremely successful and highly honored career in England. But, he wrote, "You cannot become an Englishman, as you can become an American." His daughter wrote that her father "had a great admiration for Britain and rather idealized it; he never felt English but was proud to be British." The historians I knew held quite similar sentiments. A major exception was G. R. Elton, the historian of Tudor England and Reformation Europe who was to become Sir Geoffrey Elton and Regius Professor at Cambridge. He had quickly turned more English than the English and delighted in the country's most conservative traditions. He claimed to have felt at home from the moment of his arrival as the teenage son of the classicist Victor Ehrenburg.

Although the internees were able often to pursue their educations, and although most were released well before the end of the war, it was not surprising to find some who remained quite resentful and who felt excluded from or on the edges of an English world in which it was hard not only for them, but for their parents and siblings as well, to find full acceptance.

At Oxford I was taken on by Eduard Fraenkel, an important and absolutely terrifying classics scholar. He had known both my father and my mother in Berlin when they were students. He was scandalized by my ignorance of Greek and decided that this must be corrected at once. Not, to put it euphemistically, the most popular man in Oxford, he was known to be hard and abrasive but capable, when he put his mind to it, of a heavy kind of charm. A fellow of Corpus Christi College, he showed me some of the treasures in its library, including the manuscript of Livy owned and annotated by Petrarch, an amazing and beautiful object to see and touch.

The Fraenkels invited me frequently. It was like stepping into a home in, say, Marburg. Mrs. Fraenkel, her hair in a bun and dressed like a German *Hausfrau* of the past in a shapeless dress with a large lace collar, produced German meals and German talk. She sat with a huge basket of sewing, darning stockings while the men conversed after dinner. A guest often met there was Arnaldo Momigliano, the extraordinary polymath classical scholar then teaching at Manchester who seemed to know everything there was to know. At our first meeting he asked about my research project and immediately gave me two citations useful for learning more about William Thomas, a person so obscure that no one else I knew had ever heard of him. Later Momigliano was a regular visitor to the University of Chicago, where he had a tremendous influence on colleagues and students alike.

My most frightening experience was that of spending New Year's Eve and Day with the Fraenkels. On New Year's Eve, the family (wife, grown daughters and sons) and I were assembled in the living room and furnished with a text of Horace's *Odes* in order to hear Fraenkel read to us his recently completed article on the poet. From time to time, as he referred to a particular ode, he would stop and order me to sight-read and translate the passage in question. Not only was I nervous about making a mistake, but it seemed to me that he was making a point at the expense of his children, who were not Latinists. (The youngest son, who had been interned in Canada, was a rising mathematician.) As midnight struck, we were served a thimbleful of peach wine. The next morning, when I came down to breakfast, Fraenkel was reading the New Year's Honors List in the *Times*. When he came to the name of Maurice Bowra (another Oxford classicist whom he considered a superficial, unscholarly popularizer and toady), he picked up the bread knife and sliced the page in half. It was not a pretty sight. I supposed this feud was just one of many among the gowned figures I saw from afar in the Oxford environment.

In London I became a reader in and well acquainted with the Warburg Institute, the library founded in Hamburg by Aby Warburg of the banking family and transported to London when the Nazis came to power. A central theme of the library was that of the history of the classical tradition and its *Nachbelebung*, or afterlife, its influence in different contexts and forms of art and thought, with special emphasis on the Renaissance. It was organized by subthemes—for example, the "afterlife" of Cicero—and on the shelves one found not only the books but also offprints of articles and essays related to the subject. The arrangement itself was highly instructive—one learned a great deal and came to new intellectual questions merely by browsing along the shelves. Most of the senior scholars at the institute were Jewish émigrés, with the exception of Frances Yates (a great scholar of Renaissance Neoplatonism, as well as of magic, mysticism, and the hermetic tradition). They spoke German all around.

Among them, the art historian Ernst Gombrich remains the best known. Both he and his wife were immensely kind to this youthful student, and we renewed our friendship when my husband and I lived in London in 1954–55 and again in 1963. They were broadly and humanely cultivated people whose love of music equaled their devotion to art. Gombrich was a soft-spoken man with a quiet and penetrating sense of humor, a certain wry cynicism, and a remarkable command of learning in many fields.

The best memories of all from Oxford are those of the circle of English and American friends who left the Bodleian Library every midmorning for coffee and lively conversation, of long spring days and walks across meadows in bloom that led from the town to the pub called the Trout, of the sounds of bells and the sights of robed figures moving along narrow streets to their myriad occupations. Many years later, I received an honorary degree from the university, especially pleased to share this event with Kingman Brewster, then ambassador to the Court of St. James's. I marched in the academic procession down those same streets to the Sheldonian Theatre where the ceremonies were conducted in Latin (and citations read out in his distinctive English pronunciation of Latin by the university orator).

The chancellor of the university, Sir Harold Macmillan, conferred the degrees, after which we all marched again in alphabetical order. Next to me in the alphabet and in the procession was Graham Greene who I feared might collapse at any moment but who fortunately managed to stay on his feet until he disappeared sometime in the afternoon. Having started out with a generous collation of strawberries and champagne, we ended up for lunch with plenty of wine and more strawberries and champagne and then at a garden party where strawberries and champagne were served. Dinner found us enjoying yet more hospitality with a wonderful array of wines, a dessert of strawberries and champagne, and, of course, brandy to follow. At this occasion I was seated, as the only woman present, next to Macmillan. His capacity for strong drink seemed bottomless. He told me story after story, all greatly enjoyable. Others at the table may well have heard and wearied of them, but his stories were new to me, and he appeared to relish their telling (including tales of his time as a representative of Macmillan & Co. in Chicago) with increasing gusto as the evening wore on. At some point I asked him whether after this long day he was not tired, and he replied with a somehow touching non sequitur, "You forget, my dear, that I am a very old man."

Oxford vacations were long. I spent most of the Christmas vacation in London with prosperous (and very kind) hosts from whom I learned that the wealthy could still enjoy life in the city in a quite luxurious way. It was an occasion to see the British class system in its most fully articulated form, essentially unchanged by socialism.

In the spring I went to Paris—another transformative (and how conventional that sounds!) experience. A general strike was declared on the day I arrived in Paris, with the result that the friends who were to join me there could not, and with the further, and, as it turned out, constructive consequence that the only way I could go anywhere was to walk, there being no public transportation at all. That was certainly the way to learn Paris, and even though some museums were closed for at least part of the time, it was an exhilarating introduction. The food was wonderful even at student rates in the simplest little restaurants. The life and language and feel of the city seemed exactly what literature had promised they would be; the joys of sitting at an outdoor café to watch the entertaining public show or of sitting in a park to watch children at play (speaking, it still seemed surprising to me for such young people, perfect French)—these constituted an important dimension of beginning to feel comfortable in a truly foreign country.

From Paris, once the strike was over, I set out for Germany, where I was to spend some days in Heidelberg. It was an unsettling and almost overwhelming trip that left me with deep reservations about ever going again. With a wait in Frankfurt to change trains, I went outside the station in order to see something of the city and, with a sudden and painful awareness of my innocence and ignorance, found there was nothing to see, at least in the station's vicinity. Destruction, ruin lay all around. It was my first exposure, despite what I had glimpsed in England, to the total devastation that the war's bombing had wrought.

Heidelberg had been spared the bombing, and the city had become the headquarters for the American occupying forces. My godmother, Frau Tobler, still lived there. I found her one of the most impressive people I had ever met. There were several women like her of my grandmother's generation and circle. They had lived through two world wars. They had lost their husbands and, in some cases, children, the latter either to war or to the profound difference in attitude toward the Nazi regime that drove them at least to some degree apart from one another. They had remained where they had always lived, quietly accepting what life had brought them, confronting hardship and loss, trying to help where possible.

I was told a story about one of these ladies: she had been asked by a young man who had fled to France to smuggle out his family's silver so that he would have something to sell. Searched at the border, when asked what she was doing with all those riches, she drew herself up and said, in her most regally commanding way, "I never travel without my silver." The officials saluted and left. These friends of my grandmother's seemed entirely recognizable; I could converse with them as with her and could see in them the same courage, character, and self-discipline in the face of wrenchingly changed lives that she, too, exemplified.

But too many members of the next generation (at least of those I met), contemporaries of my parents, seemed alien. They saw themselves as victims of an unfair defeat. They believed that I must be living a gay old time like everyone else in decadent Britain, enjoying tons of good food and goods, while here they suffered. In fact, people were, I thought, actually somewhat better off in Heidelberg despite the shortages about which everyone complained.

It was as though we shared no common vocabulary at all. Their attitude toward the war and to their current situation in Germany, their lack of any sense of what the British had endured and were still suffering, their silence over the horrors perpetrated by a regime they had supported or tolerated: all this was simply repugnant, as were the self-pitying envy and bitterness they expressed toward the rest of the world. The resentment shown toward those who had left Germany in the '30s was almost beyond belief—as though such émigrés had acted selfishly and self-indulgently in not remaining steadfastly loyal to their country while now enjoying a comfortable life at the expense of their own compatriots. That "their" country had offered them the stark choice between forced exile abroad and extermination at home seemed not to register.

Heidelberg University was beginning to revive. Alfred Weber (younger brother of Max Weber), in conflict with the Nazi regime, had left the university in the early 1930s. He continued to live in Heidelberg and after the war resumed his university professorship as well as becoming a politically active Social Democrat. I met Alfred Weber, together with Else Jaffe, at the apartment they shared. Frau Jaffe was Alfred Weber's longtime companion; she had also been a mistress of his brother Max. She was one of the famous trio of Richthofen sisters that included Frieda (Mrs. D. H.) Lawrence. I took them a box of chocolate and looked on as they argued over who was going to get which piece, and as Professor Weber tried to wangle a third one. Frau Jaffe was very strict and refused his entreaties. The two of them complained that the American military had taken over some of their living space. But they seemed to have a well-informed sense of what was going on in the larger world, and, despite age and weariness, to take an interest in thinking about the future.

I traveled to Italy in the summer by way of southern France, immediately captivated by the region's light and landscapes and such historic sites as Avignon and Aigues-Mortes. On the train to Italy I found myself alone with a garrulous priest in a third-class compartment and, for the first time in the real world, had reason to thank Bryn Mawr for having taught me to speak as well as read Latin with sufficient fluency. Arriving in Florence was another of those memorable revelations of my time abroad; to see what one had read so much about and viewed on slides and photographs and in one's imagination was overwhelming.

From a list of low-priced student accommodations I had chosen a room in a villa about two-thirds of the way up the steep road, lined with stone walls and olive trees, to Fiesole. The villa had seen better days, but its large garden was well kept, and its view over the city was breathtaking. An aged *contessa*, on the path to senility, tended chickens, which she brought into the house at night; her daughter, widow apparently of an executed fascist, presided over the household with an iron hand. On arrival I was shown my room and then, with proud smiles, escorted to a brand-new American bathroom, shining and modern. But its pipes were not, and apparently never would be, connected. It was merely a showpiece, and for my morning showers the houseboy, Vincenzo, turned the hose on my swimsuited self in the garden.

My mornings in Florence were spent in language class at the Università per Stranieri, my afternoons in walking, looking, and trying to learn everything I could in the churches and museums and piazzas and palazzos. At some point Felix Gilbert arrived for a research stay, and I became his student once more as he showed me things I had overlooked or failed to understand; his knowledge of the city was unparalleled.

One Sunday he took me to a lunch with Bernard Berenson. My memory is of a small man in a white suit, very well turned out, old and frail in appearance. He accepted the deference of his guests in a somewhat lordly manner, perhaps assuming (probably correctly) that everyone was present to hear him talk. After lunch, each of us was shown to a room with shutters closed for a siesta (I felt like a prisoner) until called to tea. The only other guest I can recall was Count Francesco Guicciardini. I never discovered how direct the count's lineage from his illustrious namesake of the sixteenth century might have been, but I was in awe.

When Berenson died, leaving his estate, library, art collection, and villa of I Tatti to Harvard as a study center, he had not seen his alma mater since graduation and had no idea of what its library resources had become. He had thought his own library would represent a unique gift, and so it was, but not as he imagined it. I was told that Berenson's assistant, Nicky Mariano, dissolved in tears when she visited Cambridge to help plan what became the Harvard University Center for Italian Renaissance Studies and saw the Widener Library for the first time, learning also that there were some ninety or more units in Harvard's library system to which Berenson's would be now added.

The second director of the Harvard Center was Myron Gilmore, the professor of Renaissance history at Harvard who had been my dissertation adviser and mentor. In 1964, and together with my husband, I was back again at I Tatti to spend a wonderfully enjoyable time with the Gilmores and the institute that was now taking shape—an excellent and very different kind of visit from my first, and one that involved no required siestas.

7

Graduate Study and Teaching at Harvard

I enrolled at Radcliffe in the fall of 1951. Radcliffe College was still the women's "Annex" to Harvard. Although its graduate students were in fact studying at Harvard and fulfilling the university's requirements for a degree, Radcliffe conferred the degree, distributed fellowships and any financial aid, was responsible for admissions and residential and extracurricular life, and provided its own facilities on two main quadrangles. Radcliffe had its own library (in which, it should be noted, men were allowed), classrooms, and gymnasium, its own culture and extracurricular activities and regulations of student life. Women could not enter Harvard's undergraduate Lamont Library until 1967; my own first time through its doors was as a member of the Harvard Corporation, the university's principal governing body, to which I was appointed forty-five years later, in 1996. Nor, even if they held faculty appointments, could women enter the Harvard Faculty Club by the front door.

Radcliffe had no regular faculty of its own but did have appointment power for a group of instructors in some introductory courses and for a number of graduate teaching fellows. Its students were taught by Harvard faculty. Initially these professors had first lectured in Harvard Yard and then repeated the same lecture in Radcliffe Yard, paid separately for each. During the war "joint instruction," which meant that women and men sat in the same classrooms and professors lectured once to them all, was introduced as a temporary wartime expedient. This emergency measure was then, not without some concern, made permanent in the years after the war. Harvard wanted it to be absolutely clear that joint instruction was *not* coeducation. An official explained this to the *New York Times*: "My picture of coeducation shows boys and girls whispering together in library corners and walking arm in arm under the elms . . . That's all very well, but it's not the Harvard way."[1]

While Radcliffe counted as one of the Seven Sisters women's colleges, it was, strictly speaking, not a college in the usual sense, since it lacked both a faculty and central responsibility for its own academic program. For most undergraduates, the life of the college was very rewarding: it had its own customs, was intimate in scale, and benefited from the teaching of a great scholarly faculty. But while separate, Radcliffe was not equal. Nor did graduate students gain from the special characteristics of the undergraduate college; their subordinate position was all too evident, as was Radcliffe's relative poverty as reflected in lower fellowship awards and in the attitudes encountered on the Harvard side.

It was sometimes said that Radcliffe was coeducational and Harvard was not, or, as President Conant remarked, that Harvard was "coeducational in practice but not in theory." When I arrived, women had just been given access to the main reading room of the Widener Library (they had been confined earlier behind a curtain to a small space that had now become the periodical room). My entering class was told of this privilege by Harvard's provost, Paul Buck, a man who essentially ran the arts and sciences and more at Harvard during Conant's extended absences during and after the war (from watching Buck I learned the power that could be conveyed by speaking very softly without seeming to move one's lips, so that everyone had to lean forward and concentrate totally on the speaker).

At some point Radcliffe's president, Wilbur K. Jordan, said a few words. A professor of early modern English history, he made an amiable impression on public occasions and left much of the socializing with students to his wife, Frances, an extremely competent woman of great warmth who loved doing it and did it well. She had been dean of Radcliffe for some time in the '30s. In the meantime, "Kitch" Jordan taught and did his research and writing. I suppose he was busy presiding over Radcliffe in ways I never saw—for example, dealing with budgets and board meetings—but his historian's role appeared to come first. My first teaching experience was as grader and section leader in his course on Stuart England. My husband was Jordan's PhD student, and we came to know him and Frances well. They were very kind and very hospitable to us, both in Cambridge and in Vermont, and they were helpfully persuasive in encouraging our move to the University of Chicago later on. The Jordans had spent satisfying years there.

Radcliffe's dean of the graduate school, Bernice Brown Cronkhite, hosted the welcoming reception. A majestically corseted and well-dressed woman with fashionably purplish hair who looked like a Helen Hokinson lady out of a *New Yorker* cartoon, Dean Cronkhite was a formidable presence. She had been awarded the first PhD in political science at Radcliffe, had studied abroad and at the Yale Law School, and had become a Radcliffe dean at a very young age. As dean, she was willing to take chances and to support unusual students for admission, as she did for my aunt, Louise Holborn, who was allowed to enter, at an older age, without a university degree and with a very uncertain grasp of English, to earn her doctorate. Dean Cronkhite's great ambition was to create a center for Radcliffe graduate students that would be both a dormitory and a meeting place. She sounded some of us out on her plans for this and was displeased by my reaction. It seemed to me that further segregation of women graduate students in Cambridge should not be a priority and that her vision of the center's design was too full of chintz for my taste. But she went ahead, and chintzy the center was, while certainly improving residential life for some.

The women deans at Radcliffe were determined to do their best for their students in the face of Harvard resistance or indifference, and the situation naturally made them defend their own institution and fight to prevent it from being submerged by Harvard's aloofness, wealth, and power. Their goal was to secure the recognition and survival of Radcliffe's autonomy. A small sign of this built-in tension was my becoming something of a casus belli as deans at both institutions argued for a year over whether I should have a Radcliffe or a Harvard title, and on whose payroll to place me when I was first made a tutor and teaching fellow. This bureaucratic issue caused a serious conflict that had finally to be mediated by the presidents of both institutions.

During my time there, Harvard continued to resist any talk of moving toward coeducation. Women at Harvard were, at best, second-class citizens. President Conant was skeptical about all plans that suggested the appearance of the camel's nose under the tent, even vetoing proposals to create a Harvard-Radcliffe chorus and a coeducational choir for Memorial Church. His views on the education of women can be deduced from his response when asked to speak at the fiftieth-anniversary celebration of Barnard College: "I have a good many doubts and qualms about education in general, but when it comes to the education of the fairer sex, I throw up my hands in complete despair and consternation . . . it is very much like asking a Christian Scientist to speak at the celebration of the fiftieth anniversary of a medical school."[2] Only under President Pusey, who took office in 1953, was a woman finally granted even an honorary degree (Helen Keller, Radcliffe class of 1904, in 1955). Pusey held far more positive views about Radcliffe's position vis-à-vis Harvard and after 1960 began conversations with Radcliffe's new president, Mary Bunting, about moving to coeducation.

It was, however, a long and winding road that had to be traveled as Harvard tiptoed toward coeducation, and Radcliffe toward the final merger that marked the close of its collegiate existence and its corporate transformation into the Radcliffe Institute for Advanced Study as an integral part of Harvard.

I had left Cambridge by the time Mrs. Bunting took office but soon came to know her through service on an executive committee she appointed to oversee the Radcliffe Institute for Independent Study (later renamed in her honor). She founded the institute for women who held advanced degrees and had then paused to devote themselves full-time to family responsibilities, to enable them to reenter and advance in their professions; the institute was designed to support their research and to give them space, access to necessary resources, and the encouragement of a collegial community. Creative literature and art were added to the fields welcomed at the institute, and as time went on, it developed into a center for junior scholars and writers holding competitive fellowships to renew their work and enjoy the riches of this academic setting. Mrs. Bunting's goal as president was to enhance women's educational and social experience, and she believed that a closer relationship with Harvard was not only desirable but essential, for social as well as educational purposes, for those who were in effect studying at Harvard without the recognition of a Harvard degree and who were excluded from so many of its extracurricular and social benefits. She had been struck, on coming to Radcliffe, by its subordinate position and in 1962 had initiated her conversations with a responsive President Pusey in the hope of forging a new compact.

Over the next thirty-six years things moved like the proverbial molasses. In 1962–63 all Radcliffe degrees became Harvard degrees (our PhD degrees retrospectively as well), and the Radcliffe Graduate School of Arts and Sciences disappeared; the Harvard Graduate School of Arts and Sciences had gone coeducational. Harvard took over a formal responsibility for the education of female students at all levels. In 1969 talk of a merger became public, and its consideration was assigned to what became over time a series of committees, including faculty committees, joint trustee committees, and alumnae committees piled on top of one another. From the earliest beginning of discussions, strong disagreement and resistance to the idea had come to light. Many Radcliffe trustees and alumnae, jealous for the college's independence and suspicious of Harvard's goodwill, were strongly opposed, as were many Harvard loyalists; the latter voiced a variety of reasons ranging from concern over potentially reducing the number of male students, should merger come to pass, to the belief that the distracting effects of coeducation would lead to the deterioration of a Harvard education. The two presidents, in pressing their case, were often out of sync with members of their own boards and important constituents.

In 1970 and 1971 new administrations took office at Radcliffe and Harvard, respectively; new priorities and perspectives commanded their outlook on Radcliffe's future. With the strengthening women's movement that emerged on campuses across the country, there had grown the sense that what was required for women's success and fulfillment was not simply "equality" as something that could be legislated, but, beyond that, the assimilation and institutionalization of deep, sensitive understanding for the special needs and characteristics of women's history, status, and experience, joined to a genuine will to offer powerful and continuing support and programs tailored to those needs. In a universe heedlessly and traditionally male, opponents argued, Harvard might swallow Radcliffe and fail its women students even more. Opponents of merger felt that Radcliffe should maintain its identity in order to represent and secure women students' well-being and success. Other obvious objections were voiced on both sides, but those aroused by the women's movement came to be uppermost for most Radcliffe advocates of retaining corporate independence.[3]

Having been forever a partisan of merger and long disappointed by Radcliffe's insistence on remaining a sovereign institution and Harvard's condescension toward its partner, I was extremely happy when in 1998 President Neil Rudenstine asked the Corporation to consider whether the time had finally come to rationalize the relationship with Radcliffe and to seek a full merger ending its separate corporate existence. Radcliffe was known to have severe financial troubles, and the college had embarked on several programs and centers deemed of less than first-rate quality. It was, of course, a delicate question, and reaction was mixed, but I thought, as did other Corporation fellows, that merger should be encouraged. It did indeed appear to be the right time with Neil in charge. He was widely regarded as generous, humane, tactful, and understanding, one whose style was anything but threatening, and who carried no baggage from the past on Radcliffe issues. The lengthy negotiations that followed were often agonizing. I served on a negotiating committee with the provost, president, and another Corporation fellow.

We met regularly with a Radcliffe group consisting of the board chair together with several trustees and alumni leaders. The majority were not happy to be deliberating about the closing of their college and had ambivalent opinions and very strong emotions about the matters under discussion. They made very large financial and other demands in return for Radcliffe's acquiescence in the proposal to close the college and transform its corporate form, succeeding to and building on Radcliffe's existing endowment and real estate and Bunting Institute, into a new Institute for Advanced Study that would be part of Harvard, with a dean who would be one of Harvard's deans. We gradually came to agreement on transforming what had been Radcliffe College into a center that would be open to men as well as women, while giving some special attention to women's studies, and perhaps positioned also to becoming a source, through the identification and recruitment of outstanding institute fellows, for increasing the numbers of women faculty at Harvard.

Our discussions sometimes went very badly, with one or two intransigent participants making it very difficult to move forward, and we would be back almost where we had started. Individual conversations between meetings would then help get us back on track. The Radcliffe board had hired an adviser to aid in sorting out the strategic options and the financial questions to be resolved. As it happened, their choice fell on someone I knew well and with whom I had worked at both Yale and the University of Chicago. He and I held confidential weekly phone conversations that provided a helpful back-channel path. It was very satisfying in 1999 finally to reach a conclusion, enabled at the end by the provost's and president's engagement in intensive talks that gave the Radcliffe representatives reassurance over Harvard's good faith and confidence in the high profile and value that the new Radcliffe Institute could bring. It was a hard sell for them, not a joyous outcome for everyone, but it was surely the right result, a testament above all to Neil's patience and tact and the persistence of all those involved in the face of a process that could have self-destructed at many moments. The institute has achieved its purpose of using Radcliffe's resources to productive ends, and its fellowships are prized, as is the Schlesinger Library, another Radcliffe institution that falls under the institute's jurisdiction.

When I entered graduate school, Harvard's Faculty of Arts and Sciences had exactly one female full professor, the first holder of the Zemurray chair (a chair specifically endowed for a woman). This was Helen Maud

Cam, an English medieval historian of great distinction who had already stimulated considerable discomfort in the highly segregated world of the University of Cambridge, where Girton College, the women's college of which she was a fellow, had been carefully located two miles from the university's center. In Cambridge, Massachusetts, she was of course subject to the same prohibitions against entering the Lamont Library and Faculty Club noted earlier, but she did make a controversial breakthrough by becoming the first woman to attend Morning Prayers (instituted at Harvard in 1638), simply by virtue of going and sitting down in the chapel each day. I think uneasy stirrings of shame began to permeate the hearts of her colleagues, who compensated by lavish shows of respect and affection. It was indeed impossible not to feel both, and impossible also not to be awed by Miss Cam herself.

Miss Cam was totally, single-mindedly committed to her teaching and to her scholarly project of unraveling the arcane mysteries of the Hundred Rolls. A missionary for the cause of close, thorough, painstaking reading in the sources of constitutional history with all the tools of paleography and criticism that could be mustered, she was a stern and uncompromising guide from whom one absorbed a profound sense of what scholarly dedication and discipline could mean. Her standards were demanding and her principles blindingly clear. When I served as her grader, the ablest student in the class was getting married on the final Saturday before Christmas break and asked whether she might be excused from the hour exam Miss Cam had scheduled for that morning. I brought the request to Miss Cam. "At what time is the wedding?" she inquired. At 4:00, I told her. Well, she said triumphantly, the examination is at 9:00 a.m., so Jane has no conflict. Needless to say, Jane took the exam and received an A.

On another occasion, Miss Cam arrived for her lecture looking a bit odd and summoned me into the hallway. "I can't think how I did it," she said, "but I've simply forgotten my teeth." And so she had. "I *must* begin my lectures on Bracton today," she went on, with the implication that the world would otherwise come to an end, "so would you be a dear and get them for me?" Through the blinding snow I ran, with the keys to her apartment, found the objects in question, raced back to the classroom, opened the door and beckoned her from the platform, assisted with the installation, and returned weakly to my seat as she resumed the platform to engage seamlessly with Bracton. No one seemed to have noticed anything out of the ordinary.

Outside the lecture hall and library and archive, Miss Cam was something of a sentimentalist. She took great interest in the relationship growing between Charles Gray and me and invited us to dinner—not a gourmet occasion. Miss Cam, totally unaccustomed to cooking after years of being served by others and at Girton, had brought with her to America a huge store of powdered eggs left over from World War II, and this formed the nucleus of her cuisine. Charles and I took our PhD orals one day apart, and Miss Cam occupied herself during his by drawing a sketch of him that she then presented to me. In England, after she had retired with a sister to Kent, we invited her to dinner in London at a restaurant in Soho. She was titillated, sitting at the window and asking, each time a youthful woman with makeup and high heels walked by, "Oh, is *that* one?" Miss Cam had grown up in a Victorian vicarage, and Soho had only one, sinful, connotation in her imagination.

If you had been a Harvard undergraduate, it was assumed that you had already taken pretty much all the undergraduate courses available and could therefore do as you pleased and take as many seminars as you wanted. Otherwise the history program had you take one seminar a term and three courses at the undergraduate/graduate level, usually with additional requirements of reading and essay writing assigned to graduate students. In my first term, no seminar was available in my field of Renaissance and Reformation (a yearlong general course in the field was being taught by Myron Gilmore); the closest thing was Crane Brinton's eighteenth-century seminar. Brinton, a noted historian and influential Harvard citizen, was the senior fellow of the Society of Fellows. He had us come for two sessions in the society's handsome rooms in Eliot House to talk about choosing paper topics. After that the seminar did not meet again until the deadline for drafts of the papers had been reached, and then we met to listen to each participant read his or her composition. Students wrote on a very wide variety of topics; the seminar had no central theme and its chronological limits were permeable. I remember that someone wrote on a subject dealing with twentieth-century China. (Mine was on Ludovico Antonio Muratori, the eighteenth-century Italian historian, antiquarian, and editor of major sources of Italian history.) Crane would close his eyes at the beginning of each reading (we could never tell whether he actually slept) and open them at the end, usually to ask a single question. On only one occasion did his eyes open and stay open during the paper, that of a woman who said of Hogarth that he depicted "disgusting" images of Londoners stuffing themselves at banquets, including one of a diner biting off the finger of another. "Well," said Crane, always the tolerant relativist, "what you and I might think inappropriate or vulgar was not necessarily considered bad manners in the context of that time." "Professor Brinton," she replied, "you may not think it revolting to gobble with your fingers. You might not think it appalling to bite someone's finger off. But I think it's disgusting, and I will continue to think it disgusting till the day I die." That was that; Crane said not another word. The seminar was anything but rigorous; discussion was random and diffuse. Crane did, however, read and comment on the papers with care.

Several things stand out in my memory of that first term at graduate school. One was the course in French medieval history taught by Charles Taylor. Professor Taylor was an overly modest man who never courted the conventional rewards of his calling. He had studied with (and I think was permanently intimidated by) the preeminent medievalist of his time, Charles Homer Haskins. When Taylor presented his completed PhD dissertation at the great man's Widener office on Christmas Eve, Haskins kindly said to him, "Very good, Taylor. Why don't you take tomorrow off?" Taylor was a perfectionist. He published very little, but he had a considerable influence. He was a great teacher who thought through every problem over and over again in our presence in a way that made this a shared intellectual imperative. He refused to omit any step of analysis and counteranalysis, bringing before us an example of intellectual intensity and integrity in action, insistently reminding us of the need, as well as the ultimate satisfaction, of acknowledging and grappling with complexity in history and human affairs.

My husband and I came to have another and different debt to Charles Taylor and his wife, for it was their farm in Vermont that ultimately became ours. They had suggested the lake nearby as a place where we might spend our honeymoon, and had introduced us to their surroundings of Vermont's Northeast Kingdom as well as to their own property. We thought that when we grew up we would like to have a place just like theirs. And so we did; in fact we had the very one. When the Taylors had to give up the farm, they asked whether we might be interested, knowing how much we had come to love it from our visits to them. Nearby was a small colony of Harvard professors that included Crane Brinton (he had been the pioneer there), and so we came to know him and his wife in this other way of life also.

Another memory is of the revelation I experienced when Myron Gilmore assigned the graduate students in his Renaissance history course an article by Paul Oskar Kristeller, "Humanism and Scholasticism in the Italian Renaissance." Kristeller's work opened up whole new paths of inquiry and interpretation as to the essential nature of Renaissance thought, arguing that humanism represented not a systematic "philosophy" but an intellectual orientation, an attachment to the liberal arts based in a long ancient tradition as providing a set of educational goals for the shaping of human character, conduct, and understanding. It set me on my own path of investigating the role of classical rhetoric and its adaptations in the characteristic forms of Renaissance humanism in general and in Renaissance ideas of history and of the uses of history more specifically.

I learned also that perhaps the largest and most enduring benefit of graduate school would grow from joining a cohort of very able graduate students and young instructors. Many were more senior and were often specialists in fields quite different from my own. Over the years we would all come to be acquainted with an ever-expanding group of people who would remain academic colleagues for the rest of our lives, wherever they might be located and however dispersed among different institutions. An incalculable amount of my education came from these associations with talented and stimulating contemporaries; there was a huge community of them in Cambridge. I came to know the historians, of course, most immediately. My brother, Fred, was concurrently studying at Harvard's Littauer School of Public Administration (now part of the Kennedy School of Government), and through him I was introduced also to a whole circle of political scientists, a very lively group that included such disparate people as Henry Kissinger, Samuel Huntington, Zbigniew Brzesinski, and many others. I came to know students in English, classics, economics, philosophy, and even physics, astronomy, and chemistry.

These overlapping circles included also quite a few junior faculty who seemed closer to the graduate students than to senior faculty, given the university's hierarchical structure and given the recently shared experience of graduate work. Most junior faculty knew, while hoping they were mistaken, that they were only temporary appointees at Harvard and were highly unlikely to be considered for tenure. Tenure meant being judged "the best in the world" and was usually restricted to much more senior scholars whose work was said to pass such scrutiny, and who were therefore recruited to Harvard from elsewhere (in the process sometimes bringing back to the university people who had started out there and had then moved on to other institutions).

The advantages of holding temporary junior positions were many: it was understood to be the best postdoctoral position imaginable; it was excellent for the résumé; it offered the opportunity to be working in Cambridge with its great research collections and to have outstanding colleagues and students. And afterward, at this time in the '50s, to receive an entrée into an expanding marketplace dominated by a network of their mentors, to move reliably on to first-rate positions at first-rate institutions, including the other universities of the Ivy League together with Johns Hopkins and Stanford, the University of Chicago and MIT, the great public universities and the elite liberal arts colleges. The disadvantages were evident, too, beginning with the insecurities fostered for the junior faculty around their sense of exclusion from genuinely full faculty status and the processes of faculty governance. They were generally kept from teaching graduate students. One might question, too, whether taking greater risks on the most promising of the young rather than rewarding those who might already have done their best or most original work could not have led to a livelier and more collegial intellectual community, and to retaining some excellent scholars who had already developed an institutional loyalty and a gift for institutional citizenship that would have served the university well. Observing the system over the years, I saw consequences that were not, in my opinion, always healthy for the university itself in a culture that too often exuded an aura of inflated self-importance.

We engaged every day with others of the younger generations (and some senior faculty as well) through the patterns of lunching together at the Harvard Houses and gathering together for morning coffee after class at the nondescript cafeterias on Harvard Square. Our discussions and debates were intense, as was our constant speculation (and our often erroneous claims to information) about the university, the faculty, and fellow students.

The most widely talked-about graduate student at the time was Henry Kissinger. He didn't seem like a graduate student at all but appeared already to have reached some higher stage of being. Kissinger was said to have done the impossible by becoming the protégé in the government department of its two most powerful figures, men who stood in well-known opposition to one another, Carl Joachim Friedrich and William Yandell Elliott. With Friedrich he was editing a volume of Kant; with Elliott he was already engaged in administering an international summer program and consulting in Washington. Kissinger had the air and led the life of a settled bourgeois and of an already well-positioned academic of influence when he received his doctorate in 1954. Of course he was older, a World War II veteran, but so, too, were the majority of our fellow students at the time (the mix of veterans and younger students was another of the things that made the graduate student community so interesting).

I developed a minor reputation as a mimic with a special aptitude for doing Henry Kissinger. This fact appeared many years later in a profile written of me by the *Wall Street Journal*. And years later the foreign minister of Turkey came to call on me at the University of Chicago, accompanied by very tight security that, I felt sure, was listening in on our meeting. Settling himself in my office, and after our exchange of routine courtesies, the foreign minister leaned forward and said, "I understand you do an excellent imitation of Henry Kissinger. Will you do this for me?" He had been too well briefed. Not anxious to provoke an international incident, I declined, and he left disappointed.

I had come to know Henry Kissinger quite well when we lived for a time next door to him and his then wife Ann. I saw a man who could be arrogant and domineering as well as charming, insecure as well as absolutely sure of the rightness of his opinions, a man with a powerful sense of ambition and entitlement and a need to be at the center of attention. Much later, and after he had left public office, I served together with Kissinger on a board and watched his intelligence and judgment at work on often knotty questions, usually constructively but sometimes giving a cynical attention primarily to the politics involved. At the rededication of the Statue of Liberty in 1986, he and I were among a group of naturalized citizens symbolically honored with an award at the celebratory ceremony at which the statue's torch was relit, and I saw his concern, on that cold and windy night, for the comfort of his elderly (and totally focused) mother, toward whom he showed great deference and warmth. I remember, too, that the awardees were seated alphabetically; between the two of us sat Bob Hope. It seemed an only-in-America kind of moment. We engaged in lighthearted conversation across the semifrozen comedian while beginning to feel some concern about whether he could survive the evening.

For the second term of my first year Myron Gilmore announced a seminar on the middle Latin works of Erasmus. He told me, with some excitement, that an extraordinary student who had graduated from Harvard summa cum laude and whose senior thesis in History and Literature had been published by the Harvard University Press would be a star member. My friend Frannie and I were the only other students. She and I started out doubtful about the paragon whom Professor Gilmore had described with such admiration, thinking that he would probably be arrogant and self-serious. The two of us sat on one side of the table, Myron and Charles Gray on the other. Charles turned out to be modest, gentle, and courteous, deeply intelligent and learned, intellectually restless and inquiring, with broad interests and sympathies. He could also be very funny in a deceptively understated way, and he gave no sign of the hubris we had come to associate with the smart and privileged graduate students whose undergraduate careers at Harvard gave them a status above the rest of us. On the contrary, I thought I had never encountered anyone more likable or collegial.

My own parents had met in a seminar at the University of Berlin, and I had always thought this the most unromantic thing I had ever heard of; mine would surely be a different story. I could scarcely believe it was actually happening to me amid the middle Latin works of Erasmus, but so it was. After the first few meetings of the seminar, Myron Gilmore was diagnosed with an illness that forced him to take leave for the rest of the term. I learned that I would now be reassigned to Professor Jordan's seminar on Tudor England. Charles Gray, encountered in the stacks of Widener, spoke his first words of a personal kind: "Will you be taking Professor Jordan's seminar?" He was already enrolled. I found it an excellent seminar and an increasingly fine spring as Charles and I began to see a good deal of each other outside of the classroom and library as well.

Charles and I were both academic children but from very different backgrounds. His roots were deep in downstate Illinois. Both parents had grown up on farms; they had met at the University of Illinois where Charles's father, Horace Montgomery Gray, studied economics, finally taking a PhD and becoming a professor at the university. As a young man Horace had enlisted in the navy during World War I, and his tour of duty crossing the Atlantic had been his introduction to another world. He was an outstanding baseball player and entertained thoughts of a professional career, but an uncle, John Gray, a graduate of Harvard's class of 1887 and later professor of economics at Harvard, persuaded him to go on to university. Charles's mother was one of eleven children. Her parents, whose education had ended with the eighth grade, saw to it that every one of their children graduated from college. Almost all of them became teachers. Charles's mother paid her way with secretarial jobs at the University of Illinois before settling into the role of faculty wife. Her extended family, scattered throughout the Midwest, remained close, and she somehow kept track of the infinite number of nephews and nieces and cousins in the next generation. I went on one visit to Kinmundy, Illinois, while Charles's grandmother was still alive. It put me in mind of towns in movie Westerns, with dusty main streets and old men sitting by day on the porches of the general stores and saloons and post offices. She was a very sweet and frail old lady who used to send Charles birthday cards with a dollar bill tucked inside and the admonition to "be a good boy."

Horace and Gene Gray went on their honeymoon to Washington. In those days the president greeted the public on the veranda of the White House twice a week, and a high point of their visit was shaking the hand of Calvin Coolidge. After the Depression took hold, they abandoned their inherited Republican affiliations and became New Deal Democrats. They once voted for Norman Thomas, the regular Socialist candidate for president, and they continued pretty much to favor the left wing of the Democratic Party.

Horace Gray's economic views were of a Midwestern Progressive orientation; he wrote on trusts and championed trust-busting. He held strong views and argued them with passion, and he was a great talker, as was his wife often simultaneously, which may have led to the quiet demeanors of their son and daughter. Horace's interests went well beyond economic and political matters. He was a tremendous reader. Growing up as the son of a reluctant farmer who had inherited his land and was doing his duty and led another life among the books he shared with his son, Horace had read and reread classical literature, especially history and biography (Plutarch the winner here), Shakespeare, and the poets. Burns was his favorite, and he loved all things Scottish. Proud of a genealogy that went back to Scotland, he was something of a romantic Scots nationalist. Horace was also learned in American history, particularly of the Civil War. He loved visiting battlefields and going over the military strategies and outcomes of each battle, as well as following each stage of a battle on-site.

Horace Gray was deeply committed to the University of Illinois while disdainful of its administration, its bureaucracy, and its elected board (in Illinois, candidates for the board ran in statewide elections under party labels). He used to refer to one university president only as "that little sparrow" and had harsher words for the rest. He liked to point out that the great Illinois football player Red Grange had run for a board seat on a platform that questioned plans to build a new music building on the grounds that there were already perfectly adequate pianos in the gymnasium. Horace and his colleagues generally took the view—prevalent of course in the academic world, but still more marked in the public universities where state politics played so powerful a role—that administrators were failed academics unable to make it in the world that mattered, and that trustees were nothing more than abysmally ignorant politicians.

Charles Gray looked back on his boyhood with great fondness for both his immediate and his extended family, for the rich farmland and the flat Illinois countryside with its endless vistas, for his memories of family farms and outdoor pleasures, for his schools and games and routines of play and visits. He was familiar with the houses and schoolhouses and cemeteries of his ancestors, fully connected to a remembered history that went back to the Grays' and Doolens' migrations to the Midwest from the southeastern states.

Life in Urbana, despite the insecurities embedded in the experience of the Depression, was basically stable and predictable. Charles remembered every neighbor and every friend and every teacher. His sense of duty led him to drop out of kindergarten when his sister was born, thinking that he would be needed at home to help raise her. University colleagues and their children knew one another and socialized constantly. The children were in and out of one another's houses and yards. Relations between the generations were respectful while seeming to lack the formal boundaries to which I was accustomed.

When he was old enough, Charles began to join his father and friends in their "Saturday Hikers Club," a weekly picnic and baseball game held in the countryside nearby, and listen to their talk about the university and politics. Like his father, he was an excellent athlete and continued over his lifetime to engage in running and speed walking, swimming and squash and tennis. Charles recalled Sunday afternoons on which he and his father read and discussed Shakespeare together. When I first knew them, they constantly argued about politics at great length and with great conviction, the father aghast at what he regarded as the conservatism of the son. To the degree that Charles had an adolescent rebellion, it would seem to have been in the area of politics and to represent the reverse of the usual situation, a radical son reacting to his conservative father. Both he and Horace thoroughly enjoyed their debates, and Horace never gave up his hope of Charles's potential for conversion to and salvation in the right political faith.

Charles, as a little boy, would run two blocks or so every morning to the university farm to watch the cows being milked. He was sure he wanted to be a farmer, and as an adolescent decided that maybe he would become a politician as well. But at Harvard, he said, he discovered that he was in fact a "contemplative."

Horace Gray was frugal by nature, a trait inherited by his son, who almost never spent anything on himself although he was entirely benevolent toward others. Despite his strictures on capitalism run amok and likely to ruin this country, Horace was an extremely skilled investor and did very well with his portfolio of blue-chip stocks. Money existed, he thought, to be saved against a rainy day; the poorhouse was probably just around the corner.

Money could and should, however, be used for investment in education. One day Horace saw on a university bulletin board a notice inviting applications for a summer program at Andover and asked Charles whether he'd like to go.

Charles did go and was then asked to stay. Graduating with high distinction in 1945, he went on to Harvard. Concentrating in the degree program in History and Literature with Tudor/Stuart England as his special field, he wrote and published a senior thesis on Hugh Latimer, a leading Protestant martyr in Queen Mary's reign. He then spent a year on a Commonwealth Fellowship at Oxford (the year before I did) and traveled extensively in England and Scotland, and on the Continent. He came home expecting to be drafted but was unexpectedly deferred and spent the year before returning to Harvard teaching at Andover. There, although he disliked the role of moral disciplinarian expected of Andover instructors, he found that teaching might indeed be his vocation.

But graduate school did not agree with him. When I first knew Charles, he was becoming tired of being the good student and disillusioned with the competitive atmosphere and tensions that surrounded graduate school. He was thinking of applying to law school and giving up scholarship; he was also finding law to be of growing intellectual interest. Charles was increasingly anxious to find time to paint and to write as well as to expand the breadth of his reading in literature and political theory, to give more serious attention to philosophy, and to enhance his knowledge of languages. On the other hand, his sense of duty and his love of history and attraction to teaching drew him toward completing what he had started.

His election to Harvard's Society of Fellows for a three-year term was a lifesaver. He no longer had to struggle to decide between law school and graduate study. The society's purpose was to give broad freedom and the opportunity to explore new or unusual or interdisciplinary topics without having to fulfill the specific requirements of graduate programs. Initially junior fellows were not even permitted to pursue PhD degrees, but that prohibition had lapsed by Charles's time. Among his contemporaries in the society were Noam Chomsky, E. O. Wilson, and Henry Rosovsky.

The society supported Charles's attending the first year of Harvard Law School. There he completed the basic courses and what he felt he needed in order to make legal history his specialization. He learned also that the practice of law was not for him, and confirmed that he was indeed a "contemplative." Encouraged by Samuel Thorne, professor of English legal history at the law school, he chose a topic for his dissertation, later published as *Copyright, Equity, and the Common Law*, in his new field (copyright was a form of land tenure). At his death, Charles had embarked on the fifth volume of his major work *The Writ of Prohibition: Jurisdiction in Early Modern English Law.*

A Harvard friend wrote of Charles that "he was one of the most gifted, talented people I've ever known and one of the most decent. . . . I've often thought that he embodied what was hoped for in creating the Society of Fellows: scholars absolutely independent and original, following their own creative instincts, no pretense, and somehow free of academic clannishness, vanities, and jealousies."

Charles never abandoned his many other interests, and he found ways throughout his life to satisfy them, although he never felt, even in retirement, that he would ever have enough time to accommodate everything he wanted to read or to do. Charles had started to draw and paint early, and he had spent one summer at an art school in Michigan. He painted from his teens on, moving through a number of different styles and phases to a final period in which he concentrated on creating collages of great complexity. He wrote poetry and toward the end of his life assembled a printed volume of his poems. He wrote steadily, books and articles and reviews, taking up subjects of general history, intellectual history, and the history of political thought as well as legal history. And he wrote as a way of thinking, in order to draw out the complexities and nuances, the questions and counter-questions, the arguments and counterarguments of the issues that engaged him, from current events to religion, ethics to politics, in long disquisitions written primarily to work such subjects through for himself.

At the age of forty, Charles began to teach himself ancient Greek, later joining a reading group at the university and at home reading some pages of Greek, usually Plato, every morning with his second cup of coffee. He tried also to keep up with his Latin (mostly Cicero and Seneca) and German (his German was very good, but he was shy about speaking it). He wore great erudition without a hint of pedantry. And he became increasingly interested in cooking. Charles loved good food and was enterprising in trying out new and different dishes. He was something of a wine connoisseur and a connoisseur of pipe tobacco as well.

Charles was able to do so much because some things, mostly having to do with worldly matters or with popular culture, he didn't do at all. There was nothing of the deliberate ascetic in this; he was simply pursuing what interested him. The breadth of his teaching enabled him to roam widely; he created many different courses around books and subjects that attracted him. He did, of course, regularly teach courses in English history and in legal and constitutional history, offering courses at the law school as well. The University of Chicago was the perfect place for him, with its flexibility and its undergraduate courses like Western Civilization, and the interdisciplinary text-based programs in which he also taught, like Fundamentals: Issues and Texts, and Law, Letters, and Society. Chicago gave him the freedom and opportunity to try out any number of things. He taught works of Hobbes and Dickens, Shakespeare and Blackstone, Plato and J. S. Mill, Macaulay and Sir Edward Coke.

Charles also spent an extraordinary amount of time on individual reading courses for students. He conveyed his sense of continuing discovery to the generations of students with whom he engaged in close textual analysis and discussion over his long teaching career. They responded with devotion to the kind, attentive, and always accessible professor of very high standards who stretched their capabilities and who listened carefully so that they knew they were being taken seriously. He was never unprepared for a class, always rereading, rethinking, and writing new notes. Nor did he ever go to class without a coat and tie.

A younger colleague who joined Charles in teaching a course on ancient law wrote: "I learned to teach by watching Charles. He always made me and the students feel that we had something important to say, something new to teach him. He would restate a student's or my rambling—always prefaced by some disarming remark such as 'Let me see if I understand you ...' in such a way that it actually made intelligent sense. Only much later did I come to appreciate how rare is this skill, and even rarer the generosity and grace to use it."

Charles was not much interested in, though he did not spurn, the public rewards of the academy. He sometimes wondered whether he had followed his own personal course of intellectual life so much on his own trajectory that he had somehow overlooked the ordinary tests of recognition or success. He seemed almost impervious to academic politics and brought a consistently civil voice to the often petty but excruciating conflicts of faculty meetings and relationships. To me, Charles's path was indeed out of the mainstream and absolutely right for the person he was, for the principles by which he lived, and for the independence of mind and thought central to his character. He pursued his own occupations with consistency and courage under whatever circumstances might prevail. Charles's defining strengths lay in his individuality and integrity, in a deeply humane and searching spirit, and in his refusal, despite all surrounding pressures, to conform for the sake of meeting merely conventional expectations.

Charles was entirely comfortable with women colleagues and students; he could not have been more supportive, a natural feminist of the old school. He was the most tolerant of men and found it difficult to be as tough or hard-hearted as he wished he could be in dealing with people whom he privately considered hopelessly wrongheaded or foolish. He did not take difference of opinion personally; on the contrary, he enjoyed the battle of debate while hating personal conflict of all kinds. His was a complicated outlook on the world, never sure that certainty could ever be asserted, always looking for that certainty amid the shifting and variable shades and expressions of thought and experience. He was extremely witty, and his wit was reflected in much of his painting and poetry. Over time, he became more conservative in his political views, though never quite predictably so, and more conservative in his reactions to the excesses of modern university life. He loved the country, and especially rural Vermont where we spent fifty years of summer life, and he still retained the wish to be (but not to have to do the work of) a farmer. Cities he enjoyed especially for their restaurants and museums and theaters and architecture, travel for immersion in the landscapes and cultures that helped expand one's interior and imaginative life.

We became engaged in our second year of graduate school. I was warned by some that this would likely mark the end of any chance of an academic career for me, but Charles didn't seem to think so, nor, fortunately, did the faculty with whom I worked. I did of course realize that any prospects of such a career were wholly uncertain, dependent as they would be on finding a position in my field, let alone one close to any institution at which Charles might be teaching. I was well aware of the nepotism rules that generally prevailed in the academic world and that would prevent my receiving an appointment at the same institution. The idea of a commuting marriage never crossed my mind. It was not for me.

Charles and I were married in 1954 on a beautiful June day on the Yale campus. We left several weeks later for London, where we spent the next fifteen months at work on dissertation research, Charles at the Public Records Office and I at the British Museum and the Warburg Institute. On the Continent we explored every town and every corner of Italy that we could reach as well as traveling in France, Germany, Switzerland, and Austria. When on our way to visit my parents, who were spending a semester at the University of Vienna, we passed in Austria through the Russian zone of a still-occupied country and saw both Munich and Vienna still showing the effects of the war, their museums in large part dark, their universities half-asleep.

In London we had a very good year and saw much of friends both English and American (the latter, like the historian Carl Schorske, then starting work on what became his wonderful book on fin de siècle Vienna, also engaged in archival research). Our London life did, of course, center on archives and manuscript reading rooms, but it also left plenty of opportunity to enjoy the many attractions of London and to travel more widely in England as well.

We returned to Cambridge, Massachusetts, in the fall of 1955. I became a tutor and teaching fellow in the degree program of the Committee on History and Literature and taught approximately two-thirds time.

Charles, in his final year as a junior fellow, completed his dissertation the following spring. He was now on the academic job market. In those days everything depended on one's department, on one's principal professors who were given the responsibility for placing their students, and on the professorial network through which the availability of positions was communicated from person to person, and not through advertising. One heard, of course, that a particular institution might have an opening, but waited for someone there to contact one's department or mentor or some acquaintance to inquire whether they might have anyone to recommend. It was a somewhat mysterious and highly informal process that we took pretty much for granted.

In the end, Charles accepted a position in the humanities division of MIT, then chaired by John Blum, the American historian who moved on to Yale where he became the first Jewish member of the history department. MIT's curriculum required broad courses in the humanities of all its students, as well as upper-level electives chosen from a reasonably wide range of subjects. The students were very smart and hardworking. On the other hand, they were studying to be engineers and scientists, not humanists, and these courses were not usually their first priority (although there were always a few students who did decide to shift to a major in those subjects), and their preparation in writing and in critical reading was often less than adequate.

MIT had assembled a great group of young historians who joined a small senior faculty and colleagues in related fields in lively curricular discussions and plans for the extension of the humanities at MIT. Charles ultimately chose not to accept tenure there, but he enjoyed his teaching and his colleagues immensely, and he liked the informality, the openness to thinking about change, and the democratic freshness of the atmosphere. The group of historians gradually dispersed to positions in history departments around the country.

Charles came to know some of MIT's scientists and social scientists as well. His office was close to that of Norbert Wiener, famed as the eccentric genius who had invented cybernetics. After they met in the hall one day, and after some conversation, Mr. Wiener asked Charles, "What direction was I coming from when we met?" Charles pointed out the way. "Ah," said Mr. Wiener, "then I've had lunch."

I found myself the first woman tutor in Harvard's special field of concentration in History and Literature. There was some awkwardness. The Signet Society (a Harvard club) was reluctantly forced to let me attend the obligatory tutors' lunches in its dining room. There the waiters, if not the members, made me feel at home.

In the course of the year I received an invitation to a dinner marking the fiftieth anniversary of the Committee on Degrees in History and Literature. I realized at once that since it was to be held at Boston's Tavern Club, a place I knew did not allow women in its precincts, I should send my regrets. A day or two later I was summoned to meet with two distinguished senior professors of the committee. They appeared to be giving each other support in case I should faint or become hysterical. I thought I was probably about to be fired, but no, I was being disinvited to the dinner. They apologized for the invitation having been sent out in error. I reassured them that my regrets were already in the mail, and their relief was palpable. "Maybe that night you could go over to Radcliffe and have dinner with some of the girls," said one. (I might mention, as an illustration of how things change, that I was the main speaker at the seventy-fifth anniversary dinner.)

Later, as an assistant professor in the history department, I was required to attend departmental lunches to help produce a quorum. Women were not allowed through the front door of the Faculty Club, only through a side door (and not, of course, in the main dining room). I took to going through the front door when on the way to department meetings, and everyone was too much a gentleman to stop me or say anything; the prohibition gradually faded away.

It was a big deal that caused some consternation when I was appointed a tutor at Kirkland House. What all this says is that I had unusual support from the professors with whom I studied—Charles Taylor (who was now the master of Kirkland House), Myron Gilmore, and Wilbur Jordan. These men could scarcely be described as wild-eyed radicals; they belonged to the Harvard establishment. All were steady mentors to their students, and, with their backing, I survived to take a degree. I was luckier than were all too many of the women with whom I had started graduate school. And this at a time when it was widely assumed that the education of female graduate students would likely go to waste unless they remained single and found an opening at a women's college. Of the 321 respondents to a survey of the women who had received Radcliffe PhDs between 1902 and 1951, only 32 held full-time jobs.[4]

History and Literature had been founded as a field of undergraduate concentration at a time when literature was ordinarily taught as the history of literature and as related to the historical context in which it was created. It was initially conceived as a synthetic field of what could be called cultural history. The New Criticism that was taking hold in the English department moved sharply away from that emphasis, insisting rather on the close reading and internal understanding of the text per se, quite apart from any historical context. Some students were more interested in literature, others in history, and there was frequently some confusion as to how the two disciplines might inform one another. I remember an occasion when two girls in a group being examined on the *History* of Thucydides presented a stunningly original essay titled "The Symbolism of the Ships in Thucydides." Reminded that the ships were real and belonged to navies that had fought each other in real time in the real world, they seemed surprised and dismayed by so philistine an interpretation, as also by their failing grade.

In those days History and Literature was a concentration restricted in the number of students it accepted. Three years of tutorial were intended to be the principal means of integrating their studies in their different subjects. The students were very good, but they sometimes viewed themselves as among the chosen and brighter than most. Like almost all Harvard students, they tended to postpone intensive reading and writing until the (then) quite lengthy reading period at the end of each semester. There were some Harvard students, content just to squeeze by with minimal grades, who actually managed to do almost nothing. I earned some spare change by proctoring Harvard examinations. The rule was that the examinee had to stay in the room for at least one hour of the three-hour period. A few would depart the minute this time was up. Scanning the first page of the first blue book to be returned, I found the following reply to the first identification question on a humanities exam: "Antigone was the wife of Homer." After that, his guesses became even more original.

At my first tutorial I found two students who scrutinized me, an unknown quantity, with obvious suspicion. They had little to say and were probably trying to figure out how to get reassigned. I gave them two texts to read for the following week. It was clear, when we then met, that they had not read with any care (if at all), and that they were used to winging it and getting away with that. They were shocked when I told them they should just go away and come back the following week with the assignment properly done. The next session was fine. I had commanded their attention, and we had all been tested. Both students turned out to be extremely competent, and both did excellent work. Another test in that first year was to supervise the senior thesis work of J. Carter Brown (later to be director of the National Gallery). He had expected to be working with a senior professor, not with a woman still short of her PhD. But Myron Gilmore was on leave, and this exceedingly wealthy and well-traveled young man, who had spent the preceding summer in Venice already embarked on his research, would have to deal with me instead. His manners were perfect, and his subject was of great interest, so it was not too hard to build toward cordiality and good conversation.

I completed my PhD thesis the following year and was appointed a full-time instructor for a term of three years, followed by a five-year term as assistant professor in 1959. My dissertation was on fifteenth-century humanists' discussions of the purposes of reading and writing history, and on the ways in which they adapted ancient rhetorical texts, as well as ancient works of history, to their own historical writings and their ideas about the uses of history. I had the good fortune of being asked to teach in the general education course called Social Sciences 5, basically an introduction through original sources to European history from the age of early Christianity to the twentieth century. The course was unusual in that it was offered by six junior faculty members who were given the freedom, quite rare for young faculty at Harvard at the time, to design and run their own course. My colleagues included a political scientist, an economist, and three other historians. Together we planned a common syllabus and divided the weekly lectures equally among ourselves; otherwise each of us met twice a week with our own class of thirty students. It was interesting to work with and listen to the lectures of my colleagues. The chairman when I first joined the group was the political scientist Harry Eckstein, followed by Klaus Epstein, the historian of modern Germany. Both were members of the second generation.

With great generosity Myron Gilmore invited me to share, and to give half the lectures in, his large course on the Renaissance and Reformation. I enjoyed and learned from that immensely. I was able also to give an upper-level course, The Renaissance and the Revival of Antiquity; we read classical works in conjunction with texts mainly of the sixteenth century. I had in addition become head tutor of the History and Literature concentration, a first small administrative job and one that I liked doing. My functions included assigning students to tutors (and listening to or rectifying problems that arose), overseeing the calendar and preparing agendas for our meetings, seeing to the approval of thesis topics, and organizing an examination system that included written comprehensives in the students' fields as well as final oral examinations. The orals often provided entertaining moments of student chutzpah. I remember one elegant young man who, when asked his view of the impact of social Darwinism, responded that it was like the vermouth in a very dry martini. Another, who appeared to have read no novels at all despite majoring in English history and literature of the nineteenth and twentieth centuries, finally said that he had actually sort of read one over his wife's shoulder but couldn't recall much about it. He thought it might have been by Conrad.

After our return to Cambridge in the fall of 1955 and over the following five years we were watching a series of crises and developments that affected universities in general during that period. At Harvard, Nathan Pusey had succeeded President Conant in 1953; McGeorge Bundy had become dean of the Faculty of Arts and Sciences. The Red Scare had not ended, despite the Senate's censure of Senator McCarthy. In his time of hurling reckless accusations he had singled out a number of people at Harvard as guilty of holding or having held membership in the Communist Party and of harboring subversive sympathies. Called before investigative committees of the House and Senate, some (but not all) of the accused had taken the Fifth Amendment and had refused to name names of others with whom they had been associated in their past political activities.[5]

While the allegations dated back a few years, their resonance was still very much felt in the academic year 1955–56 as court proceedings on charges of contempt of Congress were scheduled to begin in Boston in the fall. In one case, the defendant, Leon Kamin, had been a teaching fellow at Harvard; in the other, Wendell Furry was a tenured member of the physics faculty. Both, in their testimony before congressional committees, had taken the Fifth Amendment; both had refused to name names. Monies were being raised to support their legal defense costs.

Intense arguments, sparked in earlier years when congressional investigations at the height of the Red Scare went after university faculty, continued to rage on. The issues of academic freedom and of university policy and practice still provoked division as arguments arose over the questions of whether Communists or their sympathizers should be appointed to the faculty, whether such scholars could teach in a disinterested manner, and ever be open to different views and interpretations, or were inevitably seeking to overthrow the very freedom that permitted them to teach by espousing and working to further an ideology that brooked no dissent.

There was division, too, over what an appropriate response should be to those who refused to testify as requested. Harvard had gained the reputation of standing up to McCarthy and McCarthyism, and President Pusey (already a public opponent of McCarthy in his earlier incarnation as president of Lawrence College in the senator's own hometown of Appleton, Wisconsin) together with Dean Bundy had somewhat moderated President Conant's stance that Communists (or perhaps even ex-Communists who failed to tell all) should not be allowed to teach. They treated the individuals charged with subversion or contempt of Congress on a case-by-case basis. The president, dean, and Corporation had not taken action to dismiss tenured faculty who had been accused. (Furry had, however, been put on a kind of three-year probation.)

Our extended group of teaching fellows and junior faculty wondered whether the same policies held true for the nontenured as for the tenured, and whether Harvard's position regarding the few people we knew as teaching fellows and instructors under fire was quite so commendable. Several in this category who lost their appointments or were simply not reappointed disappeared from the university. Sigmund Diamond, a historian and sociologist, had been quite visible; his departure (and whether withdrawing his appointment was justified) tended to be the instance we heard most about. Robert Bellah, a sociologist who ultimately became a full professor of sociology at Harvard before leaving for Berkeley, was not, in fact, let go but judged it prudent, after having been summoned to tell his story to the dean (and then told to undergo a psychiatric evaluation), to go elsewhere in the immediate aftermath of this inquiry into his onetime political affiliations.[6] The university appeared to be asking the accused to make full disclosure to internal authorities without requiring them to cooperate fully with congressional investigators if they did so. We learned something about these instances and others without ever coming to know the full stories. Speculation and rumor abounded. The concerns in which we shared with alarm over external threats to academic freedom that had been building for so long during the McCarthy era were now directed as well to the internal policies of the university and to the integrity of its processes. It was not clear whether and, if so, to what extent, the university might have been cooperating with outside investigators such as the FBI.

There was endless talk in Cambridge about McGeorge Bundy. President Pusey seemed a bland and remote figure. He was regarded as virtuous, pious, and conscientious but not as a person of great intellectual weight. In 1958 he came under withering attack from a large segment of the faculty over his support for maintaining the exclusively Christian character and ritual of the Memorial Church in defending the denial of permission for a Jewish couple to hold their wedding ceremony in its space. The Corporation ultimately ruled that the university was now a "mixed society," and that private services of other denominations could be conducted in Memorial Church. The whole episode provoked much commentary and debate over the relation of the university to religious faith and purpose, and led to the affirmation of its mission as a secular institution. Some of this was quite interesting to historians, but it seemed rather quaint, a reversion to a vanished past in which compulsory chapel (abolished in 1886) had mattered.

Dean Bundy, on the other hand, presided over the Faculty of Arts and Sciences that regarded itself as essentially *the* university, defining its character and quality. His youthfulness, quick intellect, and energy, his reputation as an unusually effective and forceful administrator intent on bringing higher and higher levels of excellence to the faculty and student body, the stories of his triumphs, the wisecracks and put-downs ascribed to his wit—all this appealed to much of the faculty as a whole and certainly to the younger group with whom I identified. We believed that some lingering cobwebs were at last being cleared away from a tradition-bound institution. And yet we had times of doubt at significant moments when it was hard to discern consistent principles behind the dean's words and actions.

The Kamin trial of 1955 had proved conclusive; the judge ruled that the congressional committee had lacked authority to ask the questions to which Kamin refused to respond. The prosecution of Furry was dropped. For a time after the academic year 1955–56 the issues related to those cases seemed less urgent, although the environment was filled with the continuing noise of angry critics, including a number of Harvard alumni who alleged that the university was going to hell as a consequence of left-wing faculty trying to impose their dangerously radical views on innocent undergraduates. Various events—the selection of J. Robert Oppenheimer as William James Lecturer for 1957, the appearance of Fidel Castro at Harvard before a huge audience (he was introduced by McGeorge Bundy) in 1959—fueled the flames of controversy. An attempt on the part of some Massachusetts legislators to have the state cleanse all colleges in Massachusetts of Communists and other subversives on pain of losing their charters failed to win support.

By 1958, a prolonged conflict had sprung up over a loyalty oath and an affidavit certifying that a prospective grantee was not a member of any subversive organization, the completion of which were required for graduate students receiving grants under the National Defense Education Act (NDEA). This matter renewed intense discussions about how the university had come to relate, and how the university should relate, to the political order. While over time we became increasingly aware of how many very substantial matters came under this heading—the broader issues of federal funding and the conditions it might impose, of classified research and its challenge to the openness of academic work, of partnership with government in meeting political and social objectives—it was through the immediate question of the NDEA requirements that we could at that moment see a direct impact in areas outside the sciences that affected specific individuals as well as the institutions participating in the program.

As a first-year assistant professor, I had to attend FAS faculty meetings (achieving a quorum here, too, required sacrificial bodies), and I recall a standing-room-only meeting of the faculty—I'd never seen such a large one—gathered to discuss the NDEA oath and affidavit. There was heavy opposition to Harvard's continuing to accept NDEA monies. President Pusey and a group of other university presidents had tried to persuade Congress to eliminate the offensive oath and disclaimer and had lobbied hard for that purpose. Legislation to that effect had been sponsored by Senators John F. Kennedy and Joseph Clark, but it had not passed. Harvard had adopted a policy of having the student grantees decide individually whether or not to accept and comply with the conditions of NDEA grants, thus leaving the university as simply the pass-through recipient of the funds.

To most of us this seemed a cop-out, a capitulation to political pressures and a violation of the institutional autonomy essential to upholding academic freedom. We thought also that Harvard, of all universities, should be a leader of this cause. I was astonished by the attitude Bundy conveyed in the faculty's debate. He seemed surprised that the question was being taken so seriously, pointing out—and this was true—that everyone present had taken a state-mandated oath just to be there in the faculty room.

Massachusetts law, applicable to private as well as public educational institutions of all kinds and on the books since the 1930s, specified that, to obtain legal appointment, a teacher had to swear to uphold and defend the Constitution and to "oppose the overthrow of the [government] by force, violence, or by any illegal or unconstitutional method." And, of course, foreign-born faculty had sworn an oath of allegiance when becoming naturalized citizens of the United States. So, the dean asked, what was so different?

Well, quite a lot was different, of course, beginning with Harvard's being quite free to reject NDEA funds entirely and ending with the discriminatory singling out of academics as those who had to disclaim any association with any organization vaguely described as subversive. It was as though the lessons of the University of California loyalty oath wars had not been recognized, although in this instance, the issues pertained to students rather than faculty and could perhaps be separated from the corporate university. The dean, attempting to protect a policy that made each student, rather than the university, complicit in the choice of collaboration, found himself in a distinct minority. The Harvard Corporation subsequently voted to withdraw from the NDEA program and gave up the potential funds, as had a few institutions (Bryn Mawr among them) earlier.

Throughout those years, Harvard's leaders never ceased in their expressions of grave concern over financial constraints and their fears of damaging, perhaps fatal, deficits ahead. They set very large tuition increases (from $800 to $1,000 in 1956 and, only two years later, $1,250 for the college). In the fall of 1955, Harvard's endowment stood at a new high of $439 million; three years later it had risen to $535 million, and by the fall of 1960 to $621 million. In December 1956 the Ford Foundation made an astounding grant of $260 million to the nation's private colleges and universities, with Harvard's Faculty of Arts and Sciences receiving some $4.5 million to be allocated as it might choose. The principal choice made was to increase the level of faculty salaries across the board. The new infusion of money gave Dean Bundy an opportunity to pursue still more vigorously his practice of recruiting outstanding and unusual figures, like Erik Erikson and David Riesman, to the FAS faculty at his own initiative.

Riesman came to Harvard from the University of Chicago. He was regarded as a guru and reformer of higher education and in particular of general education. I recall an evening under the sponsorship of the Committee on General Education at which young social sciences faculty who were teaching courses in the general education program were treated to an enthusiastic talk given by Riesman, newly arrived as a Ford Professor, on the University of Chicago's program, which he described as more or less perfect (thus offering an implied judgment on Harvard's). General education was, as always, coming under review.

Another large debate was taking place over the size of Harvard College and, in addition, over a target size for the Graduate School of Arts and Sciences. Did Harvard have an obligation, it was asked, to educate a greater number of the enlarged cohort of those who were and would be attending college in this postwar era? Should Harvard be training a greater number of those who would be teaching this expanded college population? On the one side, a combination of noblesse oblige and, for many, the desire to make a greater contribution to society; on the other, the sense that the place was just fine, if not already overcrowded, right now, and that invaluable aspects of community life and character might fade away forever.

Sporadic debate occurred over the question of whether various extracurricular activities and organizations at Harvard and Radcliffe should be combined, without much result. In 1958, Cecilia Payne-Gaposchkin was appointed to a professorial chair in astronomy, the first woman to hold an endowed chair (other than the Zemurray chair, which was specifically limited to women) at Harvard.

The presidential campaign of 1956 and, overseas, the events of the Suez crisis and the Hungarian Uprising that same fall drove major attention to national and international politics. Within our circles, support for Adlai Stevenson ran high, but the sides were pretty evenly divided across the board within the universities we knew. A *Crimson* poll indicated that Eisenhower would have won Harvard, attributing this result to the business school and to a narrow majority of votes from students. World events made for a much-deepened set of discussions around foreign policy and for the further staking out of positions on the nature of the Soviet state and the status of the Cold War, as well as on the role and appropriate goals of the United States in Middle Eastern politics. Students initiated fund-raising efforts to bring Hungarian refugee students to Harvard, and a few came, warmly greeted and listened to by both undergraduates and graduate students for whom the engagement of these young men in the revolution was a story of heroism in a not very heroic time.

In 1959, rumblings of the next presidential campaign began to be felt around Harvard and MIT. There was much talk of faculty already signing on as advisers to Senator Kennedy (for example, Arthur Schlesinger, Jr., and John Kenneth Galbraith at Harvard, Walt Rostow at MIT). My brother Frederick had become a full-time member of Kennedy's Senate staff in 1957 and came often to confer in Cambridge, so we met many of the senator's staff and counselors as well as the senator himself. Fred had accompanied Ted Kennedy (his student when, as a Harvard senior, he was writing a thesis in his government concentration) on a trip to Algeria. Fred had written a report for Senator Kennedy that formed the basis for a highly controversial speech on Algeria; the speech brought Kennedy considerable attention for his warning about the likely catastrophe should extremism be victorious on either side, his criticism of French colonialism, and his endorsement of Algerian independence. It also provoked sharp public scoldings from the State Department and the government of France.

As the decade of the fifties and the Eisenhower administration neared their end, the air was filled with endless predictions of a new era to come and a new age of scientific exploration on the horizon. In 1959 two monkeys named Able and Baker were sent into space and (unlike previous space monkeys) came home alive. One evening before commencement, the historian John Clive, who was always the center of entertainment at the parties we shared, spun out a splendid fantasy. Harvard's fetish of total secrecy around the identities of those who were to receive honorary degrees presented a challenge to John, who tried annually to guess their names. But this time he proposed Able and Baker and pictured a certain pompous member of the faculty as their escort, holding a little simian paw in either hand at the head of the academic procession and leading them before President Pusey to receive their degrees.

A year later, Charles and I, and John as well, went off to Chicago, the two of them to share the field of English history between them at the University of Chicago. It was clearly an excellent opportunity and place for both, and we felt great anticipation about the move. I had no idea what I was going to do, but it seemed that Chicago would surely offer many possibilities of many kinds for interesting work or study. I thought again of law school and of embarking on a new profession, since I assumed that my academic career had very likely ended, and that there would be new choices to be made in the different life that lay ahead.

The First Round in Chicago and Evanston

Chicago, it turned out, was indeed different, a difference we came soon to embrace. Charles and John Clive were immediately absorbed, with a sense of great freedom, in planning their new programs of British history for both graduate and undergraduate students. Out of the blue, and thanks to Stanley Pargellis, president of the Newberry Library, whose family and mine had been friends in New Haven when he taught at Yale, I was offered a year's research fellowship at the library. Not only was this a splendid place to work on Renaissance humanism, given the library's exceptional holdings of rare books and editions in my field, but commuting to the Near North Side of Chicago allowed me to explore and become familiar with parts of the city well beyond the Hyde Park neighborhood where the University of Chicago is situated.

Hyde Park at the time felt rather like an insular village with its own culture and a fortress mentality. Its citizens were proud to have stayed on through a recent period of neighborhood decline and turmoil; they were relieved to see their surroundings improve while anxious to keep them from succumbing to some kind of suburban wasteland. Hyde Parkers did things like chain themselves to trees that were scheduled to be felled in order to straighten out a particularly dangerous curve on Lake Shore Drive close to the university. Hyde Park was often regarded as the strange home of an exotic and even alien species of left-wing do-gooders. Its reputation discouraged North Siders from visiting and getting any real knowledge of the neighborhood. When a wealthy matron from Lake Forest asked me where I lived, she responded to my answer in amazement, "Really, my dear, how *very* unusual!" and treated me as an innocent who had just stumbled into civilized society on the Near North Side, the "Gold Coast" of the city.

The presidential campaign of 1960 was cresting when we settled in Chicago. I signed up to work at the polls and later became precinct captain of our contiguous block. That initiated a great education in the political culture of Chicago, but I was viewed in our community with the suspicion cast on all persons associated with the Cook County Democratic Organization. The organization was deemed a corrupt entity directly opposed to the liberal and independent-minded reformism that characterized the majority of university and neighborhood citizens. Our upstairs neighbor, intermittently in residence when he was home from Washington, was Paul Douglas, once a university faculty member and now the most prominent proponent of Hyde Park's independent Democratic tradition both in Illinois and in the US Senate.

My brother was still serving on Senator Kennedy's staff and, just before Election Day, traveled with him to Chicago, where Mayor Daley and the organization produced a huge torchlight parade and outpouring of support for their candidate. I accompanied my brother back to Midway Airport and sat chatting with him on the candidate's plane while awaiting the senator. He finally came on board with the mayor in tow, talked with me briefly, and then commanded the mayor to give me a ride home. All of Blackstone Avenue was horrified to see the Daley limousine deposit me on our doorstep.

The next morning I attended a meeting called by our congressman, Barrett O'Hara (the last veteran of the Spanish-American War to serve in Congress—and it showed), to energize the troops for Election Day. We were addressed by Abner Mikva, a wonderful man in the Hyde Park mold who was to enter Congress, become a judge, and serve as a counselor in the Clinton White House. He was at this time an Illinois state legislator. There were, he told us, ten thousand precincts in the state, and if each of us were to bring to the polls just one voter who might otherwise not have voted, Kennedy would win Illinois by ten thousand votes. That, of course, turned out to be the actual margin of victory, and I used to tax Mikva with his forecast and ask whether he had engaged in any funny business.

Mikva knew everything there was to know about the politics of the state and city. He had, famously, when volunteering as an election aide, been asked by his ward committeeman, "Who sent you?" and when he said no one, he was told, "We don't want nobody nobody sent." When Mikva indicated that he was not looking for a job, the committeeman warned, "We don't want nobody who don't want a job." And when he'd answered the question of where he came from, the response was, "We don't want nobody from the University of Chicago."

I was fortunate to find myself greeted with open arms, so pleased was the Fifth Ward committeeman to find anyone in our notoriously stand-offish neighborhood to work a precinct for the party. When Charles and I went abroad on leave in 1963, I gave my precinct up with some regret. It had been a fascinating job that gave me an insight into the organization's role at the local ward level, where it fulfilled some of the functions of a social service agency for the faithful, as well as in the city.

I started my daily work at the Newberry Library by paying a call on its senior scholar and bibliographer, Hans Baron. A renowned scholar of the Renaissance, he had quite recently published a book, *The Crisis of the Early Italian Renaissance*, a work that had come to be, and indeed has remained, of great importance in hotly debated arguments over the origins and substance of the Renaissance as an epoch of history. A German refugee scholar and former Meinecke student, Baron had undergone a very difficult exile. His deafness had made it almost impossible to learn English well enough to lecture or to converse with any ease. His isolation had severely limited his ability to listen or be responsive to others. He was preoccupied only with his own sorrows and with the increasingly dogmatic ideas that he thought it his mission to defend in every detail.

After some preliminary courtesies, Baron asked, "You have read my book?" "Yes, indeed," I replied. "And in my book do you find things with which you disagree?" he went on. "Yes," I said, thinking we would now have a really interesting discussion. "On which pages do you find these things?" he demanded. It was terrifying; I had of course no page numbers in my memory bank. This first encounter, I learned, demonstrated how conversations with Dr. Baron tended to go.

I had also started—newly appointed at the last minute when additional bodies were needed, and at the lowest level and pay of part-time lecturer —to teach a section of the general education course History of Western Civilization, a course then required of all undergraduates in the University of Chicago's college. A schedule of regular staff meetings was announced, and I was anticipating an intellectual feast, having heard David Riesman describe the memorable excitement of staff discussions as the high point in his experience of the University of Chicago.

The chairman of our staff was Christian Mackauer, a German refugee revered for his breadth of humanistic learning and his rigorous style of teaching. He was wholly identified with the Western Civ. course's success, together with a younger colleague and protégé, Karl Joachim Weintraub, also a refugee, who had found his way to Chicago after living through the war in hiding in the Netherlands. Jock Weintraub was to become equally celebrated as a great teacher and university loyalist. Preregistration in the spring for the following academic year would find students camping out all night on the main quadrangle in order to sign up for the sections taught by these two instructors.

At our staff meeting, Mr. Mackauer presented his interpretation of the so-called archaeology of Thucydides and then called for questions. The feast would now begin! I thought. I asked whether another reading of one passage might not be possible. "*No, Mrs. Gray*," he said firmly. That was the discussion. My introduction to the vaunted Socratic method I had heard so much about was over.

The University of Chicago played host to a significant group of European refugees. Some went on to other institutions after making an imprint on their disciplines and on the university; others became permanent members of the faculty. Among the best known were several winners of the Nobel Prize: Enrico Fermi, whose widow lived down the street from us (she later wrote a book about the academic émigrés), James Franck in physical chemistry, and the physicist Maria Mayer. The first woman after Madame Curie to win a Nobel Prize, she could not be officially on the faculty because of nepotism rules. Instead she was appointed senior scientist at the Argonne National Laboratory (managed by the university) and taught in the Department of Physics (without compensation).

Other major scientists included Konrad Bloch in chemistry and Oliver Struve in astronomy, as well as the mathematician Antoni Zygmund. Among the social scientists, Leo Strauss in political philosophy and Hans Morgenthau in international relations remain identified with significant schools of thought that still command both disciples and critics today.

Two important figures at the law school were Max Rheinstein in the field of comparative legal studies and Hans Zeisel, who brought a sociologists' perspective to legal scholarship. The controversial Bruno Bettelheim, (self-taught) psychoanalyst and director of the Orthogenic School for emotionally disturbed children, developed a high public profile.

In the humanities, a number of art historians exercised a significant influence on the development of their discipline in the United States and helped bring prominence to the department: Otto von Simson, Ulrich Middledorf, and Ludwig Bachofer. The philosopher Rudolf Carnap and the classicist Werner Jaeger spent some years at the university. The Oriental Institute was home to several leading scholars of the ancient Middle East (Gustave von Grünebaum, A. Leo Oppenheim, Ignace Gelb, and Hans Güterbock). The musicologist Edward Lowinsky arrived in 1961.

Hans Rothfels joined the Department of History to teach modern European and German history. A student of Meinecke, he leaned toward conservative and nationalist views that aroused anxieties, then and now, about his political reliability in the face of National Socialism. He had indeed initially thought himself exempt from losing his position at Königsberg because he was a decorated veteran of World War I who had been seriously wounded and disabled. He was an ardent patriot who left Germany years later than some, but a Nazi he certainly was not. After his return to Germany, and without cutting his ties to the University of Chicago, he played a constructive role in the rebirth of the historical profession and its institutions in the Federal Republic.[1]

There were still other refugees, not well-known, who in their homeland had been gymnasium, advanced high school, teachers, rather than university scholars. They were men of wide and deep learning whose contributions to the college were of great weight, men like Christian Mackauer and Gerhard Meyer whose professional lives at Chicago were led entirely in the college, and who provided models of cultivation and of commitment to their mission of extending the reach of their European learning to American students.

A number of nonacademic immigrants, too, had settled in Hyde Park. On our arrival we found nearby a small department store and a German chocolate shop, both owned by refugees. Central European accents were ubiquitous in Hyde Park.

The wife of the art historian Otto von Simson, born and raised a princess in her native Austria, left behind a wonderful narrative, written for her family, that recounts their coming to America and finally to Chicago. She wrote with devotion and nostalgia of her attachment to the university and its neighborhood, the sense of freedom and opportunity she gained in America, about studying and subsequently teaching ancient Greek, her delight in becoming part of the community, and her regret in having to return to Europe where her husband ultimately directed the institute for art history at the Free University of Berlin.[2]

Both Hannah Arendt and the theologian Paul Tillich became regular visiting faculty for some years in the '60s. One could see them on Fridays lunching at the Quad Club and then talking intently as they walked, gesticulating wildly, to the lakefront, looking as though they were off on a *Spaziergang* along the Philosophenweg in Heidelberg.

The fall of 1960 saw the University of Chicago still in the throes of a long transition that had started with the departure of Robert Maynard Hutchins; its continuing problems dominated university planning and politics. Hutchins had been a charismatic and controversial figure within as well as outside the university. His ideas, always forcefully and strikingly announced to the larger world, conveyed his anger over what he thought the degraded state of American higher education and his prescriptions for the drastic remedies needed to reform it, and so also to reform a confused and troubled world that lacked all moral vision and direction. The Hutchins program of a required core curriculum of general education, implemented in the college of the university after 1942, had embodied Hutchins's belief in a liberal education grounded in the fundamental works of Western civilization that would cover the essential areas of knowledge and thought in the humanities, the social sciences, and the natural sciences—and that, in his outlook, would define the educated person. Sequences of interdisciplinary courses in each of these areas constituted the course of study, but certification for a degree depended entirely on passing fourteen comprehensive examinations written and evaluated by independent examiners, and covering what were considered those essential areas of thought and knowledge. A student might take the exams whenever he or she felt ready. On passing them, the student would receive a bachelor's degree. The curriculum did not demand a field of concentration or any electives. Such work was instead deemed the province of masters' programs taught through the departments of the university's graduate divisions.

In Hutchins's opinion, genuine education was exclusively contained in a prescribed general education; specialization in education and scholarship represented for him the anti-intellectual enemy and reflected a vocational bias that had killed the true mission of higher education at its roots. Elective systems, according to Hutchins, represented a degeneracy destructive of higher education. They had, he maintained, generated a fragmented world of knowledge that had opened the path to a meaningless collegiate education lacking in all unity, coherence, and spiritual purpose.

In order to put teaching at the center and to secure the integrity of Chicago's undergraduate program, Hutchins had placed the bachelor's degree entirely in the hands of a specially formed college faculty whose single focus was intended to be that of teaching broad staff-taught interdisciplinary courses in the humanities, social sciences, and natural sciences. This was a faculty formally separated from the graduate (or "divisional") faculty, with its own criteria of appointment and evaluation; some members were schoolteachers appointed directly from the university's Laboratory Schools. Hutchins believed that teenagers were unproductively detained to linger through the later years of high school. His plan allowed students to apply without having completed their secondary education; the Hutchins college was to cover the last two years of high school and the first two of traditional college. The college became a heady mix of World War II veterans attending on the GI Bill and very young, socially inexperienced students living for the first time on their own. A. J. Liebling was to call Chicago "the greatest magnet for juvenile neurotics since the Children's Crusade."[3] It was an exciting place of intellectual ferment that inspired them and provoked a passionate loyalty to the Hutchins college and its program. For many alumni of that period, any change or deviation was considered an unconscionable betrayal of the ideals their education had instilled and exemplified. For many college faculty, the subsequent movement under Hutchins's successors toward a more traditional four-year college, even one that still required two years of the Hutchins general education curriculum, inevitably meant the disintegration of their mission and an unwarranted attack against the greatest experiment undertaken in collegiate education since the nineteenth century.

In the immediate postwar years, returning veterans had swelled the ranks of colleges and universities across the country, resulting in some of the largest class sizes they were ever to have. The GI Bill stimulated a shift, too, in the demography of higher education. It brought students to institutions and studies they might never otherwise have contemplated, inaugurating a new era in American higher education and reflecting a widespread belief in the power of education to create a truly democratic society and in its capacity to shape the postwar universe for the good. Once the returning veterans had been absorbed, at the beginning of the 1950s, most colleges had reverted to a smaller size. At the University of Chicago, however, it had at that point become evident that the university was confronting not just the end of the postwar boom, but a dwindling pool of applicants altogether. Applications had dropped by some 60 percent, and the university found itself in crisis. That sense of crisis was still very much alive when we first came to know Chicago in 1960.

Several interconnected reasons help explain the lessening appeal of the University of Chicago in the preceding decade. The college was widely perceived as an unconventional, even eccentric institution populated by intensely intellectual, neurotic and socially inept students who would have been regarded as misfits elsewhere. Chicago's special bachelor's degrees were not well understood or always accepted by the graduate and professional schools to which its graduates sought entrance, and its curriculum was considered too far removed from the norm.

The Hyde Park neighborhood was viewed as unattractive, crime-ridden, and unsafe. It had undergone a very rapid deterioration, transformed by an influx of lower-income immigrants from the South exploited by profiteering landlords who flouted zoning and building codes, illegally converting apartment buildings into crowded substandard properties. The university had committed to investing in a major program of urban renewal, which in turn had caused enduring tensions to arise with the surrounding area. People had been displaced, and many in the surrounding communities, especially that of Woodlawn to the south—plagued by poverty, unemployment, and gang warfare—had become intensely hostile to the university, suspicious of its motives and goals, perceiving its policies as racist and as driven only by self-interest and a cynical political power exercised in collaboration with a compromised city administration. In those areas, sparks seemed always ready to blaze up, as indeed they did more than once—for example, in the riots that broke out after the King assassination.

A fear that violent crime could, as at times it did, spill over into Hyde Park pervaded the neighborhood. The South Side was reputed a place to avoid, and the university's leadership saw its goal of a stable, racially integrated neighborhood affording a pleasant place of residence for faculty and staff near the university as essential to regrounding the university's unity and tradition of collegiality. The university of the midfifties felt itself on the edge of disaster. Some faculty left, replacements were not always easy to recruit, and student numbers seemed to be in free fall.

The college's unique general education curriculum had endured while becoming of less interest to a new generation of potential students and to parents fearful for their children's safety and anxious about the effect of a nontraditional education on their futures. The college had in addition acquired a reputation for having few of the amenities or extracurricular activities that marked student life at other colleges, however good its academic quality might be, and students complained vociferously about the quality of student life, or its absence.

Inevitably, too, the intensity of fervor and commitment that had marked those serving on the core teaching staffs had in some cases begun to wane. College faculty often felt that they were expected merely to teach courses designed by others in the past and given almost no chance to express their own intellectual visions or to reshape the syllabi they had inherited. It was increasingly felt that college faculty had been consigned to a second-class citizenship in a graduate and research-oriented institution. The disciplinary departments often refused to recognize or offer joint appointments to college-based instructors who shared their fields of study. The college seemed less valued and respected, trailing unrecognized, despite its excellent students and teachers, behind other parts of a university famed for its graduate faculties and its outstanding record of research and scholarship.

Already in the 1950s Chancellor Kimpton, Hutchins's successor, had encouraged an effort to create a regular system of joint appointments between the college and the divisions and to move from an all–general education BA program to one that required in addition both a field of concentration and a number of elective courses; the new courses would be taught by divisional or jointly appointed instructors. There was considerable resistance to this plan, and that conflict, too, still stood at the center of discord in 1960. At the same time, it had become crystal clear that the university was facing very severe financial problems. The Hutchins era had left it in precarious circumstances, its resources far below those of its major competitors, and the university would have to try to play catch-up.

Lawrence Kimpton was not a major scholar or an educational innovator. His career had been essentially that of an administrator. As chancellor, he devoted himself vigorously and with considerable success to the necessary task of stabilizing the university. The university's investment in the neighborhood, about which Hutchins had shown minimal concern, came initially on his watch, and by the time of his retirement, he could see that a corner had been turned.

At the same time, and despite the many conflicts, both internal and in the public universe he had provoked, there had grown up around Hutchins a potent legend that was to shadow his successors for many years. In 1960 and in the following decade, loyalty to the legendary Hutchins persisted, along with nostalgia for what some now regarded as a golden, incredibly stimulating age of educational debate and accomplishment, which made the work of change, challenged with such fierce emotion by many alumni and faculty, extremely difficult.

Even as late as 1978 when I took office, the yearning for Hutchins, or for *a* Hutchins, remained strong. I saw his successors, including myself, often unhappily compared to the great predecessor by alumni of his era, some of whom had become alienated from the university because it was no longer *his* university. When Hutchins came to speak on campus in 1961, Rockefeller Chapel could not accommodate the huge crowd that came eagerly to listen. Students who had not known him, but who had absorbed the ideology that attached to Hutchins, expected to hear a message from on high that would confound the present philistine administration, whose leaders they thought unsympathetic to their concerns and unlikely to tolerate the higher educational ideals he would enunciate. Afterward the student newspaper found Hutchins's talk rather tame and bland but then forgave him on the grounds that most of the deservedly vilified administrators had been sitting in the front row, so that Hutchins had presumably had to be unnaturally careful not to provoke a scene and hence had been forced to watch his words.

Hutchins's prominence as an advocate for the pacifist and noninterventionist goals of the America First movement in the later 1930s was rarely mentioned. Instead, he was (and still often is) made an example of the great, and (so critics say) now-vanished university president, a true leader possessed of the courage to speak to the urgent and important issues of the day, illuminating the public's understanding and persuading to wise action in the political and social universe. One repeatedly hears a longing for such figures, preachers to the world, as universities are deemed derelict for not filling an existing vacuum of spiritual enlightenment and purpose that might once have been the province of the church.

Hutchins was indeed an extraordinary preacher and public figure, especially, I think, because of his insistence on thinking about education, and thinking about it with tremendous impact in a serious and demanding way, and on making it a topic of ongoing public discussion and argument beyond academia as well. His own views of education and of the life of the mind are most certainly debatable, and while the University of Chicago continues to champion the priority of a broad general and liberal education, the underlying ideas that animate its teachers have little to do with Hutchins's specific convictions about metaphysics or the unity of knowledge or the Great Books. But there is a legacy nonetheless, and its powerful effects can be detected in the educational debates of the last half century. Hutchins's clarity about the purpose of the university endures as well. "A university," he said, "must stand for something, and that must be something other than what a vocal minority, or majority, demand at the moment." His other great contribution, and it, too, endures, was his steadfast, courageous, and brilliantly articulated defense of the principle of academic freedom.[4]

A new president, George Beadle, took office in 1960. A Nobel Prize-winning geneticist, a man of modesty, kindness, and strong academic values, he came from the California Institute of Technology without having had any significant ties to Chicago, and he was always regarded as a bit of an outsider. With the appointment of Edward Levi, dean of the law school, to the newly created office of provost, it seemed apparent that academic leadership and planning were in fact coming from the provost's direction, and that Edward Levi was energetically at work to deal with the academic problems that had accumulated. In an early move, he inaugurated a new program of University Professorships, designed to attract distinguished scholars to Chicago at a time when the university was feared to be in some decline and when neighborhood issues loomed. From the perspective of junior faculty (who naturally thought the rebuilding of Chicago should begin with young scholars), this program had its downsides, but more positive thoughts accompanied the appointments of some very interesting new faculty. Every successful recruitment seemed to confirm for all its faculty the priority of affirming and strengthening the excellence of the university.

What we found and came to love at Chicago was a university that insisted unfailingly on its existence as a united community of scholars that understood with total clarity its mission of pursuing intellectual discovery and learning, open to intellectual ventures that crossed disciplinary lines, proud of sustaining a tradition of vigorous debate, offering unusual freedom to its members to choose their paths of teaching and research, and populated with gifted and interesting students who worked hard and were not afraid to see themselves as budding intellectuals. People actually talked without embarrassment about a mission that had to do with the life of the mind, a phrase seemingly thought a bit gauche to mention in polite society at the Ivy League universities we knew, where the official rhetoric had to do not so much with the life of the mind as with the goal of training leaders, an elite corps educated to hold positions of authority in American society.

The University of Chicago's underlying culture had, by 1960, survived the hardest of times. It was there to be built on. We were immediately impressed by its members' deep loyalty to the university, a loyalty grounded in a sense of purpose fueled by the belief that this was a "real" university, not a mix of individual sovereignties sharing only a name, and not an institution that defined itself by the externalities of public expectation or pressure or by social status, let alone by vocational aims.

Or, indeed, by athletic renown. One of Hutchins's achievements for which we should be forever grateful had been to abolish Big Ten intercollegiate football at the University of Chicago. That action was still resented by some alumni, and it was thought troublesome by others who believed it had caused a lessening recognition and appreciation for a university no longer mentioned, except occasionally in jest or for minor amusement, in sports journalism. Yet even our alumnus Jay Berwanger, the first winner of the Heisman Trophy, talked of his warm admiration for Hutchins, saying that the anonymous exam-grading system had made him feel that he had earned his marks on his own; he always spoke with great pride of his education. Elmore Patterson, Chicago's last All-American, was another admirer. He told me Hutchins had joked that, had he not abolished football, the Humane Society would have had to be called in for that purpose, given the disparities of size and educational rigor between Chicago and the league's other institutions, not to mention the enormously lopsided scores by which Chicago was losing its games.

I repeated these comments in an interview with the *New York Times* and remarked that I thought I must be the only university president in the country not to know that our football coach had left until my Christmas card was returned stamped: "Moved. Left no forwarding address." I'd asked the dean of students, to whom athletics (now in Division III) reported, whether this was indeed so, and received the reply "We didn't think we needed to bother you about this." As a result of the *Times* article, I immediately received letters from indignant alumni asking what on earth we were doing playing football, and one letter from a parent hoping I was less careless about losing students.

The reaction was not surprising; football had become a kind of litmus test, for many alumni and also for current students, of whether the university could still claim fidelity to the Hutchins legacy. Every potential athletic event other than a club or intramural game was at once suspect, revealed as the camel's nose under the tent in an ongoing conspiracy (run, of course, by the secretive administration) to restore football and make the university like every other soulless mediocre college. When the football club found it had enrolled enough players, it arranged to hold a scrimmage with North Central Park College at the old stadium, Stagg Field. But kickoff was prevented by students staging a sit-in on the fifty-yard line, and the police were eventually called to manage the ensuing riot. In our first or second year at the university, there occurred a large uproar over the university's acceptance of a prize scholarship designated for a scholar-athlete in the name of Amos Alonzo Stagg, Chicago's grand old man of football in its glory championship-winning Big Ten days. The first award was presented at a dinner given at the Quadrangle Club by the dean of the college. The building was surrounded by chanting student protesters; they were only slightly mollified by the recipient's sport turning out to be Ping-Pong.

The dean of the college was Alan Simpson, a witty Englishman and historian of early modern England who made it his mission to make final the institution of a four-year college that now required a core general education curriculum as one half, the completion of both a field of concentration and a number of electives as the other half, in its undergraduate program. This was a hard goal to accomplish. The college faculty in its plenary meetings clashed hopelessly over the curriculum it had itself legislated that required ten general education courses for all students in a curricular space that had room for only eight. The college faculty refused to sacrifice the principle of holding their requirement to the reality of numbers and instead adopted a tortuous process called "mitigation"; this exempted students who had not actually passed examinations testing their level of proficiency in the relevant areas from two of the required courses (hence "mitigated" from what they had not earned). It proved totally impossible to achieve any consensus or rational accommodation on this issue despite the best efforts of the dean and his supporters. Alan Simpson tried, but it took Edward Levi to solve the impasse. After Simpson's departure to become president of Vassar, Levi made himself interim dean, examined the college's problems with his usual penetrating acuity, and came up with a new organization for the college that created four divisions mirroring the graduate units, and adding a fifth division designed to house or develop programs that crossed conventional lines and to act as a source of curricular innovation. I was present at the college faculty meeting at which Provost Levi presented his plan. It was the first and only time that I saw the college faculty take a decisive action. Their almost unanimous vote actually put them out of business, as Levi had intended, for governance under his new structure precluded the full faculty body from acting as the legislative authority for the college and substituted a partly elected, partly appointed College Council in its place. As to curricular policies, apart from a common year of core courses specified for all students, each collegiate division as a unit of governance was to take broad responsibility for deciding the next level of specific requirements of its own curriculum.

Dean Simpson was determined to move toward faculty joint appointments with the divisions on a regular basis and to ensure a robust range of undergraduate courses beyond the kinds of introductory departmental courses then mounted by most departments. The history department, for instance, and it was not alone, often had trouble persuading its faculty to teach undergraduate courses at all.

Dean Simpson summoned me to his office early in the fall of 1960 and extended the offer of an assistant professorship to begin a year from then. The dean added that he wanted the history program strengthened and developed into a substantial field of concentration, asked me to take on something he invented out of the blue for the purpose called the College History Group, and made me its chair.

I was astonished. It had not occurred to me that a regular appointment at the university would ever be within reach. I was so grateful that I was ready to do anything I was ever asked, including taking on some extra courses I was only minimally qualified to teach and taking on innumerable committee assignments as well.

Alan Simpson's offer was unusual, given the nepotism rules of the day. At Chicago they had even been applied to Soia Mentschicoff, the first woman to teach at the Harvard Law School. She had left there to accompany her husband, Karl Llewellyn, to Chicago's law school; only after his death was her "professorial lecturer" title changed to a full professorship (she later became dean of the University of Miami's law school). The rule seemed mysteriously, but happily, to vanish in the ensuing years. The next couple to join the faculty came in the persons of our longtime friends from Harvard, the political scientists Susanne and Lloyd Rudolph, who pursued research together and coauthored work in Indian studies as an outstanding team. After 1965 Charles and I were to collaborate as coeditors of the *Journal of Modern History*, but otherwise we pursued very different research areas. I don't think our department considered us a bloc; in any case, we always made a point of never sitting near one another at departmental meetings, and I think the point took.

The University of Chicago was a far more welcoming place for women than Harvard had been. Most people seemed quite relaxed with female colleagues, and students did not seem surprised to find women instructors in their classrooms. All libraries were open to women, and it was taken for granted that women should enter the Quadrangle Club through the front door. The university had been chartered as a coeducational institution in which women would have equal access to all its academic programs. There were women on its faculty from day one. Nor was I the first or only woman in the history department, although the medievalist Sylvia Thrupp (badly treated by the department's far less distinguished senior medievalist) left for a chair at the University of Michigan and Ilsa Veith, a historian of medicine, for the University of California not long after I had joined them. Only the already-retired Bessie Pierce remained in the Social Sciences Building, working away at her research on the history of the city of Chicago, and I became the sole active female member of the department until I left for Northwestern.

The proportion of women on the faculty had declined since the university had opened its doors in 1892. In 1961 women represented only 7 percent, with a majority of the few tenured women at the university teaching in the School of Social Service Administration. The university was only slightly ahead of its peer institutions, which at the time were only just beginning to look toward coeducation. By 1969, when a university committee on the status of women chaired by Professor Bernice Neugarten examined the numbers, not much had changed. Out of a faculty of 1,189, 87 (7.3 percent) were women, 27 of them tenured (11 as full professors). The Division of the Social Sciences, home of the history department, had only 2 tenured women, of whom I was one, and 11 nontenured; the Humanities Division 5 tenured and 10 untenured female members. Twenty-nine graduate departments had no women faculty at all, nor did the divinity school.[5]

I did not feel that I was made to experience discrimination personally, although I did see some traditions and behaviors that tended to suggest a lower status for women in the university community. There must undoubtedly have been colleagues who held old-fashioned views on the subject, but I think the attitudes and practices that subordinated women were largely diminishing.

William H. McNeill was chairman of the history department in the vital years of its growth and rebuilding in the decade of the '60s, overseeing the recruitment of excellent faculty who brought renewed distinction and energy to a department that flourished greatly in the aftermath. When, engaged in a search for junior faculty, I showed him a list of three potential candidates that included a woman, he looked at it and said, "Oh, Hanna, please don't appoint a woman; they make such difficult colleagues," and then, when I began to laugh, quickly added, "Oh, I never think of you as a woman!" I could only laugh harder. This opinionated man was in fact always remarkably supportive, then and later when I had returned as president, on any issue that mattered, although he was deeply disappointed by my rejecting out of hand his perfectly serious proposal, urged more than once, that the university purchase the Chicago Bears football team. A larger public, he argued, would finally learn and recognize the attractions and accomplishments of the U of C as a consequence of this sort of bold stroke, and the university would benefit, too, from the opportunity to sponsor lectures during halftime, an excellent space for demonstrating its intellectual prowess to millions of viewers tuned in to the football game.

My colleague Eric Cochrane generously shared with me the field of Renaissance and Reformation history, he teaching the Later Italian Renaissance and Counter-Reformation, I the Early Italian Renaissance, Northern Renaissance, and Protestant Reformation. We shared students, both graduate and undergraduate, and we participated in a group of Renaissance scholars from different areas who met together to hear and discuss papers.

We had colleagues from the divinity school, the Romance language departments, and the departments of English, history of art, and music. Hans
Baron began to give a seminar for the history department, and we were
given hospitality at the Newberry Library for seminars to meet there amid
rare editions of the works under discussion. When I left the university in
1971, the Renaissance was a thriving business. When I returned to full-time
teaching in 2000, the history field called Renaissance and Reformation
had vanished as an official category of study in the department, absorbed
partly into Early Modern Europe and partly into the Late Middle Ages, a
victim of new historiographical fashions.

In the early '60s I encountered a good deal of resistance from the old-
timers in my efforts to expand the college's history program, to enable
a greater freedom and flexibility for instructors teaching Western Civ. in
their choice of texts, and also to stop depending on independently graded
multiple-choice examinations in favor of essays and questions requiring
thoughtful analysis. Both Mackauer and Weintraub were outraged when I
and other young Turks made such proposals. Finally, at a meeting in which
they were opposing even minor changes in the format of the course, I took
off a shoe, thinking a little Khrushchev joke might lighten the atmosphere,
and gained a surprise victory. Mr. Mackauer had somewhere in his makeup
a hierarchical sense of deference to authority and, ridiculous as that was,
came to act as a colleague not necessarily happy but accepting of changes.
Individual instructors now had greater control over their teaching in the
Western Civ. course and were quite happy with an expanded history program to which Western Civ. was an essential introduction, taught by a faculty jointly appointed with the Department of History.

Concern over the relatively low count of women faculty and questions
surrounding the role of women at the university became increasingly
clamorous in the decade of the '60s. Those issues constituted a significant
dimension of the political conflicts that roiled the campus as the radical
movement took shape after 1965.

It was the nonreappointment to her current rank of an assistant professor named Marlene Dixon that became the stated cause of a sit-in,

takeover, and sixteen-day occupation of the university's administration building in the winter of 1969. It was alleged that Marlene Dixon had been the victim of discrimination, not reappointed because she was a woman, a radical feminist, a radical in the field of sociology, and on the extreme left wing in her politics. To those allegations were joined all the other issues of the day—the war in Vietnam, the draft, civil rights, student power, the perceived shortcomings of universities, and the makeovers advocated for their missions, their governance, and their programs of education and research.

The sit-in took place against the backdrop of the activism that swept the country from California to the East in the '60s. Prolonged conflicts at Berkeley represented act 1, the chaos and violence of police intervention at both Columbia and Harvard followed, and the shootings at Kent State University marked a culmination. The University of Chicago had witnessed a sit-in at the president's office already in 1963—an undergraduate named Bernie Sanders was one of its leaders—over discriminatory real estate policies in the outsourced management of the university's neighborhood properties. More recently there had arisen strong protests that provoked fierce disagreements and debates within the university community over whether the university should report student grade averages to draft boards at a time when exemption from the draft depended on students' academic standing (the university policy on this issue was to allow individuals their choice as to whether their transcripts should be forwarded, but many saw this as making the institution complicit in an unfair draft system and an unjust war). Liberal faculty sympathetic to student concerns began often to draw back somewhat after more radical students, joined by several young faculty members—most prominently Richard Flacks, a sociologist and a founding member of the SDS—took leadership of the activist movement and demanded not only the reinstatement of Marlene Dixon, but a permanent role for students in the processes of faculty appointment, as well as participation in decision making on just about all major academic and institutional matters.

Marlene Dixon, an assistant professor teaching in the interdisciplinary Committee on Human Development, had been informed in December 1968 that she would not be renewed as an assistant professor. The committee, lacking independent appointment powers of its own, could make its appointments only jointly with a disciplinary department. Facing an emergency shortage of faculty to mount its program, the committee had brought Dixon to Chicago at the last moment, having received approval, pretty much as a formality, from the Department of Sociology.

Ms. Dixon, when she arrived in 1966, had not yet completed her PhD at UCLA and was not really prepared for a full-time position at a major research university where she would have to be evaluated for renewal in only two and a half years' time. As it happened, she was a radical feminist, a radical also in her politics and in her profession of sociology. Allegations immediately arose, when it was publicly known that she would not be reappointed, that these were the reasons for the decision. The dean of the social sciences, D. Gale Johnson, and the provost, John T. Wilson, were accused of having applied inappropriate considerations to deciding Dixon's case, and activists at once seized on it to unleash a broader set of attacks and demands on the university. The Committee on Human Development announced that it had voted unanimously in Dixon's favor; the Department of Sociology that it had not found sufficient merit to prolong her appointment. The dean and provost had agreed with the department.

That was the spark igniting the larger protest held in Dixon's name. The sit-in began at the end of January. At its height, it probably included about four hundred students, both graduate and undergraduate, and drew in several others, like the radical historian Staughton Lynd about whom it was alleged that he had been prevented from receiving an appointment to the history department because of his political convictions. Students were warned, as they entered the building, to leave or face disciplinary action. The administration did leave and conducted its business as well as it could elsewhere on campus. There was considerable concern over the building's office files, especially the records of the financial affairs office, that were now accessible to the protesters, a fear that they would be read and possibly destroyed. There did in the end turn out to have been some vandalism of that sort.

Edward Levi instructed the police to stay away from the campus; he would not call them in unless by a special signal under the most drastic circumstances. He would wait the sit-in out, and it went on more or less peacefully. It being the University of Chicago, some of the students sitting in periodically left to attend class and then returned. By the end their ranks had been somewhat thinned. As the sit-in continued, the women came to be increasingly aware of their lesser status, even among egalitarian radicals. They were outraged by the male leaders who lolled about in fatigues and combat boots ordering the women to prepare and serve them their peanut butter and jelly sandwiches, and expecting them to perform other submissive roles as well. One day a group of women appeared on the steps of the administration building demanding the opportunity to address female journalists only to voice their complaints about the place and role of women at the university and in society at large. Radical feminism assumed a dramatic public presence on campus from that moment on.

President Levi dealt with the crisis by holding to a consistent course of waiting the sit-in out, keeping the community well informed, and consulting throughout with the elected faculty governance institutions of the Council of the University Senate and the Executive Committee of the council. He made the crisis an occasion to offer a kind of running seminar on the questions of what a university was for, why it mattered, and why the activists' views, demands, and actions threatened its integrity and most important purposes by attempting to make the university an instrument of social and political change, confining the freedom of its members, and promoting an anti-intellectual spirit where the free life of the intellect should be paramount. His eloquent speeches and communications constitute some of the best statements on the fundamental nature and role of universities that I know.[6]

Levi appointed a committee, with me as its chair, to investigate the circumstances of the Dixon case and to determine whether fairness and appropriate process had prevailed, pledging to make available any information that we might seek and promising to abide by any conclusions we might reach or recommendations we might offer. The committee was drawn from a wide variety of faculty. Its two other women members were Susanne Rudolph from the Department of Political Science and Helen Perlman from the School of Social Service Administration. The other members were four men—Stuart Rice from the Department of Chemistry, Robert Fogel, an economist (later to win a Nobel Prize) from the Graduate School of Business, Brewster Smith from the Department of Psychology, and Jacob Getzels from the Department of Education.

Our committee worked under a good deal of pressure, and its members sometimes fell into emotional arguments that needed to be calmed. I have never learned so much in so short a time. Nor have I ever been more absorbed by the task of finding a way through the complexities of ascertaining essential facts or working through differences of opinion and perspective to reach a reasonable and explicable judgment. That process is, indeed, what I later found most compelling in the world of academic administration and in the experience of serving on boards.

In the course of our inquiry, we talked to the administrators involved, to faculty, and to students who had studied with Ms. Dixon. I twice visited the administration building to be confronted by large groups of jeering students who repeated demands and allegations that went far beyond the Dixon case to the larger issues of what role the university should take in stopping the war, in dealing with social injustice, and in transforming its governance, curriculum, and intellectual activities in order to make research and education directly and urgently "relevant" to creating a better world.

I saw the difference between protesters behaving as a crowd egging each other on and persons behaving as individuals; on each occasion I was pursued by one or two students, well-brought-up idealistic young people caught up in a cause, apologizing for the aggressive rudeness that dominated the proceedings. Genuine discussion with the assembly of jeering and shouting protesters was of course impossible, but it was not unimportant to have been there and willing to talk.

A big lesson for me came out of our interviews with the chairman of the Committee on Human Development. He assured us in the first round of conversation that its vote had been unanimous in Dixon's favor, but when we decided to question him further in a second meeting, since something seemed not quite right, he said the vote had been "virtually unanimous." This, as I recall, meant a vote of 7 to 5. The sociology department, on the other hand, was unanimous in its negative estimate of the work Dixon had done and of her now-finished PhD dissertation. Our committee enlisted several outside experts in the field to review the work; their conclusions were identical.

Dixon's students were divided: a large number thought her a very capable and caring teacher; others, especially among the more advanced students, found her disorganized, uneven, and sometimes unprepared. Her supporters were passionate in her defense, but it was her personality and the attention she gave them and not her intellectual strengths that they tended to praise.

Marlene Dixon, in our meetings with her, seemed a vulnerable and somewhat insecure and confused woman. She was conscious of being to some degree exploited by people who had bigger goals than her reappointment in mind. I think she felt that the protest, although she had to be for it, was not helping her case. In the end, we concluded that there had been no irregularities in the procedures used for her evaluation. We thought her initial appointment had been a rushed and mistaken one to start with, that in agreeing to it the Department of Sociology had paid no attention to its merits and had focused on it only much later when the need to judge the matter of her reappointment had arisen, then to find the case clearly negative. We recommended that Dixon be offered an additional year, given all that had transpired and that she had been put through.

She refused the offer, moving instead to McGill University where, oddly, the same outcome, followed by the same kind of allegations, occurred after her failure to win tenure there. She had become, in the meantime, a strong adherent of the Quebec separatist movement as well as devoting herself to radical feminist causes. Marlene Dixon finally moved to California, where she founded a cult-like political movement whose members ultimately revolted against her increasingly bizarre behavior and her autocratic and erratic leadership. She had become a sometimes delusional alcoholic.

The Dixon case brought to our attention a number of questions that our report asked be further pursued: the status of women at the university (the Neugarten Committee that published the sobering figures listed above was appointed in response); the criteria having to do with appointments made jointly in and between different disciplinary units; the problems that, we had found, most concerned junior faculty; the issue of how to evaluate and give weight to teaching; the question of whether some kind of independent board should be established to deal with cases that deserved review after a serious challenge to the integrity and fairness of procedure (such an entity was appointed and reappointed annually, and in its entire history dealt with only one case).

The sit-in ended shortly after the report's submission. Disciplinary proceedings began, and that process provoked strongly divisive conflicts within the university community over the process itself and the university's treatment of its students (eighty-one were suspended and forty-two expelled, a few placed on probation). Amnesty was not the rule at the University of Chicago as it more commonly was elsewhere. Those conflicts lasted for a very long time and drove the internal politics of the university, with factions that fought over nominations and elections to the faculty's governing bodies as well as for and against policies under consideration for student representation in advisory committees and other matters.

Edward Levi had been an outstanding leader among university presidents in his handling of the sit-in and all that it entailed, and in his eloquent statement of the university's purpose and of the overriding claims of intellectual freedom and responsibility. He had entered office as president with the ambition of expanding the academic quality and influence of an institution he had done so much as provost to restore and strengthen, and had been instead diverted to become a crisis manager. Amid the turmoil, and most significantly for the future, he had seen to it that the university's identifying culture had been sustained. That was a truly great accomplishment and, for the future of the university, an indispensable legacy.

The aftermath of 1969 turned into a difficult time. The university's economy again declined; the college experienced the effects of the preceding years of turbulence and came again to be diminished in size. The larger environment for higher education became increasingly problematic also, public faith in the prospects for higher education and its worth increasingly questioned. The culture wars were warming up, and the beliefs that had animated the sizable investment in higher education and its prospects were beginning to some extent to fade. Faith in the powers of higher education and all its works was receding, shaken by the events of the later '60s and earlier '70s, battered by a slowing academic economy and a growing skepticism over the outcomes to which higher education might lead, and society was coming to embrace other funding priorities regarded as more urgent for the health of the social order.

The occupation of the university's administration building and the events that accompanied the relatively long-lasting sit-in drew a good deal of attention, as did the report of our committee. Institutions were beginning to look for women and minority candidates. I had already had a number of inquiries and even offers from several women's colleges, but I did not want and knew I was not ready for a presidential job. Events at Chicago had made me in a minor way more visible, and without aspiring to an administrative career, I had become more interested in the substance and value of such work. I liked chairing meetings, finding ways to move toward consensus, and coming to consequential policy recommendations and actions, and I felt an acute sense of how important it was to maintain the always-fragile character of institutions whose missions would be damaged, perhaps irrevocably, were they to become politicized and lose the primary purposes and requisite freedoms that justified their existence. I was not uninterested in pursuing objectives that looked toward fulfilling the goals of academic life, and the following year away from Chicago offered time and some new experience for reflecting on those questions.

Charles and I spent the academic year 1969–70 in California, he as a fellow at the Center for Advanced Study in the Behavioral Sciences, I as a visiting professor at Berkeley. My time at Berkeley was a new and fascinating academic experience. Berkeley's history department was arguably the best in the country, and it was stimulating to be even temporarily a member.

At the time, many Berkeley faculty seemed to be suffering burnout when it came to thinking about university affairs, after the deep tensions and violent events of the previous five years had created fissures within their ranks and endless distractions from their work. The university showed the effects of its recent history. It had become the symbol of all that the radical student movement might bring into being, from the Free Speech Movement to the protests over People's Park and the restiveness that still hung over the campus. My colleagues had watched the university become the target of conservative opposition in the state and on the Board of Regents. They feared what Governor Reagan's enmity would bring as their university struggled to attain at least a modicum of peace and renewed cohesion.

From the history department's offices, one could hear drums being banged for hours down the corridor where the faculty of a new Department of Black Studies were creating their own cultural events. No one ever asked that the noise level be lowered; that could have set off disputes everyone was anxious to avoid. Outside, on Sproul Plaza and at Sather Gate, colleagues, flower children, ordinary citizens, and speakers for an infinite variety of causes mingled to protest, beg for cash, study, eat, take the sun, or simply watch what was going on. Demonstrations were mounted every day. People appeared wearing bizarre outfits to advocate far-out platforms for the revolution and for life. The lunch crowd, which I joined, was buying food from hippie vendors—at least one of whom, it later appeared, was a soldier in the Symbionese Liberation Army.

I was teaching both graduate students and a group of senior history concentrators in the honors program. The undergraduates were used to large classes, and they were touchingly grateful for the attention they received in their seminar-style honors course and somewhat surprised by having access to their instructor. I found them unfailingly courteous and very much wanting to talk, mostly about their work but also about the unrest and uncertainties to which they continued to be exposed in their collegiate lives, and the ambivalence that many of them felt in taking positions on the means and ends of the student movement.

Berkeley was a far more interesting place than Stanford, where the Center for Advanced Study in the Behavioral Sciences was located. Whatever one thought about events in Berkeley, it was a lively community where intense and serious debate prevailed in a setting that was part of an urban center. Palo Alto was, by contrast, the picture of a carefully manicured wealthy suburb, and the contrast between the two campuses, both physically and in terms of intellectual tone, mirrored that difference.

Stanford was in fact seeing its own version of radical protest. On one evening, when I was giving a paper to an audience of Renaissance scholars and students in a room at the Stanford library, a group of protesters raced through the building, snatching books from the shelves and hurling them to the floor, mocking readers at their desks, and finally disrupting our meeting. No one seemed surprised; such happenings were apparently taken for granted. We simply left and went to a professor's home to resume our discussion in his living room. Later in the year, H. Bruce Franklin, a Stanford associate professor of English and member of the leftist Venceremos Organization (who once appeared on TV carrying a rifle and wearing a Che Guevara outfit), was charged with inciting students to riot and to burn down Stanford's computation center. He was terminated on this account in a rare instance of tenure removal, one that aroused widespread controversy in the academic community at Stanford and beyond.

When I was asked in the summer of 1970 to consider the position of dean of the College of Arts and Sciences at Northwestern University, it seemed an interesting proposition. The prospective offer of a professorship in the history department made it even more attractive. I knew and thought highly of the department, for I had twice taught a course there and found an excellent department with wonderful colleagues and very able students. I could happily teach as a member of the department for life should I turn out to be not much of a dean.

I found that I was ready to try something new, and this seemed an opportunity to help build an already very good place to still greater strength. The resources to do things and the will to see them done appeared in hand, as I gathered from conversations with faculty and administrators. Both the president,

Robert Strotz (an economist who had previously been dean), and the provost, Ray Mack, a sociologist, emphasized their aim to move the university to a next level and to overcome the perception that it lagged seriously behind the University of Chicago. Strotz and Mack believed in delegating; they gave a good deal of freedom, as well as their full support, to the university's deans.

We moved to Evanston after finding a very nice house on the lakefront in a pleasant neighborhood of comfortable old houses convenient to commuting south to Hyde Park, as Charles began to do. From the outset, learning on the job, I discovered that I very much enjoyed my work. Every day I looked forward to getting to the office and to what might happen next. The first lesson of academic administration, as one quickly learns, is always to expect the unexpected.

Northwestern had an NROTC unit presided over by a naval captain. He arranged to visit, bringing his executive officer, on day one. They arrived in dress uniform and addressed me as "Sir." When offered coffee, the captain said, "My exec takes cream in his coffee, Sir." I think they felt some lack of enthusiastic interest on my part; some years later, when nominated for a seat on the board of the Naval War College (not a position I had sought), I was told that clearance had been withheld in Washington, and I supposed my naval friends in Evanston had been lukewarm when asked their opinion. The idea had been promoted by Admiral Stansfield Turner (later director of the CIA), who as commandant of the Naval War College had me spend a few days there to evaluate the humanities program he had initiated in place of his college's usual curriculum of modern military history and strategic thought. The senior officers studying for a year before being assigned their next posts were reading Thucydides and Thomas More. One of the wives asked me why the men should be studying "those Polynesian wars," but the officers, most of them veterans of Vietnam, were caught up by the ethical questions raised for deep and difficult consideration by both their experience of a war whose ends were hard to fathom or accept, and the classic texts in which they were absorbed. The program was impressive. When I asked Admiral Turner how it had taken hold so well and quickly, he smiled and said, "You forget; I give the orders of the day."

I had not been prepared for the outpouring of interest from the media, as well as from women in the academic world, when the appointment of a woman as dean of a university college was announced. The reaction certainly underscored how few women had at that time been given such opportunities at our research universities. It also initiated an endless stream of questions and interviews in which I was asked what it was like to be a woman rather than ever being invited to talk about what I might think about education. The same happened on a still-larger scale, a cascade of news stories and letters, when I was appointed provost at Yale.

The differences between Northwestern and the University of Chicago were substantial, starting with their different mix of schools. Unlike Chicago, Northwestern had schools of engineering, journalism, music, communications (theater an important component), and education (a school Chicago was shortly to eliminate). In addition, students were admitted as undergraduates and received bachelor's degrees from these professional schools. They took their liberal arts requirements in the college; some of the best students in our classes came from the school of journalism whose students were far better than average in their ability to write. Intercollegiate sports mattered at Northwestern, a Big Ten member and competitor. The graduate school of arts and sciences was relatively small; undergraduate education and undergraduate life were dominant on campus and in Northwestern's reputation.

In the early '30s, during the Depression, there had actually been serious negotiations in an attempt to merge the two universities in the interest of using limited resources efficiently and concentrating donations and support from the Chicago business and civic community on a single private research university. Had that happened, Northwestern would have been responsible for undergraduate and Chicago for graduate education.

There existed a generalized impression that in such areas as law and medicine Chicago was more focused on basic research and Northwestern on clinical training and applied investigation. What struck me most, however, was that Northwestern seemed to have much less sense of itself as a university with a common ethos and was far less integrated as an institution. It lacked a strongly defined persona. Crossing intellectual boundaries among faculties and programs was neither a tradition nor a priority.

Northwestern's schools seemed like freestanding islands with varying missions of their own. With medicine and law located in downtown Chicago, those faculties were both physically and academically separated from the Evanston campus. I argued with the dean of medicine solely by formal correspondence when he maintained, after I had approved payment for a cadaver needed for the work of a forensic anthropologist in my college's Department of Anthropology, that he alone was entitled to authorize such purchases and to approve their use. That was my first and only substantive contact with the dean; others I encountered at official events or not at all, for we had no real business with one another.

The College of Arts and Sciences had great strengths, particularly in economics, chemistry, history, African studies, and English, and a few weaknesses, astronomy among them. That department's chairman, J. Allen Hynek, was well-known to the public, since he appeared often on television as a specialist on UFOs. Having founded the Center for UFO Studies, he encouraged the belief that space aliens were on the loose in flying saucers and disseminated reports of their sightings. Another astronomer, pathologically frightened of germs, roamed Evanston wearing a face mask, casting fear into the town's pedestrians. The Department of Physics was riddled by dissent. An earlier effort to remake physics overnight by appointing a group of senior scientists all at once had failed to move the department forward and cast it into factional strife. Biology was a mélange of different fields in the life sciences that lived uneasily together. It contained an outstanding group of molecular biologists who wanted desperately to establish a department of their own. One of my principal efforts, finally achieved after much infighting, politicking, and obstruction on the part of the biologists left behind, was to make that happen. We ended up with a distinguished department that built also on the considerable strength of biochemistry in the college.

I learned how difficult it could be not only to create something new but to eliminate something old. The college had a Department of Home

Economics. The chair, a wonderful woman active in college affairs and much loved by the entire faculty, was due for retirement, and the department would be left with only a single tenured member as well as several junior faculty. I thought this the right moment to close the department. The field seemed not exactly appropriate to an institution of the liberal arts, and the remaining faculty, who specialized in such areas as nutrition, could be accommodated elsewhere. I had not fully realized how grueling the process of closing a program (a process from which I earned scars later also at Yale and the University of Chicago) would come to be, especially given the complicating personal relations that intensified the unhappiness and resentment of those who had cared for the program. After the deed was done, the Department of Home Economics held a fire sale at which I, to my shame, bought pots and pans and napkins at bargain prices. Saving the Department of Home Economics was a passionate cause for some, but I can no longer recall whether a sit-in by a nursing mother at my office door around that time was an act of protest over home economics or some other cause, for of course there were many.

Northwestern had established a new Department of African American Studies in the wake of the growing demand for such programs in the '60s and the tensions over race that challenged the university's mainstream culture. Several of its faculty were sympathetic backers of a large group of their students who were fighting for more African American faculty and more resources to fund activities, spaces, and courses of their own. They had founded an organization known as FMO, which meant "For Members Only," that had support from several leading figures in Chicago's African American community.

On several occasions FMO held demonstrations at my office, once crowding into a confrontational meeting that narrowly avoided turning into a sit-in. Their agenda, presented as a set of demands, asked for specific numbers of faculty to be appointed immediately, and for funds for the organization to mount a series of programs ranging from courses, lectures, and other events to housing and meeting places of their own. The department's faculty, chaired at the time by the writer Jan Carew, were deeply engaged mentors to their students, even as they urged the more moderate positions that ultimately prevailed. Ray Mack made the provost's office a positive force in advancing the interests of minority students in the university, and for all the tension that arose in the early '70s, Northwestern was able to recruit a greater number of African American students than was, for example, the University of Chicago.

After a Corporation meeting in the spring of 1973, I was startled by King man Brewster's asking whether I would consider becoming provost of Yale at the beginning of the academic year 1974–75. Yale's current provost, the economist Richard Cooper, would be leaving in a year's time. I was sufficiently knowledgeable about Yale and its financial problems to have some sense of what might await a provost. I also thought Kingman a great leader with whom it was already a pleasure to work. I realized that his appointing a woman would not be popular with all Yale's constituents, and I was happy in my work at Northwestern and very much concerned about whether it was right to think of leaving after a stay of only three years. The question of Charles's wishes and opportunities was of course the most pressing issue to be resolved, and the offer of a position in legal history at the Yale Law School combined with an invitation to teach in the history department proved extremely attractive at a time when he felt ready for a new landscape and more time for his research. In the end, we concluded that the move made sense for both. Once again I was struck by the unanticipated ways in which life unfolds.

Just before leaving for New Haven, we attended a retirement dinner for J. Roscoe Miller who had been president of Northwestern before Robert Strotz and then appointed chancellor, taking a special role in fund-raising and serving as an ambassador of goodwill. Dr. Miller, a surgeon, was a very good man, amiable and kind, who had done well by his university. During his time the campus had been enlarged and buildings constructed on land created by huge quantities of lake fill: sand removed from Lake Michigan's Indiana shore was used to extend the main campus out into the lake from its Evanston shoreline, a project unimaginable today. The university had prospered and grown in stature under his benign guidance. He knew everyone, and everyone knew him; the world outside the campus scarcely realized that Bob Strotz was actually president until Miller retired as chancellor. It was a memorable evening. The Empire Room of the Palmer House in downtown Chicago set up a champagne fountain that never stopped flowing. The dinner featured ten speeches, one given by Bob Hope and another by Governor Dan Walker (some fifteen years later, in the best bipartisan tradition of Illinois politicians, found guilty of fraud and perjury and hustled off to federal prison).

It was hard to leave Chicago behind as we traveled east to our next academic life.

9

The Yale Years

My knowledge of Yale was reasonably up-to-date. In August of 1970 Kingman Brewster had invited me to become a fellow of the Yale Corporation, the university's board. The Corporation was composed of ten "successor" trustees appointed for a term of twelve years each, and six alumni fellows, elected by the alumni for terms of six years. The president chaired its meetings. One member was also a senior fellow who took charge when, for example, a vacancy occurred in the president's office or when the board needed to meet in executive session in his absence.

There had been a review of governance at Yale, and a decision had been made to make women eligible to serve on the Corporation. I would be a successor fellow, and the plan was to nominate a woman candidate sure to win on the slate for alumni election, so that there would be two women fellows at the outset.

I had come to know Kingman Brewster some four or five years earlier when we attended an international conference held at the Rockefeller Foundation's center in Bellagio on Lake Como, a beautiful and serene setting for thinking about the nature, causes, and meaning of student revolutionary movements in the United States, Britain, and the Continent.

I met some shell-shocked people there, men whose liberal and tolerant outlook had been rejected by students they had hoped to assist, men like David Truman, still haunted by the turmoil he had experienced at Columbia, where he had been dean of the college, and others who felt their entire worldviews threatened by the violence and disorder they had witnessed

and could not assuage. Our conversations made evident the large differences that existed, despite some common themes of student protest, between the situation of universities in the United States and that of those
in Europe, given the basic differences of structure, culture, history, and
governance among us.

Afterward I traveled with the Brewsters to Milan for our flight to New
York, only to find it had been delayed for an entire day. We spent the time
in sightseeing and conversation, and we talked about the ideas for a coeducational Yale that Kingman was starting to consider. His notion was to
introduce coeducation by moving Vassar as an affiliated women's college
to New Haven. I told him that I thought this a terrible idea; it would only
create second-class citizenship for women students and for the Vassar faculty also. Yale, in my opinion, should become a genuinely coeducational
university; the Radcliffe/Harvard structure was the last model to imitate.
Kingman seemed a little surprised by the ferocity of my reaction but listened and argued with great politesse.

Although the university had long been admitting women to its graduate and professional schools, their presence had no particular influence on
the college. To speak of Yale or Old Eli was to refer to Yale College, not the
university. Although the Sterling Memorial Library was open to women,
its very handsome and comfortable Linonia and Brothers reading room
was open only to men until 1963, and even then its new accessibility to
women provoked a heated outcry. Mory's, the quintessential club for Old
Blues, remained firmly male until 1974, when the state liquor commission
threatened to withdraw its license if the club failed to admit women within
thirty days. The membership was polled to approve this outrage, and one
member wrote plaintively that he could not grasp why this issue had to be
solved in thirty days—after all, it had taken thirty years to put ice cream
on the menu. I arrived as provost down the street just after Mory's had
succumbed, and was later the first female recipient of the Mory's Cup, one
redesigned in a handsome glass version for ladies.

When Ray Kroc, CEO of McDonald's, visited Yale, he came to see me
and urged that the university, which he had gathered was short of funds,

17. With Kingman Brewster on our way to his farewell Baccalaureate Address at Yale in May 1977.

18. Yale Commencement Class Day 1978. From left: William Sloan Coffin, Bishop Paul Moore, Senator John Chafee, A. Bartlett Giamatti, Hanna Gray, Henry S. Chauncey, and an Old Blue.

19. With President Ford at Yale, 1976.

20. At Bart Giamatti's inauguration as president of Yale, together with Kingman Brewster. October 1978.

21. Robert Maynard Hutchins, as a very young president at the University of Chicago.

22. Amos Alonzo Stagg flanked by the university athletic director and Robert Maynard Hutchins, showing an unusual attention to athletics.

23. Hans Rothfels, distinguished German historian and refugee at the University of Chicago, who later returned to Germany without breaking his American connections.

24. Four presidents of the University of Chicago, October 1978. To my left, Edward Levi; on the right, John Wilson and George Beadle.

25. Rockefeller Chapel of the University of Chicago at the inauguration ceremony, October 1978, with Hanna Holborn Gray speaking at the left.

26. With Mayor Michael Bilandic of Chicago, 1978. University of Chicago photograph.

27. Neil Rudenstine and I look on as Nelson Mandela signs the Harvard guest book before receiving an honorary degree, October 1998.

28. Meeting with Raisa Gorbachev at the home of Pamela Harriman when the Gorbachevs were on a state visit to Washington and Mrs. Gorbachev had asked to meet some professional women. To my left: Katharine Graham, Justice Sandra Day O'Connor, Mrs. Gorbachev, Senator Barbara Mikulski, Pamela Harriman, Senator Nancy Kessenbaum, and a Russian translator. December 1987.

29. With Charles and President and Mrs. Bush when receiving the Presidential Medal of Freedom in 1994.

30. Charles and I greeting Sir George Solti, conductor of the Chicago Symphony Orchestra, at the university before an award dinner in his honor. University of Chicago photograph.

31. With David Rockefeller, grandson of the University of Chicago founder and himself a PhD in economics from the university at an October 1992 event of the university centennial celebration.

32. With Charles, June 1993, at our final Chicago commencement.

exploit a profitable new revenue source. He explained that he had been much taken by the "cute little white clapboard house with the little white fence in front." His recommendation: "Franchise, Mrs. Gray, franchise." Alas, I had to inform him that Yale did not have ownership.

Women had finally been admitted to Yale College in the fall of 1969. Coeducation still felt slightly like an experiment in the fall of 1970 when I joined the Corporation together with Marian Wright Edelman (founder and president of the Children's Defense Fund and graduate of the Yale Law School), who had, as predicted, been chosen in the alumni election. We were welcomed with pleasant cordiality. John Hay Whitney, the senior fellow, set the tone. One might have thought this Yale superpatriot would find the departure from tradition we represented difficult to accept, but he showed absolutely no qualms. I was a test case also as the first non-Yale fellow. There was a kind of irony in being embraced nonetheless as a Yalie because of my father's association and my growing up as a faculty child. I was immediately awarded an honorary MA (conferred on all those faculty unfortunate enough to possess no Yale degrees) in order to count officially as an Old Blue.

When, many years later, I became a fellow of the Harvard Corporation, I found that the Yale Corporation's size and structure made for a much more effective governing board than Harvard's, even though Harvard's met far more frequently and was defined almost as coexecutive with the president. The Harvard Corporation had only six members in addition to the president. It was hardly possible to have the robust committee structure from which boards benefit, and the frequency of its meetings caused it to focus too much on immediate day-to-day matters and too little on larger strategic questions. The administration scarcely had time between sessions to think about and plan in a more long-term fashion.

The Harvard Corporation suffered an unnecessarily difficult relationship with Harvard's other governing board, the elected Board of Overseers, which wanted always to be granted a greater authority in policy and decision making than was really permitted by its primary mandate, responsibility for the oversight of visiting committees (intended to assess the state of the departments, schools, and other units of the university). The Board of Overseers, on which I had previously served, included many members whose strengths and experience were not called on or engaged in constructive collaboration with the fellows. Only more recently has the Corporation been expanded in size and successfully reorganized to enhance the quality of Harvard's governance.

There were many impressive people and many strong personalities on the Yale Corporation during my time. Among them, Cyrus Vance (later to become secretary of state) took a special interest in and a mediator's approach to town-gown relations that, poor to begin with, had become increasingly strained over a decade that had seen the economic decline of the city, a rise in the problems of urban crime and drugs, the threatening events of the Bobby Seale trial in New Haven's courthouse, and the growing power of unionization at Yale.

J. Irwin Miller, CEO of the Cummins Engine Company, was a highly influential and outspoken member. He was once heralded by *Fortune Magazine* as a man who should be president of the United States. Irwin was born and bred in Columbus, Indiana, and at Yale had majored in classics. He continued his studies at Oxford before returning home to become a remarkable businessman, philanthropist, and patron of the arts. He owned a Stradivarius, played chamber music, and possessed a complete set of the rare and important Aldus Manutius editions of the classical texts, both Greek and Latin, published in the early sixteenth century. When I became a member of the board of what was then the Cummins Engine Company, Irwin had retired to the role of chairman of the board's executive committee, but he was still very much involved and in many ways still the company's ruling spirit. He was revered both in the company and in the community, spoken of with awe only as "Mr. Miller." Irwin conceived the company's mission not only as that of developing and manufacturing the best heavy-duty truck diesel engines possible, but of contributing to and strengthening its home community. He believed that 5 percent of the company's profits should be devoted to that cause and created a foundation within the company to make grants for projects that had primarily to do with social welfare and support. He emphasized community service and family values for his executive employees. A connoisseur of architecture, he had the company foundation underwrite architectural fees for new buildings in Columbus that made the town a showplace of modern architecture. You can visit the town and admire churches, a courthouse, a city hall, a jail, a telephone company office, the Cummins headquarters, and other structures all designed by such famous architects as I. M. Pei and the Saarinens, both father and son.

Another trustee was William Scranton. A man of great charm, judgment, and intelligence, a liberal Republican, former congressman and governor of Pennsylvania, briefly US ambassador to the United Nations, and a one-time candidate for the presidential nomination who had hoped to eliminate Barry Goldwater but lost in the primaries, he had forsworn politics forever despite being repeatedly called on to consider another presidential run. John Chafee, senator from Rhode Island, shared Scranton's moderate Republican position, and John Danforth, elected to the Senate a bit later, tended, though slightly more conservative, in the same direction.

Other trustees included William McChesney Martin, chairman of the US Federal Reserve Bank from 1951 to 1970, a man of conservative instincts and tolerant judgments; William Bundy (brother of McGeorge Bundy and married to the daughter of Dean Acheson, a former fellow), former assistant secretary of state, a lawyer and foreign affairs adviser and editor of the journal *Foreign Affairs*, published under the auspices of the Council on Foreign Affairs; Carryl Haskins, president of the Carnegie Institute of Science, a man of remarkable peacefulness, courtesy, and learning; Leon Higginbotham, an African American who served first as a Pennsylvania district judge and then as a judge of the Court of Appeals for the Third Circuit, a man of powerful presence and principle; and Paul Moore, the liberal-minded Episcopalian archbishop of New York. Another trustee, William Beinecke, a generous benefactor and successful businessman, was generally ready to close ranks with the majority, but he was dismayed by what seemed to him excessively left-leaning tendencies in the academic universe, and by the absence of a business school at Yale (he was ready to donate funds for the purpose of founding one).

We had lively, but always civil, arguments and then ordinarily came to consensus, assisted by the custom of meeting on one afternoon in plenary session as a "committee of the whole" to discuss the most significant questions before us, then allowing the night to pass before any further discussion, and voting only on the following day. This custom allowed for wide-ranging discussions and for considered judgment after a pause for reflection.

A number of Corporation fellows belonged to Skull and Bones (and all apparently belonged to one of the secret societies). Most of the fellows' undergraduate careers overlapped, and they seemed to have known one another as students, their associations often continuing after college. Kingman Brewster (class of 1941) had been at Yale with Cyrus Vance, William Scranton, William Bundy, Paul Moore, J. Richardson Dilworth, and Arthur Watson, all of whom served during my time. Kingman had been active in the college's most important extracurricular organizations, like the *Yale Daily News* and the Political Union. But he had, famously, turned down Skull and Bones; this was regarded as a quite radical statement. He was later convinced that it had affected his relations with some important Yale alumni and believed that Dilworth, chairman of the Corporation's investment committee and senior fellow after Jock Whitney's retirement, regularly bypassed him to deal directly with Yale's treasurer, John Ecklund, yet another member of the not-always-secret S&B.

Refusing Skull and Bones had not been a unique act, but it was rare and certainly nonconformist. It spoke to the fact that even those at the center of the prewar Yale tradition were not always uncritical of their world and its dominant outlook. Some were beginning to question the political allegiances customary in their backgrounds. In Kingman's undergraduate days, Yale did indeed house a few genuine radicals, like William Kunstler and David Dellinger, but they were a tiny minority. Students like Brewster and his friends were, however, increasingly caught up in the great debates of their time. Foremost among those and one that possessed an immediate relevance for all of them was, of course, the question of whether America should intervene in the war. Brewster was a leader of the noninterventionists and for a time associated with America First. This, incidentally, brought him to the attention of Robert Maynard Hutchins, a high-profile crusader for nonengagement; the two men, different as they were, developed a lifelong respect and liking for one another.[1]

His rejection of Skull and Bones became one item among a series that defined Kingman for those conservative old Elis who accused him of betraying Yale in seeking to diversify the student body with the admission of women and minority students. Kingman was viewed by a vociferous group of unhappy alumni as encouraging and supporting left-wing liberals like "Inky" Clark, the dean of admissions who initiated the new policy of his office, and Yale's chaplain, William Sloane Coffin, a highly visible leader in the civil rights movement and in the antiwar protests of the time.

Kingman Brewster became Yale's president in 1963. He had come from a professorship at the Harvard Law School in 1960 to serve as provost for his close friend A. Whitney Griswold, who died at fifty-six a few years later. Griswold was an important president, but it was Kingman who led Yale into the final stages of maturing as a genuine university in its intellectual culture. He made it a more open and democratic institution as well.

Working with Kingman was a most enjoyable and stimulating experience. He was an interesting compound of traditionalist and innovator, of idealism and worldliness, of patrician bearing and liberal sentiment, a man of immense vitality, charm, warmth, and wit, with a penetrating intellect quick to see and understand, and an insatiable urge to "save the republic," as he was fond of saying. He could be impatient for action and results, while patient and deliberate in teasing apart the intertwined strands of complex and difficult situations and in setting out goals and strategies. He was at once puzzled and amused by the irrational elements in the human comedy over which he presided, ready to take risks, sometimes impulsively, while also, on the whole, ultimately responsive to the counsels of caution.

An internationalist who had worked with the first administrators of the Marshall Plan in Paris, he was an Anglophile who admired England's historic adherence to the rule of law, as he did the English landscape and way of life. That included Savile Row. Kingman liked the good things of life without ever having quite the means to indulge them comfortably. He was ready to find fun and sociability and pleasure in almost any place or set of circumstances. His sense of humor never failed, even at the bleakest of moments.

Kingman was capacious, affectionate, and faithful in his friendships. He was loyal, sometimes to a fault, to old companions and teachers to whom he occasionally gave projects or positions not really suited to their skills or experience. He found it very difficult to fire or shift people elsewhere when it was clear that they were in the wrong role for their talents, or had failed seriously to measure up, or had behaved badly. Kingman's sense of honor was powerful and unyielding. I think he found it personally too painful to fire people and feared that dismissing them would ruin their lives and trouble his conscience. In consequence, Kingman kept in place colleagues whom he did not entirely respect or like or trust, and this was certainly not a good thing. He was by contrast strongly and steadily supportive of his closest colleagues, always accepting and publicly underscoring his own responsibility for approving unpopular policies and actions.

Kingman was a natural leader, persuader, and recruiter for his causes and for his university. Even those who disliked him on ideological grounds did not find it easy to dislike him in person. His priorities were those of academic excellence, the active maintenance of academic freedom, and the enabling of a civil environment of learning and debate. He sought to preserve what he believed had been best in the old Yale while adapting that to a newly transformed world and university.

Kingman became a leading advocate for higher education. As he observed the environment for universities, he became increasingly troubled by the problem of university-government relations as it had developed in the postwar era. He saw in the growing reach of government regulation a dangerous challenge to the autonomies of private universities. He was deeply concerned by what he thought an unprecedented exercise of unsanctioned authority in the use of the "power of the purse"—the threat of removing all federal funding, no matter for what purpose it had been granted, from an institution that had failed to satisfy some unrelated federal requirement—and feared this might be a harbinger of things to come.

Kingman was constantly dreaming up new ideas and projects. He became an enthusiast for the notion that students should shoulder at least a portion of the cost of their education and for the proposal of a student loan program in which repayment would be based on later income levels. He toyed with the idea of moving to a standard three- rather than four-year bachelor's degree program. He thought about collaborations with other colleges for teaching certain kinds of subjects, like introductory foreign language or calculus. More generally, Kingman was preoccupied with thinking about universities and their purposes, their roles in promoting public service, their legal obligations, and their contributions to the health and promise of civic life. While usually careful not to speak on political issues that might imply a corporate university position or sponsorship for his opinions, he did speak out against the war in Vietnam and landed early on the Nixon administration's enemies list. Spiro Agnew called loudly for his dismissal.

Kingman was not a great manager. His strengths lay not in the day-to-day work of administration, but in his ideas and intelligence, and in his capacity to express and carry forward his principles and to inspire others to commit to the goals and undertake the tasks that mattered for the university. Financial problems worried but bored him. He loved projects for new and renovated buildings, and his presidency, like Griswold's, added much to the architectural distinction of the campus. He took pride in the university's four schools of the arts and great pleasure in their accomplishments, hoping always to find more resources to ease their relative poverty and the draw on the university's general funds.

The university had long been under pressure to establish a business school, but Kingman was not a fan of business education. He wanted instead a professional school that, if it was to exist at all, would unite training for both for-profit and not-for-profit management with public policy studies, preparing its students to move between public service and the private sector. That reflected Kingman's own sense of the overriding importance of public service and the university's role in preparing those who would become leaders in government, diplomacy, education, philanthropy, and non-governmental organizations concerned with public welfare. When the Yale School of Organization and Management finally came into being, Kingman insisted that these were its aims, and that it not be called a business school.

In the last years of his presidency, Kingman continued to be seen by critics as a dangerous figure guilty of subverting values now under siege from the countercultural young, a charge intensified by events that had transpired in May of 1970. That spring had been a time of protest and dissent on the Yale campus. A crisis had occurred for both Yale and the city of New Haven when the Black Panther leader Bobby Seale was facing trial for murder in the courthouse on the Green. A call had gone out for demonstrators to converge on the city to protest the trial and Yale as well, citing Seale as a victim of the racism practiced by a reactionary and oppressive establishment embodied by Yale. The judge presiding over Seale's trial had issued highly controversial contempt citations, condemned as unfair and unprecedented by many legal experts, against two visiting Black Panthers. And against this background Kingman had uttered words that were endlessly to haunt him in the years to follow. "I personally want to say," he said, "that I am appalled and ashamed that things should have come to such a pass in this country that I am skeptical of the ability of black revolutionaries to achieve a fair trial anywhere in the United States."[2]

Kingman had made his statement during a special meeting of the Yale College faculty called to discuss the impending events scheduled to occur on May Day in New Haven and to debate his recommendation that the university not shut down but be as helpful and open as possible to the community and demonstrators alike, offering a peaceful and welcoming space to everyone in the vicinity. The meeting revealed sharp divergences of view over any possible suspension of university operations and over Yale's policies and practices related to minority students and faculty. In the end, Kingman's position prevailed. When the weekend came, the broad and intensive process of consultation he had followed and his colleagues' attention to meticulous planning and preparation made a considerable success (as compared to such events on other campuses) out of what could have been catastrophe. The demonstrations passed without serious violence, and Yale had helped make that possible while also maintaining the university's essential stability and unity as May Day came and went.

Nonetheless, the resonance of that time and of that faculty meeting endured. Lingering reactions to the events of the early '70s continued to form an undercurrent of restiveness and dissension, still influencing faculty opinions on university issues well into the later years of the decade. Those who disagreed with the administration's tactics in May of 1970 continued to say so. Kingman's critics regularly took the occasion to repeat their condemnation of his statement on fair trials for black revolutionaries, and to make it a symbol of all they thought wrong with Kingman's and with Yale's direction.

A little of Kingman's spirit of joy and optimism had ebbed by the later '70s. The tasks now before the university were ones in which he found duty rather than satisfaction: for example, the need to make hard choices that might entail the elimination of an entire school or program, trying to do so in such a way as to reverse financial crisis without sacrificing academic quality, and the related burden of conducting an ambitious fund-raising campaign, with the ceaseless search for major donations hovering over his agenda. Kingman liked to joke that the campaign goal could best be met through the sale of his promise of immediate resignation from the presidency to the highest bidder.

The alumni who expressed such fervent opposition to the Brewster regime represented only a fraction—if also an organized and disproportionately loudly heard one—of Yale's alumni population. Kingman had many supporters among the latter and persuaded many to his cause. One could certainly find a fairly large group of those between the two poles who were critics of one or another decision, or who felt vaguely and uneasily that Yale was going in the wrong direction. One will find this kind of outlook in any alumni body anywhere. People are likely to feel that their alma mater started on a downhill path almost immediately after their graduations. Their colleges do not remain what they were or as they remember them.

They focus on their colleges their discontents over changes that they deem threatening to the larger society, and their anxieties about the tendencies and views expressed by the younger generation, fearing that these are signs of a society in deep crisis and bemoaning the character, outlook, and practices of young people who do not behave or believe as they did.

On the other hand, I noticed how alumni who had been unhappy with the admission of women became adjusted to the new order, and how proud they became of daughters and granddaughters who attended Yale. The alumni I knew best might have initially been upset by my appointment to the provost's office, but they became reconciled to the idea and were generally both helpful and supportive.

The environment of higher education during the later years of Kingman's term was difficult for all universities: years of "stagflation," with very high, even (in several years) double-digit inflation, combined with depressed markets and poor investment performance to create severe financial stresses, diminished endowments, and negative outlooks. The all-encompassing energy crisis of that era sent energy and related costs escalating ever higher; their impact on university budgets was immense. It was not a good time to start a campaign; nor was it a good time to expand the support for financial aid and faculty appointments that hopes for a more egalitarian academic community—one more inclusive of minority and women faculty members—had engendered, and which affirmative action policies, guided by federal mandate, would require. Yale's relatively small proportion of women and minorities in the faculty ranks could not be overcome overnight. There was concern that affirmative action could too easily take the form of setting quotas under the conditions laid down for corrective plans by Washington administrators, and affirmative action itself was under critical debate. But there was no question that Yale needed to welcome and to appoint women of first-rate promise to its faculty ranks, and to build on its own long tradition of educating women scholars as well as to train and appoint minority members beyond the Department of African American Studies.

Arriving in New Haven on a sultry July afternoon, we drove up to the provost's house on Hillhouse Avenue, a street lined with large houses occupied by the president, several other university officers, and a number of academic offices. We had hardly started to unload the car when Kingman appeared with a summons to a meeting he had called on the workers' strike that had started in May and was still in full progress, with no end in sight. The union representing the skilled and unskilled employees responsible for everything from dining halls and grounds to the building crafts and maintenance skills belonged to the Hotel and Restaurants Union. Its president, Vincent Sirabella, had ambitions for higher office at the national level and was well connected in New Haven political circles. The 1974 strike was Yale's first experience of bargaining with organized labor. The negotiations proceeded slowly and badly. There was little trust on either side, and the lawyer chosen by Yale, known as a tough and belligerently adversarial labor specialist, was immediately disliked and seen as reflecting contempt for the union on the university's part. The situation reinforced ill feelings about relations with the city and strife over long-standing issues that had long plagued town-gown relations.

Yale was New Haven's biggest employer other than the Southern New England Telephone Company, and it ranked among the largest employers in the state of Connecticut as well. Perceived by those sympathetic to the strike as rich and arrogant, they insisted that Yale be a leader, not merely a market competitor, in the compensation and benefits offered its workers. The university was castigated as a wealthy, irresponsible tax-exempt institution for resisting the plea for increased payments in lieu of taxes to a city desperately in need of resources and of expanding its social services. Our meeting that July evening went over ground already covered many times before and yielded no immediate solution, although it helped clarify the options that the university might pursue in the next round of talks. Many weeks later, when a three-year contract was signed, one could not ignore the continuing sense of strain, an uneasy tension that would not be easy to mend in so short a period.

My official work as provost began the next morning. I sat down at a splendidly clean desk, was given a pad of paper and a felt-tip pen by my assistant, and sat wondering what to do, not realizing that the pile of cartons sitting on the office floor was filled with things, removed from the desktop, that had been left in considerable volume for me to do. I need not have worried, however, because quite soon an agitated assistant professor rushed in. He complained loudly and colorfully that he had just been bitten by a colleague, pointing as proof to an invisible mark on his arm. "I am San Sebastiano!" he cried. There was now plenty to do. I had, of course, learned to expect the unexpected, but this was new territory. It was abundantly clear that the melodrama being enacted was evidence of a department whose faculty were at one another's throats and needed to be placed in receivership at once. This first event of my first day ensured that absolutely nothing could ever truly surprise me again.

It was one thing to know as a trustee that Yale's finances were in a critical state, quite another to assume the responsibility of doing something about it. Although a large fund-raising campaign was underway, its hoped-for help in enlarging the endowment and providing general funds for operations would, if successful, come into play only some years off. After Kingman's departure in 1977, I had to take responsibility for the campaign, and this at a time when the next leadership of Yale and the next priorities it might announce were unknown quantities as a presidential search went forward. Bill Scranton accepted the role of my executive assistant for campaign matters; that made a lot of people chuckle! But we had a good time attending alumni gatherings together, and we raised some money as well. George H. W. Bush also reported to me at a time when he had just left public service and renewed his energetic volunteer activity at Yale in the interval before resuming his political ambitions.

In 1974, the university's budget was in deficit; the prospective size of future deficits increasing at a sobering rate even under best-case scenarios and despite current efforts to economize and to slow budget growth.

Endowment returns would not increase at this period of terrible markets, and federal funding was beginning to decline in real terms. The academic marketplace itself was shrinking; the supply of vacant positions for newly minted PhDs was drying up as institutions cut back on new appointments. The technological revolution was just beginning to hit the academic world. Developing computerized systems, purchasing the hardware, and hiring the technicians needed for the expert management of the new technologies created new costs. It was naively believed that the application of the new systems would make possible immediate savings—for example, in staff costs. The rapid growth as well as the rapid obsolescence of the developing systems kept adding both uncertainty over how and how much to invest and significant budgetary impacts to absorb. Another important issue to be addressed was that the university had accumulated a very large backlog of deferred maintenance as a consequence of trying to contain expenditures. Many campus buildings were in bad shape and overdue for upkeep or renovation; a robust capital budget had to be planned in order to meet needs that became ever more urgent.

Kingman had decided to shift budgetary responsibility from the financial office to the provost's office, but the budget staff actually remained where it had been, reporting to both in an unwieldy arrangement that caused tensions and inefficiencies in developing new systems for accurate budget data and analysis. Financial records and projections were unreliable; the level of sophistication in such matters well below what Yale should have possessed. The treasurer, who presided over financial affairs, and who was dismayed by what he took to be excessive and undisciplined spending on the university's (read, Kingman's) part, was never fully accepting of the shift Kingman had decreed. The officer in charge of business affairs was intent on running his fief as an independent realm and did not seem always in tune with Kingman's priorities. I took office in the first year of the new arrangements made for developing and overseeing the budget, so these issues lurked always in the background of the struggle to deal with the problems Yale was facing.

Kingman had asked two highly respected Yale professors, Horace Taft (physicist and dean of Yale College) and Jaroslav Pelikan (professor of church history and religion, a man of incredible learning and wide-ranging scholarship who was soon to become dean of the Graduate School of Arts and Sciences), to act as a kind of committee of two to consider creative ways that might add revenue while affirming and enhancing Yale's academic strengths. They recommended that the university institute a special summer term that would, they thought, provide additional tuition revenue; allow for growth in the student body, whose larger numbers would be spread over three semesters, affording flexible new options of time to degree for students; and provide a year-round use of facilities underused for much of the year.

That such a plan could actually succeed or make much impact on Yale's budget situation was obviously open to question, but the possibility appealed in the absence of others that would have necessitated significant reductions in faculty numbers and programs or other drastic measures, and it held interest in itself as an experiment worth trying. Kingman was quite enthusiastic and appointed a planning task force. The idea did not arouse a great deal of interest or support among the faculty; the planners soon discovered that finding instructors willing to teach in the summer was not easy. I volunteered for the first summer and enjoyed teaching a course in Renaissance intellectual history. The new summer term came with the intimate feeling of a small college, but it never achieved a large following; its success was modest at best, and it became not so much a regular semester as a term in which some basic courses could be offered for those wishing to meet such curricular requirements as language study or organic chemistry outside the regular academic year.

Events at Yale stimulated wide-ranging attention to fundamental questions about the mission of universities. The year 1974 saw the publication of the Woodward Report, a document on freedom of expression in the academy that remains an important statement on the crucial, if often uncomfortable, importance of honoring and sustaining the greatest possible freedom of thought and utterance in an academic community which can be measured in large part by the strength of its adherence to the values of such freedom and by its capacity to defend that value under challenge. The report's author was C. Vann Woodward, the great historian of the American

South, a man uncompromising in his convictions. Vann was a staunch foe of what has come to be called political correctness, scandalized by events at Yale in the early '70s that had seen several controversial speakers kept from speaking. In the most recent case, demonstrators had forced the cancellation, when he was about to speak, of a talk by the Stanford engineering professor and Nobel Prize–winning physicist William Shockley, a man who preached what he claimed a legitimate science of racial genetics that asserted the mental inferiority of blacks.

These events, and the committee's commitment to free speech as an absolute value, as well as its criticism of administrative actions and inactions and of what it found an apparent indifference on the part of many faculty to such violations, provoked intense debate over whether there can be acceptable limits to expression—whether, for example, speech deemed to be false or abusive or offensive or destructive of civility can or should be banned.

Those, of course, are questions that arise recurrently and remain central to the health and self-definition of universities. The specific contexts of their consideration may change; the basic question does not.

Another hot issue had to do with Yale's policies and guidelines governing investments and with the question, made urgent by concern over investing in companies doing business in South Africa, as to an institution's ethical and social responsibilities in such matters. I was to encounter the vehemence of this controversy for a period at Yale and then for at least a decade at the University of Chicago.

Yale, in my time, responded with two steps. The first was to create an Advisory Committee on Investor Responsibility that included students, faculty, staff, and alumni as members to consider ethical and social issues raised by particular investment choices, followed by the establishment of a Corporation Committee on Investor Responsibility to which the advisory group's recommendations were transmitted. The second step was to adopt as Yale's policies for South Africa–related investments the so-called Sullivan Principles,[3] a set of standards for evaluating such proposed investments. A trio of Yale faculty had published a book, *The Ethical Investor*, on the ethical, legal, and financial questions pertaining to institutional investments in general; its broad guidelines for all investments were adopted as policy by the Corporation.

No matter how restrictive such guidelines might be, they were not accepted by everyone. The underlying questions remained: In what ways and to what degree should a university take a position on social and political matters? If the assumption prevailed that a university should refrain from taking such positions, whether through its investment policies or in statements by those seen as speaking for the institution, did the South African question and the evil of apartheid at its heart constitute an exception to such understandings? Was the university complicit in evil to invest at all in companies associated with a regime that enforced apartheid? Where should the lines be drawn?

The central and most rewarding part of the provost's work was, of course, the oversight of academic affairs. Yale at that time did not have a dean of the Faculty of Arts and Sciences. That role was taken instead by an executive committee with the provost as chair, working together with the dean of Yale College and the dean of the Graduate School of Arts and Sciences. We met weekly and acted together as a kind of multiperson Arts and Sciences dean. We held regular meetings also with a further group of advisory section heads (faculty members who served in these positions part-time) for the humanities, social sciences, physical sciences, and biological sciences. There we discussed allocations for faculty positions and questions that were ripe for intensive discussion, as well as sharing information and coordinating planning.

Our executive committee meetings dealt with immediate matters that needed resolution—a departmental request or problem, a budget question or overrun, an appointments offer or faculty complaint. But we also took time for sharing and refining or rejecting longer-term ideas and proposals. And we spent a great deal of time on those academic areas that showed some weaknesses or potential for decline, as well as identifying attractive opportunities for appointments and programs.

The greatest strengths of Yale lay in the humanities, especially in the areas of English, comparative literature, French literature, Slavic studies, music, and history, as well as in the social sciences such as political science and economics.

The sciences at Yale presented a mixed picture, and their physical detachment from the main campus on Science Hill seemed somehow symbolic of where Yale's center lay. Yale's physicists, mathematicians, and chemists were in many ways outstanding, and yet there existed in some quarters a feeling that the sciences were less highly valued or supported than were the other disciplines of the arts and sciences. It was essential to strengthen the position of the sciences, while difficult to find the full resources of space and funding that were requested as necessary.

The school of engineering was at a low point, much reduced in enrollment and in reputation; applied science relatively weak. The biological sciences were divided between a general department of biology in the arts and sciences and a number of basic biomedical departments under the medical school's wing. Biologists in the arts and sciences suffered from the competition for resources and disciplinary priority among the subprograms their units housed, while the medical school departments were gaining in strength and funding. Yale was not unique in struggling to catch up with or to find structural solutions for organizing the rapidly changing disciplines of the biomedical sciences. These constituted a major preoccupation for all research universities with medical schools.

So, too, did the complicated and often-conflicted relationship between medical schools and their affiliated hospitals, each institution seeking its own solution and ultimately finding that there existed no perfect cures to this chronic condition of tension. Changing health-care and reimbursement policies had the effect of pulling further apart the basic interests of the two players. Medical schools exist to educate doctors and to perform research, hospitals to perform clinical care (and to break at least even in doing so). Medical faculty usually think hospital administrators care only about the bottom line and that their demands heedlessly obstruct the faculty's time and the universities' priorities for education and research in favor of increasing the volume of clinical practice. It would make no sense, of course, for a university to have a medical school and a teaching hospital, were these not part of their academic mission; it is equally obvious that it is through medical care that universities serve their communities as well as giving clinical training to medical students. In Yale's case, major difficulties arose also out of the divided governance of its affiliated hospital and badly strained relations between the academic and local medical communities.

For the humanities and social sciences, it was a flourishing, if not always peaceful, time of intellectual ferment. Each area did have a few programs not fully up to standard. Those included philosophy, Spanish, and sociology. The first two suffered from sometimes vicious internal conflicts that kept them from agreement on appointments, and even, to some degree, on the intellectual direction of their programs, the latter from a long decline in the quality of appointments and the ebbing prestige of a once-distinguished department. All came to be perceived externally as troubled departments that potential recruits might wish to avoid. Philosophy was seen as an uncomfortable home whose inhabitants were wedded to unfashionable forms of scholarship in the stream of modern Continental philosophy. The Spanish department could never reconcile those who pursued specialties in Iberian culture with those who specialized in Latin American studies as they jockeyed for positions, graduate students, and recognition. Its faculty, deeply engaged in personal feuds, could not live in harmony. Having placed the department in receivership with a chair who came from a different discipline and department, I observed a period of sullen acquiescence, but never of peace.

The departments of literature, and especially those of English and comparative literature, were marked by the increasing prominence and influence of the deconstructionist school of literary criticism, represented at Yale by some of its leading figures—Paul de Man, Geoffrey Hartman, J. Hillis Miller, and Peter Brooks (together sometimes called "the Hermeneutical Mafia") among them. They were men of international reputation and, given the heated arguments swirling around schools of critical thought, of international as well as local disputatious attention. They were eager to advance their own program of criticism in a home of its own while living in sometimes-uneasy proximity to literary scholars of what was now

a more traditional philological and historical bent and a group of very eminent scholars identified with the school known as the New Criticism that
was now giving way to other fashions. And there was Harold Bloom, prolific and, when it came to identifying his "school," sui generis, who felt
out of sorts with everyone else and for whom I invented a new position,
professor of the humanities, reporting directly to the provost so that he
would not have to make either English or Comparative Literature his primary home. Provosts and deans have a lot of pastoral work to do.

I did not know, as most people did not, of Paul de Man's unsavory background. I had encountered him first at Harvard, where he had been in my
time a tutor in the program of History and Literature and then a junior fellow. There was some slight sense of mystery about him, and rumors spread
that he was closely associated with a Belgian uncle known to have been
a collaborator during the Nazi occupation. At Yale he was revered as an
almost-saintly figure: kindly, modest, otherworldly, gentle, gracious, and
learned, the ultimate intellectual. Only after his death did the extraordinary truth become public: his lies and manipulative behavior, the stories
of his bigamy, the desertion and financial neglect of his first wife and three
children, the articles written for a pro-Nazi paper, and his commission of
fraud as well as other dishonesties before escaping from Belgium to a new
life. The argument still continues over whether de Man's critical theory
somehow reflected his fictionally constructed life. Thinking about Paul
later, I could not be sure whether, despite his quiet and calm demeanor, he
might have been haunted every day by the fear of discovery or whether he
was—hard to imagine—at peace.

The Yale Center for British Art was under construction when I arrived
in the provost's office, a wonderful project made possible by Paul Mellon's
munificent gift of British art to his alma mater. It was a difficult project,
too; the architect Louis Kahn had designed the building, as he had the Yale
Art Gallery across the street, and this was his last commission. He had died
before completing the plans, so the center would be a monument to the
architect as well. Every detail had to be reconstructed from Kahn's sometimes sketchy notes in the effort faithfully to realize his vision. In addition,

Paul Mellon was totally involved. He visited frequently. The center's founding director, Jules Prown, worked with him very successfully, but it was not always easy to do so. I was deputized to represent the central administration in dealing with Paul Mellon. Paul greatly admired and missed Whitney Griswold. He had not warmed to Kingman; they were not at ease with one another. I would don my construction helmet and tour the site with him and Jules. Paul examined everything and asked for a good many changes. We must have seen a dozen or so doorknobs before he was satisfied, and the skylights offered an unending series of problems. As a result of so many changes, we were constantly warned and scolded by the bad cop (his lawyer) for going over budget. But the good cop had excellent taste, and the building is spectacular, perfect for its purposes of displaying and studying the British art that Paul Mellon loved, and conveying the repose and the light and atmosphere of the great country houses in which its paintings were intended to hang. The opening celebration of the center was spectacular too. Mrs. Mellon spent an entire day arranging the flowers for the formal dinner; she created yet another work of art for that evening.

The new School of Organization and Management also opened in 1976. Its early days were not easy. The faculty of two departments, Organizational Behavior and Operations Research, that had been located in the arts and sciences, were shifted to the school as a kind of starter faculty. These fields (and their practitioners) were not compatible in outlook and methodology, and this made for a somewhat dysfunctional group at the outset. The political science and economics departments were not friendly toward the new school and not eager to participate in joint appointments in finance or in public policy. The public policy side of the school never developed strength, and the school increasingly emphasized the study of management, retaining an interest in public service and management and attracting unusual (and talented) students who were often looking for a nontraditional business degree. The founding dean, William Donaldson, was himself an example of the kind of graduate the school aspired to teach, having moved between the worlds of public and private management at the highest level, as he was again to do after presiding over the building of a new school that offered a distinctive choice among business schools. On the other hand, his term could only be a beginning. One cannot (and this my experience confirmed also at Chicago with the founding of the Harris School of Public Policy Studies) create a great school overnight, especially in a universe of already-existing and successful programs. It takes the work of several decades, not years, to arrive at the destination. Still, the initial directions and aims of the founding, even if their stated intentions and applications come to be modified, do remain in the genes.

Issues arising out of allegations of gender discrimination and of sexual harassment were coming to occupy the provost's office. One or two women who failed of promotion lodged complaints of unfairness based on gender, and I appointed a faculty committee headed by the widely respected economist James Tobin (later a Nobel Prize winner) that set a precedent for such investigations to come; the process originated to some degree in my experience at Chicago. It was more difficult to agree on and establish a process recognized as fair, firm, and appropriate to accusations of sexual harassment against members of the faculty and staff. Several students who represented a group of extreme feminists made such charges and asserted that their treatment reflected a prevalent indifference and hostility to women's lives at Yale. They were unhappy with the pace and form of our responses, although this did not then appear a significant concern for the majority of women students. I was never, despite many attempts to do so, able to shape agreement (for example, over issues of confidentiality) to establish an ongoing and well-accepted or well-communicated process. Instead, I found myself dealing with cases on an individual basis. My intervention led to several forced departures and a number of stiff warnings. Many members of the faculty were reluctant to believe their colleagues guilty of crass conduct and were hesitant to participate in the review of such allegations. Title IX had come into being; at the time it was not interpreted in terms of personal sexual misconduct but primarily as calling for gender equality in collegiate athletics.

When I asked Yale's popular football coach, Carmen Cozza, to become athletic director, I asked him also whether he was ready to administer the requirements of Title IX for women's equality in sports. "Oh, yes," he said, "I understand women. I know they're a different breed of cat." This was not reassuring, and Carm did not remain athletic director for long. He was definitely better off on the football field.

The potential disruption of a speaker became an issue once again when a student group invited William Shockley, presumably to test the university's resolve. Administrators pointed to everyone's right to protest, and also to the obvious fact that a simple boycott of Shockley's appearance might be the best option of all. We were determined to let Shockley say his ugly piece. The evening passed tensely and noisily, with threats, fortunately not implemented, of rushing the lecture room. When Kingman and I visited the long line of demonstrators outside the building, we were alternately screamed at and greeted. By the end of the night, the university had passed its test; there had been no disruption of a speaker whose presence on any campus posed that possibility, a major scientist who believed he could justify the worst claims of a despicable pseudoscience.

A more complicated problem arose when a longtime Russian language teacher was suddenly revealed as an anticommunist White Russian who had cooperated with the German occupiers in his region. He had held the Germans to be a lesser evil than his Soviet enemies, and had edited and written columns in a regional newspaper that toed the Nazi line, including flagrantly anti-Semitic passages. His proper name was Vladimir Sokolov, but he had adopted and at Yale was known by his pen name of Vladimir Samarin. At war's end Samarin had fled Russia and ended up in a displaced persons' camp. From there he had come in 1951 to the United States under the Displaced Persons Act, which required applicants for immigration to testify (as Samarin did) that they had had no Nazi associations.

At Yale Samarin became a senior lecturer on a rolling appointment (a position that did not confer tenure), a teacher liked and respected by his students, and a man who led a quiet life with his wife in the Hamden neighborhood. Their daughter and grandchildren were thoroughly American. Samarin presented himself in New Haven as a Zionist. The revelation of his earlier life caused a huge outcry. There were at once calls for his immediate dismissal. But these were not unanimous; there were those who thought Samarin had atoned for his sins (and that these were perhaps understandable, given his situation as an anticommunist under the Soviet regime) by the now-lengthy and blameless life he led in the United States and the service he had given through his successful teaching and unflagging helpfulness to students. Even the *Yale Daily News* supported Samarin's retention, while his Slavic department colleagues were bitterly divided.

The federal authorities began to take an interest and to investigate whether Samarin had entered the country illegally; that could subject him to deportation. He could not easily explain away what he had written, although he claimed that the Nazi censors had forced him to write as he did, and had altered some of his work as well.

Meeting with Samarin, I found an aging and seemingly broken man who felt that he was about to lose everything, and was desperately concerned about what would become of his family. He was now determined to abandon his self-defense in the face of the outraged disapproval and hostility he faced every day. Samarin could not be persuaded to accept my plan to institute an orderly internal process to ascertain the facts and deliberate on his status. The pressure surrounding him was too great, and we allowed him to resign. There were some who thought we had dealt with him too kindly. Ten years later, he was stripped of his US citizenship. The Department of Justice had brought charges to have him deported. The case dragged on through appeals and other maneuvers, and he died in 1988 before the sentence of deportation could be carried out.

Another controversy erupted in what became known as the "Aptheker case" in 1976. An appointment conferring a limited status of visiting lecturer attached to a program of semester-long residential college seminars that were intended to let the colleges offer some academic courses to their students. Students were heavily involved in choosing the subjects of such courses, which carried only half credit or no credit at all. Their choices sometimes brought controversy in their wake, as some surprising people— for example, the sportscaster Howard Cosell—turned up to give the seminars. In general, the seminars were not judged to be of great intellectual weight or even, in the eyes of some, worthy of the Yale name. As with all academic appointments, official approval was required, right up to the Corporation's sign-off, ordinarily a simple formality. The recommendation that such a position be offered to Herbert Aptheker, a Marxist historian, longtime and continuing member of the American Communist Party (he was once called by J. Edgar Hoover "the most dangerous Communist in America"), and radical activist (among other things, he had traveled, amid much publicity, with Tom Hayden to Hanoi to discuss prospects for a negotiated peace), set off tremendous controversy.

Aptheker was a prolific scholar of African American history. His editing of W.E.B. DuBois's voluminous work was judged an important contribution, and DuBois was to be the subject of his seminar. Much of Aptheker's writing revealed a political and ideological agenda, and C. Vann Woodward, enraged by the thought that he would receive a Yale title and be thought a member of the history department, even for a single semester, called for the recommendation to be rejected and for his fellow historians to join him in opposition. Its proponents responded that Woodward, author of the famous report on freedom of expression, was violating his own principles and guilty of applying his own standard of political orthodoxy to an unorthodox scholar. Others argued that appointments to college seminars did not need the detailed scrutiny or have to meet the criteria of normal Yale faculty appointments, and that the college seminars brought to Yale an alternative learning experience and contact with a range of interesting people whom students would otherwise have never encountered.

As with all such matters, the conflict over Aptheker was over more than its ostensible cause. The whole issue of the residential college seminar program and its academic quality, of the location of authority for initiating and approving any faculty appointment, of the politics of scholarship and politically directed scholarship, of what might or might not be construed as a question of academic freedom—all these became entangled. Demonstrations and protests galore followed. But this case did lead to worthwhile debates about fundamental questions of the academy across the university. In the end, the Aptheker visiting appointment was approved.

Ivy League athletics were meant to be pure. Athletic scholarships were forbidden; an athlete had to earn a scholarship on the same conditions of need and admissibility as did every other admitted student. Nonetheless, there could be no doubt that students within the acceptable range who had athletic talent were given something of an edge (no differently, it was argued, from those with other kinds of skills, such as playing the oboe). Each of the Ivies was sure that the others (unlike themselves) were busy recruiting athletes, sometimes with special exemptions from the usual standards. I saw an instance of this when the University of Pennsylvania decided to eliminate ice hockey and solicited us to admit some of the team members who were losing the sport they had relied on Penn to offer. The records sent for our review were definitely below par.

Eliminating a sport is, to put it mildly, a challenge. Yale had a varsity polo team, and it occurred to me that there was absolutely no reason why Yale should be supporting this rich person's sport, which was probably played by students who could afford to bring their own horses to New Haven and board them there. We could save some money here. My decision to eliminate polo as a varsity sport provoked a terrible outcry, and I was soon on the defensive, at war with a group of alumni who seemed to care about nothing else. Then one day came yet another call. I quailed, answered, and found at the other end a wealthy alumnus and polo enthusiast who said he certainly understood my position and offered to finance polo as a club sport, taking it off the university's budget. And that, very luckily, was that. But I was struck by the fact that, by contrast, the elimination of the graduate program in the history of science and medicine had provoked little publicity and only quiet, if deeply distressed, opposition.

It was assumed at Yale that one attended the home football games. They were rather pleasant (unless the weather failed to cooperate) social events where one enjoyed the company of friends and felt embarrassment over the half-time performance of the band. Without, I think, violating my convictions about freedom of expression, I found it possible to moderate the band's worst skits by asking to have the scripts delivered to me *after* the performances. Even Vincent Sirabella attended the games and always shook my hand; he was a great rooter for Yale and agreed that the band simply went too far in the vulgarities of its performance.

Before home games, the Brewsters gave lunch for the attending administrators and trustees of the visiting college. On a beautiful fall afternoon of 1976, I sat overlooking the garden of the president's house with Cyrus Vance as he talked about his desire to take on some important role in public service and his hopes that a Carter victory might bring such an opportunity. Carter won, of course, and in the following year Vance became secretary of state.

In the spring of 1977, Kingman Brewster was nominated and confirmed as ambassador to the Court of St. James's. On commencement day, and in the same garden, Cy swore Kingman in as ambassador. The two then invented a little ceremony in which they swore me in as interim president of Yale. Because I served for more than a year, I am counted officially in the line of Yale's presidents (my portrait, however, hangs with the provosts).

The year that followed had its painful aspects, but it taught me that you can survive anything. I was doing two major jobs at once, continuing as provost while playing president, dividing my time between the two offices morning and afternoon. An eleven-week-long strike that angered and inconvenienced our students and outraged their parents began in the fall. A presidential search was going on, surrounded by gossip and rumors that could be unpleasant to hear. I was presiding over the Yale Corporation at a time when its members were conducting the search with as much confidentiality as could be mustered, leaving its meetings when it went into executive session for that purpose. I found myself interviewed by my colleagues as though I were an outsider, given the same amount of time as were others in order to be totally fair to all, and then going on to chair their regular meetings. In the normal course of our work together nothing seemed to change at all, and the Corporation fellows were always helpful to me and highly supportive in pursuing the shared goal of keeping the university moving on important priorities.

Vinnie Sirabella did not apparently think that I was likely to take a strike of any length. It ended only when (initially because of a tip from a travel agent that Vinnie had booked post-Christmas reservations for Palm Springs) we were able to rearrange the terms to stick with the cost of our final offer by putting more in one place and less in another. But the strike was tough, and students who were affected by losing their dining halls were naturally very upset and vociferous in opposition to the university administration. Union pickets marched outside our house (although they were friendly when we left to go to work). They were the rank and file of the blue-collar workers who could not easily earn by moonlighting, as did the skilled crafts workers, the ones who depended on walking the picket line to earn the union's limited compensation. Callers phoned, shouting, "Turkey" and less quotable names at regular intervals during the early morning hours to keep us from sleep; indignant parents called to protest. Even the governor of Connecticut tried to wade in.

As the search committee of the Corporation was doing its work to review the situation of the university and select the next president, there was of course incessant speculation about their choice and inevitably about me. It was quite clear to me that I would not be the candidate. In truth I did not that much want to be, given the focus on and, in some quarters, loud opposition to the very idea of a woman, a non-Yale woman at that, as president of Yale—a specter that I thought would always continue to haunt such an outcome. I thought that the provost's role at Yale, which I found full of interest and satisfaction, suited me better, and that in any case the president would have to be an Old Blue. Nonetheless, it was not always easy to disregard what was being said, or to shrug off every negative judgment in the air, or to feel that some candidates whose names were floated about were necessarily more suitable or competent.

The search committee was certainly warned about the danger a woman's appointment would pose, but there were other compelling considerations as well. The trustees wanted, I think, to make a break with the Brewster years, not because they had not supported Kingman, but because they believed it time to reconcile the dissident alumni and other critics, and to move on with a different cast of people, with a new generation and a new mandate.

The fact that their first choice was Henry Rosovsky—the very effective dean of Harvard's Faculty of Arts and Sciences, a distinguished educator and administrator with an extraordinary sense for what a university should be—demonstrates that the Corporation was willing to break some new ground in its selection. Henry would have been the first Jewish president. He felt a lack of any real sense of connection or fit with Yale and its culture, and decided to remain in his position at Harvard. I had known Henry, yet another member of the second generation, since graduate student days. He had been a junior fellow in the Society of Fellows contemporaneously with Charles, and we had formed a lasting friendship. I thought Henry an excellent choice, and, at the behest of Yale's trustees, helped try to persuade him to take the position. It was an odd situation because Henry had told me that he thought I should be Yale's choice.

Charles and I had already made other plans. Shortly before the November Yale-Harvard game, I had had a call from Robert Ingersoll. A Chicagoan and Yale alumnus, he had been a very successful US ambassador to Japan. Active on the Yale Council, an advisory group that met twice a year with Yale's president, he served as vice chairman of the University of Chicago's board and member of its presidential search committee. He had come by to ask my views about candidates and my perceptions of the university. He now suggested that he and two other Chicago trustees (also Yale alumni) stop by to see me the following Sunday.

I assumed they were attending The Game and wanted further discussion about their search, but they had in fact come to invite me to consider the presidency of the University of Chicago. After the delegation had left, I went to Charles in his study. Would you like to go back to Chicago? I asked. Yes, he said, musing as he thought about the question with less surprise than I had expected.

The next weekend was the long one of Thanksgiving, and we traveled to London for a memorable stay with the Brewsters at the handsome ambassadorial mansion in Regents Park with peacocks strutting in the gardens. The Brewsters were full of stories about a former ambassador, Walter Annenberg, fabulously rich, whose favorite entertainment was to dress up as a Prince of the Church, red hat, robe, and all, to the consternation of the footmen. The footmen were snobs to the nth degree. They thought it totally non-U for Kingman to carve the turkey at Thanksgiving dinner, but since he insisted, the chef boned it in advance, and a very pathetic-looking bird was carried in on a gigantic silver tray.

The embassy represented a way of life made for people more prosperous than the Brewsters, and that was a problem, but they loved it. At a time when ambassadors had less and less influence in Washington, Kingman could be sure of having Cyrus Vance's ear. And he made many friends and productive connections in Britain.

A week later we visited Chicago, a supposedly secret visit. Charles was swept off by history department colleagues to be rerecruited to the position he had left several years earlier, and I to meet and talk with trustees and John Wilson, the current president who was intent, with great generosity, on persuading me to succeed him. Charles and I had dinner with the faculty committee that was working alongside the trustee group, and the conversation and collegial spirit of the occasion brought back to us how much we liked and were at home in the atmosphere of the University of Chicago. By the time we said goodbye to the chairman of the board, a wonderful man named Robert Reneker who was a joy to know and to work with, we were pretty sure about our decision.

The morning after our return to New Haven, I had to attend a meeting of Ivy League presidents in New York. We discussed athletics and Ivy policies on athletics at boring length. Looking around at the excellent presidents of the other Ivy League institutions, I wondered whether this was really how they should be spending their days (or I mine), and was moved to depart the room early. Once in the lobby, I called Bob Reneker to accept Chicago's invitation.

The next day, J. Richardson Dilworth, senior fellow of the Yale Corporation, told me that he and other Corporation fellows had just been to see Henry Rosovsky in Cambridge. He asked me to be in touch with Henry to add my voice to theirs. I did so and soon concluded that he would probably say no. In the meantime, the British ambassador to the United States had a speaking engagement at Yale and was coming with his wife to stay with us. The occasion went very well, as did the dinner that followed. As we sat at breakfast the next morning, however, all hell broke loose. Newspapers were calling to ask for comments on my appointment at the University of Chicago. There had been a leak—as it turned out, a deliberate one committed by Edward Levi, who had been told what was happening and who wanted Chicago to announce before Yale. The newspapers made a big deal out of the appointment. It was rather awkward, and not a good way for the Yale community to learn of this decision. But the ambassador was much amused by all the excitement.

At Yale, events moved rapidly in the next several weeks. The Corporation, its options having disappeared, renewed its search process. Bart Giamatti was elected Yale's next president. The strike ended. The Christmas break began, and something like quiet spread over the campus.

Bart Giamatti was a friend with whom I shared many interests, not only in Renaissance studies (it had been great fun to teach a course with him) but in the arts and in the ways of universities more generally. He lacked administrative experience, but so had Whit Griswold, and Bart was picked as a similar kind of appointment—a Yale graduate passionately devoted to the university, a fine teacher and recognized scholar, someone who would bring disaffected alumni back into the fold; someone of a new generation and quite different from Kingman Brewster. Bart wanted me to continue in my role until the end of the academic year, with him preparing and observing in the meantime.

The rest of that year was busier than ever, with several trips to Chicago in addition to the provost's and president's work. The trustees wanted me to carry on with full authority; they also wanted me to take care of some delicate things like telling several key administrators that they would not retain their positions in the new administration, leaving the trustees and Bart free to make changes. I thought this rather cowardly on their part, but I did what they asked.

Transitions of this kind can be hard; people in the place to which you are going demand your attention and want to tell you all their problems and get commitments for their projects before you are actually in office, while people at your current location want to deal with the person they know and secure the commitments they want to keep or gain while also anxious to make themselves heard by the new president or provost or dean. The retiring president may want to hold on; the president-elect not to get in the way, but to be informed. Some new presidents find that they aren't told things by their predecessors quickly enough, others that they are being told more than they might wish. Often, as in the Yale instance, they would like their predecessors to get some matters, preferably the most difficult ones, out of the way before their arrival. I was fortunate that John Wilson was clear and always helpful in educating me about what he thought I should know, fortunate also in our long acquaintance and in my past experience at the University of Chicago. Nor was there any question that he was in full charge until July 1.

In our last weeks at Yale we attended many enjoyable going-away parties given by kind New Haven hosts. We had a large circle of faculty friends, and social life in New Haven had been very pleasant. New Haven had almost no restaurants for good dining, and indeed there was constant complaining about the city's relative lack of amenities and good hotels or shopping or dining in a city too small and economically ailing to support the tastes of its university citizens. It was too far from New York to make that city one's daily port of call and too close to New York to secure confidence in lasting commercial viability for the businesses that would have been welcomed. But social life at the university was a great pleasure. Everyone entertained at home with more or less formality, and colleagues, fortified by good home cooking and a comfortable sense of familiarity, came together for occasions of great warmth. My memories of New Haven dinner parties, from helping serve at my parents' evenings when I was younger and again in our period of residence at Yale, remain among the strongest of both times.

Once again we packed the car and set off. It had been a very good four years for both of us. We were again leaving the familiar landscape of New England, but we felt were going—as we were—to the home where we really belonged.

10

President of the University of Chicago

I started my work in the president's office at the University of Chicago on another stiflingly hot July day, noticing that the air-conditioning seemed not to work very well and that the desk was crowded with documents waiting to be read and dealt with. A kind trustee who stopped by to extend his welcome described the office itself as reminding him, with its plastic couch and lack of adornment, of a Trailways bus terminal waiting area. It was a look that reflected John Wilson's modesty and unwillingness to spend but also the state of the university's resources.

On top of the paper pile lay the tenure case of Allan Bloom. John Wilson had received conflicting recommendations on Bloom's promotion, reflecting sharp disagreements among the departments with which he was associated over his strengths as a philosopher, political theorist, and scholar. John had appointed an ad hoc committee to review the case, but it split 50–50, so he decided to leave the vote to me. Allan knew this and was nervous about it. He had retained vague memories of a disastrous evening on which as a visiting guest at Yale he had attended and had a drink or two before a dinner honoring former president Ford. Ford was enjoying the visit to his law school alma mater and wanted to talk only of his happy experience there and of the legendary football coach, Ducky Pond, for whom he had served as an assistant. But he was suddenly accosted by an out-of-control Allan Bloom loudly decrying the decline of everything—America, higher education, culture in general—and, completely bewildered, he found himself unable to escape from an apparent maniac lecturing him on the collapse of Western civilization. Our host finally took charge, and Allan was not seen again that evening.

And now, remembering dimly that he had not behaved well on the only occasion of our meeting and had been observed hectoring a former president of the United States, Allan was sure that his goose was cooked. He at once sent a little group of friends to tell me that I had not seen him at the normal state of brilliance and rectitude to which they could testify. The idea that I would determine any appointments case on such grounds offended me, and I had to lean over backward in assessing the voluminous Bloom record at hand. Allan of course did receive tenure and then became famous with the 1987 publication of *The Closing of the American Mind*, an unexpected best seller containing all the themes that had so mystified President Ford.

It was no surprise to see that the university was subject to the same financial uncertainties and other conditions and trends that had come to prevail for all research universities. Commentators on higher education were making only the gloomiest forecasts about the future. Beyond raising the questions of finance and of government funding and its downward trend, they were pointing to significant shifts in the nation's demography and what that might portend for student populations; to the relative decline in numbers of college-age students and its effects for enrollments; to the investments and aggressive action needed to bring minority students to college and make their educational experience successful, as well as to recruit minority faculty; and to the urgent need for opportunity and equity for women faculty and students.

Issues common to all had differently weighted effects for each in accordance with an institution's particular structure and history. I set out to examine our own situation in the light of Chicago's recent history and in the context of the larger developments taking place in the world of higher education.

The University of Chicago continued as in the years before 1978 to struggle with acute financial distress. The endowment had taken a very hard fall; it was worth scarcely $265 million that July. Chicago's trustees had just declared an end to a faltering capital campaign in order to give a new president a clean slate. Annual fund-raising had decreased. The university was facing a decline in the flow of federal funding and the near impossibility of adequately replacing soft monies that had enabled the support of some substantial programs. The physical plant was blessed with buildings that had been extraordinarily well constructed but had now arrived at an age that required their extensive modernization and renovation. The institution lagged seriously in systems development. It lacked a budget office, had only a tiny and demoralized fund-raising staff, and could count on only minimal alumni activities. The university's budget was in deficit although made to look in balance by the device of inserting a revenue line of "money to be raised" to fill the gap, a figure that illustrated the well-known triumph of hope over experience. In addition, various deals that presumed some hefty further expenditures had been closed and stuffed into back pockets outside the approved budget process. Forecasts predicted rising deficits over the years to follow.

Over the preceding years the university had suffered a visible loss of momentum. Our undergraduate enrollment totaled only around 2,600 to 2,700 students; applications to the college were at a relatively low ebb. The undergraduates I had so greatly enjoyed teaching had, I was glad to find on my return, maintained their general profile as a self-selected group of serious-minded, nonconformist, and independent young people with intellectual ambitions and a sense that they had at last found a community of people like themselves. They were sure that they worked much harder and had far less social and extracurricular life than did their peers at other colleges, and they certainly enjoyed fewer amenities, but they also took a perverse pride in the grim austerity of which they complained. The Chicago T-shirt that defiantly declares the university the place where "fun comes to die" still says it all. I initiated an annual party for undergraduates at which everyone seemed actually to have a pretty good time. After the first of these, I was approached by a student who first thanked me politely for the evening and then fixed me with an indignant glare. "I hope you're not going to make this into a fun school," she said.

The crisis that had come to affect the academic marketplace in the later '70s, with dwindling numbers of positions available to new PhD holders, threatened the university's traditional role and self-definition as a graduate institution. At Chicago as elsewhere the question of whether fewer graduate students should be admitted or encouraged to aspire to academic careers in the arts and sciences was under anxious discussion. Some sense of guilt over continuing to admit large numbers in the face of a collapsing academic market went side by side with fear that the special character and standing of the university would be transformed for the worse were the numbers of PhD candidates to decrease.

The graduate divisions appeared dominant in the university's sense of its defining characteristics. The college, acknowledged as rigorous and as educationally distinctive in preserving its curricular requirements of a strong core program of general education when this had all but vanished elsewhere, seemed not to carry its full weight next to the graduate and professional areas in framing the university's atmosphere. Conflict between teaching and research priorities had not subsided. It retained institutional form in the semiautonomous college with authority over undergraduate education on the one side, the graduate divisions with responsibility for graduate programs on the other. Undergraduate students inevitably felt marginalized in a society that appeared to hold the prestige and rewards associated with research and graduate teaching above the claims of undergraduate teaching.

The university's organization, developed early in the Hutchins era, had neither a formal body of arts and sciences, as did most peer universities, nor a central graduate school of arts and sciences. Instead departments responsible for graduate instruction had been divided among the four graduate divisions: Humanities, Social Sciences, Physical Sciences, and Biological Sciences. Responsibility for undergraduate education resided in the college. The dean of each unit had immediate authority for the approval of positions and appointments, the evaluation of faculty, and the oversight of budgetary and programmatic priorities and planning. They were the key players in what looked like a decentralized system of governance in a university that was in fact more centralized than most, given the wide jurisdictions of the president and provost and the central institutions of faculty governance.

The structure of faculty governance was university-wide and designed for discussing issues and legislating on matters that affected the university as a whole beyond the borders of its individual units. It reminded me of the constitution of the Republic of Venice in the late medieval and early modern eras. The hierarchy—I still have to laugh when describing it—was as follows: The University Senate, consisting of all those on the tenure track, was the sovereign body. It elected the Council of the University Senate, consisting of fifty-one members. The council elected the Committee of the Council of the University Senate (seven members), and the committee elected the spokesman of the Committee of the Council of the University Senate, who acted as a link to and from the faculty at large. The president chaired monthly meetings of the council (its minutes distributed to all members of the senate), and biweekly meetings of the committee. The system and its practices offered an invaluable means of garnering advice and discussion on all kinds of issues as well as an important means of communication and sharing of information with the faculty at large. It also furnished one means of becoming acquainted with a considerable number of faculty colleagues.

The 1970s saw a major reversal in the patterns of growth to which the universe of higher education had become accustomed in the postwar era. That had meant growth in the numbers and size of its institutions, growth in student enrollments, and growth in the numbers of faculty who had benefited from the kind of sellers' market created by an expansive environment in which the need for more teachers, and the opportunities to develop new academic programs and to count on generous research support, marked a period of high ambition for research universities looking to enrich their potential as instruments of educational and scientific progress. A considerable percentage of their faculties had pursued graduate study and found academic positions in those days of growth, their outlook shaped in part by their experience of a booming higher education enterprise.

Now they were seeing what many began to consider the loss of a golden age of academic prosperity and progress. Expectations inherited from an idealized and actually very brief and even unique past moment had, however, survived. Those expectations often provoked unrealistic hopes while generating frustrations over the newer (yet much more typical) norms of academic life that now obtained. The most senior academics had known and experienced more in the way of straitened circumstances in the university world than had those who were now to become their successors and who carried in their academic DNA the mentality of growth and its assumptions at a time of increasing constraint. Chicago was not immune to these currents or to the tensions churned up in their wake.

I soon began to see not just that there was much to be done, but that the university had reached a critical point at which a difficult shift of generations had inevitably to occur, a very large transitional moment that came in the midst of a seemingly tectonic movement for higher education as a whole. We urgently needed to think and to plan for the shape and agenda of the university for the long-term future while also attending to immediate circumstances that called for action. We needed to think broadly and deeply about what we would want the university to look like and be able to accomplish in ten years' time.

The most important task—and this is surely the central task of all academic leadership—was to identify and to keep reviewing an appropriate balance between the university's traditions and committed values on the one hand, the challenges and opportunities of change on the other. Significant changes were needed to cope with the realities of a problematic environment and to take advantage of new opportunities and developments for education and the disciplines of learning. That did not mean sacrificing traditional strengths; on the contrary, preserving the best of tradition while adapting to evolving challenges and vigorously searching out new ones is an essential source of vitality, the most basic work to which academic leaders at every level of the academy are called. Their own effectiveness rests in turn on a larger engagement with colleagues throughout the university. It was clearly essential also to create an administrative team of people who would see the university as a cause for which to care, bringing a fresh energy and imagination to the support of its goals.

Above all, I had to learn and understand the range and activities, the strengths and weaknesses of our academic programs, to meet and listen to as many people as possible and learn from them about their fields, their own projects and prospects, and their views about the university itself. I had of course known the university before, and my knowledge of its culture was a tremendous help now, as it was also to have acquired some perspective born of experience at other universities. I needed to find out what might now be different at the university, what imprints had been left by the intervening years and what impacts had already proceeded, or were likely to result, from the contemporary prospects for higher education.

Edward Levi had left in 1975 to become attorney general of the United States, and his provost, John Wilson, had become acting president. Then, after a presidential search proved unproductive, John agreed to take a three-year term as president. He specified that he would not have to live in the president's house or spend major time in fund-raising or alumni affairs. John had been an excellent provost, and he was a much better president than he believed himself to have been, but his was regarded as a temporary administration that still represented the past without renewed energy or vision. He was able to call on the commitment and loyalty to the university of a remarkable generation of distinguished long-serving faculty who cared deeply for the university and its values, and who seemed always ready to take on the tasks of citizenship. The economist Gale Johnson became provost, the geographer Chauncey Harris an unlikely vice president for development. Allison Dunham of the law school accepted the job of general counsel. The ethos of these men was one of concern for the best interests of the university, of helping out and creating confidence at a time of uncertainty. They represented an extraordinary generation of faculty leaders who joined in maintaining the continuity and successful pursuit of the university's best purposes.

I do not mean to overstate the problems that I found at the University of Chicago when I became president, nor would I claim for an instant that I had somehow finally solved them. The state of the university in 1978 was certainly in some respects perilous. But it was nonetheless one of great inner strength and a cause for optimism because the university's essential endowment—its powerful sense of mission, its uncompromising intellectual spirit, its insistence on intellectual freedom, its capacity for interdisciplinary discourse and scholarship, its exceptional students and the breadth and rigor of education they had on offer—remained robust, preserved in the face of the huge changes that were shaping the world of higher education. The loss of this essential endowment would have been irreparable (the other endowment could, after all, be replenished). I had the good fortune, together with my colleagues, of inheriting a great institutional legacy from predecessors whose astonishingly generous service had furthered and protected the university at its core.

When one embarks on executive responsibility, it is tempting to decide what needs to be done, take a deep breath, and try to do everything right away. But a sense of pace and a sense of priorities—of what to concentrate on at the outset and over what length of time to distribute and accomplish those priorities—had to overcome this impulse. It was essential to listen, to discover the nature and state of the institutional culture and where it seemed to be heading, to talk with as many people as possible and listen with an open mind in order to understand the issues on people's minds: their intellectual interests and ideas and hopes for their institution, the quality of the scholarly and scientific work they observed around them, the trends and directions of their disciplines, and the projects that held the most promise in their thinking. The great rewards of this process were those of coming to know many of one's colleagues and coming to grasp more of the range and variety and excitement of the university, its activities, and the possibilities that lay before us.

I spent time in my first year doing this kind of questioning and listening and becoming better educated. The faculty I talked with showed great openness and seemed pleased to have the lights back on in the president's house after its deserted appearance had made it a minor symbol of something missing at the university for those who passed it every day on their way to and from campus. Much interest was shown in my domestic life and arrangements. I could not shop for groceries at the neighborhood co-op without having people look with undisguised curiosity into my shopping cart, and one day I surprised a distinguished professor of law in the act of peering from the shrubbery into our garage window, presumably to find out what kind of car we drove.

On the administrative side, the delicate process of moving some people on—people who liked being at the university and who had hoped to stay in their positions—was not entirely easy, and each case was sui generis, but in the end the process was concluded more or less gracefully and without appearing to inflict permanent wounds on people who generally went on to good positions elsewhere. By year's end I had been able to assemble a very able, energetic, and congenial group of administrative colleagues, several already in place when I arrived and others recruited from outside.[1] The newcomers were young, all in their thirties, with the ambition and readiness to take on broad executive responsibilities of their own and the goal of doing so in the service of a consequential end, which they saw as that of the university. They were generalists in outlook and in background, committed to the university and its mission and to the broadening of their own horizons in its environment, anxious to become acquainted with and to be active in the university community. The familiar tensions that characterize the "we versus they" relationship between faculty and administration were not absent, but they were far less pronounced at Chicago than I had observed elsewhere. We worked together with considerable ease and developed long-standing friendships. We tended to informality, running in and out of one another's offices to consult, or share the latest news or a joke, or just to schmooze. Over time, each of my colleagues developed growing interests and skills in a host of directions and expanded their portfolios to new areas of management. Helping that to happen, helping career paths to unfold, and recognizing with pride one's colleagues' growth and accomplishment, is, I think, one of the obligations and joys of presidential office. Two of my associates left to become university presidents; another two became presidents of liberal arts colleges.

In university management, the less bureaucratic, the better, in the interests of effective decision making and the flexibility that can make things move quickly, whether a response to a faculty offer from another institution or a request for special assistance. Anything that looks like bureaucracy— for example, the attempt to enforce reporting requirements imposed by federal mandate on recipients of federal research grants—raises the most powerful animus and resistance from academics, who see in it a violation of their freedoms inflicted by petty university tyrants lacking all respect for the higher things of the intellect. We tried to avoid organizational hierarchy and complexity and to act with flexibility as much as possible. That sometimes became harder as regulatory requirements emerging from Washington increased over the years, or as the inherent drive to protect one's turf threatened to overtake one or another unit.

By late 1979 we had established a budget office and a professionally staffed development office. We had started work on new systems and had initiated a program of building renovation on the university's main quadrangle that was in part made possible by an Illinois program that allowed institutions of higher education within the state to borrow up to $150 million at favorable rates. A campus plan, setting the guidelines for future building and landscaping, with the quadrangular models of the main campus at its heart, was under development in consultation with the architectural and design firm Sasaki Associates.

On the budget side, our work was focused on the university's underlying financial condition, with the assistance of analytical studies conducted by Cambridge Associates, a group specializing in not for-profit institutions and in assessing their financial situations, laying out comparisons with other institutions, and considering the routes that might be traveled to achieving financial equilibrium. Their findings tended to confirm our view of an overstretched university economy more limited than its peers in the key resources of endowment and tuition revenue. Our undergraduate college was smaller and brought in less income; in addition, a larger proportion of our students needed financial aid from general funds.

The good news was that despite the relatively lesser contribution made by endowment funds to our annual budget, a larger portion of those funds was unrestricted than was the case elsewhere, and that meant a degree of flexibility in allocating such revenue to our chosen priorities with greater freedom. Those priorities throughout my time included strengthening faculty compensation and sustaining a need-based program of financial aid for undergraduates and improved aid for graduate students. All this would carve a healthy amount annually out of general funds and, when endowments were in place or could be raised, restricted funds as well.

We needed to find ways not just of reducing expenditures but of substantially increasing the university's revenues, and the first big move in that direction was to raise the level of tuition quite aggressively (our price had lagged that of our competitors, so there was some room to do this). Over time the problem of funding financial aid through general tuition revenue has created a significant dilemma for all colleges in elevating the "discount" price of tuition to a level that has steadily diminished the net value of the revenue realized from high tuitions. And no matter how often institutions try to make clear to students and their families that they will not be paying the ticket price, but a considerably reduced one, it is the ticket prices that are out there, frightening prospective applicants and causing public uproar over the cost of higher education. In addition, those families at the edge of the line separating those eligible from those not qualifying for financial aid may feel deep resentment that their high payments are supporting those on aid.

We did of course begin to make budget reductions where possible right away. An energy conservation program that remained in effect for many years produced major savings. We left some positions open and slowed the rate of new appointments, achieved some consolidations in administrative offices, and cut our own expense budgets, while beginning to look at programs that could be eliminated and other steps that could be taken for the following year. We closed several centers that were not showing very much of real value to the university. For the longer term, we were busy with identifying questions that would require more extensive deliberation and planning, such as the size of the faculty and the enrollment targets we should establish for the future. By the 1990s we had somewhat reduced the size of the faculty, a very large one compared to Chicago's enrollment and to the faculties of peer institutions. The urgency of keeping that level more or less constant had increased with the elimination of mandatory retirement, a serious obstruction in the path of the desirable turnover that keeps fresh talent and new intellectual directions moving through the academy. University faculty have no particular incentives to retire. Retired scholars within reach of a library, or with their computer accounts, can go on doing their research and writing—although this is harder for scientists who rely on laboratory space and, usually, federal funding and may not always find those available to them—and may have some teaching opportunities as well. But being unretired and compensated is better. The end of mandatory retirement accelerated the aging of the faculty throughout higher education.

The provost and I met with an ad hoc group of faculty to discuss the financial situation and solicit their ideas of what might be done. This set of discussions was only partially successful; the committee members inevitably wanted to gore oxen other than their own. Some argued that investing more money—for example, in additional appointments that would generate more grants and their accompanying indirect cost recovery—would be the best (and pleasantest) way to increase income. The discussions were nonetheless useful and helped to communicate the issues of the day to a larger audience. We devoted a great deal of effort to communicating the university's situation to the university community through reports to the Council of the University Senate, through the president's annual State of the University talk, through meetings with the faculties of the schools and divisions, and through the university's publications. Transparency in sharing the data we had gathered and reporting on the planning underway was vital to keeping the community informed and engaged. From the first days of the university there had existed a *University of Chicago Record*. All commissioned reports were published there, as were also such items as the annual State of the University talks and annual reports on the budget, on capital projects, and on development. This publication was sent to sister institutions as well as to our own community; colleagues in other places found it interesting and even useful for sharing ideas. We soon added a new and more informal publication. The *Chronicle* was distributed around the university every two weeks, bringing news, features, announcements, and calendars of events to the entire community in the days before websites took over.

On the development side, the university's annual fund-raising totals were considerably below those of our competitors. Our alumni body differed in its profile. A much smaller number of Chicago's alumni in recent decades had been Chicago undergraduates, and these were alumni who were not so likely to identify themselves as members of a particular class, as did, for example, the class of 1939. Chicago's alumni had graduated when they were ready to do so, after completing curricular requirements defined not by numbers of courses taken but by comprehensive examinations passed, which often occurred at a wide variety of times for students who had entered the college the same year. Class spirit had not been especially encouraged. A larger proportion of our alumni as compared to those of other major universities had chosen professions, including the academic and public service professions, that led to lives of satisfaction and accomplishment but not to substantial incomes or very high average gifts. In addition, there existed serious disaffection among alumni who believed the Hutchins college they loved had been callously destroyed, and others whose memories were of unhappy and difficult years in the '60s and early '70s. On the other hand, the university had many alumni who were ardent in their loyalty and ready to become more involved.

We asked Arthur Schultz, a devoted alumnus and trustee, to chair a commission on alumni affairs. He conducted it with great skill and wrote a most informative and helpful report that guided our steps. By late 1979 we had been able to re-create an office of alumni affairs. Alumni activities were beginning to awaken and stir. I found that visits to alumni groups in various cities brought out alumni from every part of the university who always asked one question in particular, just as one would have hoped: Was the university maintaining its educational and scholarly standards?

Planning our fund-raising strategy, we took into account the somewhat dismal results of the university's most recent efforts and decided to concentrate on raising the level of annual giving and to launch not a university-wide campaign but a series of smaller ones that by their success might not only aid their individual beneficiaries but inspire a mounting confidence in the university's capacity to attract giving in the years ahead, when a broader campaign would become feasible. Each of these minicampaigns, for the arts and sciences (in support of the college and divisions), the law school, the medical school, and the Graduate School of Business, did indeed achieve its goals. Annual giving also increased by a welcome percentage.

I had returned to Chicago with several ideas in my mind of things I wanted to investigate and act on. In my earlier time at the university I had thought the college too small and student life too narrow. It seemed to me the college and the excellent education it provided had unused capacity; it might grow without damage to its small class size and unusual ratio of faculty to students. I had found the university-wide requirements for awarding the PhD degree too rigid and fellowship aid well below par. To be eligible for the degree, a candidate had to have completed twenty-seven courses, and I noted the remorseless application of this and other rules to an area that I thought would benefit from a greater flexibility that could take into account divergences among fields and support whatever stage of scholarly ambition and preparation a student had achieved.

Those questions melded into two larger ones as we thought about the long term; they bore directly on the university's character and culture. What should be the shape and size of the university and what the balance of its different parts? Should we continue to admit so many graduate students? How could we improve the lives of graduate students? And how might we encourage departments, each responsible for setting and running its own graduate curriculum and program, to initiate searching reviews of their specific curricula and practices?

Two faculty committees began deliberating these questions. I asked one, chaired by Norman Bradburn, to consider the desirable size, composition, and balance of the university going forward. The other, chaired by the historian Keith Baker, was charged with surveying and assessing graduate education in the divisions and the divinity school. Both committees presented thorough and substantive reports that did much to determine plans for the university's future. Both were subjected to heated debate before their principal conclusions entered the mainstream of university policies.

The mandate to recommend an appropriate size for the college prompted anxiety and alarm, both among those college faculty who felt that any increase would destroy its special qualities and among those who interpreted the question as somehow signaling a lessened commitment to the enterprises of research and graduate training. The Bradburn Committee's report and recommendations intensified these concerns and provoked wide-ranging argument. The committee had examined the university's enrollments and the considerable variation over time in the numbers of students distributed among its different areas. It drew attention to the fact that undergraduate enrollments in the university, from the beginnings and right through the 1930s, had actually represented the dominant proportion of the university's total population. The college had been larger in the 1930s than during the past two decades. The Bradburn report argued that over an entire history, the university's composition, on average, consisted of one-third collegiate education, another third graduate education. A final third belonged to the professional schools. It recommended that this general distribution by thirds, the precise figures naturally varying from year to year, be embraced as the target defining the university's balance of programs. The committee recommended that the university seek to maintain its numbers in graduate programs while increasing the size of the college to 3,200 students. This was a number, we thought, that could be accommodated without major increases in facilities or faculty size. This plan was adopted with the unqualified understanding that admissions standards would not in any way be altered for the sake of numbers and that we would be working hard to increase the pool of qualified applicants. We were able to recruit Dan Hall, an outstanding leader in his profession, as director of admissions and began to see a gradual increase in applications and a gradually rising college enrollment that included steady increases in the proportion of entering women students but only frustratingly small changes in the recruitment of minority students. Later in my term I asked another faculty group, chaired by David Greenstone, to take a look at further increasing the size of the college; it recommended an increase to 3,400 and set a maximum of 3,600.

Many projects were in motion to support and strengthen extracurricular and social life in the college; there was always more to be done. Chicago was among the founding institutions, selective private universities with relatively small colleges, of the Division III's University Athletic Association. This athletic conference became to some degree a model for the pursuit of intercollegiate sports without any compromise of academic priorities. I set up a committee of students from across the university, with college students in the majority, that met monthly to discuss their ideas and concerns and to exchange information about the university and the state of things. I heard a lot of repetition in the questions and concerns voiced in our meetings, but I learned quite a lot too, and so, I think, did the students. The committee had an impact on some of the decisions that affected student life, helping us better to understand students' attitudes and priorities as we planned renovations of the spaces that housed their daily and social lives, their organizations, meeting places, theaters, and cafés.

I have always thought it strange that students can learn about the constitutions and laws and political processes of just about any place in the world but never receive much of an education in how universities are organized, how they work, and how their policies and procedures are intended to support the purposes and obligations for which they exist. My little advisory committee's members came to know quite a lot about all of this and found it interesting. It would make a difference, I think, in our society's understanding and in support for higher education were more attention given to providing its graduates-to-be with an informed sense for the basic structures and practices of its institutions.

It was an unusual move to launch from the administrative center an effort like that of the Baker Commission. In undertaking to assess the quality and effectiveness of graduate education in the divisions, we were in effect setting out to evaluate the strengths and weaknesses of the divisions themselves. From the start there arose suspicions that I was intruding into departmental business, meddling where I should not, that I had predetermined the outcome of the Baker project in order to impose my own conclusions, and that these were to be discovered lodged implicitly in the questions I had raised.

As the process moved forward, I undertook a series of discussions with a number of departments, meeting with their faculties to moderate those concerns, to explain the commission's charge and its bearing on the university's planning, and to elicit their views on the issues before us. I met also from time to time in informative sessions with the commission and with the subcommittees it created to study in depth specific areas within its comprehensive survey.

The Baker Commission's report had influence even beyond our university. In examining the conditions of graduate student life, the report pointed to the isolation and loss of intellectual support and fellowship that could overtake students, most often doctoral candidates in the humanities and social sciences, once they had finished their course work, passed their oral examinations, and begun work on their dissertations, too many of them never completed and too many hopes for the doctoral degree abandoned. The commission recommended establishing a program of workshops in which graduate students could present their research in progress for discussion by both fellow students and faculty, thus offering a collegial setting that recognized these doctoral students as participants in the academic profession to which they aspired. The workshop program spread and flourished. The commission's ideas for revising the university's PhD programs were implemented setting residence requirements at two years of coursework, followed by years of research residence with lowered tuition.

The Baker Commission's report urged that graduate fellowship support be greatly expanded and systematized, a priority on which we continued to work steadily over all the years that followed. We had long been behind the competition and had first to make aid available to a larger number of students and guarantee secure support for a given period of years from the outset of their studies. We hoped to establish more dissertation fellowships as well. The commission also addressed the issue of graduate student teaching and the need for students who aimed for an academic career to learn something about how to teach and to gain some experience in doing so. Everyone could agree that it would be helpful to devise some means of introducing graduate students to teaching, perhaps in the form of selective teaching internships, but there was no general agreement as to how it might be done, or how important it was taken to be in the larger scheme of graduate programs, and whether the college, which had prided itself on having mostly full-time faculty in the classroom, should move to appointing more graduate students as instructors. A variety of opportunities began to be offered, differing according to departmental needs and interests and differing in their duration and effectiveness as well. The commission had pointed out also that not all PhD students were necessarily planning or able, in a constrained academic market, to embark on academic careers (already, of course quite a number of degree holders, especially in such fields as economics or chemistry, regularly chose to work in research institutes or museums or the corporate sector). The commission emphasized the importance of looking beyond the academic world, and to the value added by a background of graduate training. But such exhortations tended to get little notice. Most faculty inhabited a culture which took it for granted that graduate students were being trained for academic futures. While mourning the decline of opportunity, they could not easily imagine alternatives.

The Baker Commission based many of its recommendations and programmatic judgments on the candid appraisals it had rendered on the four divisions; these appraisals accompanied its published and widely shared report. This degree of transparency was, I think, unusual in the university world.

In the meantime, and through many discussions with the provost and deans, I had been seeking to identify the questions requiring special attention in the university's schools and divisions.

The most urgent and most tenacious of these, not only then but for my entire time in office, related to the School of Medicine and the University's Medical Center (comprising three hospitals and a large number of specialty clinics), both part of the Division of the Biological Sciences and reporting to its dean.

John Wilson had made the Division of Biological Sciences his special cause. The division was an inclusive home for medical education, research, and practice, as well as for the basic biological sciences and also for undergraduate instruction in biology. Despite the outstanding departments, clinicians, and scientists the division could claim, it was not fulfilling the ambitious promise of this intended integration. The organization in one space of all biological and biomedical programs, and their unusually close relation to other parts of the university, would seem on the surface to offer unique possibilities and interdisciplinary breakthroughs, but the division had somehow fallen short of the highest rank. George Beadle's presidency had been expected to advance the university's prominence on the cutting edge of the modern biological sciences, but, as he himself sadly observed, the division had during his time managed to miss turning the big corner toward the molecular revolution in a timely fashion.

John Wilson felt proud and relieved to have recruited a dean, Daniel Tosteson, who, both he and the faculty believed, would forcefully lead a new era of increasing strength and distinction. To his dismay, Dean Tosteson appeared in John's office after less than two years with the news that he would be leaving the following June to become dean of the Harvard Medical School. No, said John, you are leaving right now. John was enraged, not only at the departing dean, but at Harvard's president for not having informed him of their negotiation. He never forgave either of them. In Tosteson's place, he appointed the then dean for academic affairs in the Division of the Biological Sciences, a very decent man who did not have a medical degree and came into immediate conflict with the powerful chairmen of surgery and medicine, as well as suffering a lukewarm reception from the divisional faculty. The school fell into a morass of disunity and competing ambitions for control.

All this took place amid a rapidly shifting landscape of health care that imposed a heavy impact on the university. Its hospitals served the largest uninsured population, mostly on Chicago's South Side, of any private hospital in the state of Illinois (only Cook County Hospital served more). The income derived from reimbursement for medical care had been counted on to produce revenues that the medical center could allocate in part to research and educational purposes at the medical school; that was typical in the economy of all academic medical centers. As policies governing reimbursement and expenses allowable for health care tightened steadily, these revenues decreased. The immediate interests of the medical center partners, of medical schools and their hospitals, came more and more to diverge as the hospitals strove for financial health and stability, their medical schools for support of their academic goals. Universities became more and more vulnerable to very large and potentially devastating swings in the financial performance of their owned or affiliated teaching hospitals. There was every reason to worry about the structure and governance of a medical center that reported to an academic dean. The hospitals posed huge management problems that required first-rate skills and a special talent for strategic thinking and decision making. It was unlikely that one could find a hospital director of that quality without giving him or her a fuller executive responsibility. Hospital directors were likely to chafe at reporting to a dean whose primary mandate had to do with education and research, however critical also the role of first-rate clinical practice.

The dean had not asked for the trouble that bedeviled the division, nor was he well suited for managing its complexity. I should have replaced him in that first year, but I failed to do so. It would surely have saved him a lot of stress. He was a very conscientious man who worked hard and faithfully at a pretty thankless task, a loyal citizen of the institution who wanted to protect it and to make things work. He had made a commitment that he was anxiously determined to honor. I had no desire to humiliate him or to give in to those who were demanding his head. I could see no internal candidates to succeed him, and I thought a search could well be fruitless at a time when it would be very hard to find outstanding candidates in the wake of the Tosteson departure and the questions it raised about what had gone wrong at Chicago, not to mention the widespread knowledge of the division's internal conflicts disseminated through the chattering networks of the biomedical establishment. I thought it best first to let things cool down and put the house in order, and then to begin a search process in two years' time. But this was, I think, a mistake. I should have considered compelling arguments on the other side and tried, despite all the perfectly rational reasons to wait, to explore further how we might move in more constructive directions as soon as possible.

I thought also that before a new dean took office, we should be looking at the complicated issues of management and governance that surrounded the hospital and its relation to the medical school and university. A committee of the university board had been trying to play some role of oversight there without, so far as I could tell, any really useful results. I organized a group that included several trustees to examine what kind of governance structure might make most sense for our situation. We visited and learned a great deal from other academic medical centers, especially Johns Hopkins, Stanford, and Duke. Each had a different structure; no one deemed wholly satisfactory by its institutional leaders. Those who did not own their hospitals wished they did; those who did own them wondered whether affiliation arrangements might not be better. Those whose hospitals had boards of their own wanted more control over them; others wanted more focused oversight and more protection for the university through the institution of independent hospital boards with genuine fiduciary obligations. In short, we found no one model and certainly no perfect one. Our discussions of these questions continued over the years. Ultimately a hospital board subject to the university board's authority came into existence. The hospital was made a separate corporation; its board, composed of selected university trustees and other members from outside nominated by the university, which thus retained ultimate control. The hospital director became a full-fledged CEO. The new structure came into being with the thought that it would preclude the university's having to bear full faith and credit for the hospitals, and would provide legal safeguards for the university under damaging circumstances. But of course the university's name is on the door. The new arrangement did not cure—nor could it have cured—the tensions spawned inevitably by the sometimes-conflicting mandates of medical schools and their teaching hospitals in any academic medical center. Periods of constraint and the effects of public policy changes in the health-care system aggravate such differences and the difficulties of reconciling their goals.

Despite my previous exposure to academic medical centers, I was amazed by the enormous amount of time one spent on this area of university administration. Presidents of universities with medical schools greatly envy their peers whose universities are not so constituted; the former are given to repeating the story about the president who goes to Hell and finds himself on a splendid campus with gorgeous buildings, manicured grounds, and wonderfully courteous and well-behaved students. The Devil turns up to say hello, and the president expresses astonishment that this beautiful, perfect campus is actually Hell. Ah, says the Devil, you don't realize: this is a university with *two* medical schools. My own notion of Hell imagines a place where one's life is given over to trying to merge two hospitals, as we attempted unsuccessfully to do over a year of negotiations with the Michael Reese Hospital and Medical Center, already (if somewhat uneasily) affiliated with our medical school. Located not far off, Michael Reese was a logical partner to share in advanced education and clinical service on the South Side of Chicago; combining our strengths would seem a winning proposition for both partners. Michael Reese ended up going out of business altogether (having entered a brief shotgun marriage with another medical school) after its physicians and trustees demanded conditions (for example, 50 percent of all departmental chairmanships) unacceptable to the university.

Our medical center underwent considerable changes during this period and later. The medical school had begun its existence as an almost pure example of the blueprint outlined in the Flexner Report of 1910, which had advocated educational and scientific standards and structures for medical schools that had an enduring influence. At Chicago, hospital privileges were confined to a full-time salaried faculty responsible for the entire range of education, research, and clinical care. In order now to strengthen and expand clinical service, the medical school moved to create a new series of clinical faculty tracks (a model familiar in other academic medical schools), doing so over considerable opposition from faculty who saw this trend as a threat to the university's criteria for faculty status. Debate in the Council of the University Senate was heated, but the proposals were finally approved. The new titles assigned to the clinical practitioners made clear that they were not regular faculty or appointed by the usual measures of research quality and productivity. Titles at once became a huge issue, since the clinical professors, predictably, did not want to be treated as second-class citizens, and there ensued long internal struggles over titles and privileges.

The law school was in the process of searching for a new dean when I took office. Its faculty search committee recommended two excellent internal candidates, with Gerhard Casper accepting appointment to the great benefit of the law school and the university. He was a first-rate dean, a man of broad cultivation and outlook who cared greatly for the university, and who encouraged the close connections and joint programs between the school and, especially, the Division of the Social Sciences. He himself held an appointment in the Department of Political Science in addition to his law school chair. He was a wise and generous adviser on a wide array of complex university questions, and he was ultimately to become provost of the university before moving to Stanford as its president.

I asked the other candidate, Kenneth Dam, to become provost in succession to Gale Johnson. He served for two years with impressive calm and competence, making a notable contribution and finding it fascinating to discover the scope of the university's intellectual landscape beyond the law school. Ken left to become deputy secretary of state for George Shultz (once professor and dean of our Graduate School of Business). He was in turn succeeded by Robert McCormick Adams, an esteemed anthropologist and archaeologist, a onetime dean of the Social Sciences Division and former director of the Oriental Institute. He brought an uncompromising scholarly sensibility to the office, fiercely independent and single-mindedly concerned with academic standards. He, too, left for Washington, in his case to become secretary of the Smithsonian Institution. I had worked with three different provosts over my first seven years and learned from each one. While the rotation spun much faster than I would have wished, I gained each time from the fresh perspectives and expertise brought by each of the provosts, and from their different insights and ways of thinking that helped form my own as we debated our views, proposals, and options. Each provost brought new questions to the table.

The divinity school was in good hands under the leadership of Joe Kitagawa as it expanded the range of its programs in the areas of comparative religion and world religions. As a center for the advanced study of religion, its close ties to the Divisions of the Humanities and of Social Sciences (where the Department of History was located) were of tremendous importance in the enrichment of scholarly and educational activities in their respective departments as well.

The Graduate School of Business (now the Booth School) maintained close ties to the Department of Economics and to the law school and its program of law and economics. I found an air of mounting discontent over the school's dean, a man who seemed deaf in matters of human relations and autocratic in his administrative style to the point where I finally found it necessary to ask that he step down. His successor, John Gould, was almost his opposite, a man sensitive to others, open in his thinking to the views of others, capable of delegating and sharing. He was committed to the interests of the university as a whole and ready to initiate ventures with other faculties. Business schools have a tendency to strive for autonomy within the universities whose names they bear, and to achieve as much distance as possible from any central control. Our school was not free from these common tendencies, but Gould's leadership, and the colleagues he especially relied on, saw the strengths of the school as closely linked to those of the larger university.

At the other extreme, the professional Schools of Social Service Administration and of Library Science held a far higher ranking and respect in their fields externally than they did in the life of the university. In the case of SSA, the school was having to cope with some tough financial and programmatic problems after the withdrawal of a major federal grant. Its new and relatively inexperienced dean was struggling with controversies that had arisen over the balance of priorities between its traditional mission of educating leaders in the social work profession and recent initiatives that, under its previous dean, had moved increasingly toward a concern with research and with incorporating programs related to public policy in matters of social welfare. The school's longest-serving faculty and older alumni and supporters thought their school needed to reassert the understanding that its central purposes had to do with training in the practice of social work and the management of social service organizations.

A certain tension between the goal of training professional practitioners and the academic interests associated with a more theoretical and research-driven orientation is a common thread in the lives of professional schools more generally. Many donors, supporters, and alumni of these institutions want to see their graduates becoming leaders of their professions in the "real" world rather than qualifying for think tanks. Those critics question what they regard as excessively "academic" directions.

Within the university, there were many who thought the school's students and programs not really up to the university's standards. However highly ranked among schools of social work, SSA in its own home was judged as off the university's central track, despite the presence among its faculty of much-respected colleagues active in university affairs.

The library school seemed a relatively quiet backwater. It was highly ranked among library schools. Yet as the library world was undergoing an immense transformation in a world of new technologies, new tools of information retrieval and digitization, and new networks of libraries and collections, the school did not appear to lead on the issues that were raising the biggest questions of all throughout an academic universe which often celebrated the university library as the "heart" of the institution: Where were libraries headed? What would be the library of the future? How would the subjects and methods of scholarship be affected? What kinds of skills and what kinds of training should librarians of the future possess, and for what kind of institution? For what ongoing and relentless changes in a newly developing and highly uncertain future should their education prepare them? The growing concern with these issues was certainly not confined to library schools or to libraries. They needed to be addressed well beyond the traditional universe of libraries, and the school gave no signs of leadership within the university to that cause, nor did it substantially contribute to the university's broader intellectual activities. I became convinced that we had either to invest very large resources in a reinvigorated school or eliminate it altogether, and I chose the latter path.

The point was not primarily to save money now, although we were making a decision that would save us from expenditures that would be required in the future were we to re-create a major professional school. The criteria we tried consistently to apply in reviewing any program, including a number of centers we closed, had to do with whether it met the university's standards of quality and added or contributed to the strengths of the academic enterprise as a whole. On this scale the conclusion reached on the library school seemed clear. Any resources we could muster would better be allocated to other more promising priorities that built on the university's greatest strengths.

Closing the school involved endless time and discussion. The deed was eventually done after the proposal underwent extensive deliberation and attained final approval by the Council of the University Senate. In this process faculty participation had ground slowly but well. Another closure, that of the Department of Geography, aroused even noisier dissent from interested observers and outside groups making it their business to lobby and protest. The president of the National Geographic Society sent me a balloon of the globe with a testy note alleging that I probably wouldn't be able to recognize what this was. One professor of geography swore never to speak to me again, nor has he, even to say "excuse me" in order to push his way out of the elevator.

The discipline of geography was changing drastically; departments at other universities were disappearing also. In the department's place an interdisciplinary committee—including economists, political scientists, environmental scientists, and others interested in the evolving breadth of a subject that was taking new forms—became a new scholarly center.

The university had long had an effective custom of establishing interdisciplinary committees that could experiment with new configurations of scholarly interests that crossed traditional borders (for example, foreign area studies committees brought together many different areas of the social sciences and the humanities with the goal of understanding the totality of a culture or civilization in its many dimensions), or provided a foundation for investigating and developing topics of scholarship in innovative ways, or offered homes for scholars whose work and interests could not easily be categorized in the usual disciplinary terms (hence the Committee on Social Thought, already founded in the Hutchins era, famous for faculty members such as Saul Bellow and offering graduate degrees to a very able and selective group of students). Some of these committees over time began to offer degrees, while others remained exclusively dedicated to research. Committee structures afforded flexible opportunities. They were not necessarily translated into permanent programs but might become the basis for such programs. Or they might simply go out of business after their raison d'être ceased to command serious support.

One such degree-granting committee in place when I took office was the Committee on Public Policy Studies. The idea that the university should have a school of public policy had a long history. Funds for creating one had been offered by a wealthy donor and had been declined, to the prospective donor's fury, by Edward Levi, who did not want the kind of program the donor had in mind (something similar to Harvard's Kennedy School), and questioned whether there was in fact a genuine discipline in the study of public policy per se. After being named president, I immediately heard from the rejected donor insisting that I do something, and do it right away. He was not mollified by my replying that I would have to learn about and consider the state of things once I had taken office some months later, and he did not give up his repeated attempts to persuade me.

The Committee on Public Policy Studies sponsored and cross-listed a number of courses relevant to its interests and enlisted in its membership faculty from different areas. The committee went on to receive formal approval to grant degrees and soon proposed it become the nucleus of a new professional school. A number of distinguished faculty members, including the sociologists William Julius Wilson and James Coleman and the economist James Heckman, urged me to take action. I impaneled a committee of faculty to consider the many questions involved, to make a recommendation on whether or not we should establish a school, and, if it favored doing so, to describe what its mission, educational goals, and university-related intellectual horizons might look like. The final committee report recommended, but not unanimously (a sign of problems to come), the creation of a School of Public Policy Studies that would build on the university's interdisciplinary and scholarly traditions.

There was a complicated decision to be made. Those opposed to a school were skeptics about whether the study of public policy possessed genuine intellectual substance or would gain by being pursued separately from existing faculty offerings across the university; those in favor thought such a school would fill an unfortunate gap in the university's range of education, scholarship, and influence, and that a rigorous program of training and research incorporating the university's academic expectations and strengths could differentiate it from other schools of public policy. Our trustees were strongly in support, the more so as their fellow trustee, Irving Harris, an extraordinary philanthropist, offered a gift of some $6 million as an initial endowment. He wanted to see the new school happen right away, as did the board. Pressures to approve and begin on the project became intense.

We acted, I think, prematurely. It would have been wiser to insist on raising additional resources and on a longer planning horizon. The school was named, most appropriately, for Irving Harris. His interest and attention never flagged, but he had hoped that others would join in donating to the cause and was disappointed that it proved difficult to raise additional funds from other sources; once the naming was announced, potential donors thought it his business to give financial support. It turned out, too, as serious preparation began, that some of the senior faculty who had argued so passionately for a school had in fact different agendas in mind—some, it seemed, had primarily envisaged a center at which their research interests could be pursued with a community of like-minded colleagues; others had wanted a professional school designed to educate a cohort of public servants well versed in analytic and quantitative skills, whose expertise would contribute to the betterment of government both local and national. Irving Harris himself hoped for some special attention to be given to his abiding concern with issues of child development, education, and welfare. Some key faculty players began to withdraw from major engagement with the project, finding themselves perhaps unsympathetic to its initial priorities and losing patience with colleagues as they argued over setting the school's identity. It proved predictably difficult to find a dean for a school in which these varying agendas and differences over directions had not been adequately resolved, a school that would require greater financial security to realize the university's ambitions to attract a high level of students and faculty and become competitive in its field. That would require a decade or two in any case. I think we should have resisted the pressures to move swiftly and should have taken two years or so before its actual launch to plan for the school and sort out the issues at hand. Happily, after its rocky start the ship began to be righted under the patient and constructive administration of its founding dean, Robert Michael. The Harris School is now thriving, almost thirty years after its founding. Its early history, as I look back, presents a cautionary tale.

I was being introduced also to a whole range of affiliated enterprises of which I had had little or no knowledge at all. Of these, the Argonne National Laboratory was the largest and most demanding of time and attention. There were others, like the National Opinion Research Center, which had times of acute financial stress and of leadership issues that called for one's involvement, and the Orthogenic School (Bruno Bettelheim's school for autistic children) that came under critical scrutiny as Bettelheim came to be accused of abusively controlling the children under his care, and of having exaggerated the effects of his theories and practices as well as of falsifying his own already-controversial history. His successor as the school's director had a very difficult time, and the question of the school's survival had to be addressed. We decided to preserve the school but reorient its mission so as to serve a wider range of troubled children.

The Argonne National Laboratory had been founded as a multipurpose center for conducting research related to the peaceful uses of atomic energy. It was managed under renewable five-year contracts with the Department of Energy. In 1978 the university shared responsibility with a consortium of universities under an arrangement in which the president of the consortium and his board had a formal role in policy and program decisions. They tended to suspect that the university might try to reap all the rewards of the contract and monopolize Argonne's facilities for its own purposes, and they wanted to ensure the sometimes-conflicting interests of their members. This was not a recipe for efficient planning or harmonious oversight. Argonne's director at the time was a highly respected professor of physics at the university, wholly devoted to science and somewhat innocent when it came to dealing with the human and political things of the world.

Argonne West (now the Idaho National Laboratory), located north of Twin Falls, Idaho, also fell under the management contract. I went that first year and every year thereafter to spend a day or two at the lab, and to act as host of an annual dinner for its scientists, held in the Rotarians' hall. It featured huge slabs of roast beef and plump Idaho baked potatoes and generous helpings of pie for dessert. Couples arrived early for this well-attended social event of the year, the men wearing fancy boots. In my initial visit, I stood at the entrance with Argonne director Bob Sachs to greet each guest and was saluted by many of them, to Bob's embarrassment, as Mrs. Sachs. The word had definitely not reached Twin Falls.

Shortly after my arrival in office I was summoned to Washington to meet with DOE's director of research, John Deutsch (later director of the CIA). It was one of the most painful meetings I can remember. I felt under assault from an arrogant critic with a seemingly antifeminist bias. Deutsch was relentless in making me feel that I was to blame for what he scorned as the mediocre quality of Argonne, its leadership, its science, its governance and management. He ordered me to do something about all this quickly, or else. We did indeed do quite a lot in the succeeding couple of years, recruiting Walter Massey (later Chicago's vice president for research and ultimately president of Morehouse College) as laboratory director, negotiating the dissolution of the consortium and Chicago's assumption of sole responsibility for management, and creating a successful system of governance by establishing a board to which we were able to recruit eminent scientists, engineers, and executives of technology and other firms. This actually became a model for other national laboratories; the DOE liked it. The department's reviews of the laboratory began to improve significantly. But the political issues swirling around DOE and national science policy, as also around the relationship between university and federal oversight, were always with us, and dealings with the secretary of DOE and with the department's difficult bureaucracy, its constantly changing leadership, and its shifting policies often a nightmare.

The university's Division of Continuing Education was, to put it simply, a mess. A Center for Continuing Education designed by the architect Edward Durrell Stone and sited on the south side of the Midway was in need of extensive renovation. More important, its programs were failing to attract people to its South Side location. In order to raise income, the center was offering programs, such as wine tasting, that were entirely unsuitable for the university's sponsorship. I had finally to ask for the dean's resignation and surprised the Kellogg Foundation, which had funded the building originally and was ready to support its renovation, by telling its president we would not want the money he was ready to give us for refurbishing the center's facilities, informing him that we intended to turn it to new purposes. And so we did, to his reluctant assent (the original grant had specified continuing education, then the Kellogg Foundation's principal interest, as the building's purpose) and on our own nickel. The division of continuing education came under new leadership, its programs recast to conform to university standards. New programs that in some cases offered degrees, such as the master of liberal arts, were added to the portfolio. All were now assembled under the umbrella of the Graham School of

Continuing Liberal and Professional Studies, housed in Chicago's Gleacher Center downtown. Programs that aimed to award degrees had to be approved by the Council of the University Senate, and queries were raised there about whether a master's degree from an extension program might lower or dilute the status of corresponding divisional degrees, but these objections were overcome as it was established that the courses were to be taught by university faculty with the same rigor and expectations as obtained on campus, and that degree titles would be differentiated. Having taught a course on Renaissance intellectual history in the master of liberal arts program, I can testify to the interesting mix of older students who brought an intense motivation and an enlarged scope of life experience to their discussion of the texts we read. Their reactions were often fresh and illuminating, their responses differing in fascinating ways from those of the undergraduates I was used to teaching. I can testify also to the very good work that most of them submitted at the end. I saw a growing hunger for an expanded liberal education on the part of professionals still engaged in their jobs and others now in retirement who in their college days might have been more vocationally directed, a growing interest in intellectual exploration and an immersion in culture. I think this phenomenon will continue to grow as people live longer and look for meaningful knowledge and a broadened experience as they age. The liberal arts, shrinking in the world of collegiate education, may become in part the province of older generations.

In my earliest days I had imagined that capital projects would be centered almost entirely on the needs for continuing maintenance and major renovation. We did indeed do extensive work on all the quadrangle buildings with the exception of the dreadful Administration Building constructed after the war, its austere functionalism (not that it functioned very well) clashing with the neo-Gothic harmony of the main quadrangle.

My time in office saw more new building than I had ever anticipated. The Court Theater, to house the university's repertory program, and the Smart Museum's exhibition space came first, together with the new Mitchell Hospital, which had already been on the drawing board but needed, for reasons of cost, to be reduced to an affordable scale. One very popular project, to build a natatorium, a priority strongly advocated by John Wilson and constantly urged on me by everyone—we had a lot of recreational swimmers in our community—we never managed to realize, despite many preparations for doing so. We came close, even leaving behind a complete architect's design. But every time we were ready to move, something more important for academic purposes came into sight.

First came a unique opportunity to take over the John Crerar Library, a private research library, founded in 1894 and then housed at the Illinois Institute of Technology, its rich collections focused on science and technology and on their histories. Merging our collections with Crerar's, it became our principal science library. A new building bearing the John Crerar name anchored a new science quadrangle (that his name be on his library building was a requirement laid down in Crerar's will; he specified also that there be no immoral books, by which he meant French novels, in his library). People understood, with a touch of sadness, that this cause had clear precedence over a swimming pool. Next came a generous gift that allowed us to build the Kersten physical sciences teaching center at the corner of the new quadrangle; later an equally innovative teaching facility for the biological sciences rose across the street. In the meantime the law school had completed an addition of considerable size to its Saarinen building, cleverly designed by his protégé Kevin Roche to maintain the style and look of Saarinen's building. The Graduate School of Business needed more downtown space for its executive and other off-campus programs that had become too numerous and well attended to be contained in its existing location. The school wanted to establish a visible and welcoming presence in the city, and the Gleacher Center provided facilities that could also be used for conferences and dinners by outside groups attracted to the center's services and its setting near the confluence of Lake Michigan and the Chicago River.

There were other building projects of lesser size, but all were generally great fun as we interviewed and chose architects, watched as blueprints became limestone (actually sometimes concrete produced to look exactly like Indiana limestone, the university's dominant physical fabric) and mortar. Always hopeful, we went on visiting recently constructed natatoria at other universities. I was stunned to find that some had been designed solely for varsity teams. I remember watching a young man doing laps up and down, over and over, in the otherwise empty varsity pool at the University of Michigan; I was told that he would be there for most of the day. It seemed an unrewarding way to spend four years of college.

Early in my time a proposal to establish a department of computer science came under discussion. Faculty interested in the field were housed in the Department of Mathematics. We had neither a department nor a field of concentration in computer science. The absence of a school of engineering at the university helped explain the university's late entry into the field. The deliberations of the Council of the University Senate reflected nervousness that a program of concentration in this area would be overrun by students flocking to it for vocational reasons. Some wondered whether it belonged to the liberal arts. It was decided to approve only a joint concentration in which students were required to add a second subject to their study of computer science. The council members were given to understand also that the new department's thrust would be toward the basic and theoretical dimensions of its studies, thus giving what was considered a distinctive "Chicago" cast and justification to its program.

The university's practice is to select deans, with advice from a faculty search or review committee, largely from among the most productive faculty members of their divisions. The deans serve five-year terms that can, on review, be renewed; after their service they normally return to their faculty roles. The Division of the Physical Sciences, where I initially encountered a rather lethargic dean, progressed and flourished and saw a series of first-rate appointments under the leadership of a new dean, Stuart Rice, a distinguished chemist and a man of very high standards, ambitious for his highly ranked division and for the university as well. He was careful, imaginative, and determined in setting goals, relentless and purposeful in their accomplishment, and persuasive in his advocacy for the best of science in his division.

William Kruskal, professor of statistics and also a distinguished scholar, had become dean of the Division of the Social Sciences, long regarded as perhaps the strongest area of the university and frequently identified by the outside world with its Department of Economics. Many people identified the university with the "Chicago School," admiring or detesting it according to their political persuasion and unaware of the immense diversity of views actually represented across the institution. Bill's view of the dean's role was confined exclusively to his main goal of recruiting the most promising scholars one could find and evaluating candidates for appointment, renewal, and tenure with the utmost rigor. Nothing else mattered; he was simply uninterested in the other aspects of decanal administration. Bill had little sympathy for human irrationality or for subjects that in his opinion failed to meet his requirements of a scientific grounding and precision of method. He was a scrupulously fair-minded man, and the work of historians therefore presented him with special dilemmas. Our system of appointment and promotion calls for recommendations to move from a department to the dean to the provost and the president. Bill disagreed with a number of departmental recommendations and would meet with the provost and me in an attempt to resolve such cases; our discussions were both strenuous and stimulating. Bill's successor, the sociologist Edward Laumann, also an eminent scholar, had a broad knowledge of trends and developments across the entire range of the social sciences, a strategic outlook on the division as a whole, and a sociologist's interest in organizational structures and behaviors that made the administrative work he took up with unfailing energy and competence an intellectual challenge he enjoyed as well.

The Division of the Humanities offered some serious problems. The reasons were in part internal and in part related to increasingly contentious arguments concerning the humanities well beyond the borders of any single university.

On the larger stage of professional scholarship, the humanities were thought universally to be undergoing a deep crisis. Long experience had taught me that the humanities are always in crisis, but there could be no doubt—as the culture wars raged and battles over schools of critical thought intensified, and as new programs of cultural, multicultural, ethnic, and women's studies came into being—that the crisis of this time had in significant part to do with a loss of confidence and a painful uncertainty over the definition and worth of the humanities themselves. In addition, the rapid spread of new technologies raised deep concerns about how these would affect, and how they might be assimilated into, humanistic scholarship. And, as always, but with rising attention, the value of humanistic study was under question by those who thought education should give greater attention to imparting "useful" knowledge with some relevance to the "real" world.

The position of the humanities at the center of a liberal education had become less secure; faith in liberal education and its benefits, always regarded with some suspicion in the thread of American culture, appeared increasingly challenged. Humanists were excoriated for their use of an esoteric language inaccessible to those outside their sectarian circles, the humanities accused of having lost their way in a maze of trivial and abstruse scholarship and in curricula that no longer posed the truly important questions of life and ethics or taught the most important texts and subjects. A widening chasm had emerged between the expectations and interests of those wanting to study literature, philosophy, and other humanistic areas and those of a growing corps of professional scholars and critics who were going in new directions, ones that their own more traditional colleagues might reject as well.

Academic humanists were on the defensive. They felt underappreciated and overworked, misunderstood and underfunded. They envied what they saw as the more generous support given to the sciences and social sciences. The anxieties and insecurities and conflicts that swirled around the humanities provoked some very interesting writing and debate, as well as some that was drearily predictable and repetitious. The conviction of crisis inevitably created pessimistic attitudes and sharp divisions within faculties of the humanities everywhere.

The Division of the Humanities embraced a very large number of departments and degree-granting interdisciplinary committees, many quite small. Each was competing with the rest for limited resources and unwilling to defer to the division's interests as a whole, or to consider any consolidation of programs or changes in the usual ways of doing things. The dean had accepted the position at John Wilson's request as an act of citizenship. His own views on the academy were deeply conservative. A traditionalist totally committed to the university as an ideal that drove his life, he was often unhappy with the behaviors he observed among his colleagues. They in turn found him severe and uncompromising. While he attempted conscientiously to adapt to new and unfamiliar tendencies and trends, it was a struggle. His analysis of what needed to be done was convincing, but his respect for the existing practices and rights asserted by the division's units kept him from pressing for action. As his term drew to an end, I found it almost impossible to replace him. It seemed as if an entire generation of leadership had gone missing, as if the profession of the humanities had failed to develop scholars who cared for the work of tending to its health and welfare. The most senior faculty had to be called on to fill a disturbing vacuum. Some six years later it had become possible to appoint an outstanding dean from the faculty's ranks, the musicologist Philip Gossett, whose energy, intensity, and vision initiated a very productive era for the division. Even so, a profound sense of crisis still lingered among humanists everywhere, as did their fear of becoming marginalized in the larger scheme of things that mattered to universities and to their publics.

The Oriental Institute draws from scholars of many different disciplines in the humanities and social sciences as a center of studies in ancient Near Eastern civilization and its languages. It is home to a very well-attended museum (I received letters from several children writing, after their visits, that they wanted to grow up to be Egyptologists) and a sponsor of important archaeological expeditions throughout the Middle East. A leader of research and archaeological discovery in its field, the institute also maintains a research center in Egypt, Chicago House at Luxor, where the Epigraphic Survey—directed to documenting, reproducing, and publishing the inscriptions and relief scenes found on Luxor's temples and tombs—has been conducted since its beginnings in 1924. There was much to worry about during the times of political tumult in Egypt; the preservation of Luxor's temples and of Chicago House itself came under serious threat.

The Oriental Institute's linguistic projects are immense works of scholarship that possess long time horizons. The *Assyrian Dictionary*, launched in 1921, was completed in 2011. The *Hittite Dictionary*, initiated in 1945, still has a way to go. The patient scholars responsible for these projects have opened to view and made it possible to expand our knowledge and understanding of entire civilizations. Universities exist for the purposes of education and discovery, and also for the imperative of keeping alive subjects that might otherwise vanish and studies that may not be in fashion or attract large numbers but that are indispensable to preserving and interpreting the heritage of the past and its meaning in the present.

11

Finale

University presidents are conventionally expected to bemoan their lot and to tell you of their hard life: on call twenty-four hours every day, under constant pressure to raise more funds, torn away from the classrooms and laboratories or libraries for which they pine, harassed by their many constituencies, embroiled in the controversies and petty politics of academia, subjected to incessant and conflicting waves of unsolicited advice and attack, and treated as responsible for the derelictions of the young and the controversial opinions of their faculty, as well as for the evident decline or laxity or total failure of higher education and its institutions.

Such complaints contain some truth, but I will admit to having greatly enjoyed my work. Not that every hour or day or task was one of joy or significant accomplishment, but the association with a remarkable institution, the appeal of its powerful sense of mission, and the satisfactions that arose from every first-rate appointment and every special achievement or contribution of its individual members certainly outweighed the stresses and difficulties and strengthened an absorbing sense of working toward worthwhile purposes.

A president's day-to-day life is of course not simply occupied with high-minded thought and dialogue or strictly academic matters. Personnel matters dominate. In dealing with those, I found it often necessary to make and to communicate hard decisions and to be tough-skinned without, I hoped, becoming insensitive or overly thick-skinned. That was a concern as I encountered the impact of some unhappiness or opposition or unpopularity;

these needed not to be callously brushed off, but lived with, accepting that some things come with the territory. Anyone seeking uninterrupted popularity and support would definitely be in the wrong place. One needed to be as understanding as possible of the people and points of view involved, careful not to allow one's instinctive reactions to the discomforts of dissent and protest to prevent revisiting an issue when new developments and arguments made it clear one should do so.

Academic administration carries with it a function similar to teaching, given the role of speaking to a wide variety of audiences about the value of the higher learning, and given also the importance of explaining decisions that will never be to everyone's liking and that require clear explication in terms of the considerations, judgments, and contexts that underlie the arguments on different sides of their deliberation. Opponents who disagree with the outcomes will, in the main, respect reasoned explanation and discussion. Unanimity on any issue is the last thing one expects in a university. Nor should it be otherwise. The ideal academic environment is, after all, a space for competing views and independent voices; one's duty is to keep it that way.

The academic world is home to some large egos engaged in a restless, never-sated search for ever more attention and recognition. Their demands may at the same time be masking large insecurities. Scholars have great independence in their teaching and research, but that freedom is not entirely easy. Most are working in a greater or (as with scientific research teams) lesser isolation on their own to meet high, and perhaps never quite reachable, standards they have set for themselves, engaged in an uncertain competition for acknowledgment, judgment, and reward, not absolutely sure of how they might be viewed by students and peers. Each lecture, each publication, each grant proposal is a kind of test. Every review or critique may be a source of reinforcement or enhanced confidence or of injured pride or self-doubt. Those conditions of academic life and its drive for excellence in performance and scholarly discovery can produce both insecurity and creativity in combination.

The majority of faculty are reasonably comfortable with these features of their profession, but a small minority of prima donnas take up a disproportionate amount of time. Distinguished scholars can make some startling demands. A memorable case involved a candidate who refused appointment unless and until he and his teenage son could meet Michael Jordan. We arranged for this to happen, and the candidate finally accepted our offer. A few years later he was gone to another university that lacked a successful professional basketball team in its location but could extend much by way of compensation, recognition, and affection. In a short while he departed there and went on to yet another institution, presumably needing a fresh dose of excitement in being again an acclaimed center of attention in a drawn-out process of seduction.

There is a pastoral side to a president's role, much of it invisible and usually delicate. You learn things about colleagues that you'd rather not know, and in some instances you become familiar with the unhappy, sometimes disabling problems that can overcome their lives and begin to shadow or even ruin their professional careers, once so promising. One of the hardest, not always successful tasks I undertook was that of offering counsel and assistance when difficulties arose with people (often in denial) suffering from alcohol abuse, or intractable family problems, or loss of ambition or interest in their work. In a number of cases it was necessary to convince people who could no longer cope, and whose colleagues and students found it no longer possible to help or continue a relationship with them, to retire. Each case was different, but almost every year one or two faculty members had to be persuaded or required to give up their tenure.

The university was generally regarded as a kind of welfare state with a safety net for all contingencies. And it is, of course, a political organism that shapes another presidential role, one somewhat similar to that of mayor of a small city. The academic city is meant to provide a considerable range of services for its residents. These include basic infrastructure, housing, transportation, medical and counseling services, child-care facilities, recreational and meeting facilities, museums and concert halls and theaters, benefits and amenities of many kinds. The city's bureaucracy oversees it all, and the mayor is held responsible when any of it goes wrong, expected to respond quickly to a variety of vociferous constituents. It is very helpful not only to possess political and diplomatic skills but to find some real enjoyment in using them in order to deal with the generally anarchic internal life of the academic city, and to deal with the surrounding community on matters of town and gown.

Some purists in the academy bristle at the very thought of "political" behavior or of presidents as managers. My own view is that their work is to enable the university's members to do their best thinking, learning, teaching, and research in an environment of the greatest freedom, free to be purists on behalf of the goals that define the city of the intellect. Needless to say, that calls not only for decisions on academic programs and appointments but for finding, allocating, and preserving resources, for attending to student life, for tending relationships with alumni, donors, and friends and neighbors of the university, and for managing the corporate affairs of a very complex institution.

My days were therefore filled also with those issues and in addition with negotiations of all sorts, with never-ending meetings, with ceremony and speech making, receptions and dinners and fund-raising events. I felt like a speaking machine, having to say words for one occasion or other, so it seemed, almost daily, and spending late nights toiling over speeches and lectures that would soon be forgotten or would perhaps not have been listened to at all, like the commencement talks I gave in profusion.

There was a certain irony in this, since the University of Chicago does not allow outside speakers at its own convocations, choosing a faculty member to present a talk instead. For this reason President Clinton was told he could not deliver the address when the White House informed the university out of the blue that he planned to come and do so, but he came anyway and was allowed to make a few remarks after the main faculty speaker. He then quickly disappeared to a Cubs' game at Wrigley Field (perhaps the real motive behind his visit).

Convocations brought honorary degree recipients to be celebrated on campus. The University of Chicago awards honorary degrees only to scholars nominated by the faculty. Legend has it that when Edward Levi was dean and suggested to the law faculty that they nominate Queen

Elizabeth II on her visit to the city, they responded by asking, "What has she published?"

All year long there were guests to be entertained and introduced to the university, many of them well-known, visitors from the worlds of politics, science, scholarship, and the arts (and even of sports, like Arthur Ashe) whose presence enriched university life. Helmut Schmidt, former chancellor of West Germany, was regarded by many as the last genuine statesman of the Western world and attracted overflow crowds that began to melt away as his public lecture reached the two-hour mark. For me, the most memorable moment of his visit came at my dinner table where, after Schmidt had delivered a bitter attack on American economic policies, which he blamed for the terrible state of the world's economy, the economist George Stigler, who had just received the Nobel Prize in economics, ventured a mild objection and was immediately interrupted by Schmidt, who snapped, "You know *nothing, nichts* of economics."

Several annual occasions stirred a special resonance within the university community. Convocations, needless to say, were among those, but also such events as the Ryerson Lecture, which featured members of the faculty chosen by a committee of peers to discuss their scholarly work, each lecture and its accompanying gathering reaffirming the sense of a prized intellectual environment. We held black-tie dinners to honor faculty who won Nobel awards, eight in my fifteen years as president (two in physics and six in economics). I always asked the honoree what he would most like in the way of menu and program. The great astrophysicist Subrahmanyan Chandrasakhar said he would like macaroni and cheese and a Beethoven quartet.

Charles and I found the official duties of social life and hospitality generally quite enjoyable. He did not attend every event, having plenty to do in the long evenings required for his own work, nor did this seem to arouse concerns, as it would likely have done had he been a female spouse. People recognized the demands of his full-time profession and respected his privacy. He went about his business like everyone else, as usual impervious to gossip and wholly absorbed in his extensive teaching and writing and other pursuits. No one acquainted with Charles could possibly have thought of him as a person who might interfere in or try to influence university matters. Not having a wife, I did the planning and oversight of dinners and receptions, selected the menus, and arranged the seating. I like doing those things, and I had plenty of help. Charles and I especially enjoyed dinners at home with colleagues from different fields and generations. I also regularly held lunches to meet and hear from young faculty, and found these opportunities both pleasant and a source of helpful insights into the younger faculty's experience of the university.

Ours was a social life downtown as well, often but not always connected to the university. I was expected to join in the circle of Chicago's civic leadership, an expectation that caused some glitches. The Commercial Club, which held monthly lunches to hear and discuss talks on subjects of current interest, had always held its meetings at the Chicago Club, a venerable home for the male elite of Chicago. The president of the University of Chicago was automatically made a member of the Commercial Club. What to do? The Commercial Club told the Chicago Club it could no longer meet there. The Chicago Club asked for time in which it would hold a vote to allow women to pass through its doors as visitors and, if that were positive, would construct a ladies' room. All this was done, and I entered the sacred space without incident. The skies did not fall, and the dining business of the Chicago Club showed new signs of life as wives could now join their husbands inside its walls for dinner before the symphony.

The club's board next took the still-bolder step of admitting two women (a prominent lawyer and me) to membership, not without controversy and the threat of lawsuits, and only after raising the initiation fee. Over the years, it was my fate to coeducationalize more than one club. But when I turned an invitation down, as I mostly did for clubs in other cities, seeing no reason to pay fees for a club I might never or rarely use, it was thought mean and ungrateful, as though I had rejected an honor extended for my sake only after the most painful and selfless struggle on the part of those generous and courageous enough to ask me in.

I traveled frequently on short trips for alumni and development activities and for board meetings, talks, and the meetings of organizations

like the American Association of Universities at which one met and com-
miserated with the presidents of other major research universities. They
afforded excellent opportunities to see friends; I always profited especially from conversations with such leaders as Derek Bok of Harvard, Bill
Bowen of Princeton, and Michigan's Harold Shapiro (later at Princeton).
The AAU meetings could be useful in terms of discussing problems shared
among all universities, but disappointing in the association's ultimately
watered-down statements and recommendations for addressing them—for
example, on such questions as pork-barrel funding. The bland documents
that issued from 1 Dupont Circle, the rather depressing headquarters for a
whole coterie of higher education associations, reflected the differences of
interest (or, at times, courage) among institutions reluctant to offend the
Washington powers that be or to risk losing sources of political and financial support they had hoped to secure.

In national campaign years, the AAU and the ACE (American Council
on Education) had the custom of sending their chairs to brief presidential
candidates on matters affecting higher education. In 1980, when I chaired
the ACE, President Carter had no desire to talk to us, but Ronald Reagan's
advisers invited the AAU's chairman, Sandy Boyd (then president of the
University of Iowa), and me to the Reagans' home in Pacific Palisades
where he was taking a break.

Sandy and I arrived at a comfortable and tastefully decorated house that
afforded an air of calm and a fine view. There Mr. Reagan, dressed in chi-
nos and polo shirt, greeted us with the sociable warmth of a man who had
nothing much to do and was delighted to have neighbors drop in. "How
are you, Mrs. Nixon?" he asked me. This was puzzling—later I remembered
that Nixon's mother had been named Hannah; perhaps that was the connection. Mr. Reagan apparently noticed his error and went on to show that
he did know who I was by telling us that when he was very young, his family had lived for a while on the South Side of Chicago on Cottage Grove Avenue, quite close to the University of Chicago. He and his brother had run
away one day, had crossed the Midway (Mr. Reagan remembered the dips
built into its grounds), and ended up on the university's main quadrangle;

here they were discovered and returned to their home. What struck me was Reagan's memory of having seen horses pulling fire engines up and down the Midway, a reminder of his age.

Shortly after we had settled into the living room, his chief of staff and others arrived, breathless and alarmed that their boss might already have said something. Mr. Reagan was unperturbed and gracious to the nth degree, listening patiently to what we had to say. He seemed in no hurry for us to leave. The next day he was in Texas, questioning the theory of evolution.

I was unexpectedly to see President Reagan several times again in the following year. In his presidential campaign of 1980, Ronald Reagan had promised that he would abolish the National Endowments for the Arts and Humanities, but when he arrived at the White House he found its switchboard lighting up with calls from Los Angeles friends pleading for their museums and symphony not to lose endowment funding. He was faced also by the prospect that Sidney Yates, a staunch advocate for the endowments (and a loyal graduate and friend of the University of Chicago), might use his power as chairman of the subcommittee responsible for their budget authorizations to stall other initiatives the administration might want supported.

It became clear to the White House that a rescue operation was needed to allow the president to step back gracefully. To that end a Presidential Task Force on the Arts and Humanities was appointed in May 1981, with two cochairs: Charlton Heston for the arts and me for the humanities. It was not a pairing I could ever have imagined. Later, after the task force's work was well underway, a third cochair was added in the person of Daniel Terra, a wealthy Chicago businessman and art collector who had, as a reward for serving as finance chairman of the Reagan campaign, been given the title (never used before or since) of "ambassador at large for cultural affairs." What it meant, no one, including the undiplomatic ambassador himself, was sure, and he was paid little attention.

Charlton Heston and I got on well. We never discussed politics, or guns, and found ourselves in agreement on most of the matters before us. Charlton was intelligent, fair-minded, and hardworking, always courteous and tolerant, never full of himself, a good colleague. He wanted to ensure that the humanities received equal time and attention with the arts and deferred to me on that topic. A graduate of Northwestern, he believed in the importance of a liberal arts education founded on the classics of thought and literature.

Walking around or riding an elevator with Charlton Heston was an adventure as people became excitedly aware of his presence (and baffled by mine). A staff gathered helpful data. In the end, after four busy months of discussions and of hearings open to the public in different parts of the country, we concluded, with surprising agreement among committee members who actually represented a wide range of initial positions, that the federal government did indeed have a role, that private-public partnerships and collaboration in funding should be the still-more-encouraged wave of the future, and that the White House should be host to events that showcased the arts and the humanities. The former was easily arranged, and a program of televised "Performances at the White House" was soon initiated. The latter was not so easy; everyone could say what the arts were, but few could define or think of similar ways to represent the humanities.

We met several times with President Reagan in the course of our work, and each time he told the same story, underscoring his skepticism over public financing of the arts, about a grant of two thousand dollars made during his governorship by the California Arts Council for the purpose of having chamber music performed in laundromats statewide.

We pursued sometimes-difficult discussions with fellow members, some of them strong conservatives who had professed opposition to the endowments, believing that government should not stick its nose into cultural activities: men like David Packard (cofounder of Hewlett Packard and deputy secretary of defense in the Nixon administration), Joseph Coors (of brewery fame, an ardent rightist and contributor to right-wing causes), Richard Mellon Scaife (the same), and George Roche (president of Hillsdale College, an evangelical institution that took pride in accepting no federal funds for any purpose, ever). All except Roche, who abstained, signed on to the final product. Quite a few other members, among them the wonderful and outspoken Beverly Sills, had supported the endowments from the out-set. The president was an amiable host of the White House lunch at which I presented the task force report (Heston was detained on location), and accepted it with seeming enthusiasm. Another of our recommendations led to the formation of a committee, still in existence, to support and advocate for the arts and humanities under White House sponsorship.

During the 1980s and '90s I served on a number of other national committees concerned with higher education and a few with the humanities, and on a series of boards, often as their first woman director or trustee, since boards were only just beginning to appoint women members. Service on boards, both corporate and not-for-profit, was interesting in itself and also afforded instructive experience. Participation in other organizations allowed one to see one's own institution from broader and fresher perspectives. The academy tends too easily to insularity and to letting its own provincial preoccupations blot out other portions of the world's larger canvas.

Among my numerous not-for-profit commitments, I was particularly active on the boards of the Andrew W. Mellon Foundation and the Howard Hughes Medical Institute for many years. These were important and deeply satisfying associations for me. Each of these organizations set a philanthropic standard. Each made a unique contribution to the world of higher education, Mellon above all in the humanities and Hughes in science.

I learned from service on boards a great many things not unrelated to the work of academic administration. I came to know more about areas of management relevant to every kind of organization and to gain increased understanding of the weight borne by distinctive institutional cultures and their sustenance in very different kinds of organizations in the midst of major change and uncertainty. I learned a great deal, too, about how boards could be effective, and how to understand the line between board oversight and management responsibility. I saw that first-rate directors spoke when they had something to say and not otherwise, penetrated to the heart of the questions they addressed, were never reluctant to raise, and to raise with constructive civility, the hard ones, and provided quiet leadership to their colleagues, never claiming, but being granted, a special authority by their peers. I saw how often directors observed a kind of sen-atorial courtesy, especially if they were themselves CEOs, and how fre-quently they were thankful to have someone else ask the questions they might want answered but were reluctant to raise publicly.

As president I became an ex officio member of the university's board of trustees. It was a very large board; its committees therefore were es-pecially important in the oversight of the different areas of board's re-sponsibility. The majority of its members were Chicagoans; only perhaps a third held degrees from the university. Some trustees were significantly more involved than others and were likely to be members of the executive committee, which functioned in many ways as the real governing board, meeting monthly and coming to decisions for immediate action, and to recommendations that required (and generally received) ratification from the full board.

Our board had a well-deserved reputation of standing firm, in the past as now, on the critical matters of academic freedom and university auton-omy. The trustees honored the faculty's responsibilities for curricular mat-ters, standards of appointment, and the conduct of teaching and research. Those who had an itch to take a more direct role in such matters usually learned to exercise restraint, although I was of course sure to hear their opinions voiced forcefully in private conversation. The board had long ago delegated final approval of academic appointments to the president (in most universities, at least formal approval by the board is required before an appointment takes effect), a key symbol of academic authority.

A university board's greatest responsibility is that of looking to the fu-ture, of asking how decisions made now will affect that future, of ensuring that short-term considerations will not ransom long-term goals, that the future is not sacrificed to the present, and that the activities and actions of the institution are consistent with its mission, its integrity of purpose, and its own best values. Trustees have an obligation to ensure that long-term planning is taking place and to participate in defining its assump-tions and conclusions. They have the duty of reviewing and assessing the institution's programmatic directions and redirections, of helping set its priorities. They are charged with ensuring its adherence to the policies and procedures that they have approved, with seeing to the financial health of the institution, setting investment policies and approving those major capital projects that create the physical endowment in their charge. Above all, it is essential that trustees be clear about, ready to affirm and reaffirm, the mission to which all are pledged. While trustees ideally bring with them different forms of specialized expertise, the hope is that their concern is for the whole of an organization's purpose, and that they bring their best thinking to bear on how its different parts can function most effectively and with the greatest degree of coordination to realize and sustain that overriding goal.

Chicago's board was both very supportive and prepared to ask the hard questions, ready also to argue through different views to assist with difficult decisions at the critical junctures we confronted. I was fortunate (more than were some of my peers) to work with trustees who stayed united over issues that were sharply divisive for a number of boards elsewhere.

Those issues included such matters as the extension of equal benefits to gay couples during an era in which they could not legally marry. Ours was one of the first universities to make equal benefits the rule, a step unanimously approved by Chicago's trustees.

The board's responsibility for investments caught it up in the controversies raging over investing in shares of corporations doing business in South Africa. Those controversies had had a long history, stretching back to the 1960s, and the movement for divestment continued until the ending of apartheid. Such investments, it was argued, were unethical violations of an institution's professed values and had the effect of associating it with the support and reinforcement of the evils of apartheid; their divestment would represent an expression of the university's responsibility to promote the larger social good and would help put pressure on South Africa's governing powers to effect change. Proponents of divestment maintained that defenders of the status quo failed to recognize or act on the obligations that educational institutions above all should rightly assume to speak out on the most profound and significant issues of a world yearning for freedom and justice. At one level, the arguments had to do with South Africa per se; at another, with the recurring question of the university's role in taking corporate positions on matters other than those that affect the mission of higher education directly, such as threats to academic freedom or to basic institutional autonomies.

That question had been eloquently addressed at the university in 1967 by a faculty committee charged with preparing a statement on the university's role in political and social action. Known as the Kalven Report, it remains the best statement I know of why the university needs to resist speaking as a corporate entity when its own principal purpose is to create the conditions under which its members can speak individually and freely for themselves, whatever their views on topics of common concern.

"To perform its mission in the society," the report declares, "a university must sustain an extraordinary environment of freedom of inquiry and maintain an independence from political fashions, passions, and pressures. A university, if it is to be true to its faith in intellectual inquiry, must embrace, be hospitable to, and encourage the widest diversity of views within its own community. It is a community but only for the limited, albeit great, purposes of teaching and research. It is not a club, it is not a trade association, it is not a lobby. Since the university is a community only for these limited and distinctive purposes, it is a community that cannot take collective action on the issues of the day without inhibiting that full freedom of dissent on which it thrives. It cannot insist that all of its members favor a given view of social policy; if it takes collective action, therefore, it does so at the price of censuring any minority who do not agree with the view adopted." Kalven added that "this neutrality has its complement in the fullest freedom for its faculty and students as individuals to participate in political action and social protest. It finds its complement, too, in the obligation of the university to provide a forum for the most searching and candid discussion of public issues."[1]

At the same time, the Kalven Report took note of the fact that there could arise exceptional instances posing conflicts with social values so extreme that the university might decide to act in its corporate capacity. Here, clearly, even those in agreement with the report's major conclusions could disagree among themselves as to whether a given issue should qualify as such an exception. Adherents will always see their cause as so compelling as to count it an exception of this kind; its opponents maintain the opposite view. That represents the central point of argument in each instance of major contention. Each case becomes generalized once again to the question of the university's mission. There are and can be no precise rules to invoke; there can only be a set of principles and precedents subject to differences of interpretation and judgment to guide their application to individual cases as they arise. Every controversy is rendered still more complex as related but sometimes peripheral questions inevitably get attached to the cause with which it all began.

The movement for divestment of university-held shares in companies doing business in South Africa had many adherents in the university community. It lasted throughout my time in office. I was opposed to total divestment and in favor of subscribing to the Sullivan Principles as guidelines; the board of trustees was in agreement. We sided strongly with the principles laid out in the Kalven Report while believing that special caution and detailed analysis were required in considering any potential investments. It seemed to us that the companies whose shares were held in the university's portfolio, major blue-chip corporations like GM and IBM, were, in following their own workplace rules and the Sullivan guidelines, to some degree actually subverting the rules of apartheid, and that prospects for foreign investment by large international corporations could perhaps make some difference in persuading the South African business community to put pressure on their government. As investors, we should of course not be selecting companies that were likely to perform badly or behave unethically in their corporate operations. We thought, too, that were we to divest our holdings, we might feel very clean and virtuous and pat ourselves on our collective back, but any shares we discarded would in all likelihood be purchased by investors who had no concern at all for the racial politics of South Africa. By divesting, we would have forfeited what little we could have done by voting on shareholder resolutions that might exercise some positive influence on a company's policies and practices.

I recall a conversation with the editor of our student newspaper who was editorializing relentlessly in favor of divestment. Why, I asked him, did the *Maroon* take advertising from companies, like General Motors or IBM, the very companies from which he was passionately urging the university to divest? You don't understand, he replied; it's about the freedom of the press.

Debates, protests, petitions came in waves. I participated in a number of public debates, one with a black South African labor leader, others with faculty and students, in addition to talking with individuals and smaller groups, and arranging two or three occasions on which students met with trustees. In a final public outpouring, a faculty group called for a meeting of the University Senate for the purpose of discussing and voting on whether the university should divest (such a vote could only, of course, be advisory). The faculty's Committee of the Council negotiated an agreement on the rules of the game for the meeting: the spokesman would preside; there would be two speeches of no more than ten minutes on each side; members unable to attend the meeting would receive ballots that would count in the final totals so that the fullest response of all interested faculty could be heard.

The occasion was an example of faculty governance at its most effective in designing and mounting a serious and orderly debate. I stated my case for the university's position. People voiced their views in sharp words but in a civil fashion, the rules for discussion obtained, and at the end those present voted to support the university's stance. The professor who had organized the call for a senate meeting said that, while he disagreed with the outcome, he would accept it, satisfied that a fair and searching process and a full opportunity to be heard had taken place.

In the spring of my first year a recommendation from a faculty committee landed on my desk. It urged that Robert McNamara be invited to receive a new prize called the Albert Pick Award for International Understanding.

I was unaware of the award, established and funded in the name of a former trustee, or of the selection committee appointed the previous year. McNamara was now president of the World Bank and preoccupied with issues of poverty, hunger, and economic development in the Third World, but he remained the most visible and detested symbol of the war in Vietnam and its wrongs. The reaction against his speaking, not to mention the award, was intense. Demands that I cancel the invitation came from many quarters. Studs Terkel appeared on the quadrangle with a megaphone to condemn my behavior and express his outrage over the university's sad decline (he was a graduate). A protest movement gathered strength and numbers; its stated plan was to hold a peaceful demonstration outside the hall where McNamara was to speak.

The dinner took place on a beautiful warm spring evening, perfect for demonstrators and dinner guests alike. The guests passed through a reasonably good-natured phalanx of protesters at the entrance; the demonstrators then assembled across the street and did their thing. Once inside, the guests were happy to have seen real protesters, having heard so much about campus unrest and seen so many pictures of chanting students on TV.

Several of the seats assigned to members of the committee that had nominated McNamara were vacant. It was very disappointing that those colleagues lacked the courage of their convictions, not wanting to be seen associating with the wrong side. Ironically, McNamara's speech on international economic development would have been far more appreciated by those outside than it was inside by an audience of pretty conservative Chicagoans, some of them finding the speaker a little liberal for their taste.

The program ended, and the audience streamed out just as the demonstrators began to disperse, many of them headed down University Avenue. At this point, an activist Vietnam war veteran confined to a wheelchair rolled himself into the middle of the street and started to taunt students walking by, daring them to sit down in the street to show solidarity with him and contempt for all that McNamara represented. A number of students did so. Police appeared; the commanding officer called on the sitters to cease their obstruction of a public thoroughfare and, when few obeyed, made his request again, to little effect. Finally, he announced that this was now the third and last warning before they faced arrest.

Fate then intervened in the form of a bystander who threw—and here accounts vary—either a partially frozen cherry or (say some) strawberry Sara Lee cheesecake and succeeded in hitting the commander. He was not amused. Paddy wagons carried away the protesters who remained. They were soon released and taken home by staff from the dean of students' office, all but the veteran, who was left alone in his wheelchair on the sidewalk outside the police station.

In the meantime things had turned ugly at the house on University Avenue where the McNamaras were staying with us, surrounded by angry people shouting loudly and banging on the windows as if to break them. It was not a happy occasion, and it was surely stressful for Mr. McNamara. Nonetheless, he had been willing to endure trouble, and we had made the point that speakers were not to be disinvited, that unpopular figures who might express very unpopular views (as in fact his speech certainly did not) were to be heard and, if opposed, opposed in a way consistent with the norms of an academic community.

In the aftermath a faculty committee was charged with looking at the entire question of awards, and of what kinds of awards, if any, it was suitable for the university to sponsor. Conferring an award too easily seems to imply comprehensive endorsement of its recipient's actions and opinions. The committee released a report suggesting clear criteria for aligning any awards the university might make with areas clearly within the university's own competence and concern. On this basis, existing awards were reviewed, their precise purposes restated, and a consistent process for selection and bestowal adopted. It may sound a not very important matter, but, as the whole McNamara affair revealed, it was one of wider implications and repercussions than one might think.

A delegation of colleagues knowledgeable about the university's history came to see me that same spring with the message that it was time to start thinking about the university's centennial. I protested weakly that the anniversary was more than ten years away, and we had more urgent things to do right now. It was not too soon to start thinking, they insisted; a faculty committee should get going at once. I did as instructed, and the committee began its deliberations over what one might assume the easy question of when the centennial might actually be. The university was chartered in 1890, and a board was appointed and in turn appointed the founding president, William Rainey Harper, in 1891; he spent a year in planning and recruiting, and classes began on October 1, 1892. The original board had decided on the year 1891 as the founding date, and while the fifth and tenth and twenty-fifth anniversary celebrations counted from then, later anniversaries were inconsistent in their chosen dates. By my time sweatshirts bearing the university's seal proclaimed that the university was founded in 1892. Establishing a centennial date turned into a contentious and time-consuming issue. In the end we agreed to recognize our hundredth birthday during the academic year 1991–92 and stage a grand finale on October 1 of 1992. Yet another committee had then to be charged with suggesting guidelines for the year's program.

The University of Chicago is relatively young. There were still two or three people around who had met President Harper, and others who had witnessed the greater part of the university's history, living sources for a past still very much alive. Self-conscious about its own history, the university stressed the seriousness of its primary commitments to scholarship and discovery, to the life of the intellect, and to thinking about what that meant and about the nature of higher education and its goals. The guidelines developed for centennial programs emphasized the opportunity of a year dedicated to demonstrating those traditions through scholarly conferences, symposia on the higher learning, lectures by prominent academicians, exhibitions, and commemorative publications focused on the university's history, its faculty, and its architecture. As the year drew closer, various departments and schools planned their own contributions of conferences and lectures, while an oversight group of faculty and staff suggested the addition of musical and theatrical performances, special student events, and some moments of lighthearted entertainment. The university was, after all, the birthplace of Second City, and the spirit of satire continued to run strong in its veins.

The White Sox gave us a University of Chicago night at their ballpark. The Rockefeller Chapel choir sang the national anthem; I threw out the first ball (it reached the plate, just barely) and visited the announcers for an interview in their broadcasting booth. The night was clear, starlit and moonlit; everything seemed perfect. The White Sox lost.

For October 1 and the centennial's conclusion, I proclaimed that classes were canceled for the day, an edict that upset many students and faculty. A number of well-attended classes took place secretly—this was indeed the University of Chicago. The morning began with a convocation in Rockefeller Chapel. David Rockefeller spoke for the founder's family; Lord Roy Jenkins, as its chancellor, for Oxford University (the oldest university of the English-speaking world); and Derek Bok, president of Harvard, for American's oldest university. We then conferred honorary degrees on a group of scholars that included some distinguished Chicago alumni. Afterward we sponsored a huge picnic on the quadrangle to which everyone in the university community was invited. The free lunch lured even those who had been clandestinely attending class, and the occasion culminated with a rousing performance of the *1812 Overture* in which I was permitted to play the world's largest drum, originally an instrument proudly displayed at football games in the good old days and now returned for the present occasion from Texas, where it had found a new home after Chicago had banished Big Ten football. As the last note sounded, it began to rain. The centennial was over, and classes resumed.

It had been a day to recall the words Harper spoke in 1892 when he insisted that the work of the university would "begin October 1 as if it were the continuation of a work which had been conducted for a thousand years." Yet despite his reverence for tradition, Harper had set out to challenge tradition. He had announced his plan to "revolutionize College and University work in this country. It is 'bran splinter new,' and yet solid as the ancient hills." His ambition was to create a university, not a college from which might evolve a university, as happened in the case of most older universities, like the Ivies, as they began gradually to add graduate and professional programs.

The University of Chicago did not just happen. It had a plan. It was born as a university, and this proved decisive. Harper wanted to make the whole of his university somehow larger than the sum of its parts. It was his goal to make that sense of the whole triumph in the service of intellectual risk taking and innovative scholarship, to make it an organic dimension of the university's permanent culture. In that he had succeeded.

All told, however, the history of the university had not been, even in Harper's time, a story of unbroken progress. The university had seen times of trouble, constraint, and unresolved conflict, and was forced to renew and reconstitute itself in their wake. That helped lead the university at critical junctures to think about the nature of higher education, its goals, and the institutional conditions for their fulfillment. In this process, the university had repeatedly built on the particular mix of characteristics that constituted its DNA, reaffirming its core values amid the larger shocks and aftershocks that had affected all of higher education.

It was important that the anniversary not give way to indulgence in insular self-regard or romantic nostalgia but afford an occasion for serious reflection on the state of the higher learning. The celebration occurred at a moment in which the quality, the performance, and the directions of higher education were under intensive, often hostile, questioning. Universities had become more complicated and more central to the larger society than could have been imagined at the fiftieth anniversary, when Robert Hutchins asked whether the private research university could even survive, or at the seventy-fifth, when Edward Levi heard at his back the mounting volume of protests that were to mark his era and to cause deep rifts within the academic community. But their fundamental convictions were as pertinent at the one hundredth as they had been earlier. "A university," said Hutchins, "must stand for something, and that must be something other than what a vocal minority, or majority, demand at the moment." And Edward Levi, confronting a movement that aspired to remake the university into an instrument of social and political protest and action, was equally steadfast in speaking to his profound belief that universities are "the custodians not only of the many cultures of humanity, but of the rational process itself."

Looking around the universe of higher education, one saw too frequently an evident pursuit of the faddish or conformist, or the mere desire to avoid trouble at all costs or to engage in forms of competition among our universities that could scarcely enhance the robust quality and autonomy of distinctive centers of educational excellence. It appeared too often overcome by capitulation to ratings wars and to the distractions of a creeping consumerism. The view that its institutions should be models of harmony and virtue, protecting its members against discomfort with words or ideas that might offend, seemed to be gaining at the expense of rigorous adherence to the dictates of free expression and critical debate. A growing epidemic of self-promotion and preoccupation with rankings stimulated investment in new programs, buildings, services, and amenities that in turn required increased numbers of administrative personnel to deal with them. To manage a growing portion of undergraduate teaching, full-time faculty were gradually being replaced by part-time adjunct appointments.

The trends we witnessed in the early 1990s persisted and spread in the decades that followed. I watched them accumulate from my newly reclaimed position as a professor of history. I had retired in July 1993 and, after a year's leave, returned to full-time teaching. The transition was easier than I had thought possible. Somewhat nervous about returning to the classroom, I found myself in familiar surroundings, comfortable at once and thoroughly enjoying an experience of intellectual renewal and association with serious students eager to learn, debate, and explore.

Coming back after all those years away, I felt like a newly minted assistant professor with all the energy and excitement of embarking on a new course and syllabus, but in my case no longer having to suffer the anxieties of the quest for tenure. Sitting in my faculty office, I rarely wondered about what might be going on in the administration building. When headquartered there, we all thought the faculty were probably thinking all the time about what we might doing. It is in fact a sign that things are on the whole going pretty well when people are not thinking about what the administration is up to now. It suggests the administration is doing its assigned job to help free everybody else to do theirs.

It is almost impossible to generalize about students of different eras; one can only speak of some visibly shared behaviors, assumptions, or attitudes, and even then one is all too aware of a huge host of exceptions and variations. My students were polite, smart, somewhat more cautious and grade conscious than in earlier days, a pleasure to teach, eager for serious learning and discussion, committed to intellectual inquiry. They appeared at one level more sophisticated and experienced in the world than in the past, at another more inclined to assume that the institution owed them sanctuary. Students here and elsewhere seemed to be demanding full independence and full protection at the same time. Colleges no longer spoke of being in loco parentis, but students seemed to want them to act like their notion of *perfect* parents: tolerant, permissive, and caring—parents who would, should their exercise of freedom have unpleasant results, be there for them and make things right again.

Our students worked hard but did not, I thought, study quite as hard as they believed they did, perhaps because they were so incredibly busy, occupied with internships and community service and jobs, as well as with surfing the Internet and their extracurricular activities. The majority had had or were anticipating at least some study and travel abroad. Multitasking and résumé building were the order of the day. Students felt the pressures and insecurities of preparing for a world plunged into recession and an unpredictable future; old bets were suddenly off. They could hear, voiced ever more loudly, the widening public skepticism over liberal education and its asserted failure to provide the tools needed for the work and expectations of the world after college.

The defense of the liberal arts had come increasingly to be couched in instrumental terms. In advocacy for universities and their missions, their supporters argued increasingly that their existence and their privileges were justified by their important and useful contributions to the economy, and to the skills they provided for performing well in the tasks of employment and career. While all those claims surely have merit, the emphasis on such arguments by themselves reflected the weakness of a posture that failed to state sufficiently the fundamental importance of extending and transmitting a life-enriching culture that deepens the quality of social existence, or the goals of cultivating intellectual interests precisely because they matter greatly in themselves and are of enduring value in defining the animating spirit and vitality of civilization itself.

As I peered out from my observation post to the larger world of higher education, it appeared to me that universities were speaking of their mission in the formulaic phrases of tradition even as they were submitting to the new consumerism in the competitive search for public regard, and in a competition with their peers for prestige and for resources to support an institutional lifestyle that could not endure for the long term. The rising costs of knowledge, of its discovery and transmission and preservation, of its support in technologies and facilities, would, quite clearly, continue to outstrip the resources available for their support. This truth was most visible in the exploding costs of the sciences. One sign was that the expense of setting up newly appointed scientists with laboratory and other requirements had become often prohibitive.

There is a compelling need, I think, to simplify and stabilize by building more selectively on what an individual institution can do well, by encouraging a willingness to decide on priorities rather than proceed merely by adding without ever subtracting, and by speaking to the central purposes by which their choices are in the end to be measured.

To urge that universities be more modest and more realistic in what they undertake beyond the academic core is not to diminish the university's unique value to society. Nor does it mean that universities should abandon public service. But I would argue that the kinds of service they undertake or sanction should proceed from their educational and scholarly purposes, from what they do best or from what they can do that other institutions cannot do or do as well. The insistent demands for universities to make a difference in every important good cause that merits attention will only divert them from the long-term contributions that are theirs specifically to make. So, too, does the idea that the university's goal is to exemplify social virtue.

The desire that the university be an ideal community, a Garden of Eden from which the serpent has been banished, a model for bettering the social order beyond its borders as well: this has gained at the expense of a university's underlying raison d'être. For universities, the demands that they provide more and more assistance and direct more of their time to economic development, and concentrate their intellectual resources on the urgent need to find solutions for mitigating the social and educational problems of the world, have intensified the pressures that universities have always experienced to take up tasks that they are not well equipped to perform, spreading their programs and resources too thin.[2]

The air today is filled with melancholy diagnoses of the state of higher education and still gloomier prognostications about the future. The questions of spiraling costs and debt, of preparation for work in the real world, of access, of the worth of college attendance, dominate public discussion. And once again the fundamental principles of the academic universe—the commitment they require to freedom of thought and expression—are under scrutiny and debate.

I have experienced the university world today as one that has undergone a profound transformation in my lifetime, but also as one that has demonstrated the same basic struggles of self-definition and freedom as those of the past, and those struggles continue. Contemporary calls for divestments (for example, in companies associated with Israel or the production of fossil fuels and still other causes) or to boycotts of other institutions (as in the call for boycotting Israeli universities) are again raising issues of censorship and politicization, as are the calls for speakers to be disinvited or prevented from speaking. The political repression of universities on a massive scale continues to repeat itself in different parts of the world (as, for example, in Turkey) in a seemingly international contagion.

It is disturbing to see so much disregard for freedom of expression on campuses (not only in the United States) and dismaying to observe the extent to which its meaning is not only misunderstood but even distorted to justify disruptive behavior or defend rules outlawing speech deemed offensive. On the other hand, in the rising chorus of voices on the other side of the arguments over academic freedom we can observe some heartening signs that this foundational requirement continues to exercise a genuine power. They underscore, too, as they did in the past, that academic freedom is at its strongest when it can flourish in an environment of political freedom.

The belief that universities should be, above all, the homes of searching and critical intellectual vigor and thought needs recurrent renewal and reaffirmation. Universities have always been vulnerable to outside influence and to the threat of control and manipulation, and they have been vulnerable, too, to conformities imposed from within.

My parents and their fellow refugees survived the most extreme assault ever launched against universities from a totalitarian regime bent on reconfiguring the German universities, and the disciplines they taught and studied, into its own ideological image, distorting their purposes to serve its own ideological ends. The academic refugees had witnessed also the passivity and widespread complicity of the professoriate from which they had been dismissed. These émigrés brought with them to America a faith in the prospects of academic freedom and its goals. They were hopeful about the potential of the still-youthful universities of their new country to be freer, more democratic, and more open than the rigid and conservative institutions they had known at home even in better days, and they found those hopes in many ways fulfilled. They understood the fragility of all such institutions, revealed at critical times like those of the McCarthy years, and were determined to help keep intact the sometimes-wavering ethos of their existence.

I am grateful to have seen and learned so much through their eyes, to have had such rewarding guidance through their example, and to have been allowed, in the brighter circumstances of their adopted home, the satisfactions of an academic life.

Notes

Preface

1. Two useful handbooks: Hagemann and Krohn, ed., *Biographisches Handbuch*; Strauss and Roder, eds., *International Biographical Dictionary*. Coser, *Refugee Scholars*, remains the best general study (other than for the scientists); Krohn, *Intellectuals in Exile*, gives an overview in his early chapters. Other important accounts: Duggan and Drury, *The Rescue of Science and Learning*; *German Refugee Historians*, ed. Ritter; Jackman and Borden, eds., *The Muses Flee Hitler*; Lamberti, "The Reception of Refugee Scholars"; Lehmann and Melton, *Paths of Continuity*; Schale, Thümmler, and Vollmer, *Intellektuelle Emigration*. See also Heilbut, "The Intellectuals' Migration."

2. On the second generation: Daum, Lehmann, and Sheehan, eds., *The Second Generation*; Sonnert and Holton, *What Happened to the Children*. Daum's volume includes my "Some Reflections" (102–13), and I have borrowed from these comments on my life as a member of the second generation in the first several chapters of this memoir while going well beyond their scope.

Chapter 1. From Berlin and Heidelberg to Exile in London

1. Gerhard, "Reminiscences," 10.

2. Gerhard Ritter provides a good introduction to Meinecke and the considerable literature on him in his introduction to his *German Refugee Historians and Friedrich Meinecke*, 1–22. See also Felix Gilbert, "The Historical Seminar of the University of Berlin in the Twenties," in Lehmann and Sheehan, eds., *An Interrupted Past*, 67–76, and Gilbert, "Friedrich Meinecke," in *History: Commitment and Choice*, 67–87.

3. Masur, *Das ungewisse Herz*.

4. On the German historians who emigrated to the United States, see especially Epstein, *A Past Renewed*; *German Refugee Historians*, and Ritter, "Meinecke's Protégés"; Coser, *Refugee Scholars*, 278–96; Eakin-Thimme, *Geschichte im Exil*; Faulenbach, *Ideologie des deutschen Weges*; Kessler, ed., *Deutsche Historiker im Exil*; W. J. Mommsen, "German Historiography during the Weimar Republic and the Émigré Historians," in Lehmann and Sheehan, eds., *An Interrupted Past*, 32–66; Mitchell, *Fleeing Nazi Germany*; Sheehan, "Three Generations of German *Gelehrtenpolitik*"; Stern, "German History in America"; Wolf, *Deutsch-jüdische Emigrationshistoriker*.

5. October 14, 1924, trans. in *German Refugee Historians*, ed. Ritter, 237.

6. Gilbert, "Hajo Holborn: A Memoir," 8.

7. Remy, *The Heidelberg Myth*.

8. On the Hochschule: Korenblat, "The Deutsche Hochschule für Politik" and "A School for the Republic?"; R. Eisfeld, "From the Berlin Political Studies Institute to Columbia and Yale: Ernst Jaeckh and Arnold Wolfers," in Rösch, ed., *Émigré Scholars*, chap. 11.

9. See Gemelli, ed., *The "Unacceptables"* (essays on foundations in the interwar period).

10. On the New School refugee faculty: Krohn, *Intellectuals in Exile*. See also Lyman, "A Haven for Homeless Intellects."

11. English translations in *Germany and Europe*.

12. Noakes, "Ivory Tower," 376, 377.

13. Korenblat, "The Deutsche Hochschule für Politik," 425, 428.

14. Holborn, *Weimarer Reichsverfassung and Freiheit der Wissenschaft* (Leipzig: Meiner, 1933), 30: "Wenn Herr v. Papen eine tiefgreifende Initiative des autoritären Staates auf dem Felde der Kulturpolitik ankundigt, so sehen wir faktisch ein neues Verhältnis von Staat und Wissenschaft postuliert: die staatlichgebundene Wissenschaft im neuen Obrigkeitsstaat, der halb bürokratischer, halb Einparteienstaat sein wird. . . . Wird das Volk oder warden die Parteien sie zwingen können, den besseren ort zu Wählen? Kein Zweifel, dass die freie Wissenschaft heute mit dieser Grundabsicht der Weimarer Verfassung steht und fällt."

15. P. 9.

16. Jaeckh, *The War for Man's Soul*, 89–90, 109–22. Jaeckh was director of the Hochschule. His memoir recounts his attempt to find a way to preserve the school in a conversation held with Hitler on April 1, 1933; his account has been questioned as inaccurate and his behavior as self-serving. Jaeckh became a refugee in New York. My father's dismissal letters are in his Yale Papers, Folder 5.

17. See Reichert, "Hans Bettmanns Freitod," 539–42.

18. Noakes, "Ivory Tower," 380–81.

19. Ibid., 382.

20. September 1933, to Dietrich Gerhard, in *German Refugee Historians*, ed. Ritter, 237, 255. I have slightly modified the translation.

Chapter 2. The Search for Academic Work in Exile: London and New York

1. Refugees in England: Alter, ed., *Out of the Third Reich*; Seabrook, *The Refuge and the Fortress*; Snowman, *The Hitler Émigrés*; B. Wasserstein, "Intellectual Émigrés in Britain, 1933–1939," in Jackman and Borden, *The Muses Flee Hitler*, 249–56.

2. Quoted in Snowman, *The Hitler Émigrés*, 89.

3. On the AAC: Marion Berghahn, "Women Emigrés in England," in Quack, ed., *Between Sorrow and Strength*; Snowman, *The Hitler Émigrés*, 101–4. Among other refugee historians who moved on to the United States from England were Hans Baron, Fritz Epstein, Dietrich Gerhard, Felix Gilbert, Ernst Kantorowicz, George Mosse, Hans Rosenberg, and Hans Rothfels.

4. Franz L. Neumann in *The Cultural Migration*, 18.

5. Emergency Committee: Duggan and Drury, *The Rescue of Science and Learning*, offers a comprehensive account of its work and outcomes, including statistics.
6. Quoted in Keller and Keller, *Making Harvard Modern*, 155. See also Conant, *My Several Lives*, on these issues, and Norwood, *The Third Reich in the Ivory Tower*, 29–33, 36–74.
7. Edward R. Murrow, Einstein Commemorative Award Acceptance Speech, 1957, 4–5, MS in *The Life and Work of Edward R. Murrow, an Archives Exhibit*, Tufts University, 2008.
8. Louise Wilhemine Holborn (1898–1975). Her last and best-known book, published in 1975, was *Refugees, a Problem of Our Time: The Work of the United Nations Commissioner for Refugees, 1950-1972*. Her voluminous papers contain a good deal about the international refugee issues of her time, issues on which she served often as a consultant.

Chapter 3. The Academic Émigrés in America

1. September 23, 1946, in *German Refugee Scholars*, ed. Ritter, 266–67.
2. The report on German universities: Hahn, "Hajo Holborn: Bericht zur deutsche Frage," 146ff.
3. It is difficult to determine precise numbers, and some fluctuations arise from including different populations, whether only German-speaking or all or some part of Central Europe as a whole. See especially Krohn, *Intellectuals in Exile*, 11–13; Sonnert and Holton, *What Happened to the Children*, 19; and Herbert A. Strauss, "The Movement of Peoples," in Jackman and Borden, *The Muses Flee Hitler*, 54.
4. Coser, *Refugee Scholars*, 14–15. He calls the émigrés in the United States "people without a history."
5. See summary of findings in Sonnert and Holton, *What Happened to the Children*, 66ff.
6. *Beyond Swastika and Jim Crow*, Museum of Jewish Heritage Exhibition, 2009; Edgcomb, *From Swastika to Jim Crow*.
7. H. Stuart Hughes, "Social Theory in a New Context," in Jackman and Borden, *The Muses Flee Hitler*, 111–20; Kenneth Barkin, "German Émigré Scholars in America," in Lehmann and Sheehan, *An Interrupted Past*, 149–69; Carl Schorske, "The Refugee Scholar as Intellectual Educator: A Student's Recollections," in Lehmann and Sheehan, *An Interrupted Past*,140–45; and L. Krieger, "European History in America," in Higham, *History*, 282–83.
8. On refugee historians and the OSS: Katz, *Foreign Intelligence*; Laudani, ed., *Secret Reports*, introduction. H. Stuart Hughes, "Social Theory in a New Context," in Jackman and Borden, *The Muses Flee Hitler*, 118.
9. Kelley, *Yale: A History*, 371. Also on Yale in the '30s: Pierson, *Yale: The University College*.
10. February 1935, in *German Refugee Historians*, ed. Ritter, 261.
11. Vagts, "Memoir," in Hajo Holborn Papers, Yale University Library, Folder 5. Vagts also writes here about my father's success in America, calling him a skillful academic politician, and about Meinecke as his patron, all in a rather spiteful tone, writing probably in or around 1976.

12. "German Idealism in the Light of Social History," in *Germany and Europe*, 1–32; "The History of Ideas," *American Historical Review* 73 (1968): 683–95, repr. in *History and the Humanities*, 196–212.
13. *Inter Nationes* publication, 21.

Chapter 4. Growing up in New Haven and in Washington, DC

1. Kabaservice, *The Guardians*, 68–85, on Skull and Bones and America First at Yale; Bird, *The Color of Truth*, 59–64.
2. Pierson, *A Yale Book of Numbers*, 676–77.
3. This led to his writing *American Military Government: Its Organization and Policies*, as noted earlier, and to his involvement as an adviser to the American Occupation leaders and to the State Department.

Chapter 5. An Education at Bryn Mawr College

1. *Offerings to Athena: 125 Years at Bryn Mawr College*, ed. Anne L. Bruder (Friends of the Bryn Mawr College Library, 2010), 146.
2. On Bryn Mawr and President Park: Norwood, *The Third Reich in the Ivory Tower*, 110–11, 234, 238–39.
3. Lane, "Felix Gilbert at Bryn Mawr College," 16; Gilbert, "Desirable Elements," 73–86.

Chapter 6. A Year at the University of Oxford

1. Seabrook, *The Refuge and the Fortress*, 38.
2. Perutz, "That Was the War," 36, 50; Seabrook, *The Refuge and the Fortress*, 38.

Chapter 7. Graduate Study and Teaching at Harvard

1. *Harvard Class Report of 1949*, xxvi.
2. Keller and Keller, *Making Harvard Modern*, 53–55, 52.
3. On coeducation and the Ivy League: Malkiel, *"Keep the Damned Women Out"*; on Harvard, see also Keller and Keller, *Making Harvard Modern*, 277–84.
4. Keller and Keller, *Making Harvard Modern*, 278.
5. Ibid., 201–7; Schrecker, *No Ivory Tower*; Bird, *The Color of Truth*, 121–33.
6. Diamond became a professor at Columbia and in 1992 published a book, *Compromised Campus: The Collaboration of Universities with the Intelligences Community*, about his experience (questioned for its accuracy by a number of Harvard contemporaries, as in the *New York Review of Books*, below). Many passages of Diamond's book, in which he cites government files painfully extracted under the FOIA, are so heavily blacked out as "classified" by government censors that it is almost unreadable. See Diamond in the *New York Review of Books*, April 28, 1977, and Bellah, on his experience, in the *New York Review of Books*, July 14, 1977, as well as the contentious interchange of letters between Diamond and Bundy, joined by Clark Kerr and a group of Harvard professors, that follows in the same *NYRB* issue under the heading " 'Veritas at Harvard.' "

Chapter 8. The First Round in Chicago and Evanston

1. On Rothfels: see especially Mommsen, "Hans Rothfels."
2. Von Simson, *Happy Exile.*
3. A. J. Liebling, in his "Chicago: Second City," first published in the *New Yorker* in 1952 and later as a book (augmented by Liebling and republished, Lincoln: University of Nebraska Press, 2004) added memorably to this view of the university by calling it a "foundling asylum" (115) and describing the college as "the greatest magnet for juvenile neurotics since the Children's Crusade, with Robert Maynard Hutchins . . . playing the role of Stephen the Shepherd Boy," 100.
4. There is a considerable literature on Hutchins; for two recent interpretations and for bibliography, see Boyer, *The University of Chicago: A History,* and Gray, *Searching for Utopia,* chap. 1.
5. The "Neugarten Report": *Women in the University of Chicago. Report of the Committee on University Women. University Record,* May 1, 1970, University of Chicago, Regenstein Library, Special Collections.
6. On Edward Levi: H. Gray, "Biographical Memoir," *Proceedings of the American Philosophical Society* 146 (2002): 297–302. For selections from his speeches: Murphy and Bruckner, eds., *The Idea of the University of Chicago.*

Chapter 9. The Yale Years

1. Kabaservice, *The Guardians,* 68–85; Bird, *The Color of Truth,* 59–64.
2. On May Day: Henry S. Chauncey, in *May Day at Yale, 1970,* 10–31.
3. The Sullivan Principles called for nonsegregation in the workplace; equal employment practices; equal pay for equal work; training programs for blacks for clerical, supervisory, technical, and administrative positions; increased numbers of nonwhites in managerial and supervisory positions; improving the quality of life for nonwhites outside the workplace in such areas as housing, transportation, school, health, and recreation; and (added in 1984) working to eliminate "laws and customs that impede social, economic, and political justice."

Chapter 10. President of the University of Chicago

1. My new colleagues: Jonathan Fanton, with whom I had worked at Yale and who was indispensable in his work as vice president for resources and planning in creating the new development and alumni programs as well as presiding over the complicated Crerar merger and construction (he went on to become president of the New School); Alexander Sharp, a man of broad experience and interests with a deep understanding of the academic mission, served as vice president for finance and administration (he went on afterward to earn a divinity degree and to found an organization dedicated to work on behalf of social justice); Arthur Sussman, a fine legal counsel and wise counselor who took on many special projects as well as responsibility for human resources and for the oversight of the Argonne National Laboratory (afterward vice president of the MacArthur Foundation); Jonathan Kleinbard, who became vice president for public communications

and community relations, had served for some years already at the university as special assistant in the president's office. William Cannon (vice president for administration) and Gale Johnson (provost) stayed on until their successors took office. Both were men of great competence and altogether helpful, not least in offering continuity through their comprehensive knowledge of the university and of its recent history.

Chapter 11. Finale

1. *Kalven Committee Report*, 1–2.
2. I have discussed these questions at somewhat greater length in and have drawn here on two of my publications, *Searching for Utopia* and "The Leaning Tower of Academe."

Select Bibliography

Primary Sources

Family Letters

I have in my possession a large collection of family letters and photographs dating from the early years of the twentieth century and extending through my father's death in 1969. Some are from and to my aunt Louise W. Holborn. The bulk of her correspondence and other papers are held in the Schlesinger Library on the History of Women at the Radcliffe Institute for Advanced Study at Harvard University.

I have relied for my account of the years in Germany and London on my father's letters to his wife (still in Heidelberg) and to his mother (in Berlin) and sister (mostly in Berlin), written from London and later from New York, Washington, Cambridge, New Haven, and Cedar Grove, New Jersey, and from my mother's letters to him and to her mother-in-law and sister-in-law.

Archival Materials

A small collection of my father's papers is housed at the Yale University Library. A full bibliography of his published work to 1970 is offered in the tribute volume *In Memory of Hajo Holborn, 1902–1969, Central European History* 3, nos. 1/2 (1970). It also contains a listing of students who received their PhD degrees under his supervision, together with tributes by Felix Gilbert ("Hajo Holborn: A Memoir," 1–8) and Dietrich Gerhard ("Reminiscences," 9–16). Two posthumous volumes of my father's selected articles, some originally published in German and here translated into English, appeared in 1970 (Hajo Holborn, *Germany and Europe* [New York: Doubleday]) and 1972 (Hajo Holborn, *History and the Humanities* [New York: Doubleday]). A festschrift, edited by Leonard Krieger and Fritz Stern, *The Responsibility of Power: Historical Essays in Honor of Hajo Holborn* (New York: Doubleday), appeared in 1967. In 1969, Inter Nationes published Hajo Holborn, *Inter Nationes Prize 1969* (Bonn/Bad Godesberg) with the text of his last talk at the ceremony in which he was honored and several tributes together with selections from his writings.

COLUMBIA UNIVERSITY LIBRARIES, RARE BOOK AND MANUSCRIPT LIBRARY
Records of the Carnegie Foundation for International Peace.

NEW YORK PUBLIC LIBRARY, MANUSCRIPTS AND ARCHIVES DIVISION (MSS. 922)
Records of the Emergency Committee in Aid of Displaced Foreign Scholars.

ROCKEFELLER FOUNDATION ARCHIVES (AT THE ROCKEFELLER ARCHIVE CENTER)

Secondary Works

Alter, Peter, ed. *Out of the Third Reich: Refugee Historians in Post-War Britain.* London: I. B. Tauris, 1998.

Aschheim, Steven E. *Beyond the Border. The German-Jewish Legacy Abroad.* Princeton, NJ: Princeton University Press, 2007.

Ash, Mitchell G., and Alfons Söllner, eds. *Forced Migration and Scientific Change: Émigré German-Speaking Scientists and Scholars after 1933.* Cambridge: German Historical Institute, 1996.

Ball, Philip. *Serving the Reich: The Struggle for the Soul of Physics under Hitler.* Chicago: University of Chicago Press, 2014.

Bauerkaemper, Arnd. "Americanisation as Globalisation? Remigrés to West Germany after 1945 and Conceptions of Democracy: The Cases of Hans Rothfels, Ernst Fraenkel and Hans Rosenberg." *Leo Baeck Institute Yearbook* 49 (2004): 153–70.

Bendix, Reinhard. *From Berlin to Berkeley.* New Brunswick, NJ: Transaction Books, 1985.

Bird, Kai. *The Color of Truth: McGeorge Bundy and William Bundy, Brothers in Arms.* New York: Simon & Schuster, 1998.

Boyer, John. *The University of Chicago: A History.* Chicago: University of Chicago Press, 2015.

——, *'We Are All Islanders to Begin With': The University of Chicago and the World in the Late Nineteenth and Twentieth Centuries.* Occasional Papers in Higher Education, 17. Chicago: College of the University of Chicago, 2007.

Brecht, Arnold. *The Political Education of Arnold Brecht: An Autobiography 1884-1970.* Princeton, NJ: Princeton University Press, 1970.

Breiner, Peter. "Translating Max Weber: Exile Attempts to Forge a New Political Science." *European Journal of Political Theory* 3 (2004): 133–49.

Brint, Steven, ed. *The Future of the City of the Intellect: The Changing American University.* Stanford, CA: Stanford University Press, 2002.

Cahan, David. *An Institute for an Empire: The Physicalisch-Technische Reichsanstalt 1871–1918.* Cambridge: Cambridge University Press, 1989.

Chauncey, Henry S., John T. Hill, and Thomas Strong. *May Day at Yale 1970: Recollections. The Trial of Bobby Seale and the Black Panthers.* New Haven, CT: Prospect Books, 2015.

Clark, Mark W. *Beyond Catastrophe: German Intellectual and Cultural Renewal after World War II, 1945–1955.* New York: Rowman & Littlefield, 2006.

Conant, James Bryant. *My Several Lives: Memoirs of a Social Inventor.* New York: Harper & Row, 1970.

Cornwell, John. *Hitler's Scientists: Science, War, and the Devil's Pact.* London: Penguin, 2003.

Coser, Lewis A. *Refugee Scholars in America: Their Impact and Their Experience.* New Haven, CT: Yale University Press, repr. 1984.

The Cultural Migration: The European Scholar in America. Philadelphia: University of Pennsylvania Press, 1953.

Daum, Andreas, Hartmut Lehmann, and James Sheehan, eds. *The Second Generation: Émigrés from Nazi Germany as Historians.* New York: Berghahn, 2016.

Displaced German Scholars: A Guide to Academics in Peril in Nazi Germany during the 1930's. Studies in Judaica and the Holocaust, no. 7. San Bernardino, CA: Borgo Press, 1993.

Duggan, Stephen, and Betty Drury. *The Rescue of Science and Learning: The Story of the Emergency Committee in Aid of Displaced Foreign Scholars.* New York: Macmillan, 1948.

Eakin-Thimme, Gabriela. *Geschichte im Exil: Deutschsprachige Historiker nach 1933.* Munich: Peter Lang, 2005.

Edgcomb, Gabrielle S. *From Swastika to Jim Crow: Refugee Scholars at Black Colleges.* Malabar, FL: Krieger Publishing Co., 1993.

Epstein, Catherine. *A Past Renewed: A Catalog of German-Speaking Refugee Historians in the United States after 1933.* Cambridge: Cambridge University Press, 1993.

Evans, Richard J. *The Coming of the Third Reich.* New York: Penguin, 2003.

———. *The Third Reich in Power.* New York: Penguin, 2005.

Fair-Schulz, Axel, and Mario Kessler, eds. *German Scholars in Exile.* Lanham, MD: Lexington, 2011.

Faulenbach, Bernd. "Hajo Holborn." In *Deutsche Historiker*, ed. H.-U. Wehler, 4:114–32. Göttingen: Vandenhoeck & Ruprecht, 1982.

———. *Ideologie des deutschen Weges. Die deutsche Geschichte in der Historiographie zwischen Kaiserreich und Nazionalsozialismus.* Munich: H. Beck, 1980.

Fermi, Laura. *Illustrious Immigrants: The Intellectual Migration from Europe 1930–41.* Chicago: University of Chicago Press, 1968.

Fleck, Christian. *Etablierung in der Fremde. Vertriebene Wissenschaftler in der USA nach 1933.* Frankfurt: Campus Verlag, 2015.

Fleckner, Uwe, and Peter Mack, eds. *The Afterlife of the Kulturwissenschaftliche Bibliothek Warburg: The Emigration and the Early Years of the Warburg Institute in London.* Berlin: De Gruyter, 2015.

Fleming, Donald, and Bernard Bailyn, eds. *The Intellectual Migration.* Cambridge, MA: Harvard University Press, 1969.

Friedlander, Saul. *When Memory Comes*. Trans. Helen Lane. New York: Farrar, Straus and Giroux, 1979.

Gay, Peter. *My German Question: Growing Up in Nazi Berlin*. New Haven, CT: Yale University Press, 1998.

———. "Reflections on Hitler's Refugees in the United States." *Leo Baeck Institute Yearbook* 53 (2008): 117–26.

———. *Weimar Culture: The Outsider as Insider*. New York: Harper & Row, 1968.

Geiger, Roger. *Research and Relevant Knowledge: American Research Universities since World War II*. New York: Oxford University Press, 1993.

———. *To Advance Knowledge: The Growth of American Research Universities, 1900–1940*. New York: Oxford University Press, 1986.

Gemelli, Giuliana, ed. *The "Unacceptables": American Foundations and Refugee Scholars between the Two Wars and After*. Brussels: Peter Lang, 2000.

German Refugee Historians and Friedrich Meinecke: Letters and Documents, 1910–1977. Ed. Gerhard Ritter. Trans. Alex Skinner. Leiden: Brill, 2010.

Gilbert, Felix. "Desirable Elements: Refugee Professors at Bryn Mawr in the Thirties and Forties." In *A Century Recalled: Essays in Honor of Bryn Mawr College*, ed. Patricia H. Labalme, 73–86. Bryn Mawr, PA: Bryn Mawr College Library, 1987.

———. *A European Past: Memoirs 1905–1945*. New York: Norton, 1988.

———. "Friedrich Meinecke." In *History: Commitment and Choice*, 67–87. Cambridge, MA: Harvard University Press, 1977.

Governing Academia. Ed. Ronald I. Ehrenberg. Ithaca, NY: Cornell University Press, 2004.

Gray, Hanna H. "Aims of Education." In *The Aims of Education*, ed. John Boyer. Chicago: University of Chicago Press, 1997.

———. "The Challenge of Leadership and Governance in the University." In *Knowledge Matters*, ed. Paul Axelrod, 93–100. Montreal: McGill-Queen's University Press, 2004.

———. "The Leaning Tower of Academe." *Bulletin of the American Academy of Arts and Sciences* 46 (1996): 34–54.

———. "On the History of Giants." In *Universities and Their Leadership*, ed. W. G. Bowen and H. T. Shapiro, 101–15. Princeton, NJ: Princeton University Press, 1998.

———. "Overgrowth and Undergrowth in the Groves of Academe." *Proceedings of the American Philosophical Society* 158 (2014): 128–35.

———. "Prospects for the Humanities." In *The American University: National Treasure or Endangered Species?*, ed. R. G. Ehrenberg, 115–27. Ithaca, NY: Cornell University Press, 1997.

———. "Some Reflections on the Commonwealth of Learning." In *AAAS Science and Technology Yearbook 1992*. Washington, DC: American Association for the Advancement of Science, 1993.

———. "Some Reflections on the Second Generation." In Daum, Lehmann, and Sheehan, eds., *The Second Generation*, 102–11.

———. *Searching for Utopia: Universities and Their Histories*. Berkeley: University of California Press, 2011.

Greenberg, Karen. "Academic Neutrality: Nicholas Murray Butler, James B. Conant and Nazi Germany, 1933–1938." *Annals of Scholarship* 3, no. 2 (1984): 63–76.

——. "The Search for the Silver Lining: The American Academic Establishment and the 'Aryanization' of German Scholarship." *Simon Wiesenthal Center Annual* 2 (n.d.).

Greenberg, Udi. *The Weimar Century: German Émigrés and the Ideological Foundations of the Cold War.* Princeton, NJ: Princeton University Press, 2014.

Hagemann, Harald, and Claus-Dieter Krohn, eds. *Biographisches Handbuch der deutsch-sprachigen Wirtsschaftswissentlich Emigration nach 1933.* 2 vols. Munich: De Gruyter, 1999.

Hahn, Erich J. "Hajo Holborn: Bericht zur deutsche Frage. Beobachtungen und Empfehlungen von Herbst 1947." *Vierteljahrshefte für Zeitgeschichte* 35 (1987): 135–66.

Heilbut, Anthony. *Exiled in Paradise: German Refugee Artists and Intellectuals in America from the 1930s to the Present.* Plunkett Lake Press, 1973. Repr., Berkeley: University of California Press, 1997.

——. "The Intellectuals' Migration: The Émigré's Conquest of American Academia." *Change* 16 (1984): 24–36.

Hershberg, James. *James B. Conant: Harvard to Hiroshima and the Making of the Nuclear Age.* New York: Knopf, 1993.

Herz, John. "The Fiasco of Denazification in Germany." *Political Science Quarterly* 63 (1948): 569–94.

Higham, John, with Leonard Krieger and Felix Gilbert. *History: The Development of Historical Studies in the United States.* Englewood Cliffs, NJ: Prentice Hall, 1965.

Hobsbawm, Eric. *Interesting Times: A Twentieth-Century Life.* London: Allen Lane, 2002.

Holborn, Hajo. Full bibliography to 1969 in *In Memory of Hajo Holborn, 1902-1969, Central European History*, vol. 3 (see "Archival Materials," above).

Holborn, Louise. "Deutsche Wissenschaftler in den Vereinigten Staaten in den Jahren nach 1933." *Jahrbuch für Amerikastudien* 10 (1965): 15–26.

Horowitz, Joseph. *Artists in Exile.* New York: HarperCollins, 2008.

Iggers, Georg G. *The German Conception of History: The National Tradition of Historical Thought from Herder to the Present.* Rev. ed. Middletown, CT: Wesleyan University Press, 1983.

——. "Refugee Historians from Nazi Germany: Political Attitudes toward Democracy." Center for Holocaust Studies, 2005. Repr. in Fair-Schutz and Kessler, eds., *German Scholars in Exile*, chap. 10.

Jackman, Jarrell, and Carla Borden, eds. *The Muses Flee Hitler: Cultural Transfer and Adaptation 1930-1945.* Washington, DC: Smithsonian Institution Press, 1983.

Jaeckh, Ernest. *The War for Man's Soul.* New York: Farrar & Rinehart, 1943.

Jay, Martin. *Permanent Exiles: Essays on the Intellectual Migration from Germany to America.* New York: Columbia University Press, 1985.

Kabaservice, Gregory. *The Guardians: Kingman Brewster, His Circle, and the Rise of the Liberal Establishment.* New York: Holt, 2004.

Kalven Committee Report on the University's Role in Political and Social Action. University of Chicago Record, November 11, 1967.

Katz, Barry. "The Accumulation of Thought: Transformation of the Refugee Scholar in America." *Journal of Modern History* 63 (1991): 740–52.

——. *Foreign Intelligence: Research and Analysis in the Office of Strategic Services, 1942-1945.* Cambridge, MA: Harvard University Press, 1989.

Katz, Ethan. "Displaced Historians, Dialectical Histories." *Journal of Modern Jewish Studies* 7, no. 2 (2008): 135–55.

Keller, Morton, and Phyllis Keller. *Making Harvard Modern: The Rise of America's University.* Oxford: Oxford University Press, 2001.

Kelley, Brooks M. *Yale: A History.* New Haven, CT: Yale University Press, 1974.

Kennedy, Donald. "Making Choices in the Research University," *Daedalus* 122 (Fall 1993): 127–56.

Kerr, Clark. *The Uses of the University.* 5th ed. Cambridge, MA: Harvard University Press, 2001, 2004.

Kessler, Mario, ed. *Deutsche Historiker im Exil (1933-1945): Ausgwählte Studien.* Berlin: Metropol, 2005.

Kettler, David. *The Liquidation of Exile: Studies in the Intellectual Emigration of the 1930s.* London: Anthem Press, 2011.

Kettler, David, and Gerhard Lauer, eds. *Exile, Science, and Bildung: The Contested Legacies of German Émigré Intellectuals.* New York: Palgrave Macmillan, 2005.

Kettler, David, and Thomas Wheatland. "Contested Legacies: Political Theory and the Hitler Era." *Journal of European Political Theory* 3 (2004): 117–20.

von Klemperer, Klemens. *Voyage through the Twentieth Century: A Historian's Recollections and Reflections.* New York: Berghahn, 2009.

Korenblat, Steven D. "The Deutsche Hochschule für Politik: Public Affairs Institute for a New Germany 1920–1933." PhD diss., University of Chicago, 1978.

——. "A School for the Republic? Cosmopolitans and Their Enemies at the Deutsche Hochschule für Politik." *Central European History* 39 (2006): 394–430.

Krieger, Leonard. Introduction to Hajo Holborn, *History and the Humanities*, 1–10. New York: Doubleday, 1972.

Krohn, Claus-Dieter. *Intellectuals in Exile: Refugee Scholars and the New School for Social Research.* Trans. Rita and Robert Kimber. Boston: University of Massachusetts Press, 1993.

Kunoff, Hugo. "Émigrés, Emigration Studies, and Libraries." *Library Journal* 45 (1975): 141–49.

Lamberti, Marjorie. "German Antifascist Refugees in America and the Public Debate on 'What Should Be Done with Germany after Hitler.'" *Central European History* 40 (2007): 279–305.

——. "The Reception of Refugee Scholars from Nazi Germany in America: Philanthropy and Social Change in Higher Education." *Jewish Social Studies: History, Culture, Society,* n.s., 12 (2008): 157–92.

——. "Returning Political Scientists and America's Democratization Program in Germany after the Second World War." *German Studies Review* 31 (2008): 263–84.

——. Review of *German Refugee Historians and Friedrich Meinecke,* ed. Ritter. *Central European History* 44 (2011): 536–42.

Lane, Barbara. "Felix Gilbert at Bryn Mawr College." In Lehmann, *Felix Gilbert as Scholar and Teacher,* 11–16.

Langer, William L. *In and Out of the Ivory Tower.* New York: N. Watson, 1977.

——. Review of Hajo Holborn, *A History of Modern Germany. Journal of Modern History* 42 (1970): 286–90.

Laqueur, Walter. *Generation Exodus: The Fate of Young Jewish Refugees from Nazi Germany.* Hanover, NH: University Press of New England, 2001.

———. *Worlds Ago: A Memoir of My Journeying Years.* New Brunswick, NJ: Transaction Books, 2016.

Laudani, Raffaele, ed. *Secret Reports on Nazi Germany: The Frankfurt School Contribution to the War Effort.* Princeton, NJ: Princeton University Press, 2013.

Lehmann, Hartmut. *Felix Gilbert as Scholar and Teacher.* German Historical Institute Occasional Papers, no. 6. Washington, DC: German Historical Institute, 1992.

Lehmann, Hartmut, and James Van Horn Melton, eds. *Paths of Continuity: Central European Historiography from the 1930s to the 1950s.* New York: Cambridge University Press, 1994.

Lehmann, Hartmut, and James Sheehan, eds. *An Interrupted Past: German-Speaking Refugee Historians in the United States after 1933.* Cambridge: German Historical Institute, 1991.

Lemmerich, Jost. *Science and Conscience: The Life of James Franck.* Trans. Ann M. Hentschel. Stanford, CA: Stanford University Press, 2011.

Lerner, Gerda. *A Death of One's Own.* New York: Simon & Schuster, 1978.

Lerner, Robert E. *Ernst Kantorowicz: A Life.* Princeton, NJ: Princeton University Press, 2017.

Levine, Emily J. *Dreamland of Humanists: Warburg, Cassirer, Panofsky, and the Warburg School.* Chicago: University of Chicago Press, 2013.

Lowenthal, Leo. *An Unmastered Past: The Autobiographical Reflections of Leo Lowenthal.* Ed. Martin Jay. Berkeley: University of California Press, 1987.

Lyman, Stanford M. "A Haven for Homeless Intellects: The New School and Its Exile Faculties." *International Journal of Politics, Culture and Society* 7 (1994): 493–512.

Malkiel, Nancy Weiss. *"Keep the Damned Women Out": The Struggle for Coeducation.* Princeton, NJ: Princeton University Press, 2016.

Mann, Golo. *Reminiscences and Reflections: A Youth in Germany.* Trans. Krishna Wilson. New York: Norton, 1990.

Mann, Klaus. *The Turning Point: The Autobiography of Klaus Mann.* 2nd ed. New York: L. B. Fischer, 1984.

Marcuse, Herbert. "Der Einfluss der deutschen Emigranten auf das amerikanische Geistesleben, Philosophie und Soziologie." *Jahrbuch für Amerikastudien* 10 (1965): 27–33.

Masur, Gerhard. *Das ungewisse Herz: Berichte aus Berlin über die Suche nach dem Freien.* Holyoke, MA: Benheim Publishing, 1978.

Mitchell, Allan, ed. *Fleeing Nazi Germany: Five Historians Migrate to America.* Trafford Publishing, 2011.

Molho, Anthony. "The Italian Renaissance: Made in America." In *Imagined Histories*, ed. Anthony Molho and Gordon S. Wood, 263–94. Princeton, NJ: Princeton University Press, 1998.

Mommsen, Hans. "Hans Rothfels." In *Deutsche Historiker*, ed. H.-U. Wehler, 9:127–47. Göttingen: Vandenhoeck & Ruprecht, 1982.

Monfasani, John, ed. *Kristeller Reconsidered: Essays on His Life and Scholarship.* New York: Italica Press, 2006.

Mosse, George. *Confronting History: A Memoir.* Madison: University of Wisconsin Press, 2000.

Muir, Edward. "The Italian Renaissance in America." *American Historical Review* 100 (1995): 1095–118.

Murphy, William, and D.J.R.B. Bruckner, eds. *The Idea of the University of Chicago: Selections from the Papers of the First Eight Chief Executives.* Chicago: University of Chicago Press, 1976.

Noakes, Jeremy. "The Ivory Tower under Siege: German Universities in the Third Reich." *European Studies* 23 (1993): 371–407.

Norwood, Stephen H. *The Third Reich in the Ivory Tower: Complicity and Conflict on American Campuses.* Cambridge: Cambridge University Press, 2009.

Peck, Abraham, ed. *The German-Jewish Legacy in America 1938-1988.* Detroit: Wayne State University Press, 1989.

Perloff, Marjorie. *The Vienna Paradox: A Memoir.* New York: New Directions, 2004.

Perutz, Max. "That Was the War: Enemy Alien." *New Yorker*, August 12, 1985, 35–54.

Pierson, George W. *A Yale Book of Numbers.* New Haven, CT: Yale University Press, 1983.

———. *Yale: The University College, 1921-1937.* New Haven, CT: Yale University Press, 1955.

Popkin, Jeremy D. *History, Historians, and Autobiography.* Chicago: University of Chicago Press, 2005.

Prochnik, George. *The Impossible Exile: Stefan Zweig and the End of the World.* New York: Other Press, 2014.

Pross, Helge, and Franz Neumann. *Die deutsche akademische Emigration nach den Vereinigten Staaten, 1933-1941.* Berlin: Dunker & Humblot, 1955.

Quack, Sybille, ed. *Between Sorrow and Strength: Women Refugees of the Nazi Period.* Cambridge: Cambridge University Press, 1995.

Reichert, Folker. "Hans Bettmanns Freitod und das Ende der deutsch-jüdischen Symbiose." *Zeitschrift für die Geschichte des Oberrheins* 159 (2011): 531–53.

Remy, Steven P. *The Heidelberg Myth: The Nazification and Denazification of a German University.* Cambridge, MA: Harvard University Press, 2002.

Richardson, Malcolm. "Philanthropy and the Internationality of Learning: The Rockefeller Foundation and National Socialist Germany." *Minerva* 28 (1990): 21–58.

Rietzler, Katharina. "Philanthropy, Peace Research, and Revisionist Politics: Rockefeller and Carnegie Support for the Study of International Relations in Weimar Germany." *Bulletin of the German Historical Institute*, Supplement 5 (2008): 61–78.

Ritter, Gerhard A., ed. *Friedrich Meinecke: Akademischer Lehrer und emigrierte Schüler. Briefe und Aufzeichnungen 1910-1977.* Munich: Oldenbourg, 2006. Translated by Alex Skinner as *German Refugee Historians and Friedrich Meinecke.* Leiden: Brill, 2010.

———. "Meinecke's Protégés: German Émigré Historians between Two Worlds." *Bulletin of the German Historical Institute* 39 (2006): 23–38.

Rösch, Felix, ed. *Émigré Scholars and the Genesis of International Relations: A European Discipline in America?* New York: Palgrave Macmillan, 2014.

Rutkoff, Peter, and William Scott. *New School: History of the New School for Social Research.* New York: Free Press, 1986.

Schale, Frank, Ellen Thümmler, and Michael Vollmer, eds. *Intellektuelle Emigration. Zur Aktualität eines historischen Phänomens.* Wiesbaden: Springer VS, 2012.

Schrecker, Ellen. *No Ivory Tower: McCarthyism and the Universities.* Oxford: Oxford University Press, 1986.

Scott, Joanna Y. "Alien Nation: Hannah Arendt, the German Émigrés and America." *European Journal of Political Theory* 3 (2004): 167–76.

Seabrook, Jeremy. *The Refuge and the Fortress: Britain and the Flight from Tyranny.* London: Palgrave Macmillan, 2009.

Sheehan, James J. "Three Generations of German *Gelehrtenpolitik.*" *Bulletin of the German Historical Institute* 39 (2006): 39–44.

Sherratt, Yvonne. *Hitler's Philosophers.* New Haven, CT: Yale University Press, 2013.

von Simson, Louise Alexandra. *Happy Exile.* Darmstadt: Rötherdruck, 1986.

Smelser, Neil. *Dynamics of the Contemporary University: Growth, Accretion, and Conflict.* Berkeley: University of California Press, 2013.

Snowman, Daniel. *The Hitler Émigrés: The Cultural Impact on Britain of Refugees from Nazism.* London: Chatto and Windus, 2002.

Söllner, Alfons. *Deutsche Politikwissenschaftler in der Emigration: Studien zu ihrer Akkulturation und Wirkungsgeschichte, mit einer Bibliographie.* Opladen: Westdeutscher Verlag, 1996.

Sonnert, Gerhard, and Gerald Holton. *What Happened to the Children Who Fled Nazi Persecution.* New York: Palgrave Macmillan, 2006.

Stapleton, Darwin H. "Intellectuals Flee from Fascism: Rockefeller Support of Social Scientists, 1933–1945," 2010. http://rockarch.org/publications/resrep/stapleton1.pdf.

Stern, Fritz. *Five Germanys I Have Known.* New York: Farrar, Straus and Giroux, 2006.

———. "German History in America." *Central European History* 19 (1986): 131–63.

Stourzh, Gerald. "Die deutschsprachigen Emigration in den Vereinigten Staaten: Geshichtswissenschaft und Politische Wissenschaft." *Jahrbuch für Amerikastudien* 10 (1965): 59–77.

Strauss, Herbert A. *In the Eye of the Storm. Growing up Jewish in Germany 1918-1943: A Memoir.* New York: Fordham University Press, 1999.

Strauss, Herbert, Klaus Fischer, Christhard Hoffmann, and Alfons Söllner, eds. *Die Emigration der Wissenschaften nach 1933: Disziplingeschichtliche Studien.* Munich: K. G. Saur, 1991.

Strauss, Herbert, and Werner Roder, eds. *International Biographical Dictionary of Central European Refugees 1933-45.* Munich: K. G. Saur, 1983.

Timms, Edward, and Jon Hughes, eds. *Intellectual Migration and Cultural Transformation: Refugees from National Socialism in the English-Speaking World.* Vienna: Springer, 2003.

The University of the Twenty-First Century: A Symposium to Celebrate the Centenary of the University of Chicago. Special Issue, *Minerva* 30 (1993).

Urbach, Karina. "Zeitgeist als Ortsgeist: Die Emigration als Schlüsselerlebnis Deutscher Historiker?" In Herman Hiery, *Der Zeitgeist und die Historie*, 161–81. Dettelbach: J. H. Röll, 2001.

Weinreich, Max. *Hitler's Professors: The Part of Scholarship in Germany's Crimes against the Jewish People.* 2nd ed. New Haven, CT: Yale University Press, 1999.

Weitz, Eric. *Weimar Germany: Promise and Tragedy*. Princeton, NJ: Princeton University Press, 2007, 2013.

Wheatland, Thomas. *The Frankfurter School in Exile*. Minneapolis: University of Minnesota Press, 2009.

Wolf, Heinz. *Deutsch-jüdische Emigrationshistoriker in den USA und der Nationalsozialismus*. Bern: Verlag Peter Lang, 1988.

Wolin, Richard. *Heidegger's Children: Hannah Arendt, Karl Löwith, Hans Jonas, and Herbert Marcuse*. Princeton, NJ: Princeton University Press, 2001.

Zimmer, Heinrich. *Heinrich Zimmer: Coming into His Own*. Ed. Margaret Case. Princeton, NJ: Princeton University Press, 1994.

Index

Academic Assistance Council, 26–30
academic émigrés, 41–42, 44–63; academic
  ideals and disillusionments of, 42, 298;
  adaptation of, 51–52, 65, 71; attitudes of,
  toward Germany, 46–48; autobiographical writings of, 50–51; background of, 51;
  at Bryn Mawr College, 99–101; common
  experiences of, 48–49; communal ties of,
  60–61, 68; in England, 124–25, 127; historians among, 54–55; at Holborn household,
  65–69; impact of, 53–54; numbers of, 48;
  in OSS, 56; professionals among, 52–53;
  resentment of Germans toward, 130;
  responses of, to American higher education, 50; at University of Chicago, 172–74;
  at Yale, 57–59
academic freedom, 18–19, 21, 50, 102, 103,
  161–65, 218–19, 297–98
academic placements, 155–56
Acheson, Dean, 107, 207
Adams, Robert McCormick, 258–59
Adams, Walter, 27, 28, 31–32, 36–37
Adenauer, Konrad, 99
administrative career: considerations
  concerning, 194; Harvard University, 160;
  Northwestern University, 196–201; Uni-
  versity of Chicago, 232–93; Yale University,
  201–2, 214–35. See also teaching career
Adorno, Theodor, 47
Ady, Cecilia, 122
African American Studies Department,
  Northwestern University, 200–201
Agnew, Spiro, 211
Albert Pick Award for International Under-
  standing, 288–90
Algeria, 167
All About Eve (film), 77

SS America, 116
America First movement, 179, 209
American Association of Universities, 280
American Communist Party, 228
American Council on Education, 280
American Historical Association, 59
American Historical Review (journal), 37
American University, 34, 37
Amherst College, 58, 67
Andover. See Phillips Academy Andover
Andreas, Willy, 11
Andrew W. Mellon Foundation, 283
Angell, James Rowland, 57–58, 78–79
Angell, Kay, 79
Annenberg, Walter, 232–33
anti-Americanism, 118–19
anti-Semitism, 27, 30, 41, 50, 57, 71, 124
Applebee, Constance, 94
Aptheker, Herbert, 228
Aptheker case, 227–28
Arendt, Hannah, 67, 174
Argonne National Laboratory, Chicago, 173,
  264, 265–66, 303n1
Argonne West, 265
Armstrong, C.A.J., 122
Assyrian Dictionary, 273
athletics. See sports and athletics
Attlee, Clement, 117
Auerbach, Erich, 66

Bachofer, Ludwig, 173
Bailyn, Lotte, 69
Baker, Keith, 250
Baker Commission, 252–53
Barker, Ernest, 25
Baron, Hans, 8, 54, 171–72, 187, 300n3; The
  Crisis of the Early Italian Renaissance, 171–72

Beadle, George, 180–81, 254
Beard, Charles, 32, 60, 69
Beecham, Thomas, 118
Beinecke, William, 207
Bellah, Robert, 162
Bellow, Saul, 262
Bemis, Samuel Flagg, 59
Berenson, Bernard, 131–32
Berlin: family background in, 2, 4–5, 12–19, 23, 42; postwar, 6–7, 46
Berlin, Isaiah, 123–24
Bernheimer, Richard, 99
Berwanger, Jay, 182
Bettelheim, Bruno, 173, 264
Bettmann, Gertrude (maternal aunt), 4, 43, 76
Bettmann, Hans (maternal uncle), 20
Bettmann, Rosa (maternal grandmother), 2, 43–44, 65, 84–85, 118
Bettmann, Siegfried (maternal grandfather), 2–4, 43–44, 65, 71
Beveridge, William, 26
Bildungsbürgertum (educated upper bourgeoisie), 1
Billington, Jim, 124
birth, 11
Black Panthers, 212
Black Studies Department, University of California, Berkeley, 195
Bloch, Konrad, 173
Bloom, Allan, 236–37
Bloom, Harold, 223
Blum, John, 156
Bok, Derek, 280, 292
Bondi, Hermann, 125
Booth, Albie, 79
Bowen, Bill, 280
Bowra, Maurice, 126
Boyd, Sandy, 280
Bradburn, Norman, 250
Brearley School, 95
Brewster, Kingman, 127, 201, 203–4, 208–18, 224, 226, 230–34
Brinton, Crane, 141–42, 143
British Museum, 155
Broch, Hermann, 66
Brooklyn College, 67
Brooks, Peter, 222

Brown, J. Carter, 159
Brüning, Heinrich, 16–17
Bryn Mawr College, 87, 91–114; academic requirements of, 92–93; admission to, 88–90; board of trustees of, 113–14; culture of, 91–95; curriculum of, 108–9; faculty of, 108; Flexner Lectures at, 100, 107; Foote School associations with, 80, 81; graduate students and study at, 111–12; internationalism of, 98–101; and loyalty oath controversy, 165; male-female relations at, 94; personal academic experience at, 109–11; and politics, 101–3; postgraduate associations with, 112–13; postwar environment of, 97–98; prominent scholars and writers at, 107–8; race at, 97; reputation of, 89; sports at, 94–95; student jobs at, 93–94; student life at, 93–97; students of, 95, 97, 99, 101, 106; surroundings of, 95–96
Bryn Mawr School, Baltimore, 95
Brzesinski, Zbigniew, 144
Buck, Paul, 134
Bundy, McGeorge, 80, 160–65, 207, 208
Bundy, William (Bill), 80, 207
Bunting, Mary, 136–37
Bush, George H. W., 216
Butler, Nicholas Murray, 26, 40–41

California Institute of Technology, 180
Cam, Helen Maud, 139–41
Cambridge University, 28, 140
Cannon, William, 304n1
Carew, Jan, 200
Carnap, Rudolf, 173
Carnegie Endowment for International Peace, 12, 14, 16, 26, 32–33, 40
Carpenter, Rhys, 93, 108
Carter, Jimmy, 230, 280
Casper, Gerhard, 258
Cassirer, Ernst, and wife, 66
Castro, Fidel, 163
Center for Advanced Study in the Behavioral Sciences, Stanford University, 194, 196
Center for UFO Studies, Northwestern University, 199
Central Intelligence Agency (CIA), 85

Chafee, John, 207
Chambers, Whittaker, 102
Chandrasakhar, Subrahmanyan, 278
Chatham House. *See* Royal Institute for International Affairs
Chiang Kai-shek, 87
Chicago, politics in, 170–71. *See also* Hyde Park, Chicago
Chicago Bears, 186
Chicago Club, 279
Chicago House, Luxor, Egypt, 272–73
Chicago School, 270
Chicago White Sox, 292
childhood, 26, 64–90; academic refugees encountered during, 66–69; birth, 11; emigration in, 64–65; English language learning in, 69, 70; friendships during, 69; German influences in, 65, 69–72; housekeeping instruction during, 70; music education during, 75–76; neighborhood life during, 72–73; New Haven during, 73–77; New York exposure during, 76; rules and customs of, 70–72; Washington, DC, during, 85–88; World War II exposure during, 82–88; Yale University during, 77–80
Chomsky, Noam, 151
Christianity, conversion to, 1, 2
Churchill, Winston, 85
Clark, Joseph, 164
Clark, Russell Inslee "Inky," Jr., 209
Clay, Lucius D., 62
Clinton, Bill, 277
Clive, John, 69, 167–69
Cochrane, Eric, 90, 186
coeducation: at the Foote School, 80; Harvard and, 134, 136–39; St. Anne's College and, 120; University of Chicago and, 185; women's colleges in context of, 103, 112, 113; Yale and, 204–5, 209, 214
Coffin, William Sloane, 209
Cold War, 102, 118–19, 167
Cole, G.D.H., 123–24
Coleman, James, 263
collegiality, 143–45
Columbia University, 16, 26, 34, 37, 67, 188
Columbus, Indiana, 206–7
Commercial Club, 278–79

Committee on Degrees in History and Literature, Harvard University, 157
Communist Party, 161, 163–64. *See also* American Communist Party
computer science, 269
Conant, James B., 30–31, 134, 136, 160, 161
concentration camps, 20, 43
Connecticut College for Women, 42
continuing education, 266–67
Cook County Democratic Organization, 170
Coolidge, Calvin, 148
Cooper, Richard, 201–2
Coors, Joseph, 282
Cosell, Howard, 227
Cozza, Carmen, 225–26
Cronkhite, Bernice Brown, 135
Culinary Institute of America, New Haven, 79

Daley, Richard J., 170
Dam, Kenneth, 258
Danforth, John, 207
Dartmouth College, 95
David Dean Smith record store, New Haven, 74
Dellinger, David, 208
de Man, Paul, 222–23
Depression, 5, 16, 27, 30, 198
Deutsch, John, 265–66
Dewey, Thomas, 101
Diamond, Sigmund, 162, 302n6
Dilworth, J. Richardson, 208, 233
Diogenes (escort), 96
Displaced Persons Act, 226
Dixon, Marlene, 187–93
Dixwell, John, 76–77
Donaldson, William, 224–25
Douglas, Paul, 170
DuBois, W.E.B., 228
Duggan, Stephen, 28, 32
Duke University, 256
Dunham, Allison, 242

Ecklund, John, 208
Eckstein, Harry, 160
Edelman, Marian Wright, 205
Edelstein, Ludwig, 67

education, of the author: at Bryn Mawr
    College, 87, 91–114; elementary, 69, 80–82;
    informal, 65; in music, 75–76; parents'
    emphasis on, 72; secondary, 86–87, 89–90.
    See also higher education; liberal education
Edward Malley department store, New Haven,
    74
Egypt, 272–73
Ehrenburg, Victor, 125
Einstein, Albert, 1
Eisenhower, Dwight, 166, 167
Eliot, T. S., 107
Elliott, William Yandell, 145
Elton, G. R., 125
Emergency Committee in Aid of Displaced
    German (later, Foreign) Scholars, 28–34,
    37, 40–41, 99
émigrés. *See* academic émigrés
enemy aliens, 84–85, 124–25
Epigraphic Survey, 272
Epstein, Fritz, 67, 300n3
Epstein, Klaus, 69, 160
Erasmus, Desiderius, 5, 37, 146–47
Erikson, Erik, 165
Exeter. *See* Phillips Exeter Academy

Fantasia (film), 71
Fanton, Jonathan, 303n1
Federal Bureau of Investigation (FBI), 102
feminism and the women's movement, 103,
    137–38
Fermi, Enrico, and wife, 172–73
Fiesel, Eva, 99
Flacks, Richard, 188
Flexner Report, 257
Florence, visit to, 131–32
Fogel, Robert, 191
football, 181–83, 229–30
Foote, Mrs. (school founder), 80
Foote School, 72, 74, 80–82
Ford, Gerald, 236–37
Ford Foundation, 165
Foreign Affairs (journal), 61
Fraenkel, Eduard, 125–27
Fraenkel, Mrs. Eduard, 126
Franck, James, 173
Frank, Erich, 11, 67, 100–101

Franklin, H. Bruce, 196
freedom of speech, 219, 226, 228, 290, 297–98
Free University of Berlin, 7, 46, 174
Friedrich, Carl Joachim, 32, 38, 41, 145
Friedrich Wilhelm University of Berlin, 4, 12
Fuchs, Klaus, 125
Fulbright Scholarship, 115–18
Furry, Wendell, 161–62, 163

Galbraith, John Kenneth, 167
Gamble, Isabel, 116
gay couples, equality of benefits for, 285
Gelb, Ignace, 173
General Education in a Free Society (Red Book),
    103–4
Geneva School for International Affairs, 14
geography, discipline of, 261–62
George Washington University, 34, 37, 43
Gerhard, Dietrich, 8, 9, 21, 67, 300n3
Germany: family background in, 1–20; visit to
    postwar, 129–31
Getzels, Jacob, 191
Giamatti, Bart, 234
GI Bill, xi, xii, 97, 176
Gilbert, Felix, 8, 10, 25, 54, 67, 99–100, 108,
    112, 131, 300n3
Gilmore, Myron, 132, 141, 143, 146, 157, 159,
    160
Gleacher Center, Chicago, 267, 268
Goebbels, Joseph, 11, 20, 85
Goetze, Albrecht, 58
Goffe, William, 76–77
Goldwater, Barry, 207
Gombrich, Ernst, and wife, 127
Gossett, Philip, 272
Gould, John, 259
government-university relations, 102, 164–65,
    210–11, 266
graduate education, issues in, 252–53
graduate study, at Harvard University, 99,
    133–36, 139–46
Grange, Red, 149
Gray, Charles (husband): background of,
    147–51; character and personality of, 147,
    150, 151–52, 154; *Copyright, Equity, and the
    Common Law*, 151; courtship involving,
    141, 147, 154–55; death of, 151; education

of, 150–51; graduate study of, 135, 147, 151, 155; intellectual and artistic interests of, 151–53, 154; marriage of, 155; at MIT, 156; other academic stints of, 185, 194; social occasions and travel shared with, 76, 99, 110, 127, 132, 141, 143, 155, 278–79; as teacher, 151, 153, 156, 168–69, 197, 201, 278–79; at University of Chicago, 153, 168, 197, 233, 278–79; *The Writ of Prohibition: Jurisdiction in Early Modern English Law*, 151–52; at Yale, 201

Gray, Gene (mother-in-law), 147–48

Gray, Horace Montgomery (father-in-law), 147–50

Gray, John, 147

Greene, Graham, 128

Greensboro, Vermont, 73

Greenstone, David, 251

Griswold, A. Whitney, 209, 211, 224, 234

Groton School, 67

Grünebaum, Gustave von, 173

Guevara, Ernesto "Che," 196

Guicciardini, Francesco, Count, 132

Güterbock, Hans, 173

Hall, Dan, 251

Hamden, Connecticut, 64, 72–73, 235

Harnack, Adolf, 4

Harper, William Rainey, 291, 292–93

Harris, Chauncey, 242

Harris, Irving, 263–64

Hartman, Geoffrey, 222

Harvard Board of Overseers, 205–6

Harvard Corporation, 133, 138, 161, 162, 165, 205–6

Harvard Faculty Club, 133, 140, 157

Harvard Law School, 151

Harvard University: and academic émigrés, 30–31, 59; Berenson's bequest to, 132; Bryn Mawr students' visits to, 95; Charles Gray's studies at, 135, 147, 150–51, 155; and coeducation, 134, 136–39; Committee on Degrees in History and Literature, 157; finances of, 165; first tenured couple at, 116; Frederick Holborn's attendance at, 79, 88, 144; graduate study at, 99, 133–36, 139–46, 157–59; Hajo Holborn's visit to, 34, 37–38; History and Literature, 158–59, 160; honorary degrees conferred by, 67, 167–68; junior faculty at, 144–45, 159–60, 162–63; Kennedy School of Government, 144, 262; Kirkland House, 157; Lamont Library at, 133, 140; Littauer School of Public Administration, 144; Memorial Church, 162–63; Morning Prayers at, 140; Radcliffe's relationship with, 133–39, 166; Red Scare and associated internal politics at, 160–65; and religion, 162–63; report on postwar educational mission produced by, 103–4; size of, 166; Society of Fellows, 151–52; student protests at, 188; students of, 77–78; teaching at, 80, 155, 157, 159–64; tenure process at, 144–45; Widener Library at, 67, 132, 134; women's status at, 115, 133–34, 136, 140, 157; Yale compared to, 38, 40

Harvard University Center for Italian Renaissance Studies, 132

Haskins, Carryl, 207

Haskins, Charles Homer, 142

Haverford College, 95, 109

Hayden, Tom, 228

Heckman, James, 263

Heidegger, Martin, 21, 100

Heidelberg: family background in, 2–3, 10–12, 20; visit to postwar, 129–30

Hepburn, Katharine, 25, 95

Heston, Charlton, 281–83

Heuss, Theodor, 12, 48

Higginbotham, Leon, 207

higher education: administrator's life and duties in, 274–79, 294–95; American approach to, 30, 38–39, 44–45, 48, 50, 53–54; Brewster's advocacy for, 210–11; corporate capacity of institutions in, 286–87; costs of, 246; crises of 1970s in, 216–17, 237, 240–41; culture of, 275; émigrés' impact on, 53–54; English approach to, 27–28, 120–21; German approach to, 10, 12–14; government role in, 102, 164–65, 210–11, 266; Hutchins legacy affecting, 179–80; investment policies of institutions in, 219–20, 285–88, 297; postwar emphasis on, and the GI Bill, xi–xii, 97–98, 176; professional organizations of, 280; public attitude toward, xii,

higher education (*continued*)
194, 295; purpose and mission of, 103–7, 218–19, 271, 273, 293–98; recent trends in, 294–98; responsibilities of boards of trustees in, 284–85; students of, 295; teaching placements in, 155–56; women's plans for utilizing, 105–7. *See also* liberal education; *individual institutions*

Hillsdale College, 282

Hindemith, Paul, 66

Hiss, Alger, 102

Hiss, Priscilla, 102

historically black colleges, 52

Historische Zeitschrift (journal), 6, 62

History of Western Civilization course, University of Chicago, 172, 187

Hitchcock, Margaret, 81, 88

Hitler, Adolf, 16, 19, 68, 84, 85

Hittite Dictionary, 273

Hochschule für Politik (Berlin), 12–20, 42

Hofmannsthal, Hugo von, 66

Holborn, Annemarie Bettmann (mother): character and personality of, 4–5; class background of, 1; education of, 4; family background of, 2–3; friend of, 99; letters to, concerning emigration, 35, 38; in London, 23, 25; marriage of, 4; OSS work of, 85; and politics, 4; scholarship of, 5–6; social and cultural context of, 3–4, 5

Holborn, Frederick (brother): birth of, 11; childhood and education of, 64, 66, 68, 69, 72–73, 80, 88; at Harvard University, 79, 88, 144; as Kennedy Senate staff member, 167, 170

Holborn, Friedrich "Fritz" (paternal uncle), 32, 64

Holborn, Hajo (father): academic influence of, 59, 63; American career of, 32–41, 57–60, 78–79, 301n11; *American Military Government: Its Organization and Policies*, 56; character and personality of, 9–10; class background of, 1; death of, 63; education of, 4; emigration of, 20–22, 24, 31–41, 46; family background of, 1–2; family life in America, 68; German academic ties of, 47–48, 62–63; *History of Modern Germany*, 54, 62; at Hochschule für politik, 12, 15–16;

in London, 23–28; marriage of, 4; name of, 2; as parent, 82–83; *The Political Collapse of Europe*, 61; and politics, 2, 12, 16, 19, 37, 62; scholarship of, 6, 8–12, 18–19, 37, 54, 61–62, 107; social and cultural context of, 3–4; war service and OSS work of, 56, 68, 84–85

Holborn, Helene (paternal grandmother), 2, 42, 65

Holborn, Louise (paternal aunt), 23–24, 35, 40, 42–43, 60, 85, 88–89, 135, 301n8

Holborn, Ludwig (paternal grandfather), 1–2

Holl, Karl, 4

Home Economics Department, Northwestern University, 199–200

Hoover, J. Edgar, 228

Hope, Bob, 146, 202

Hopkins School, 89

Horkheimer, Max, 47

Horton, Mildred McAfee, 106–7

hospitals, 221–22, 254–58

House Un-American Activities Committee (HUAC), 102

Howard Hughes Medical Institute, 283

HUAC. *See* House Un-American Activities Committee

Hughes, H. Stuart, 56, 85

humanism, 143

humanities, 270–72

Humboldt University of Berlin, 4

Hungarian Uprising (1956), 166

Huntington, Samuel, 144

Hutchins, Robert Maynard, 79, 174–76, 179–82, 209, 248, 293

Hutten, Ulrich von, 10–11

Hyde Park, Chicago, 169, 174, 177

Hynek, J. Allen, 199

Idaho National Laboratory, 265

Illinois Institute of Technology, 268

Imperial Historical Commission, 6, 11

Imperial Institute of Physics and Technology, 1–2

Ingersoll, Robert, 232

Institute for Advanced Study (Princeton), 29, 66, 67, 100

Institute for International Education (New York), 28

Institute for Social Research (New York), 67–69
Institute of Fine Arts, NYU, 29
interdisciplinary studies, 262
International Refugee Organization, 42
international relations, 98–99
investment policies, of universities, 219–20, 285–88, 297
Italy, visit to, 131–32
Ivy League athletics, 229, 233

Jaeckh, Ernst, 300n16
Jaeger, Werner, 173
Jaffe, Else, 130–31
Jaspers, Karl, 11
Jenkins, Roy, Lord, 292
Jews: blamed for postwar German crisis, 16; conversion of, to Christianity, 1, 2; dismissed from universities, 19; harassment of, in Germany, 17, 43; harassment of professional, 20; Harvard policy and, 162; at Hochschule für politik, 13; Meinecke's treatment of, 7, 8; repression of heritage by, 124
John Crerar Library, Chicago, 268, 303n1
Johns Hopkins University, 67, 256
Johnson, D. Gale, 189, 242, 258, 304n1
Jordan, Frances, 134–35
Jordan, Michael, 276
Jordan, Wilbur K. "Kitch," 134–35, 147, 157
Journal of Modern History, 185
Journey for Margaret (film), 71
Judson, Harry Pratt, 78

Kahn, Louis, 223
Kalven Report, 286–87
Kamin, Leon, 161, 163
Kantorowicz, Ernst, 67, 300n3
Keller, Helen, 136
Kellogg Foundation, 266
Kennan, George, 14
Kennedy, Edward (Ted), 167
Kennedy, John F., 164, 167, 170–71
Kent Falls State Park, Connecticut, 68
Kent State University, 188
Khrushchev, Nikita, 187
Kimpton, Lawrence, 178–79

King, Martin Luther, Jr., 177
Kirchheimer, Otto, 68, 85
Kirkland House, Harvard University, 157
Kissinger, Ann, 146
Kissinger, Henry, 144, 145–46
Kitagawa, Joe, 259
Kleinbard, Jonathan, 303n1
Korean War, 118
Kraus, Hertha, 99
Krautheimer, Richard, 66
Krieger, Leonard, 85
Kristallnacht, 30, 43
Kristeller, Paul Oskar, 54, 67, 143
Kroc, Ray, 204–5
Kruskal, William (Bill), 270
Kunstler, William, 208

Lamont Library, Harvard University, 133, 140
Langer, William, 85
Latimer, Hugh, 150–51
Lattimore, Owen, 102
Lattimore, Richard, 102
Laumann, Edward, 270
Lawrence, Frieda, 130
Lawrence College, 161
League of Nations, 14
Leavis, F. R., 117
Lessing, Gotthold Ephraim, *Nathan der Weise*, 65
Levi, Edward, 180, 183–84, 190, 193, 234, 242, 262, 277, 293–94
liberal arts colleges, 52
liberal education, 103–6, 175–76, 267, 271, 282, 295–96
Library of Congress, 86
library science, 260–61
Liebling, A. J., 176
Llewellyn, Karl, 184
Loewenstein, Karl, 52, 58, 67
Lohmann, Carl Albert, 80–81
London: dissertation research in, 155; experience of postwar, 117–18; parents' emigration to, 23–28; reading at Warburg Institute in, 127
London School of Economics, 15, 26, 27, 42
Lowinsky, Edward, 173
loyalty oath controversies, 50, 67, 102, 164–65

Lutheranism, 2
Lynd, Staughton, 189

MacArthur Foundation, 303n1
MacCaffrey, Wallace, 116
Machiavelli, Niccolò, 110, 122–23; *History of Florence*, 123; *The Prince*, 122–23
Mack, Ray, 197, 201
Mackauer, Christian, 172, 174, 187
Macmillan, Harold, 128
Manning, Helen Taft, 92
Manutius, Aldus, 206
Marcuse, Herbert, 50, 67, 68, 85
Margaret, Princess, 119
Mariano, Nicky, 132
marriage, 155
Marschak, Jakob, 66
Martin, William McChesney, 207
Massachusetts Institute of Technology (MIT), 156
Massey, Walter, 266
Masur, Gerhard, 7, 8
May, Karl, 69
Mayer, Maria, 173
McBride, Katherine, 88–89, 93, 100
McCarthy, Joseph, 102, 112, 160–61, 298
McGill University, 192
McNamara, Robert, 288–90
McNeill, William H., 186
medical schools, 221–22, 254–58
Meinecke, Friedrich, 4, 6–9, 11–12, 32, 46, 59–60, 67–68, 100, 171, 173, 301n11
Mellon, Paul, 223–24
Mellon, Rachel "Bunny," 224
Mentschicoff, Soia, 184
Metropolitan Opera, New York, 75–76
Meyer, Eduard, 4
Meyer, Gerhard, 174
Michael, Robert, 264
Michael Reese Hospital, 257
Middledorf, Ulrich, 173
Mikva, Abner, 170–71
Miller, J. Hillis, 222
Miller, J. Irwin, 206–7
Miller, J. Roscoe, 201–2
Milton Academy, 95
Miss Day's School, 89

MIT. *See* Massachusetts Institute of Technology
Mohawks, 69
Momigliano, Arnaldo, 126
Mommsen, Theodor, 67
Moore, Marianne, 108
Moore, Paul, 207, 208
More, Thomas, 197
Morgenthau, Hans, 173
Moro, Peter, 118
Mory's, New Haven, 204
Mosse, George, 300n3
Muratori, Ludovico Antonio, 142
Murdoch, Iris, 121–22
Murrow, Edward R., 33–34, 37, 40
Mussolini, Benito, 68
Mutter's kleine Hilfsreiche (Mother's Little Helper), 70

Nahum, Mrs. (piano teacher), 75
Nallinger, Mrs. (housekeeper), 70
Nangle, Bobby, 84
natatoria, 268, 269
Nathan der Weise (Lessing), 65
National Defense Education Act (NDEA), 164–65
National Endowments for the Arts and Humanities, 281–83
National Gallery of Art, Washington, DC, 86, 159
National Geographic Society, 261
National Opinion Research Center, Chicago, 264
National Socialism (Nazism): criticisms of, 19; German historians' preoccupation with, 55; public disturbances involving, 17; revelations of professors' collaborations with, 223, 226–27; and the universities, 6, 11, 17–21, 173, 298
Naval War College, 197
NBC Symphony, 71
nepotism rules, 155, 173, 184–85
Neugarten, Bernice, 185
Neugarten Committee, 193
Neumann, Franz, 15, 16, 25, 28, 52, 67, 68, 85
Neumann, Sigmund, 15, 40, 67
Newberry Library, 169, 171–72, 187
New Criticism, 158, 223

New Deal, 58, 148
New Haven, 73–77, 235
New Haven Arena, 74–75
New Haven Lawn Club, 75
New School for Social Research, 15, 29, 34, 52, 67, 69, 303n1
New York, New Haven and Hartford Railroad, 73, 76
New York City: childhood exposure to, 76; father's emigration to, 33–35
New York Philharmonic, 71
New York Times (newspaper), 40, 182
Nixon, Richard, 211
Noether, Emmy, 99
Norden, Eduard, 4
Northwestern University, 185, 196–202, 198
Notestein, Wallace, 36, 37, 58
nuclear weapons, 118–19
Nuremberg Laws, 19

Obermann, Julian, 83
Office of Strategic Services (OSS), 6, 56, 68–69, 85
O'Hara, Barrett, 170
SS Olympic, 32, 33, 64
Oppenheim, A. Leo, 173
Oppenheimer, Jane, 108
Oppenheimer, J. Robert, 100, 163
Orthogenic School, Chicago, 173, 264–65
OSS. See Office of Strategic Services
O'Sullivan, Mademoiselle (Sidwell Friends teacher), 87
Oxford University, 82, 115–28; Charles Gray's studies at, 151; fond memories of, 116, 127–28; honorary degree conferred upon author by, 127–28; St. Anne's College, 115, 119–22; student life at, 120–21; students of, 119; studies at, 122–26; women's status at, 115

Packard, David, 282
Panofsky, Erwin, and wife, 66
Paoli Local train line, 96
Papen, Franz von, 17, 18
Pargellis, Stanley, 169
Paris, holiday in, 128–29
Park, Marion Edwards, 99

Passerin d'Entrèves, Alexandre, 122
Patterson, Elmore, 182
Payne-Gaposchkin, Cecilia, 166
Peabody Museum of Natural History, Yale University, 77
Pei, I. M., 207
Pelikan, Jaroslav, 217–18
Perlman, Helen, 191
Perutz, Max, 124–25
Phelps, William Lyon, 57–58
Phi Beta Kappa, 92–93
Phillips Academy Andover, 77–78
Phillips Exeter Academy, 78, 150–51
Pierce, Bessie, 185
Planck, Max, 1
Plumer, Eleanor, 120
Podhoretz, Norman, 116
politics: Annemarie Holborn and, 4; of Bryn Mawr students, 101, 102–3; childhood exposure to, 68, 75; Hajo Holborn and, 2, 12, 16, 19, 37, 62; Harvard University and national, 160–67; of 1950s, 160–67; of 1960s, 170–71; participation in local, 170–71; on university campuses, 187–93, 195–96, 203–4, 212, 289–90, 297
polo, 229
Pond, Raymond W. "Ducky," 236
popular culture, 71–72
presidency of University of Chicago, 232–93; academic program issues during, 260–67, 269–73; administrative personnel associated with, 244–45, 303n1; anecdotes and memorable incidents of, 278–82; campus planning during, 245; centennial celebration during, 290–93; controversies during, 285–91; expanded academic offerings during, 262–64; financial concerns during, 237–38, 245–49; leadership challenges of, 241–44; national committee work during, 281–83; new construction during, 267–69; period of listening and discernment at beginning of, 243–44; personnel matters during, 274–77; popular curiosity about, 243; professional school matters during, 254–60; search process for, 232–34; social and official life of, 278–79; transition to, 234–35; travel during, 279–80

Presidential Task Force on the Arts and Humanities, 281–83
Princeton University, 34, 39–40, 95
Prospect Hill School, 89–90
Prown, Jules, 224
Prussia, 14, 17
Public Records Office, London, 155
publishing industry, 105
Pusey, Nathan M., 136–37, 160–62, 164, 168

Quakers, 23, 86–87, 91, 97

Radcliffe College, 42, 115, 133–39, 166
Radcliffe Institute for Independent (now Advanced) Study, 42, 136–37, 139
radio, 71, 72, 83, 84–85
Reagan, Nancy, 280
Reagan, Ronald, 195, 280–83
Red Book, 103–4
Red Scare, 102, 160–65
Reeves, Marjorie, 121
Renaissance history, discipline of, 186–87
Renaissance intellectual history, 110, 115, 122, 143, 267
Reneker, Robert, 233
reparations, war, 16
research fellowship, Newberry Library, 169, 171–72
Rheinstein, Max, 173
Rhoads, James, 91
Rhodes Scholars, 119
Rice, Stuart, 191, 269
Richthofen sisters, 130
Riesman, David, 165–66, 172
Roche, George, 282
Roche, Kevin, 268
Rockefeller, David, 292
Rockefeller Foundation, 14–15, 29–33, 41, 203
Roosevelt, Eleanor, 37, 88, 107
Roosevelt, Franklin Delano, 37, 58, 68, 83, 87–88
Rosenberg, Hans, 8, 54, 67, 300n3
Rosovsky, Henry, 69, 151, 233
Rostow, Walt, 167
Rothfels, Hans, 8, 173–74, 300n3
Royal Festival Hall, London, 118

Royal Institute for International Affairs (Chatham House), 14, 25, 26
Rudenstine, Neil, 138–39
Rudolph, Lloyd, 184
Rudolph, Susanne, 69, 98–99, 184, 191

SA. See *Sturmabteilung*
Saarinen, Eero, 207, 268
Saarinen, Eliel, 207
Sachs, Bob, 265
Salomon, Albert, 67
Samarin, Vladimir (pen name of Vladimir Sokolov), 226–27
Sanders, Bernie, 188
Sargent, John Singer, 92
Sasaki Associates, 245
Saturday Review of Literature (journal), 61
Saxby, Amelia Naseby, 120
Sayers, Dorothy, *Gaudy Night*, 115
Scaife, Richard Mellon, 282
Schlesinger, Arthur, Jr., 167
Schlesinger Library, Radcliffe Institute for Advanced Study, 139
Schmidt, Helmut, 278
Schorske, Carl, 54, 85, 155
Schubert, Hans von, 11
Schultz, Arthur, 248
Scranton, William (Bill), 207, 208, 216
SDS. *See* Students for a Democratic Society
Seale, Bobby, 206, 212
Second City (comedy troupe), 292
second-generation émigrés, ix, 49, 69, 124, 160, 232
Seven Sisters colleges, 88–89, 113, 134
sexual harassment, 225
Seymour, Charles, 36, 57, 78
Seymour, Mrs. Charles, 89
Shapiro, Harold, 280
Sharp, Alexander, 303n1
Shaw, George Bernard, 98
Shklar, Judith, 69
Shockley, William, 219, 226
Shotwell, James, 26
Shubert theater, New Haven, 77
Shultz, George, 258
Sidwell Friends School, 81–82, 86–87
Signet Society, 157

Sills, Beverly, 283
Simpson, Alan, 183–84
Simson, Mrs. Otto von, 174
Simson, Otto von, 173, 174
Sirabella, Vincent, 215, 229–31
Skull and Bones, 77, 208–9
Smith, Brewster, 191
Smith College, 88–90
Society for the Protection of Science and
    Learning. *See* Academic Assistance Council
Society of Friends. *See* Quakers
Socratic method, 172
Soong, T. V., 87
South Africa, 219–20, 285–88
Soviet flag flying incident, 93
Spengler, Lazarus, 11
sports and athletics, 79, 94–95, 181–83,
    225–26, 229–30, 233, 251
Spring Glen. *See* Hamden, Connecticut
Stagg, Amos Alonzo, 183
Stanford University, 256; Center for Advanced
    Study in the Behavioral Sciences, 194, 196
St. Anne's College, Oxford University, 115,
    119–22
Statue of Liberty, 33, 146
Stella Dallas (radio program), 72
Sterling Memorial Library, Yale University, 204
Stevenson, Adlai, 166
Stigler, George, 278
Stone, Edward Durrell, 266
Strauss, Leo, 107, 173
Strotz, Robert, 197, 201–2
Struve, Oliver, 173
Students for a Democratic Society (SDS), 188
Sturley, Winifred, 82
Sturmabteilung (SA), 18, 19, 20
Suez crisis (1956), 166
Sullivan Principles, 219–20, 287, 303n3
Sussman, Arthur, 303n1
Swarthmore College, 109
Symbionese Liberation Army, 195

Taft, Horace, 217–18
Taft Hotel, New Haven, 77
Tavern Club, Boston, 157
Tawney, R. H., 25
Taylor, Charles, 142, 157

Taylor, Lily Ross, 108, 109–10
teaching career: Bryn Mawr College, 112;
    Harvard University, 80, 155, 157, 159–64;
    Northwestern University, 196; University
    of California, Berkeley, 194–96; Univer-
    sity of Chicago, 172, 184–87, 294–95; Yale
    University, 218, 234. *See also* administrative
    career
tenure, 144–45
Terkel, Studs, 289
Terra, Daniel, 281
Thomas, Dylan, 108
Thomas, M. Carey, 91–94, 107
Thomas, Norman, 58, 148
Thomas, William, 123, 126
Thorne, Samuel, 151
Thrupp, Sylvia, 185
Thucydides, 172, 197; *History of the Peloppone-
    sian War*, 158
Tillich, Paul, 35, 67, 174
Title IX, 225–26
Tobin, James, 225
Tobler, Frau (godmother), 129
Tosteson, Daniel, 254
Townsend, Emily. *See* Vermeule, Emily
Toynbee, Arnold, 25, 107
Trevor-Roper, Hugh, 121, 122
Trilling, Lionel, 116
Troeltsch, Ernst, 4, 12
Truman, David, 203
Truman, Harry S., 101
Tufts University Fletcher School of Law and
    Diplomacy, 39, 59
tuition, 246
Turkey, 297
Turner, Stansfield, 197
tutorial system, 120–21

Überparteilichkeit (being above parties), 13
UN High Commission for Refugees, 42
Union Theological Seminary (New York), 67
United Nations, 98
United States: anti-American sentiments in
    England, 118–19; approach to higher edu-
    cation in, 30, 38–39, 44–45, 48, 50, 53–54;
    emigration to, 30–41, 41–42, 44–63
University in Exile, 15, 29

University of Berlin, 12, 19
University of California, 50, 164, 185
University of California, Berkeley, 67, 188, 194–96
University of Chicago, 34, 99, 126, 169–94; academic émigrés at, 172–74; alumni of, 248–49; athletics at, 181–83, 251; board of trustees of, 284–85; campus plan of, 245; centennial of, 290–93; Charles Gray's teaching at, 153, 168–69, 197, 233, 278–79; Committee on Human Development, 188–89, 191–92; Committee on Public Policy Studies, 262–63; Committee on Social Thought, 262; Council of the University Senate, 190, 240, 247, 258, 261, 267, 269; Court Theater, 267; crises of, 174, 176–79, 193–94; culture of, 175–76, 181, 193, 242–43, 249; curriculum of, 166, 174–78, 180, 183–84, 187; deans of, 269–70; Department of Geography, 261–62; divinity school of, 259; Division of Biological Sciences, 254–56; Division of Continuing Education, 266; Division of the Humanities, 270–72; faculty of, 175–76, 178, 180–81, 184–93, 247; finances of, 237–38, 245–49; graduate education at, 239, 249–50, 252–53; Graduate School of Business, 259, 268; Graham School of Continuing Liberal and Professional Studies, 266–67; Harris School of Public Policy Studies, 225, 263–64; honorary degrees conferred by, 277–78, 292; Hutchins legacy at, 179–80, 248; Hutchins model of education at, 174–76; interdisciplinary studies at, 262; investment policies of, 219, 285–88; John Crerar Library, 268, 303n1; law school of, 258, 268; medical school and hospitals of, 254–58; mission of, 181, 292–93; Mitchell Hospital, 267–68; Northwestern compared to, 198; organizational structure of, 239–40; Oriental Institute, 173, 272–73; Ryerson Lecture, 278; School of Library Science, 259–61; School of Social Service Administration, 259–60; size of, 249–51; Smart Museum, 267; student life at, 251; student protests at, 187–93, 289–90; students of, 238; teaching at, 172, 184–87, 294–95; tuition of, 246; urban context of, 177, 179,

188; women at, xi, 185–93, 279. *See also* presidency of University of Chicago
University of Chicago Record, 247–48
University of Chicago Roundtable of the Air (radio program), 71
University of Heidelberg, 2, 3, 10–11, 130
University of Illinois, 147–49
University of Miami, 184
University of Michigan, 185, 269
University of Pennsylvania, 229
University of Vienna, 155
US Energy Department, 265–66
US Justice Department, 84, 226
US State Department, 30, 62, 84, 85

Vagts, Alfred, 32, 60, 301n11
Vance, Cyrus, 206, 208, 230, 233
Vassar College, 66, 113, 183, 204
Veith, Ilsa, 185
Venceremos Organization, 196
Vermeule, Emily (née Townsend), 98
Vermont farm, 143, 154
Versailles Treaty, 16
Vietnam War, 188, 191, 197, 208, 211, 289

Wagner, Richard, 2
Walker, Dan, 202
Wallace, Henry, 101
Warburg, Aby, 127
Warburg Institute, 124, 127, 155
Washington, DC, 68–69, 85–88
Washington University (St. Louis), 67
Watson, Arthur, 208
WAVES (Women Accepted for Volunteer Emergency Service), 107
Weber, Alfred, 11, 130–31
Weber, Marianne, 3
Weber, Max, 3, 12, 130
Weimar Circle of German University Teachers, 18
Weimar Republic, 2, 4, 5, 12, 16–18
Weintraub, Karl Joachim "Jock," 172, 187
Wellek, René, 66
Wellesley College, 88–89, 106
Wesleyan University, 15, 40, 67
West Point, international relations conference held at, 98–99

Whalley, Edward, 76–77

White, Mrs. (Sidwell Friends teacher), 81

Whitney, Eli, 73

Whitney, John Hay "Jock," 205, 208

Widener Library, Harvard University, 67, 132, 134

Wiener, Norbert, 156

Wilamowitz-Moellendorff, Ulrich von, 4

Wilder, Thornton, 73

Wilson, E. O., 151

Wilson, John T., 189, 233, 235, 236, 242, 254, 268, 272

Wilson, William Julius, 263

Winchester Repeating Arms factory, 74

Wolfers, Arnold, 16, 32, 35, 41, 58

Wolfers, Doris, 35

women: as administrators, 198, 201; discriminatory treatment of, 115, 133–34, 136, 140, 157, 186, 188, 190, 204, 225, 279; at Harvard, 115, 133–34, 136, 140, 157; at Oxford, 115; scholarship and career issues and opportunities, x–xi, 105–7, 136–37, 158; among student protestors, 190; at University of Chicago, xi, 185–93, 279; at Yale, 204, 214, 225–26, 231

women's colleges, 103–8, 113, 134

women's movement. See feminism and the women's movement

Woodward, C. Vann, 218–19, 228

Woodward Report, 218–19

Woodworth, Mary, 108

Woolf, Virginia, 115

World Federalists, 98

World War I, 3–4

World War II, 82–88, 124–25, 208–9

Wyatt's Rebellion, 123

Yale Art Gallery, 77, 223

Yale Center for British Art, 223–24

Yale Corporation, 203, 205–8, 228, 230–34

Yale University, 203–35; academic émigrés at, 16, 32, 58, 67; arts and sciences at, 220–23; athletics at, 225–26, 229–30; Brewster's presidency of, 209–14, 231; Bryn Mawr and, 95; Charles Gray's teaching at, 201; childhood exposure to, 77–80; and coeducation, 204–5, 209, 214; controversial issues at, 225–28; culture of, 57, 208; faculty of, 214, 225; finances of, 213, 216–18; Hajo Holborn and, 34–41, 57–59, 78–79; Harvard compared to, 38, 40; interim presidency of, 230–35; investment policies of, 219–20; medical school of, 221–22; provost position at, 201–2, 214–35; racial issues involving, 212–13; Rosovsky, Henry, 232; School of Organization and Management, 211–12, 224–25; Sterling Memorial Library, 204; student protests at, 212–13, 226; teaching at, 218, 234; and town-gown relations, 206, 215; undergraduates of, 77–78; as wedding site, 155; women at, 204, 214, 225–26, 231; workers' strikes at, 215, 230–31

Yale University Library, 12

Yates, Frances, 127

Yates, Sidney, 281

Young Men's Christian Institute, New Haven, 74

Zeisel, Hans, 173

Zemurray chair, Harvard University, 139, 166

Zimmer, Heinrich, and wife, 11, 66

Zimmern, Alfred, 25

Zygmund, Antoni, 173